MW01196971

Multiculturalism and Diversity in Clinical Supervision

Multiculturalism and Diversity in Clinical Supervision

A COMPETENCY-BASED APPROACH

Edited by
Carol A. Falender, Edward P. Shafranske,
and Celia J. Falicov

American Psychological Association • *Washington, DC*

2nd printing, July 2016

Published by
American Psychological Association
750 First Street, NE
Washington, DC 20002
www.apa.org

To order
APA Order Department
P.O. Box 92984
Washington, DC 20090-2984
Tel: (800) 374-2721; Direct: (202) 336-5510
Fax: (202) 336-5502; TDD/TTY: (202) 336-6123
Online: www.apa.org/pubs/books
E-mail: order@apa.org

In the U.K., Europe, Africa, and the Middle East, copies may be ordered from
American Psychological Association
3 Henrietta Street
Covent Garden, London
WC2E 8LU England

Typeset in Goudy by Circle Graphics, Inc., Columbia, MD

Printer: Maple Press, York, PA
Cover Designer: Naylor Design, Washington, DC

The opinions and statements published are the responsibility of the authors, and such opinions and statements do not necessarily represent the policies of the American Psychological Association.

Library of Congress Cataloging-in-Publication Data

Multiculturalism and diversity in clinical supervision : a competency-based approach / [edited by] Carol A. Falender, Edward P. Shafranske, and Celia J. Falicov.
    p. ; cm.
Includes bibliographical references and index.
ISBN 978-1-4338-1685-7 — ISBN 1-4338-1685-7
I. Falender, Carol A., editor of compilation. II. Shafranske, Edward P., editor of compilation. III. Falicov, Celia Jaes, editor of compilation. IV. American Psychological Association, publisher.
[DNLM: 1. Psychotherapy—methods. 2. Cultural Competency—education. 3. Cultural Competency—psychology. 4. Mentors. WM 420]
HV40.54
362.2'04250683—dc23
                              2013036885

British Library Cataloguing-in-Publication Data

A CIP record is available from the British Library.

Printed in the United States of America
First Edition

http://dx.doi.org/10.1037/14370-000

To my ever-supportive husband, Marty; my mentors, Beverly Golden and Michela Gunn; and the generations of supervisees and colleagues who have taught me so much.

—*Carol A. Falender*

To my wife, Kathy, and to the many supervisors, colleagues, students, supervisees, and clients who have contributed in countless ways to my learning and professional development.

—*Edward P. Shafranske*

To my daughters, Tamara, Yael, and Anna; to my partner, Peter; and to my siblings, Beba and Pablo—for the love and support you all give me.

—*Celia J. Falicov*

CONTENTS

CONTRIBUTORS

Kathleen J. Bieschke, PhD, Pennsylvania State University, University Park

Kelly A. Blasko, PhD, Pennsylvania State University, University Park

Shannon Chavez-Korell, PhD, University of Wisconsin–Milwaukee

Jean Lau Chin, EdD, ABPP, Adelphi University, Garden City, NY

Jennifer A. Erickson Cornish, PhD, ABPP, University of Denver Graduate School of Professional Psychology, Denver, CO

Carol A. Falender, PhD, Pepperdine University, Los Angeles, CA, and University of California, Los Angeles

Celia J. Falicov, PhD, University of California, San Diego

Nadya A. Fouad, PhD, University of Wisconsin–Milwaukee

Shelly P. Harrell, PhD, Pepperdine University, Los Angeles, CA

Jeff King, PhD, Western Washington University, Bellingham

Samantha Pelican Monson, PsyD, Denver Health, Denver, CO

Hui Mei Nan, MA, Adelphi University, Garden City, NY

Leah Nicholls, MA, Adelphi University, Garden City, NY

Kirsten Petersen, MA, Adelphi University, Garden City, NY
Natalie Porter, PhD, California School of Professional Psychology, Alliant University, San Francisco
Edward P. Shafranske, PhD, ABPP, Pepperdine University, Los Angeles, CA
Joseph E. Trimble, PhD, Western Washington University, Bellingham
Melba Vasquez, PhD, ABPP, Independent Practice, Austin, TX
Susan S. Woodhouse, PhD, Lehigh University, Bethlehem, PA

FOREWORD

MELBA VASQUEZ

Multiculturalism and Diversity in Clinical Supervision: A Competency-Based Approach provides a significant, rich, and unique enhancement of the clinical training literature by describing key elements involved in attending to multicultural and sociopolitical differences between supervisors and supervisees, and between supervisees and their clients.

Multicultural competence is no longer a marginal topic of interest. Understanding the cultural context of behavior is critical to competent and ethical interventions in all areas of mental health work. Regardless of one's theoretical orientation, it is important to understand how culture and other aspects of identity influence the experiences of distress, dysfunction, strength, and resilience. For supervisors, diversity and multicultural competence includes an understanding and awareness of the many strands of supervisees' and their clients' identities, including sex and gender, race and ethnicity, socioeconomic status, social class, sexual orientation, heritage, immigration and generational experiences, ableness, religion, and spirituality. Such an understanding also involves an awareness of one's own identities and how those influence one's work. We as clinicians must understand how those strands of identity combine for supervisor and supervisee, and for therapist and client, and we must be able to engage in interventions on the basis of that understanding. It may be especially challenging for us to relate to those who are different from us. We tend to relate most easily to, and have more knowledge and understanding of, those most similar to us in regard to identity variables.

For several years now, I have routinely provided continuing education workshops to practitioners throughout the country on multicultural ethics in psychotherapy. I have been encouraged that experienced practitioners are willing to learn, explore their biases, and develop skills to provide competent services to those different from them. I have also hoped that multicultural and diversity clinical training and supervision are being conducted in graduate programs, practicum, and internship settings, but I have not been certain about the extent to which this has become a reality.

Sociopolitical activism and social movements, such as civil rights, women's equity, and those who have fought oppression of other populations, have had an impact on the study of human behavior. Scholars have produced evidence-based literature on diverse populations that has influenced the field significantly. The explosion of evidence-based and theoretical multicultural literature has enhanced the possibility for mental health providers to meet the ethical requirements to attain competency in the provision of services to members of diverse groups. Guidelines and standards have evolved that provide parameters for the treatment of multicultural and other diverse populations. Policies of major organizations, such as the American Psychological Association and the American Counseling Association, have likewise been influenced.

The reality of increasing numbers of international and immigrant populations has also contributed to the increase of global consciousness and the integration of global perspectives in mental health. The goal of the integration of diversity and multiculturalism in supervision is to enhance the competency and the chances for success for supervisors with their supervisees and for supervisees with their diverse clients. This book provides invaluable insights into the impact of the multiple identities of each participant in the supervisory and therapeutic processes. It presents models for conducting competency-based multicultural clinical supervision.

One way to understand the success of psychotherapy is to study utilization rates and attrition or early withdrawal (Barrett, Chua, Crits-Christoph, Gibbons, & Thompson, 2008). Various diverse clients, especially racial/ethnic minority and poor clients, have a higher than typical rate of early treatment withdrawal (Barrett et al., 2008; S. Sue, 1977). Studies have also indicated that the negative attitudes of psychotherapists influence dropout rates and negative outcomes (Smith, 2005). If this is the case, how should psychotherapists be trained to acquire positive attitudes toward clients about whom they may have—sometimes not consciously—negative attitudes? Studies have indicated that clients who dropped out of treatment viewed the therapist as less expert, less competent, or less trustworthy and less attractive (Acosta, 1980). What are the factors that influence retention in psychological treatment for racial/ethnic minority clients, for the poor, and for individuals who represent various identity variables different from one's own?

One of the most consistent findings in psychotherapy research is that a strong therapeutic alliance predicts positive treatment outcome (Baldwin, Wampold, & Imel, 2007; Barrett et al., 2008). The alliance accounts for more than nearly any other identified factor in psychotherapy outcome research. Yet, social biases of psychotherapists, along with a complex array of cultural, attitudinal, and experiential differences between providers and consumers, present obstacles to engagement and retention in therapy (Griner & Smith, 2006).

How do we as supervisors and instructors teach trainees to develop a positive therapeutic alliance with clients of diverse backgrounds? Psychotherapists must develop knowledge, skills, and attitudes that facilitate that alliance with a wide range of clients (D. W. Sue, Arredondo, & McDavis, 1992). They must, for example, have an appreciation for the hardships of poverty, social class, and race/ethnicity. They must understand the oppression of having to hide one's sexual orientation or gender identity because of fear of rejection or even violence. This knowledge may be most important during the process of therapeutic engagement (Whaley & Davis, 2007). Throughout treatment, moment by moment, the practitioner's position shifts, and decisions about how to intervene depend on what she or he has come to understand about the client (Stark, 1999).

The continued acquisition of competency in general, and cultural competence in particular, is a lifelong process, but it is in clinical training and supervision that psychotherapy is taught and the foundation for multicultural competence is established. This edited volume provides roadmaps for increasing one's competency in developing a strong working alliance with clients from diverse populations. Multicultural competence includes awareness, knowledge, and appreciation of the three-way interaction of the client's, the supervisee's, and the supervisor's values, assumptions, biases, expectations derived from worldviews, and the integration of practice assessment and intervention skills.

The editors and the authors make a strong point of demonstrating how a commitment to social justice and advocacy is a critical element of multicultural competence. Many agree that such commitment underlies the attitude necessary for effective diversity and multicultural competence (Vasquez, 2012). Understanding the environmental contributions to human development, including pathology, is critical. For example, in the discussion of eating disorders, intimate partner violence, or sexual harassment, understanding the social construction of gender and role expectations for both women and men is critical. An appreciation of the humanity of each client in those contexts is an important goal; as clinicians address the often highly complex and emotionally charged issues that arise in therapy.

Cultural humility (as opposed to ethnocentricity or White privilege) is crucial in supervisory–supervisee/therapist–client dynamics (see Chapter 1). Various models of multicultural supervision—as well as various strategies, techniques, and identification of key points at which the infusion of diversity perspectives is important—are addressed throughout this book.

I suspect that most of diverse populations may underutilize mental health services, but researchers do not have the data to confirm this. Research has shown that clients working with clinicians of similar ethnic backgrounds and languages tend to remain in treatment longer than do clients whose therapists are neither ethnically nor linguistically matched with them (D. W. Sue & Sue, 2003). However, even that is not a guarantee, because unless we as clinicians have ourselves developed the knowledge, skills, values, and attitudes addressed in this book, we have not established competency in working with members of our own identity groups (Vasquez, 2007).

This volume is an invaluable resource for all supervisors and also for all trainers and providers of mental health services. It provides critical, up-to-date evidence-based information, as well a variety of models with which to teach and learn. It is intellectually stimulating, emotionally moving, and gratifying. I am proud to see this quality product available. It is my hope that readers will be stimulated to learn, inspired to integrate new skills, and encouraged to look honestly at themselves, especially in the context of their work with those different from themselves.

REFERENCES

Acosta, F. X. (1980). Self-described reasons for premature termination of psychotherapy by Mexican American, Black American, and Anglo-American patients. *Psycho- logical Reports*, *47*, 435–443.

Baldwin, S. A., Wampold, B. E., & Imel, Z. E. (2007). Untangling the alliance–outcome correlation: Exploring the relative importance of therapist and patient variability in the alliance. *Journal of Consulting and Clinical Psychology*, *75*, 842–852.

Barrett, M. S., Chua, W., Crits-Christoph, P., Gibbons, M. B., & Thompson, D. (2008). Early withdrawal from mental health treatment: Implications for psychotherapy practice. *Psychotherapy: Theory, Research, Practice, Training*, *45*, 247–267. doi:10.1037/0033-3204.45.2.247

Griner, D., & Smith, T. D. (2006). Culturally adapted mental health interventions: A meta-analytic review. *Psychotherapy: Theory, Research, Practice, Training*, *43*, 531–548. doi: 10.1037/0033-3204.43.4.531

Smith L. (2005). Psychotherapy, classism, and the poor: Conspicuous by their absence. *American Psychologist, 60*, 687–696.

Stark, M. (1999). *Modes of therapeutic action: Enhancement of knowledge, provision of experience and engagement in relationship*. Northvale, NJ: Aronson.

Sue, D. W., Arredondo, P., & McDavis, R. J. (1992). Multicultural counseling competencies and standards: A call to the profession. *Journal of Multicultural Counseling and Development, 20*, 64–88.

Sue, D. W., & Sue, S. (2003). *Counseling the culturally diverse* (4th ed.). Hoboken, NJ: Wiley.

Sue, S. (1977). Community mental health services to minority groups: Some optimism, some pessimism. *American Psychologist, 32*, 616–624.

Vasquez, M. J. T. (2007). Cultural difference and the therapeutic alliance: An evidence-based analysis. *American Psychologist, 62*, 878–886.

Vasquez, M. J. T. (2012). Psychology and social justice: Why we do what we do. *American Psychologist, 67*, 337–346.

Whaley, A. L., & Davis, K. E. (2007). Cultural competence and evidence-based practice in mental health services: A complementary perspective. *American Psychologist, 62*, 563–574.

Multiculturalism and Diversity in Clinical Supervision

1

DIVERSITY AND MULTICULTURALISM IN SUPERVISION

CAROL A. FALENDER, EDWARD P. SHAFRANSKE,
AND CELIA J. FALICOV

If we are to achieve a richer culture, rich in contrasting values, we must recognize the whole gamut of human potentialities, and so weave a less arbitrary social fabric, one in which each diverse gift will find a fitting place. (Margaret Mead, 1935/2001, p. 322)

As psychologists, we are called to become aware of individual differences and engage in a process of discovering and entering into the "cultural labyrinth in which clients present their lived experience" (Hoshmand, 2001, p. 106). We do so because, at its heart, psychology "respects the dignity and worth of all people" (American Psychological Association [APA], 2010) and values the multiverse of individual and cultural factors that shape a person's worldview. Developing multicultural competence ensures that all clients will be respected and their unique cultural identities will find a fitting place in clinical understanding. It is in clinical training and supervision that multicultural competence is initially developed and applied, which sets a foundation for lifelong practice. The development of multicultural competence is integral to the formation of clinical competence.

The challenges supervisors face in infusing multiculturalism and diversity in supervision traverse all general training. These challenges include facilitating

http://dx.doi.org/10.1037/14370-001
Multiculturalism and Diversity in Clinical Supervision: A Competency-Based Approach, C. A. Falender,
E. P. Shafranske, and C. J. Falicov (Editors)

the development of an effective supervisory relationship; fostering supervisee self-reflection; and encouraging full participation in accurately assessing, developing, and applying knowledge, skills, and values or attitudes essential to clinical practice. To accomplish these tasks, supervisors require a solid conceptual foundation to guide their interventions and evidence-based practices.

This book provides this conceptual foundation (Chapters 1–2) and examples of best practices (Chapters 3–11). The conceptual foundation integrates two major theoretical approaches: competency-based clinical supervision (Falender & Shafranske, 2004) and the multidimensional ecological comparative approach (MECA; Falicov, 1998; see also Chapter 2, this volume). The contributing authors describe examples of supervisor–supervisee interaction and consider their shared and differing multiple identities. In these chapters, the authors focus on conceptualization, diagnosis, and treatment, as well as values, attitudes, and personal factors as forces in both supervisory and therapeutic relationships.

A FOUNDATION: DEFINITIONS AND APPROACHES TO CLINICAL SUPERVISION AND MULTICULTURALISM

The practice of clinical supervision is based on theory and research and is influenced by personal experiences of supervision, as well as specific training and supervision of supervision. By *supervision of supervision*, we mean that the supervisor herself or himself is supervised to ensure that she or he is providing effective supervision to the supervisee. Effective supervision practice requires a clear understanding of what supervision is. Clinical supervision, "a distinct professional activity in which education and training aimed at developing science-informed practice are facilitated through an interpersonal process" (Falender & Shafranske, 2004, p. 3), provides a structure integral to clinical practice and supervision: superordinate values of integrity-in-relationship, ethical values-based practice, appreciation of diversity, and science-based practice (Falender & Shafranske, 2004).

Defining multicultural and diversity competence is complex, even without factoring in supervision. This is because culture is woven throughout all human experience in ways that are clearly obvious and in ways that are less easily observed, obscured in the routines of daily life. Implicit in the definition of *multicultural competence* is the definition of culture. Falicov (1988) defined *culture* as

> those sets of shared world views and adaptive behaviors derived from simultaneous membership in a variety of contexts, such as ecological setting (rural urban, suburban), religious background, nationality and ethnicity, social class, gender-related experiences, minority status, occu-

pation, political leanings, migratory patterns and stage of acculturation or values derived from belonging to the same generation, partaking of single historical moment, or particular ideologies. (p. 336)

More recently, descriptions of culture have considered

the dynamic and active process of constructing shared meaning, as represented by shared ideas, beliefs, attitudes, values, norms, practices, language, spirituality, and symbols, with acknowledgement and consideration of positions of power, privilege, and oppression. (Vargas, Porter, & Falender, 2008, p. 122)

Multicultural Competence

With these and related conceptions of culture as a foundation, psychologists have developed approaches to describe and define what is entailed in becoming culturally competent and to apply that understanding in the clinical arena. Most definitions of *multicultural competence* are derived from Sue, Arredondo, and McDavis's (1992) description of *competence:* knowledge, skills, and attitudes in domains of therapist awareness of personal values and biases; understanding the worldview of the "culturally different"; and developing cultural intervention strategies and techniques. Generally, two components of competence, knowledge and skills, have been primarily addressed in the literature on multicultural supervision. However, increasingly, concern has been raised that attitudes, which are at the core of competence, have been given inadequate attention.

In addition, multicultural competence is today seen to be inseparable from social justice and advocacy and, increasingly, the terms are used interchangeably (Pieterse, Evans, Risner-Butner, Collins, & Mason, 2008). *Advocacy* is a competency in benchmarks (Fouad et al., 2009), and *social justice* is "the scholarship and professional action designed to change societal values, structures, policies, and practices, such that disadvantaged or marginalized groups gain increased access to these tools of self-determination" (Goodman et al., 2004, p. 795). Guidelines for addressing social justice at the practicum level were provided by Burnes and Singh (2010). American Counseling Association (ACA) advocacy competencies include a self-assessment and a strength-based set of counselor competencies revolving around client/student empowerment, advocacy, community collaboration, systems advocacy, public information, and social/political advocacy (Ratts, Toporek, & Lewis, 2010).

Cultural knowledge, awareness, and skills alone may not ensure affective, cognitive, and behavioral learning processes (Toporek & Reza, 2001) nor lead to the proactive stance involved in social justice. Attention to values or attitudes, the often neglected component of competence, may hold the key to the development of multicultural competence. The powerful metaconcept *of cultural humility (Tervalon & Murray-Garcia, 1998) is a valuable tool to incorporate a commitment to critical self-reflection, self-evaluation, and self-critiquing, essential to multicultural awareness. Further, genuinely adopting a stance of cultural humility offers an approach to address and redress power dynamics and imbalances in client–therapist–supervisor dynamics, instilling humility in relationship with both clients and supervisees that are respectful of individual and community-contextual mores and practices.

Even when attempting to take such a position, clinicians may not ultimately understand the impact of such factors as privilege and oppression, or they may understand them but not change their professional behavior accordingly. *Privilege* refers to perceived status arising from advantages such as socioeconomic or racial, of which the individual may not be consciously aware. Further, a clinician might observe her privilege as a White, middle-class individual but might not truly understand the affective impact of her privileged status on her supervisees or clients. An example is a supervisor who always wears designer clothing but feels that any effect is mitigated by verbally acknowledging the clothing and explaining that she got it at thrift shops. Her supervisees still perceived it as a representation of privilege that increased the power differential and perceived distance between them—and cyclically reduced her effectiveness relating to them while she continued to be adamant that her clothing was not a factor with supervisees or her very-low-income clients, ignoring the pattern of client no-shows. Related to privilege, *oppression* is the exercise of power or authority in an unjust or cruel manner. Privilege and oppression are implicit in many supervisory interactions and heighten the power differential.

In addition to the challenges of incorporating cultural humility, the recognition of difference often poses difficulty. Acknowledgement of difference may be difficult because of the emotional response of minimizing risk to the experience of difference (Harrell, 2006; see Chapter 4).

Supervision Diversity Competence

In addition to considering an individual's multicultural competence, we find it useful to extend discussion to the process of clinical supervision in terms of *diversity* (rather than only *multicultural*) to reflect the vast range of multiple identities (e.g., language, educational level, religion, gender identity, sexual orientation), worldviews, and perspectives. Falender and Shafranske (2004) defined *supervision diversity competence* as follows:

> Incorporation of self-awareness by both supervisor and supervisee . . . an interactive encompassing process of the client or family, supervisee–therapist, and supervisor, using all of their (multiple) diversity factors. It entails awareness, knowledge, and appreciation of the interaction among

the client's, supervisee–therapist's, and supervisor's assumptions values, biases, expectations, and worldviews; integration and practice of appropriate, relevant, and sensitive assessment and intervention strategies and skills; and consideration of the larger milieu of history, society, and sociopolitical variables. (p. 125)

Although multicultural competence is considered an ethical and practice imperative, attaining such competence as individuals and within the supervision relationship has proven to be daunting. Having discussed culture and multicultural competence, we turn now to the historical context in which psychology as a profession has responded to the call for multicultural competence.

HISTORICAL PERSPECTIVE

Focus on diversity and multicultural identities in supervision training has grown exponentially since the 1960s and 1970s. Sociopolitical activism and social movements (e.g., women's liberation) nationally and internationally focused attention on power and oppression and their relationships with race, ethnicity, gender, socioeconomic status (SES), gender identity, sexual orientation, age, and disability.

The APA (2003a) *Guidelines on Multicultural Education, Training, Research, Practice, and Organizational Change for Psychologists* (hereinafter, APA *Multicultural Guidelines*) trace origins to the U.S. Supreme Court decision *Brown Versus the Board of Education* in 1954 and the Civil Rights Act of 1964. These guidelines also cite the Vail Professional Training in Psychology Conference in 1973 for highlighting both the lack of attention to diversity in psychology and the ethical imperative. Sue (2009) credited the Dulles Conference for bringing together African American, American Indian, Asian American, and Hispanic groups as the foundation for APA's Office on Ethnic Minority Affairs that was instituted in 1979, the Board of Ethnic Minority Affair in 1980, the Society for the Psychological Study of Ethnic Minority Issues in 1986, and the National Multicultural Summit in 1999. APA's *Guidelines and Principles for Accreditation of Programs in Professional Psychology* (hereinafter, APA *Accreditation Guidelines*) have required multicultural education for doctoral programs since 1986. The ACA's *Multicultural Counseling Competencies and Standards* (Arredondo et al., 1996) operationalized components of multicultural competence for practitioners and educators. The APA *Multicultural Guidelines*, approved in 2002, were in development for 22 years and, as guidelines, are aspirational. APA's (2008) *Report of the APA Task Force on the Implementation of the Multicultural Guidelines* (hereinafter, APA *Implementation of the Multicultural Guidelines*) emphasized the urgency of infusing the guidelines into all aspects of practice, accreditation, research, and publications.

Olkin (1999) traced the history of legislation regarding disabilities. In 1990, the Americans With Disabilities Act was passed, following the Rehabilitation Act in 1973 that was not enacted until 1977. Public Law 94-142, Education For All Handicapped Children (later enacted as the Individuals With Disabilities Education Act, 2004), authorized education and services for handicapped students. Olkin described the watershed moment as the passage of the 1990 Americans With Disabilities Act, which addressed social and economic barriers and obstacles to employment.

In 1975, the APA adopted the resolution to remove the stigma of mental illness from homosexual orientations. Garnets (2007) cochaired a task force in 1986 charged with surveying practices with gay men and lesbians that revealed therapist negative biases and misinformation causing harm in therapy. In 1998, APA adopted the *Resolution on Appropriate Therapeutic Responses to Sexual Orientation;* in 2000, the *Guidelines for Psychotherapy With Lesbian, Gay, and Bisexual Clients* were adopted and were revised 11 years later (APA, 2011b). In 2009, ACA for Lesbian, Gay, Bisexual, and Transgender Issues in Counseling adopted competencies for counseling clients (ACA, 2010).

In 1975, the APA Task Force on Sex Bias and Sex-Role Stereotyping developed guidelines regarding the failure of psychotherapy to effectively meet the needs of women or people of color (Porter, 1995). APA has published *Guidelines for Psychological Practice With Older Adults* (2003b), *Psychological Practice With Girls and Women* (2007), and *Guidelines for Assessment of and Intervention With Persons with Disabilities* (2011).

Kaslow (2000) described the historical progression of family therapy, highlighting feminist family therapy in the 1970s and 1980s; multicultural family therapy through McGoldrick, Giordano, and Pearce's classic text *Ethnicity and Family Therapy;* and the paradigm shift toward multidimensionality in the work of Falicov (1988, 1995, 1998), among multiple other contributors. Efforts to enhance multicultural competence have not been limited to the United States; in the next section, we discuss such international efforts.

INTERNATIONAL ARENA

Global perspectives necessitate movement from ethnocentric views and require a diversity lens through which supervisors and supervisees view clients and experiences. International supervisees, supervisors, and clients' worldviews and experiences encompass global linkages, consciousness, and world society (Leong, Pickren, Leach, & Marsella, 2012) and are critical components of multicultural supervision. The increasing numbers of international clients, supervisors, and supervisees and the increasing global consciousness through technology all mandate competence (Marsella, 2012). Attention to ethics through a global lens resulted in *The Universal Declaration of Ethical Principles for Psychologists* (hereinafter, *Universal Declaration*; International Union of Psychological Science, 2008), a document that has been adopted by multiple international associations, including the Canadian Psychological Association (CPA). The *Universal Declaration* provides a global frame for ethical practice in psychology to guide practice with diverse clients, supervisors, and supervisees. Its principles are as follows: Respect for the Dignity of Persons and Peoples, Competent Caring for the Well-Being of Persons and Peoples, Integrity, and Professional and Scientific Responsibilities to Society. Generally, the *Universal Declaration* defines a primary and focal attention to the welfare of the client, using an ethical-decision-making model to address the intersection of personal conscience and rule-governed behavior, a shift from risk protection of the clinician (Gauthier, Pettifor, & Ferraro, 2010). Principle I of the *Universal Declaration*, Respect for the Dignity of Persons and Peoples, states,

> Respect for the dignity of persons is the most fundamental and universally found ethical principle across geographical and cultural boundaries, and across professional disciplines. . . . Respect for dignity recognizes the inherent worth of all human beings, regardless of perceived or real differences in social status, ethnic origin, gender, capacities, or other such characteristics. This inherent worth means that all human beings are worthy of equal moral consideration. (p. 1)

We believe the *Universal Declaration* is a frame for excellent practice and for this casebook. It addresses the tensions in culture-specific concepts of autonomy and self-determination and those of harmony, cooperation, interconnectedness, and the collective good (Pettifor, 2009).

Another important lens is indigenous psychology (IP), an approach to produce and define local psychologies within a specific cultural context. Practitioners of IP define *culture* as a "a set of background features within which a group of people has developed over the course of their history, including a set of institutions (social, political, economic, religious) and a shared set of meanings and values" (Allwood & Berry, 2006, p. 263). In this context, local culture is a source of inspiration, producing inputs of language, history, philosophical and ethical frames, sacred beliefs, and social structures and gives shape to the IP (Allwood & Berry, 2006). Practitioners of IP provide perspective in which to view clinical and supervision interactions. The multicultural competence movement has produced important guidelines and standards to encourage, as well as mandate, ethical practice (Pettifor & Ferrero, 2012).

GUIDELINES AND STANDARDS

Parameters for multicultural competence are defined in the *APA Accreditation Guidelines* (Domain D, Cultural and Individual Differences and Diversity), APA's (2010) *Ethical Principles of Psychologists and Code of Conduct* (hereinafter, *APA Code of Ethics*), APA's *Guidelines on Multicultural Education,* and Fouad et al.'s (2009) *Competency Benchmarks: A Model for Understanding and Measuring Competence in Professional Psychology Across Training Levels.* The CPA (2009) has adopted *Ethical Guidelines for Supervision in Psychology: Research, Practice, and Administration* (hereinafter, CPA *Ethical Guidelines*).

APA's *Implementation of Multicultural Guidelines* (Guideline 1) encourages psychologists to increase their awareness of thoughts, assumptions, and beliefs about others and when these are detrimental to others. General recommendations in Guideline 1 include increasing self-awareness and knowledge of worldview and personal and cultural biases. Guideline 2 urges increasing knowledge about the history, worldviews, and values of groups other than their own, historical forms of oppression, immigration patterns, and the impact of stigma (APA, 2008, p. 7).

Multicultural competencies are infused in benchmarks (Fouad et al., 2009). The section "Individual and Cultural Diversity-Awareness" (p. S13) provides three categories:

A. Self as shaped by individual and cultural diversity (e.g., cultural, individual, and role differences, including those based on age, gender, gender identity, race, ethnicity, culture, national origin, religion, sexual orientation, disability, language, and SES) and context.

B. Others as shaped by individual and cultural diversity (e.g., cultural, individual, and role differences, including those based on age, gender, gender identity, race, ethnicity, culture, national origin, religion, sexual orientation, disability, language, and SES) and context.

C. Interaction of self and others as shaped by individual and cultural diversity (e.g., cultural, individual, and role differences, including those based on age, gender, gender identity, race, ethnicity, culture, national origin, religion, sexual orientation, disability, language, and SES) and context. (Fouad et al., 2009, pp. S13–S14)

The CPA *Ethical Guidelines* and the accompanying *Resource Guide for Psychologists: Ethical Supervision in Teaching, Research, Practice, and Administration* (Pettifor, McCarron, Schoepp, Stark, & Stewart, 2010) proposes "respect for the dignity of persons" as their first ethical standard. This corresponds to the

CPA *Ethical Guidelines*, as it is essential to all aspects of supervision and clinical practice and a set of ethical guidelines for supervision practice.

Although guidelines, benchmarks, and ethical codes prescribe multicultural standards, adoption has not been swift or universal. For clinical supervision, guidelines are in development through Association of State and Provincial Psychology Boards and APA's Board of Educational Affairs.

STATE OF THE ART OF DIVERSITY COMPETENCE IN SUPERVISION

The development of competence as a counseling or clinical psychologist involves the confluence of academic education and clinical training. In theory, graduate education provides a foundation of knowledge, drawn from theory and empirical research, on which applied practice is initiated. New knowledge and evolving practices as well as new questions are then generated and reciprocally influence both the academic and the practice communities.

Academic Preparation in Multiculturalism and Diversity

Graduate schools have improved multicultural training, but attention is still lacking with respect to gender; being a lesbian, gay, bisexual, or transgendered (LGBT) person; older adult; lower SES; and having other diversity statuses (Lyons, Bieschke, Dendy, Worthington, & Georgemiller, 2010; Miville et al., 2009). Training in multicultural competence most often relies on a single course (Falicov, 1988; Pieterse et al., 2008) with effectiveness based on student satisfaction. Personal changes, resulting from multicultural courses, were described by graduate students with the words, awareness, knowledge, and understanding used almost interchangeably (Sammons & Speight, 2008), but there were only minimal behavioral or attitudinal changes (Dickson, Angus-Calvo, & Tafoya, 2010).

Teachers of multicultural counseling courses encounter multiple difficulties. These include identifying students' multicultural competence level, engaging in emotionally charged dialogue and the resistance that ensues, and feeling unprepared but understanding the potential benefit to emotionally loaded group dynamics. All of these are challenges to teachers in providing a safe learning environment (Reynolds, 2011). Not simply faculty behavior but also the culturally sensitive ambience of a graduate program predicted positive cognitive attitudes toward cultural diversity (Dickson, Jepsen, & Barbee, 2008). Participatory training strategies predicted greater comfort with interracial contact (Dickson et al., 2008).

Multiculturalism and Diversity in Clinical Supervision

In practicum training and internships, the impact of a supervisor's lack of competence in diversity is multiplied because of the power differential between supervisee and supervisor (a function of supervisor evaluation and gatekeeping) and by the supervisee often having greater cultural competence and training than the supervisor (Gloria, Hird, & Tao, 2008). Harm may result to supervisees and their clients, and strains or ruptures may occur in the clinical and the supervisory relationship. Further, lack of integrated training and guidelines for multicultural practice and supervision is a deterrent to practice (Falender, Burnes, & Ellis, 2013). Supervisees have reported LGBT nonaffirming supervision (Burkard, Knox, Hess, & Schultz, 2009), a lack of preparation and competence in treating LGBT clients despite the availability of guidelines (Lyons et al., 2010), and lack of training in religion and spirituality (Crook-Lyon et al., 2012) and social class (Smith, 2009). Further, supervisees have reported supervisors using a theoretical or other model that is not resilience-oriented with queer people of color (Singh & Chun, 2010); not instilling safety to introduce privilege, power, or race (Jernigan, Green, Helms, Perez-Gualdron, & Henze, 2010); not addressing their own affirming or nonaffirming behavior (Burkard et al, 2009); and directly misusing power and making disrespectful comments about gender identity or sexual orientation (Hernández & McDowell, 2010). Furthermore, supervisors initiated discussion regarding ethnicity, sex, and sexual orientation with their supervisees only infrequently (Gatmon et al., 2001), leaving the initiation to supervisees (Duan & Roehlke, 2001).

Supervisors often neglect to fully consider the impact of client, therapist, and supervisor factors on therapeutic and supervisory processes. For example, assumptions about similarities (or differences) may limit examination of the influences of background involving culturally embedded experiences and beliefs. Supervisors may be less likely to consider their own personal worldview, attitudes, or historical or current oppression or privilege as factors in their clinical supervision, shifting focus to the client and supervisee–therapist interpersonal or process factors. However, competence entails developing knowledge, skills, and attitudes, which infuse global and historical context into consideration of client, supervisee, and supervisor relationships and interactions, including the impacts of geographic transitions, political setting, conceptions of ethical behavior, and cultural values. In effective competency-based supervision, the supervisor's self-assessment and reflective stance model openness to identifying personal cultural identities and presentations that are dystonic, addressing these, and using them as powerful tools to guide the supervision process, as well as the therapy with the client, modeling reflection and self-awareness.

Telepsychology and Clinical Supervision

How communication occurs is culturally relevant. As communication is increasingly digital, clinicians and supervisors need to enhance competence and openness to *telepsychology*, the provision of psychological services using telecommunication technologies (APA, 2013). Telepsychology for psychotherapy and clinical supervision is growing in frequency, but little attention has been directed to the multicultural aspects of practice. Supervisors bear the responsibility for, on the one hand, determining what services, populations, and competencies of the supervisee are appropriate for distance therapy, distance supervision, and supervisee preparation, and on the other hand, how to provide informed consent regarding limits of confidentiality, security, and emergency contact (Fitzgerald, Hunter, Hadjistavropoulos, & Koocher, 2010). Supervisors must also effectively communicate with diminished nonverbal cues or emotional response and address diversity among participants and contexts. Supervisors model ethical practice and ethical decision-making regarding use of social networking, online communication, and Internet searches of clients and supervisees (Myers, Endres, Ruddy, & Zelikovsky, 2012), considering multiple factors (including diversity). *Competency-based supervision* provides the structure for such consideration and practice.

Self-Assessment

Self-assessment is the most common measure of multicultural competence, but self-assessment is not necessarily accurate, nor does it correspond with specific self-reports of behavior (Hansen et al., 2006; Sehgal et al., 2011) or supervisor assessments (Ladany, Inman, Constantine, & Hofheinz, 1997; Worthington, Mobley, Franks, & Tan, 2000). Competency-based approaches with attention to small increments of behavior and self-monitoring of self-efficacy are alternative approaches to enhance accuracy of self-assessment (Eva & Regehr, 2008, 2011).

Difficult Conversations

Difficult conversations may ensue from multicultural discussion in general and from intersections of concerns about supervisee competency, personal belief structures, and multicultural considerations. Many supervisors are not prepared for these types of conversations (Miller, Forrest, & Elman, 2009; Sanchez-Hucles & Jones, 2005).

These tensions have moved into the legal arena (Behnke, 2012) in the case of practicum students who either refused to provide a client therapy because it was contrary to their own deeply held views or imposed their own values upon clients. This issue is particularly relevant for students when treating sexual minority clients or clients holding religious or spiritual beliefs and values dissimilar to their own. Bieschke and Mintz (2012) described the profession as being at a "high-stakes crossroad for the training of professional psychologists" (p. 202), as these issues are at the heart of training in professional psychology and may be discordant from the model training values statement. Behnke (2012) concluded that courts concur that training programs may prohibit students from imposing their own values on clients. However, intersections of the First Amendment of the U.S. Constitution and professional ethics are more complex. Trainees should be expressly advised that the expectation is not that they should give up their personal and/or religious values but that they should "attain both demographic competency and demonstrate the competence of dynamic worldview inclusivity" (Bieschke & Mintz, 2012, p. 202) and demonstrate cultural humility.

Multicultural Supervision Competence and Its Converse

Researchers have described successful versus unsuccessful multicultural supervision (Dressel, Consoli, Kim, & Atkinson, 2007), responsive versus unresponsive cross-cultural supervision (Burkard et al., 2006), regressive versus progressive dyads (Helms & Cook, 1999; Ladany, Brittan-Powell, & Pannu, 1997), and helpful versus hindering multicultural events in group supervision (Kaduvettoor et al., 2009). In culturally unresponsive supervision, supervisors ignored, discounted, or dismissed culture within supervision, negatively impacting supervisee satisfaction with supervision and their clients' outcomes (Burkard et al., 2006). Conversely, culturally responsive supervisors identified and appreciated multicultural aspects of client presentation and the ensuing supervisee–client relationship (Burkard et al., 2006).

Racial identity, a developmental concept, refers to the psychological response to one's race not only in relation to interactions with one's own racial or cultural group but also to identification in the larger social setting with one's own racial group and how this influences thinking, perceptions, emotions, and behaviors toward persons from other groups (Carter, 1995; Helms, 1990). When supervisor and supervisee had common belief systems (high racial identity ratings), more emphasis on culture in supervision resulted, and when supervisors had higher racial consciousness than their supervisees, they raised culture in supervision, creating a culturally receptive environment (Ladany, Brittan-Powell, & Pannu, 1997).

Multicultural Supervision Models

When Leong and Wagner reviewed 20 years of cross-cultural supervision[1] literature in 1994, they concluded that most research was theory based rather than empirically based. Many theories were derivatives of developmental models (Bernard & Goodyear, 1992; Loganbill, Hardy, & Delworth, 1982), with unknown efficacy with ethnic and racially diverse supervisory dyads. Simply incorporating multicultural issues into developmental models may neglect cultural dynamics of the supervisory relationship and culture of individual participants (Ancis & Ladany, 2001; Miville, Rosa, & Constantine, 2005).

Many models address multicultural complexities in general (e.g., Miville et al.'s, 2009, integrative training model), whereas others focus on a particular diverse group and are culture specific. Models have been critiqued for narrow focus (race or ethnicity excluding other factors) and lack of both a comprehensive framework to approach multicultural supervision issues and empirical support (Ancis & Ladany, 2010). Ancis and Ladany (2010) proposed a heuristic model of nonoppressive interpersonal development that includes affective/emotional components. In that model, an individual may belong to a combination of socially oppressed and socially privileged groups, so an essential aspect is understanding each member's level or stage of development. Other supervision models are group specific (e.g., Field, Chavez-Korell, & Rodriguez, 2010; Halpert, Reinhardt, & Toohey, 2007; Hernández & McDowell, 2010; Singh & Chun, 2010).

Linguistic competence is relevant to multicultural competence, as increasing numbers of supervisees are providing therapy to diverse clients with a language and/or culture that is not shared by the supervisor. This raises the significant ethical issue (Schwartz, Rodriguez, Santiago-Rivera, Arredondo, & Field 2010) of competence in general, as the supervisor cannot observe therapy live or understand the cultural nuance.

MECA and Reflective Practices in Therapy and in Supervision

Many models and processes emphasize both the importance of self-awareness and the process of cultural reflection. Falicov's MECA model (see Chapter 2, this volume) entails a process of reflection and continual consideration of multiple aspects of the client, supervisee–therapist, and supervisor cultural context and relationships. The supervisee and supervisor organize

---

[1]*Cross-cultural supervision* is defined as a supervisory relationship in which supervisor and supervisee were from culturally different groups (Leong & Wagner, 1994).

the parameters of personal cultural experience through use of cultural maps focused on client cultural identities. The approach provides an important tool to consider attitudes and values toward the client's presentation and therapy into the supervision process through a structural and systematic process. Combined with competency-based clinical supervision, the supervision process is transformed to make explicit many implicit beliefs and to use these in planning and executing successful treatment interventions.

Consider the intersection of cultural values with ethical decision-making, such as when a therapist receives a gift from a client. Institutional and personal ethical standards may preclude the therapist from accepting the gift. However, a broader spectrum of cultural humility would encourage careful processing of the meaning of the gift, considering not simply the value but also adding the cultural aspect, balancing respect and doing no harm to the client (Brown & Trangsrud, 2008).

Competency-Based Clinical Supervision

A competency-based approach to clinical supervision provides a framework that informs multiculturally competent clinical supervision. Competency-based supervision provides a structure for systematic self-assessment, feedback, and evaluation and is defined as

> an approach that explicitly identifies the knowledge, skills, and values that are assembled to form a clinical competency and develop learning strategies and evaluation procedures to meet criterion-referenced competence standards in keeping with evidence-based practices and the requirements of the local clinical setting. (Falender & Shafranske, 2007, p. 233)

As emphasis on competencies for performance increases, the role of clinical supervision plays an increasing role in supporting supervisees' development of competency benchmarks (Fouad et al., 2009). Competency-based clinical supervision and MECA provide a framework to understand the complexity of the interaction of diversity and worldview among supervisor, supervisee, and client or clients and apply it to the clinical and supervision contexts. We remain mindful that supervisor and clinician's understanding is always perspectival—influenced by personal interests, commitments, and cultures, out of which personal meanings are constructed (Falender & Shafranske, 2004).

The steps implicit in the combined models' implementation are the development of a supervisory alliance through collaboratively determining goals and tasks for the training period, a process resulting in an emotional bond between supervisee and supervisor. In the process of establishing the supervisory alliance, supervisor and supervisee will develop a shared vision of supervision; general supervisory expectations; and the importance of identifying conflicts, disagreements, or strain, normative parts of clinical and supervision process. A supervisory contract is developed in which elements of informed consent for supervision are defined.

The supervisor models openness and self-assessment of relevant belief structures, biases, and preferences with relation to specific clients and contexts and encourages greater self-awareness and integration of the multiple frames of shared and overlapping identities between client, supervisee/therapist, and supervisor. Sociopolitical and interpersonal cultural borders and perspectives include the context of the setting and the respective worldviews of client, supervisee, and supervisor. Essential to the process is addressing privilege, oppression, and social justice—and the experiences of the client that impact relationships and the therapy with the supervisee/therapist—as well as with the supervisor. A priority is the recognition that diversity is infused in all aspects of relationship, assessment, treatment planning and implementation, and outcome assessment. A significant role of the supervisor is to provide a safe environment in which the supervisee can disclose personal factors and reactivity to clients and context, always in keeping with ethical standards regarding supervisee disclosure (APA, 2010, 7.04). The supervisor models identification and management of reactivity (or countertransference). Supervisor competence includes knowledge, skills, attitudes, and values regarding the empirical base of multicultural, diversity, and clinical supervision research and practice, including from an international frame (Falender et al., 2013; Falender, Ellis, & Burnes, 2012).

The supervisor provides ongoing and specific formative feedback, based on behavioral observations of clinical work, timely and targeted to the supervisee's goals and performance. The supervisor ensures transparency in all aspects of feedback to the supervisee, sharing the monitoring of progress on the supervisee's development of competencies, as well as areas in which competency expectations are not being met.

The supervisor (and supervisee) will face challenges along the way, several of which are highlighted in the chapters in the volume. For example, not all supervisees will be self-aware or motivated or have the capacity for in-depth self-examination. Not all supervisees will be trusting of the supervisor or the supervisory process to disclose diversity or multicultural factors that the supervisor views as relevant to client's or clients' clinical progress. We suggest that adopting an intentional framework is essential to facilitate supervisory processes that enhance diversity and multicultural competence and can be initiated by the following:

1. informed consent in the supervision contract regarding the important role cultural diversity factors—multicultural and

diversity features (specifically identifying that multiple identities intersect) and personal reactivity play in clinical supervision and services;

2. modeling appropriate targeted self-disclosure of cultural or diversity impact of clients on the supervisor to the supervisee opening the door to reflections (e.g., "This might be a generational difference in our attitudes toward this client" or "The fact that I share a cultural/religious background with this client may be a factor in our different viewpoints");

3. allowing time for the supervisory alliance to be developed and allowing that supervisees may have had previous experiences in supervision that were insensitive;

4. facilitating a process marked by respect and noncoercion with regard to disclosure—with focus on the impact of specific behavior on the client or the clinical process;

5. seeing clearly that multiculturalism and diversity are part of the competencies expectations, and specific goals may need to be introduced to facilitate development (e.g., recognizing impact of self on others; articulating attitudes, values, and beliefs toward diverse others; Fouad et al., 2009, S10) or demonstrating this self-knowledge, awareness, and understanding (e.g., articulates how ethnic group values influence who one is and how one relates to other people; Fouad et al., 2009, S14);

6. understanding that strains and even ruptures in the supervisory relationship may occur if misunderstandings occur and that it is a supervisory responsibility to identify and address these; and

7. committing to providing a multiculturally/diversity affirmative supervisory environment that will facilitate clinical training and client treatment.

Supervision of Supervision

The competence to be effective in diversity and multicultural supervision is a developmental process. With the recognition that clinical supervision is a distinct professional practice comes the necessity for specific training (Falender et al., 2012; Falender & Shafranske, 2007). To achieve competence, supervision of supervision is one of the most generally cited training procedures. To supervise, one must complete the requisite training that includes training in the process of being an effective supervisee (Falender & Shafranske, 2012), specific coursework on clinical supervision, and supervision of supervision— that is, supervision directed at ensuring the quality and integrity of supervision practice, including observation of the process of clinical supervision between the supervisor-in-development and the supervisee.

GOING FORWARD

Although *paradigm shift* may be an overused phrase, we believe that the infusion of diversity perspectives is a larger paradigm shift for supervisors than may have been anticipated. Taboos regarding introducing discussion of diversity, discomfort, and the competence to address them once the topics are introduced may increase supervisor anxiety and fear. Significant training is essential. The importance of this volume is in providing exemplars of infusion of diversity in all levels of the supervision process to enhance strength-based multicultural practice.

Each chapter in this volume provides perspective on the infusion of diversity into the supervision process. Although each contributor focused on a primary diversity characteristic, multiple identities are woven into each chapter. Through the use of supervision examples and dialogues, the contributing supervisors describe supervisor interaction with supervisees regarding their clients in the context of the shared and differing multiple identity statuses. Many chapters address and illustrate strategies to approach the unspoken diversity statuses of client, supervisee/therapist, and supervisor in the supervision context.

- In Chapter 2, Falicov provides an introduction to the concept of supervision as a cultural encounter and to MECA, a systematic approach to incorporation of culture of client, therapist–supervisee, and supervisor. In combination with competency-based clinical supervision, MECA provides a framework for multicultural/diversity clinical supervision.
- In Chapter 3, Porter provides a feminist, gendered, multicultural, ecological, and antiracist framework, considering the dialectic of power and demonstrating its benevolent use in the supervision process.
- In Chapter 4, Harrell describes paths and complexities of race-related multicultural competence and demonstrates a developmentally sensitive three-step process instilling race into the supervision process that artfully demonstrates the integration of knowledge, skills, attitude assessment, and formation in the supervision process.
- In Chapter 5, Falicov addresses the oft-neglected issues of immigration and migration, demonstrating the intricate weaving of

client history, life experience, and a strength-based approach to a graphic representation (genoecogram) of the client/families' multiple cultural milieus and transitions using stories of struggles and triumphs.

- In Chapter 6, Fouad and Chavez-Korell address social class and the psychological factors of power and privilege that are amplified in the supervisory relationship. They use benchmark competencies (Fouad et al., 2009) to track the development of the supervisee with attention to the multiple factors of competency-based supervision and the critical importance of attitudes and inference.

- In Chapter 7, Cornish and Monson describe a strength-based approach to disability and a competency-based approach to addressing disability in supervision, another under-addressed training area, including attitudes, skills, and knowledge and a skillful approach enlisting parallel process and supervisee and client reactivity.

- In Chapter 8, Shafranske describes an affirmative, respectful approach to religion and spirituality, identifying the general lack of preparation to competently integrate these cultural features into therapy or supervision; he recommends strategies in keeping with principles of evidence-based practice.

- In Chapter 9, Bieschke, Blasko, and Woodhouse address sexual minority issues and the intersection of religion and sexual minority concerns in an application of the integrative affirmative supervision model (Halpert et al., 2007), considering instances when sexual orientation differences differ in the supervisory triad (clients or clients, supervisee/therapist, supervisor) and the multiple identities of each member.

- In Chapter 10, Trimble and King contextualize the competencies required for clinical work with American Indian and Alaska Native clients, addressing principles of respect and requisite historical knowledge and skills and reflecting on the role of supervisor and supervisee and the supervisory relationship and parallel process.

- In Chapter 11, Chin, Petersen, Nan, and Nicholls describe an innovative approach to culturally sensitive group supervision.

- In the final chapter, Chapter 12, we (the editors) describe the reflective process, reiterate the critical importance of metacompetence (i.e., knowing what one does not know), and provide specific steps to enhance multicultural competence, a sine qua non of clinical supervision.

REFERENCES

Allwood, C. M., & Berry, J. W. (2006). Origins and development of indigenous psychologies: An international analysis. *International Journal of Psychology, 41*, 263–268. doi:10.1080/00207590544000013

American Counseling Association. (2010). Competencies for counseling with transgender clients. *Journal of LGBT Issues in Counseling, 4*, 135–159. doi: 10.1080/15538605.2010.524839

American Psychological Association. (1998). Resolution on appropriate therapeutic responses to sexual orientation. *American Psychologist, 53*, 934–935.

American Psychological Association. (2000). Guidelines for psychotherapy with lesbian, gay, and bisexual clients. *American Psychologist, 55*, 1440–1451. doi:10.1037/0003-066X.55.12.1440

American Psychological Association. (2003a). *Guidelines on multicultural education, training, research, practice, and organizational change for psychologists.* Retrieved from http://www.apapracticecentral.org/ce/guidelines/multicultural.pdf

American Psychological Association. (2003b). *Guidelines for psychological practice with older adults.* Retrieved from http://www.apa.org/practice/guidelines/older-adults.pdf

American Psychological Association. (2007). *Guidelines for psychological practice with girls and women.* Retrieved from http://www.apa.org/about/division/girlsand women.pdf

American Psychological Association. (2008). *Report of the APA Task Force on the implementation of the* Multicultural Guidelines. Retrieved from http://www.apa.org/about/policy/multicultural-report.pdf

American Psychological Association. (2009). *Guidelines and principles for accreditation of programs in professional psychology.* Retrieved from http://www.apa.org/ed/accreditation/about/policies/guiding-principles.pdf

American Psychological Association. (2010). *Ethical principles of psychologists and code of conduct (2002; amended June 1, 2010).* Retrieved from http://www.apa.org/ethics/code/index.aspx

American Psychological Association. (2011a). *Guidelines for assessment of and intervention with persons with disabilities.* Retrieved from http://www.apa.org/pi/disability/resources/assessment-disabilities.aspx

American Psychological Association. (2011b). *Guidelines for psychological practice with lesbian, gay, and bisexual clients.* Retrieved from http://www.apa.org/pi/lgbt/resources/guidelines.aspx

American Psychological Association. (2013). *Guidelines for the practice of telepsychology.* Retrieved from http://www.apa.org/

Americans With Disabilities Act of 1990, Pub. L. No. 101-336, § 2, 104 Stat. 328 (1990).

Ancis, J. R., & Ladany, N. (2001). A multicultural framework for counselor supervision. In J. R. Bradley & N. Ladany (Eds.), *Counselor supervision: Principles, process, and practice* (3rd ed., pp. 63–90). New York, NY: Brunner-Routledge.

Ancis, J. R., & Ladany, N. (2010). A multicultural framework for counselor supervision. In N. Ladany & L. J. Bradley (Eds.), *Counselor supervision* (4th ed., pp. 53–94). New York, NY: Routledge.

Arredondo, P., Toporek, R., Brown, S. P., Sanchez, J., Locke, D. C., Sanchez, J. & Stadler, H. (1996). Operationalization of the multicultural competencies. *Journal of Multicultural Counseling and Development, 24,* 42–78. doi:10.1002/j.2161-1912.1996.tb00288.x

Behnke, S. H. (2012). Constitutional claims in the context of mental health training: Religion, sexual orientation, and tensions between the first amendment and professional ethics. *Training and Education in Professional Psychology, 6,* 189–195. doi:10.1037/a0030809

Bernard, J. M., & Goodyear, R. K. (1992). *Fundamentals of clinical supervision.* Needham Heights, MA: Allyn & Bacon.

Bieschke, K. J., & Mintz, L. B. (2012). Counseling psychology, model training values statement addressing diversity: History, current use, and future directions. *Training and Education in Professional Psychology, 6,* 196–203. doi:10.1037/a0030810

Brown, C., & Trangsrud, H. B. (2008). Factors associated with acceptance and decline of client gift giving. *Professional Psychology: Research and Practice, 39,* 505–511. doi:10.1037/0735-7028.39.5.505

Burkard, A. W., Johnson, A. J., Madson, M. B., Pruitt, N. T., Contreras-Tadych, D. A., Kozlowski, J. M., . . . Knox, S. (2006). Supervisor cultural responsiveness and unresponsiveness in cross-cultural supervision. *Journal of Counseling Psychology, 53,* 288–301. doi:10.1037/0022-0167.53.3.288

Burkard, A. W., Knox, S., Hess, S. A., & Schultz, J. (2009). Lesbian, gay, and bisexual supervisees' experiences of LBG-affirmative and nonaffirmative supervision. *Journal of Counseling Psychology, 56,* 176–188. doi:10.1037/0022-0167.56.1.176

Burnes, T. R., & Singh, A. A. (2010). Integrating social justice training into the practicum experience for psychology trainees: Starting earlier. *Training and Education in Professional Psychology, 4,* 153–162. doi:10.1037/a0019385

Canadian Psychological Association. (2009). *Ethical guidelines for supervision in psychology: Teaching, research, practice, and administration.* Retrieved from http://www.cpa.ca/cpasite/userfiles/Documents/SupervisionGuidelinesfinal25Jan09.pdf

Carter, R. T. (1995). *The influence of race and racial identity in psychotherapy.* New York, NY: Wiley.

Crook-Lyon, R. E., O'Grady, K. A., Smith, T. B., Jensen, D. R., Golightly, T., & Potkar, T. A. (2012). Addressing religious and spiritual diversity in graduate training and multicultural education for professional psychologists. *Psychology of Religion and Spirituality, 4,* 169–181. doi:10.1037/a0026403

Dickson, G. L., Angus-Calvo, B., & Tafoya, N. G. (2010). Multicultural counseling training experiences: Training effects and perceptions of training among a sample of predominantly Hispanic students. *Counselor Education and Supervision, 49,* 247–265. doi:10.1002/j.1556-6978.2010.tb00101.x

Dickson, G. L., Jepsen, D. A., & Barbee, P. W. (2008). Exploring the relationships among multicultural training experiences and attitudes toward diversity among counseling students. *Journal of Multicultural Counseling and Development, 36,* 113–126. Retrieved from http://www.counseling.org/Publications/Journals.aspx doi:10.1002/j.2161-1912.2008.tb00075.x

Dressel, J. L., Consoli, A. J., Kim, B. S. K., & Atkinson, D. R. (2007). Successful and unsuccessful multicultural supervisory behaviors: A Delphi poll. *Journal of Multicultural Counseling and Development, 35,* 51–64. doi:10.1002/j.2161-1912.2007.tb00049.x

Duan, C., & Roehlke, H. (2001). A descriptive "snapshot" of cross-racial supervision in university counseling center internships. *Journal of Multicultural Counseling and Development, 29,* 131–146. doi:10.1002/j.2161-1912.2001.tb00510.x

Education for All Handicapped Children Act of 1975, Pub. L. No. 94-142 . §1400, Stat. 274 (1977).

Eva, K. W., & Regehr, G. (2008). "I'll never play professional football" and other fallacies of self-assessment. *Journal of Continuing Education in the Health Professions, 28,* 14–19. doi: 10.10020chp.150

Eva, K. W., & Regehr, G. (2011). Exploring the divergence between self-assessment and self-monitoring. *Advances in Health Science Education, 16,* 311–329. doi: 10.1007/s10459-010-9263-2

Falender, C. A., Burnes, T., & Ellis, M. (2013). Introduction to major contribution: Multicultural clinical supervision and benchmarks: Empirical support informing practice and supervisor training. *The Counseling Psychologist, 41,* 8–27. doi:10.1177/0011000012438417

Falender, C. A., Ellis, M. V., & Burnes, T. (2012). Response to reactions to major contribution: Multicultural clinical supervision and Benchmarks. *The Counseling Psychologist, 41,* 140–151. doi:10.1177/0011000012464061

Falender, C. A., & Shafranske, E. P. (2004). *Clinical supervision: A competency-based approach.* Washington, DC: American Psychological Association. doi:10.1037/10806-000

Falender, C. A., & Shafranske, E. P. (2007). Competence in competency-based supervision practice: Construct and application. *Professional Psychology, Research and Practice, 38,* 232–240. doi:10.1037/0735-7028.38.3.232

Falender, C. A., & Shafranske, E. P. (2012). *Getting the most out of clinical training and supervision: A guide for practicum students and interns.* Washington, DC: American Psychological Association. doi:10.1037/13487-000

Falicov, C. J. (1988). Learning to think culturally in family therapy training. In H. Liddle, D. Breunlin, & D. Schwartz (Eds.), *Handbook of family therapy training and supervision* (pp. 335–357). New York, NY: Guilford Press.

Falicov, C. J. (1995). Training to think culturally: A multidimensional comparative framework. *Family Process, 34,* 373–388. doi:10.1111/j.1545-5300.1995.00373.x

Falicov, C. J. (1998). *Latino families in therapy: A guide to multicultural practice.* New York, NY: Guilford Press.

Field, L. D., Chavez-Korell, S., & Rodriguez, M. M. D. (2010). No hay rosas sin espinas: Conceptualizing Latina–Latina supervision from a multicultural developmental supervisory model. *Training and Education in Professional Psychology, 4,* 47–54. doi:10.1037/a0018521

Fitzgerald, T. D., Hunter, P. V., Hadjistavropoulos, T., & Koocher, G. R. (2010). Ethical and legal considerations for Internet-based psychotherapy. *Cognitive Behaviour Therapy, 39,* 173–187. doi:10.1080/16506071003636046

Fouad, N. A., Grus, C. L., Hatcher, R. L., Kaslow, N. J., Hutchings, P. S., Madson, M. B., . . . Crossman, R. E. (2009). Competency benchmarks: A model for understanding and measuring competence in professional psychology across training levels. *Training and Education in Professional Psychology, 3*(4 Suppl.), S5–S26. doi: 10.1037/a0015832

Garnets, L. (2007). Foreword: The "coming of age" of lesbian, gay, bisexual and transgender-affirmative psychology. In K. J. Bieschke, R. M. Perez, & K. A. DeBord (Eds.), *Handbook of counseling and psychotherapy with lesbian, gay, bisexual, and transgender clients* (pp. xi–xvi). Washington, DC: American Psychological Association.

Gatmon, D., Jackson, D., Koshkarian, L., Martos-Perry, N., Molina, A., Patel, N., & Rodolfa, E. (2001). Exploring ethnic, gender, and sexual orientation variables in supervision: Do they really matter? *Journal of Multicultural Counseling and Development, 29,* 102–113. doi:10.1002/j.2161-1912.2001.tb00508.x

Gauthier, J., Pettifor, J., & Ferrero, A. (2010). The Universal Declaration of Ethical Principles for Psychologists: A culture-sensitive model for creating and reviewing a code of ethics. *Ethics and Behavior, 20,* 1–18.

Gloria, A. M., Hird, J. S., & Tao, K. W. (2008). Self-reported multicultural supervision competence of White predoctoral intern supervisors. *Training and Education in Professional Psychology, 2,* 129–136. doi:10.1037/1931-3918.2.3.129

Goodman, L. A., Liang, B., Helms, J. E., Latta, R. E., Sparks, E., & Weintraub, S. R. (2004). Training counseling psychologists as social justice agents: Feminist and multicultural principles in action. *The Counseling Psychologist, 32,* 793–836. doi:10.1177/0011000004268802

Halpert, S. C., Reinhardt, B., & Toohey, M. J. (2007). Affirmative clinical supervision. In K. J. Bieschke, R. M. Perez, & K. A. DeBord (Eds.), *Handbook of counseling and psychotherapy with lesbian, gay, bisexual, and transgender clients* (2nd ed.; pp. 341–358). Washington, DC: American Psychological Association. doi:10.1037/11482-014

Hansen, N. D., Randazzo, K. V., Schwartz, A., Marshall, M., Kalis, D., Frazier, R., . . . Norvig, G. (2006). Do we practice what we preach? An exploratory survey of multicultural psychotherapy competencies. *Professional Psychology, Research and Practice, 37,* 66–74. doi:10.1037/0735-7028.37.1.66

Harrell, S. (2006). *Dynamics of difference*. Unpublished manuscript.

Helms, J. E. (1990). *Black and White racial identity: Theory, research and practice*. New York, NY: Greenwood Press.

Helms, J. E., & Cook, D. A. (1999). *Using race and culture in counseling and psychotherapy: Theory and process*. Needham Heights, MA: Allyn & Bacon.

Hernández, P., & McDowell, T. (2010). Intersectionality, power, and relational safety in context: Key concepts in clinical supervision. *Training and Education in Professional Psychology, 4*, 29–35. doi:10.1037/a0017064

Hoshmand, L. T. (2001). Psychotherapy as an instrument of culture. In B. D. Slife, R. N. Williams, & S. H. Barlow (Eds.), *Critical issues in psychotherapy: Translating new ideas into practice* (pp. 99–114). Thousand Oaks, CA: Sage. doi:10.4135/9781452229126.n9

Individuals With Disabilities Education Act, 20 U.S.C. § 1400 (2004).

International Union of Psychological Science. (2008). *Universal declaration of ethical principles for psychologists*. Retrieved from http://www.am.org/iupsys/resources/ethics/univdecl2008.html

Jernigan, M. M., Green, C. E., Helms, J. E., Perez-Gualdron, L., & Henze, K. (2010). An examination of people of color supervision dyads: Racial identity matters as much as race. *Training and Education in Professional Psychology, 4*, 62–73. doi:10.1037/a0018110

Kaduvettoor, A., O'Shaughnessy, T., Mori, Y., Beverly, C., Weatherford, R. D., & Ladany, N. (2009). Helpful and hindering multicultural events in group supervision: Climate and multicultural competence. *The Counseling Psychologist, 37*, 786–820. doi:10.1177/0011000009333984

Kaslow, F. W. (2000). Continued evolution of family therapy: The last twenty years. *Contemporary Family Therapy, 22*, 357–386.

Ladany, N., Brittan-Powell, C. S., & Pannu, R. K. (1997). The influence of supervisory racial identity interaction and racial matching on the supervisory working alliance and supervisee multicultural competence. *Counselor Education and Supervision, 36*, 284–304. doi:10.1002/j.1556-6978.1997.tb00396.x

Ladany, N., Inman, A. G., Constantine, M. G., & Hofheinz, E. W. (1997). Supervisee multicultural case conceptualization ability and self-reported multicultural competence as functions of supervisee racial identity and supervisor focus. *Journal of Counseling Psychology, 44*, 284–293. doi:10.1037/0022-0167.44.3.284

Leong, F. T. L., Pickren, W. E., Leach, M. M., & Marsella, A. J. (Eds.). (2012). *Internationalizing the psychology curriculum in the U. S.* New York, NY: Springer. doi:10.1007/978-1-4614-0073-8

Leong, F. T. L., & Wagner, N. S. (1994). Cross-cultural counseling supervision: What do we know? What do you need to know? *Counselor Education and Supervision, 34*, 117–131. Retrieved from http://www.unco.edu/ces/ doi:10.1002/j.1556-6978.1994.tb00319.x

Loganbill, C., Hardy, E., & Delworth, U. (1982). Supervision: A conceptual model. *The Counseling Psychologist, 10*, 3–42. doi:10.1177/0011000082101002

Lyons, H. G., Bieschke, K. J., Dendy, A. K., Worthington, R. L., & Georgemiller, R. (2010). Psychologists' competence to treat lesbian, gay, and bisexual clients: State of the field and strategies for improvement. *Professional Psychology: Research and Practice, 41*, 424–434. doi:10.1037/a0021121

Marsella, A. J. (2012). Internationalizing the clinical psychology curriculum: Foundations, issues, and directions. In F. T. L. Leong, W. E. Pickren, M. M. Leach, & A. J. Marsella (Eds.), *Internationalizing the psychology curriculum in the U. S.* (pp. 179–200). New York, NY: Springer.

McGoldrick, M., Giordano, J., & Pearce, J. K. (1996). *Ethnicity and family therapy.* New York, NY: Guilford.

Mead, M. (2001). *Sex and temperament in three primitive societies.* New York, NY: HarperCollins. (Original work published 1935)

Miller, D. S. S., Forrest, L., & Elman, N. S. (2009). Training directors' conceptualizations of the intersections of diversity and trainee competence problems: A preliminary analysis. *The Counseling Psychologist, 37*, 482–518. doi:10.1177/0011000008316656

Miville, M. L., Duan, C., Nutt, R. L., Waehler, C. A., Suzuki, L., Pistole, M. C., . . . Corpus, M. (2009). Integrating practice guidelines into professional training: Implications for diversity competence. *The Counseling Psychologist, 37*, 519–563. doi:10.1177/0011000008323651

Miville, M. L., Rosa, D., & Constantine, M. G. (2005). Building multicultural competence in clinical supervision. In M. G. Constantine & D. W. Sue (Eds.), *Strategies for building multicultural competence in mental health and educational settings* (pp. 192–211). New York, NY: Wiley.

Myers, S. B., Endres, M. A., Ruddy, M. E., & Zelikovsky, N. (2012). Psychology graduate training in the era of online social networking. *Training and Education in Professional Psychology, 6*, 28–36. doi:10.1037/a0026388

Olkin, R. (1999). *What psychotherapists should know about disability.* New York, NY: Guilford Press.

Pettifor, J. (2009). Commentary on value-based ethical decision-making. *Psychoanalytic Psychotherapy in South Africa, 17*, 96–100. Retrieved from http://csaweb116v.csa.com/ids70/results.php?SID=kj2tit2k0us0lhr6frrrsivsp2&id=5

Pettifor, J., & Ferrero, A. (2012). Ethical dilemmas, cultural differences, and the globalization of psychology. In M. L. Leach, M. J. Stevens, G. Lindsay, A. Ferreo, & Y. Korkut (Eds.), *The Oxford handbook of international psychological ethics* (pp. 28–41). New York, NY: Oxford University Press. doi:10.1093/oxfordhb/9780199739165.013.0003

Pettifor, J. L., McCarron, M. C. E., Schoepp, G., Stark, C., & Stewart, D. (2010). *Resource guide for psychologists: Ethical supervision in teaching, research, practice, and administration.* Ottawa, Ontario, Canada: Canadian Psychological Association. Retrieved from http://www.cpa.ca/docs/file/Ethics/CPAcoeEthicalSuper-GuideApprovedNovember2010.pdf

Pieterse, A. L., Evans, S. E., Risner-Butner, A., Collins, N. M., & Mason, L. B. (2008). Multicultural competence and social justice training in counseling psychology and counselor education: A review and analysis of a sample of multicultural course syllabi. *The Counseling Psychologist, 37*, 93–115. doi:10.1177/0011000008319986

Porter, N. (1995). Integrating antiracist, feminist, and multicultural perspectives in psychotherapy: A developmental supervision mode. In H. Landrine (Ed.), *Handbook of cultural diversity in the psychology of women* (pp. 163–176). Washington, DC: American Psychological Association.

Ratts, M. J., Toporek, R. L., & Lewis, J. A. (2010). *ACA Advocacy competencies: A social justice framework for counselors.* Alexandria, VA: American Counseling Association. doi:10.5330/PSC.n.2010-11.90

Reynolds, A. L. (2011). Understanding the experiences and perceptions of faculty who teach multicultural counseling courses: An exploratory study. *Training and Education in Professional Psychology, 5*, 167–174. doi:10.1037/a0024613

Sammons, C. C., & Speight, S. L. (2008). A qualitative investigation of graduate-student changes associated with multicultural counseling classes. *The Counseling Psychologist, 36*, 814–838. doi:10.1177/0011000008316036

Sanchez-Hucles, J., & Jones, N. (2005). Breaking the silence about race in training, practice, and research. *The Counseling Psychologist, 33*, 547–558. doi:10.1177/0011000005276462

Schwartz, A., Rodriguez, M. M. D., Santiago-Rivera, A. L., Arredondo, P., & Field, L. D. (2010). Cultural and linguistic competence: Welcome challenges from successful diversification. *Professional Psychology: Research and Practice, 41*, 210–220. doi:10.1037/a0019447

Sehgal, R., Saules, K., Young, A., Grey, M. J., Gillem, A. R., Nabors, N. A. . . . Jefferson, S. (2011). Practicing what we know: Multicultural counseling competence among clinical psychology trainees and experienced multicultural psychologists. *Cultural Diversity and Ethnic Minority Psychology, 17*, 1–10. doi:10.1037/a0021667

Singh, A., & Chun, K. Y. S. (2010). "From the margins to the center": Moving towards a resilience-based model of supervision for queer people of color supervisors. *Training and Education in Professional Psychology, 4*, 36–46. doi:10.1037/a0017373

Smith, L. (2009). Enhancing training and practice in the context of poverty. *Training and Education in Professional Psychology, 3*, 84–93. doi:10.1037/a0014459

Sue, D. W. (2009). Racial microaggressions and worldviews. *American Psychologist, 64*, 220–221. doi:10.1037/a0015310

Sue, D. W., Arredondo, P., & McDavis, R. J. (1992). Multicultural counseling competencies and standards: A call to the profession. *Journal of Multicultural Counseling and Development, 20*, 64–88. doi:10.1002/j.2161-1912.1992.tb00563.x

Tervalon, M., & Murray-Garcia, J. (1998). Cultural humility versus cultural competence: A critical distinction in defining physician training outcomes in multicultural education. *Journal of Health Care for the Poor and Underserved, 9,* 117–125. doi:10.1353/hpu.2010.0233

Toporek, R. L., & Reza, J. V. (2001). Context as a critical dimension of multicultural counseling: Articulating personal, professional, and institutional competence. *Journal of Multicultural Counseling and Development, 29,* 13–30. doi:10.1002/j.2161-1912.2001.tb00500.x

Universal Declaration of Ethical Principles for Psychologists. (2008). Retrieved from http://www.cpa.ca/cpasite/userfiles/Documents/Universal_Declaration_asADOPTEDbyIUPsySIAAP_July2008.pdf

Vargas, L. A., Porter, N., & Falender, C. A. (2008). Supervision, culture, and context. In C. A. Falender & E. P. Shafranske (Eds.), *Casebook for clinical supervision: A competency-based approach* (pp. 121–136). Washington, DC: American Psychological Association. doi:10.1037/11792-006

Worthington, R. L., Mobley, M., Franks, R. P., & Tan, J. A. (2000). Multicultural counseling competencies: Verbal content, counselor attributions, and social desirability. *Journal of Counseling Psychology, 47,* 460–468. doi:10.1037/0022-0167.47.4.460

2

PSYCHOTHERAPY AND SUPERVISION AS CULTURAL ENCOUNTERS: THE MULTIDIMENSIONAL ECOLOGICAL COMPARATIVE APPROACH FRAMEWORK

CELIA J. FALICOV

As a nation of immigrants, the United States has always faced the challenge of understanding and integrating racial, social class, and ethnic diversity. This challenge has never been greater than now. Increasingly, psychotherapists provide mental health care to a wide range of families of diverse ethnicities, races, socioeconomic levels, nationalities, and religions, among other cultural variables. In training settings, supervisors must take into account cultural differences among clients, therapists, and supervisors. The fit between the culture of therapy and the culture of the therapist and the supervisor must be considered with the recognition that psychotherapy and supervision are cultural encounters. This chapter describes systemic and postmodern concepts and tools that can guide a multicultural approach to supervision.

Portions of this chapter are adapted from Chapter 1 of *Latino Families in Therapy, Second Edition*, by C. J. Falicov, 2014, New York, NY: Guilford Press. Copyright 2014 by Guilford Press. Adapted with permission.

http://dx.doi.org/10.1037/14370-002
Multiculturalism and Diversity in Clinical Supervision: A Competency-Based Approach, C. A. Falender, E. P. Shafranske, and C. J. Falicov (Editors)

PSYCHOTHERAPY AS CULTURAL ENCOUNTER

There are many obstacles to the integration of cultural perspectives in therapy and in supervision. Psychotherapists are sometimes unsure about what cultural heritage and sociopolitical context have to do with human suffering and mental health care. Although they may acknowledge that clients are deeply connected to their cultural roots in ways that bolster or limit their resources, clinicians are unclear as to how to incorporate these issues in theory and practice. Even less acknowledged is the fact that mainstream cultural ideals may create conflicts and contradictions for individuals and families that may be in cultural transition or do not fit those mainstream ideals for a variety of reasons, such as class, religion, race, sexual orientation, ethnicity, or political ideology. An additional obstacle is that mental health providers are necessarily limited in the treatments they offer by the very concepts and methods they use, because their training is imbued with the constructions and ideologies of mainstream Euro-American culture. This fact is seldom recognized because until recently, therapists and supervisors have been largely trained with the assumption that psychological knowledge has universal application; further, systematic efforts have not been taken to critically appreciate that psychology as a science inherently reflects cultural values. A common assumption of supervisors and supervisees based in psychological theory centers on the universality of mother–child as the primary attachment dyad. This is certainly the most frequent form of attachment in Euro-American cultures. In many collectivistic ethnic cultures and lower socioeconomic classes, however, the presence of and caretaking by many significant adults call into question this universality, as it is possible to theorize about the effects of multiple significant early attachments.

A culturally attuned postmodern position requires the recognition that the professional values and perspectives of the therapist inform the therapeutic encounter as much as the values of the client. The therapist also brings to this encounter the personal values acquired in the cultures of his or her own families. In spite of a long-standing psychoanalytic tradition of questioning therapists' objectivity and encouraging self-examination, not much attention has been paid to the notion of *cultural countertransference* (Foster, 1998) that takes into account clients' and therapists' perceptions of each other's' groups. Supervisors must recognize that therapists' subjectivity is a vital component in the treatment of clients whose race, class, or ethnicity varies from that of the therapist. Clinicians' and clients' cultural histories and social contexts are not neutral or irrelevant to the therapeutic relationship and have a profound impact on treatment outcome and process (La Roche, 1999).

But how is one to approach the incorporation of these exceedingly complex sets of cultural variables in therapy theory and practice? What is the actual place of culture in therapy and in supervision? When, what for, and how are cultural dimensions to be articulated with the therapeutic and supervisory context? Some approaches advocate the need for a priori knowledge of ethnic or other cultural traits (e.g., Italians may value very close family ties). Others prefer to focus on universal invariants in families' predicaments (e.g., children need to be raised by adults) and consider cultural differences to be tangential to the therapy situation. There are also many in-between positions. Less common but necessary are approaches that sensitize therapists to the cultural underpinnings of their own theories and interventions and encourage modifying or developing theories to fit different cultures (Falicov 1995, 1998). Others have begun to search for new concepts and methodologies to detect and make use of cultural values and behaviors as they emerge during the treatment process and thus rely minimally on a priori knowledge of the particular culture of the client (Lappin, 1983; Montalvo & Gutierrez, 1983).

There are also risks to take and problems to resolve when entering this area. One of the difficulties is that the use of broad generalizations about cultural norms and values learned through anthropology or sociology may have some validity at the macrosocial level but may always need refinement and qualifications at the microsocial level. In fact, when therapists apply sociocultural norms to clients, they tend to use stereotypes and clichés that hamper rather than facilitate therapeutic work. It may be equally problematic, however, to ignore cultural norms and expectations when they have relevancy for the client's issues and therefore apply to the therapeutic situation in crucial aspects of clinical practice.

Including cultural perspectives in therapy and in supervision implies a constant vigilance in navigating between the Scylla of cultural ethnocentrism that ignores basic cultural differences and the Charybdis of cultural stereotyping that misses crucial individual differences. Like the statistician who starts with a null hypothesis and determines significance in a probabilistic framework, so the therapist and supervisor must approach the clinical relevance of cultural issues as a balancing of risks between two errors: (a) underestimating the impact of culture and incorrectly attributing dysfunction to a pattern that is normative in the individual's or family's culture (false positive, or Type I error) or (b) overestimating and magnifying the importance of culture at the expense of failing to recognize dysfunctional individual or family processes (false negative, or Type 11 error; Falicov, 1983). The approach offered in this chapter attempts to address these complexities of cultural inclusion in the therapeutic and supervisory situation. In Chapter 1 of this book, the definition of *supervision diversity competence* (see also Falender & Shafranske, 2004, 2007, 2012) set the foundation for the approach central to this book. This approach stresses the importance of self-awareness of supervisor and supervisee in each one's multiple dimensions of culture and social location. Diversity competence includes awareness, knowledge, and appreciation of the three-way interaction of the client's, supervisee's and supervisor's values, assumptions, biases, expectations derived from worldviews, and the integration of practice assessment and intervention skills.

In this chapter, I expand those ideas further by presenting a model that integrates knowledge, values, or assumptions and specific skills in diversity supervision and that is also incorporated in the chapters of this book. This model is the multidimensional ecological comparative approach (MECA). The conceptual systemic and postmodern basis for this model is discussed in the next two sections.

SUPERVISION AS CULTURAL ENCOUNTER

The supervision encounter is really an encounter between the supervisor's, the therapist's, and the client's theoretical and personal *cultural maps* (see Figure 2.1). A therapist's views about each client, as well as a supervisor's view of each supervisee, stem from his or her cultural maps, which include a preferred brand of theory and professional subculture (Fancher, 1995). The therapist's maps are further affected and organized by personal values, views,

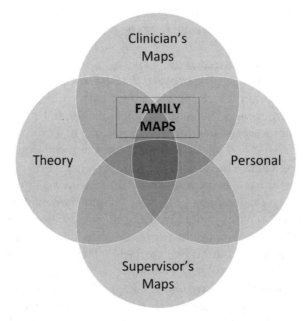

Figure 2.1. The supervision encounter is multicultural. From *Latino Families in Therapy* (2nd ed., p. 22), by C. J. Falicov, 2014, New York, NY: Guilford Press. Copyright 2014 by Guilford Press. Reprinted with permission.

and preferences acquired in his or her family of origin and other life influences (see, e.g., Aponte et al., 2009). For instance, a therapist who upholds a prochoice ideology may have difficulties separating her views from those of her prolife client who is feeling depressed and overwhelmed by her fifth pregnancy. Similarly, the supervisor's maps about the therapist-in-supervision stems from his or her theoretical position and personal culture. The supervisor as observer becomes part of the cultural equation, together with the supervisee. He or she is no longer the privileged outsider looking in, perceiving patterns not apparent to those within the system. Like the therapist in the supervisee role, the supervisor must practice cultural self-reflection and cultural humility.

The concept of *cultural humility*, used more commonly among family physicians (Juarez et al., 2006; Rust et al., 2006; Tervalon & Murray-García, 1998) than among psychotherapists, captures more accurately than the concept of cultural competence the reality that the client is the expert who is uniquely qualified to educate the therapist about his multiculturalism, that is, his membership in multiple cultural groups and his life stressors, which in turn affect his or her treatment priorities. The supervisor must help the supervisee assume the role of student who is willing to learn what cultural issues are relevant to each client. In a parallel process, the supervisor needs to be open to learning from the supervisee about his or her cultural location rather than assuming cultural knowledge based on preconceived identity labels. This points to the importance of the value dimension, which complements knowledge and skills, in competency-based supervision. Supervisors play a unique role in instilling this value rather than simply imparting knowledge about cultural variables.

Rather than presupposing objectivism or the notion that reality can be grasped through direct knowledge and experience, the approach offered in this chapter is based on a systemic presupposition of *perspectivism* (Von Bertalanffy, 1968), that is, that one's views of reality depend on one's perspective, which even organizes the observations themselves. This is consistent with the postmodern sensibility that all knowledge is perspectival (see Chapter 1) and the values and life experiences of the individual shape what can be known, as well as ways of knowing.

Perspectivism requires that one adopt a relational understanding of all descriptions when working with culturally diverse clients. An example given by anthropologists (Sampson, 1993) refers to the notion that when an observer, such as a therapist, describes the child-rearing practices of a client of another culture as being too strict, the therapist does so by building a comparison with an implicit standard, hidden from his or her view and provided by his or her own dominant culture. Strictness and indulgence are not essential or intrinsic qualities possessed by individuals of that culture. Rather, strictness or indulgence emerges as a result of a comparison that includes the vantage point of the observer. For instance, a Middle Eastern therapist may find an American family too indulgent with their children while the same family may appear on the normative side to an American therapist. Sluzki's (1982) analysis of the Latin lover further expands a similar observation in terms of how cultural stereotypes, on the part of observers, trigger culturally predictable behavior in the observed. If a therapist or a supervisor believes that the client or supervisee comes from a culture, for example, Asian, that favors privacy over self-disclosure, he or she may be overly careful in conducting inquiries, thus confirming the stereotype of shyness or private style in the client's or supervisee's preference. Bruner (1986) went further when he said,

> The Pueblo Indians are performing our theory; they are enacting the story we tell about them in our professional journals. We wonder if it is their story or ours. Which is the inside or the outside view. (pp. 148–149)

THE PLACE OF CULTURE: A SPECTRUM OF CHOICE

From a dynamic process-oriented perspective, culture becomes either background or foreground, depending on the issue at hand. Culture can also be an organizational reality, a defensive mask, or a powerful myth for the client, requiring that the therapist explore the connections between the presenting problem and cultural issues under the guidance of the supervisor. The following provides brief comments on the impact of perspective in considering the role of culture. One important task in supervision is to assist trainees to better recognize the fundamental or commonly used stance (e.g., background or foreground, as described next) they take to the role of culture.

Culture as Background

Therapists can, and have, made the choice to consider cultural influences as either tangential and optional or as central and necessary to the theory and practice of family therapy. For some clinicians, culture provides a background narrative and is seen as one of a multitude of forces that shape a family's predicament. Therapist and client have the choice to reflect upon these cultural forces, or not. For instance, a 42-year-old mother of two young children who has just heard about her diagnosis of fatal ovarian carcinoma may not find it relevant to examine the momentous implications of her untimely shortened life against the backdrop of her culture and religion but may prefer, along with her therapist, to focus on her emotional devastation.

Culture as Foreground

Therapists who view culture as an overpowering foreground narrative believe that many emotional problems are connected either to dominant, constraining self-definitions imposed by socialization or, alternatively, to alienation from one's ethnic identity and traditions or to disempowering social forces. For this last group, the healing potential lies in emotionally and ideationally reconnecting clients with their cultural myths, legacies, and sense of belonging to their cultural community. A therapist who adopts this position may feel compelled to discuss further with the dying client cultural resources and strengths that may provide comfort.

Four Possible Positions

Clinicians are further guided in the way they approach culture by taking certain positions—more implicit than explicit—about the relationship between culture and therapy. It is possible to summarize these positions into four categories: universalist, particularist, ethnic focused, and multidimensional ecological comparative. Each position has very different implications for multicultural supervision (see Exhibit 2.1).

1. The Universalist

A *universalist* position maintains that individuals and families are more alike than different. A universalist position emphasizes similarities rather than differences in both intrapsychic and interpersonal processes. Some therapists who believe in the stable universality of psychic and interactional processes claim that contextual variables such as race, gender, or ethnicity are irrelevant distractions from basic individual and family processes (Friedman, 1994). Indeed, most psychological concepts and theories are based on universalist

EXHIBIT 2.1
The Place of Culture in Supervision

Position	Multicultural supervision
Universalist	• No use
Particularist	• No use
Ethnic focused	• Cultural literacy in a separate course/lecture with specific content
Multidimensional ecological comparative approach	• Integrates culture with all learning • Distills diversity in basic systems parameters • Generic comparative maps

Note. From *Latino Families in Therapy* (2nd ed., p. 20), by C. J. Falicov, 2014, New York, NY: Guilford Press. Copyright 2014 by Guilford Press. Reprinted with permission.

assumptions: object relations, multigenerational transmission, attachment, triangulation, and life-cycle transitions, to name a few. Those who assume a universalist position regard culture as tangential to therapy and therefore to supervision.

It is undoubtedly correct that many shared biological and social imperatives create similarities across cultures. It is also crucial for therapists and supervisors to appreciate the sameness between groups. The danger, however, lies in therapists' committing ethnocentric errors, such as assuming that late adolescent separation from family is normative and indicative of healthy individuation when there are many cultural variations of this universal developmental process. However, the therapist may believe that his or her stance is objective and impartial.

2. The Particularist

At the other extreme is the *particularist* position, which states that all individuals and families are more different than they are alike. Each individual and family's idiosyncrasies make their culture unique unto itself. From a particularist perspective, no generalizations can be made about the relationship between an individual or a family and the larger culture, and therefore each individual's history and the interior of the family become responsible for the total dynamics of each case. For example, multigenerational family-oriented approaches might frame an individual's depression in the light of a family culture of unresolved secrets, without considering the effects of workplace racial discrimination on the client's mood. Similarly, similar schools of therapy can be regarded as cultures of healing in themselves (Fancher, 1995). Within the field of family therapy, Anderson and Goolishian's (1993) "not-knowing" position within postmodern language-based collaborative practices approximates a particularist position.

3. The Ethnic Focused

This third position stresses predictable diversity of thoughts, feelings, and behavior and also of attitudes toward health or illness, as well as of customs and rituals among different ethnic groups. This position speaks to the tendency of Irish people to marry late, the panic disease called *Koro* among the southeastern Chinese, or the acknowledgment of native healers such as *curanderos* or *shamans*, among myriad other collective patterns. This position has been pivotal in developing sensitivity to ethnic differences. It requires therapists to have knowledge about the characteristic traits of different ethnic groups and provides information along those lines (McGoldrick, Giordano, & Garcia-Preto, 2005).

The *ethnic-focused* position does not truly address other dimensions of collective identities, such as race, class, sexual orientation, disability, or nationality.

There is little room for cultural inconsistencies, dilemmas, or contradictions. It also assumes that the observer is culture free. Another limitation is that ethnic-focused generalizations tend to portray culture as static and stable rather than changing and unstable, which is true of most contemporary cultures. Even the most culturally isolated societies are in constant flux, largely moving toward Western ways. The danger is to fall into biases of ethnic stereotyping—exaggerating differences between therapists, clients, and supervisors.

The ethnic-focused approach advocates cultural literacy by educating the therapist on specific features of the culture of the client. As discussed in Chapter 1, the most common training in cultural competence has relied on a single course that, even though it covers knowledge, skills, and attitudes, has multiple obstacles to being incorporated by students as real, personally relevant, and necessary to the therapeutic encounter. It is certainly useful to alert therapists to ethnic differences, but stressing only general guidelines presents a number of pitfalls that need to be counteracted with the therapist's knowledge of his or her own culture and his or her prejudices, together with a stance of respectful curiosity, cultural naïveté, and a willingness to cede the role of expert to the client as narrative therapists have proposed (Dyche & Zayas, 1995). The three positions above do not consider the impact of social injustice in various forms of lack of access to resources, racism, and prejudice and many forms of income, education, and health service inequities in the lives of minorities. Thus, they disregard a huge source of mental distress for minority clients.

The approach taken in the fourth position, described next, presents a broader and more complex approach that results on a greater integration of culture and social justice to all aspects of knowledge, assumptions, and assessment and intervention skills. Furthermore, MECA stresses that all cultures have many strengths to be tapped, rather than therapists becoming agents of cultural change and promoting the values and assumptions of the dominant cultural discourses acquired in mainstream theory and practice.

4. A Multidimensional, Ecological, Comparative Approach

For more than 15 years, I have presented a framework (Falicov, 1995, 1998, 2003, 2014) for incorporating culture in therapy with a different approach than the add-on, ethnic-specific framework that defined cultural competence as becoming proficient with the cultural specifications of single or discrete ethnic groups. Instead, MECA attempts to provide a cultural-generic framework that focuses on the broad outlines of differences and similarities by using constructs and domains that are relevant to assessing and treating diverse clients. The MECA model presented here moves away from specific generalizations about various ethnic groups and attempts a more generalist model that incorporates sensitivity not only to culturally diverse values but also to the effects of social stresses in all aspects of psychotherapy assessment, intervention, and supervision.

A POSTMODERN DEFINITION OF CULTURE AS ECOLOGICAL NICHES AND CULTURAL BORDERLANDS

MECA encompasses the ability to hold the previous three positions: universalist, particularist, and ethnic focused. It offers a comprehensive definition of culture, a method for making meaningful comparisons, and room for multiple and evolving cultural narratives. The definition of culture is multidimensional and complex.

Definition of Culture

One of the first challenges is how to define culture and context in a nonstereotypic or formulaic fashion. I have always been opposed to static ethnic or cultural descriptions (Falicov, 1983, 1988, 1995) because they are more reflective of social science simplifications than of the true complexity of human behavior and experience. Indeed, static descriptions have never been more antithetical to reality than today, when cultural movement is truly vertiginous and the intersections of class, race, gender, religion, and other cultural contexts have never been more complex. MECA goes beyond the unidimensional culture-as-ethnicity framework toward a more comprehensive definition of culture, one that encompasses multiple variables; similarities and differences; the past and the present; and continuity and change in values, beliefs, and meanings over time.

As discussed in Chapter 1, the following definition underlines the multidimensionality and fluidity of culture:

> Culture is those sets of shared world views, meanings, and adaptive behaviors derived from simultaneous membership and participation in a variety of contexts, such as language; rural, urban or suburban setting; race, ethnicity, and socioeconomic status; age, gender, sexual orientation, religion, disability, nationality; employment, education and occupation, political ideology, stage of migration/acculturation, partaking of similar historical moments and ideologies. (Falicov, 1983, pp. xiv–xv)

Further, exclusion from various contexts can also be part of the cultural experience (Falicov 1995, 2003). This multidimensional view reflects more fairly the meaning of the word *diversity* than any one dimension alone. Individuals and families partake of and combine features of the many contexts listed in the definition. The contexts provide particular experiences and bestow certain values. It is the combination of multiple contexts and partial perspectives that shapes and defines each person's culture rather than any of those separately, nor does some monolithic "culture" exert an inexorable influence upon the individual. Each person is raised in a plurality of cultural subgroups that exert a multiplicity of influences depending on the degree of contact with each subcultural context. Culture can then be thought of as a community of individuals and families that partially share particular views, or dominant stories, that describe the world and give life meaning (Howard, 1991). Cultural similarities and differences reflect inclusion in or exclusion from various groups.

Because individuals and families partake and combine features of several of the contexts, it is necessary for therapists and supervisors to consider membership in all of the relevant contexts simultaneously. This exploration of culture should also include examining therapists' racist, sexist, or classist views, as well as countering their heterosexism and homophobia—that is, therapists should socialize their own critical consciousness and that of their clients (Burton, Winn, Stevenson, & Clark, 2004; Lawless, 2008).

Ecological Niches and Cultural Borderlands

Each person participates in diverse and multiple contexts. These contexts span languages, places, preferences, and subjective experience. Each person has a culture comprising a number of collective identities—groups of belonging, participation, and identification that make up his or her *ecological niche*. For example, Exhibit 2.2 shows my personal ecological niche, as well as my theoretical niche (related to my professional identity). Recent studies

EXHIBIT 2.2
Personal and Theoretical Ecological Niche

My personal ecological niche	My theoretical niche
• Argentine, naturalized American • Woman • White • Second generation middle-class • Psychologist • Liberal Democrat • Daughter of Eastern European Jews • Immigrant to the U.S. in the 1960s • Married for 30 years to a physician • Mother of 3 daughters; grandmother • Widow	• Human development (anthropology, sociology, psychology, and biology—life span development in cultural context) • Clinical psychology • Psychoanalysis • Client-centered Rogerian • Family therapist (structural, strategic, narrative)

Note. From *Latino Families in Therapy* (2nd ed., p. 25), by C. J. Falicov, 2014, New York, NY: Guilford Press. Copyright 2014 by Guilford Press. Adapted with permission.

acknowledge the intersections of race, gender, ethnicity, and class and thus, stress multiple identities (Kosutic & McDowell, 2008).

Each person's ecological niche shares *cultural borderlands,* or zones of overlap of similarity and difference with others by virtue of race, ethnicity, religion, occupation, or social class (Anzaldúa, 1987; Rosaldo, 1989). Such points of contact and divergence can be both limiting and enriching. A middle-class Chinese experimental psychologist who is an agnostic Democrat may have more in common with a similarly politically and religiously minded Jewish research psychologist than with a Catholic Chinese shopkeeper, because the first two share a greater number of cultural borderlands with each other. Rather than restricting oneself to one ethnic identity, one can talk about multicultural identities.

In a pluralistic society, one learns about cultural differences in myriad ways. As an outsider, one may rely on books, movies, radio, television, or firsthand contact at work, in the neighborhood, or at school to learn about cultural groups. It is virtually impossible for Latinos not to know something about African Americans or for Catholics not to know something about Mormons. Bateson, in her illuminating book *Peripheral Visions: Learning Along the Way* (1994), made a distinction between *identity multiculturalism,* which supports individuals in their own ethnic or social identities, and *adaptive multiculturalism,* which increases everyone's capacity to adapt by offering exposure to a variety of other cultural traditions.

Integrating Culture at All Levels

Rather than making culture marginal to theory and practice, a multi-dimensional, ecosystemic, comparative approach takes culture into the mainstream of all teaching and learning. It maintains that it is possible and desirable to integrate cultural awareness at every step in the process of learning how to observe, how to conceptualize, and how to work therapeutically, regardless of theoretical orientation. For example, if the issue being considered is divorce, remarriage, or stepparenting, what are the ethnic, social class, or religious differences one may expect to see reflected on these events? And what are the universals that transcend particular group variations? Culture is then discussed in the context of a specific issue rather than in the abstract. With MECA, issues of culture and social location can also be applied to one specific configuration, such as the metanarrative of *machismo* for Latino men, to deconstruct its origins and variability (Falicov, 2010).

Although suggestions and illustrations of culturally attuned therapeutic interventions are given in supervision, MECA does not prescribe a particular approach to conducting therapy. Rather, it introduces sufficient cultural relativism that it can be applied to many established schools of therapy and practice.

With MECA, the therapist is encouraged by the supervisor to always view families in a comparative, sociocultural context. Therapists make a quick holistic assessment of all the contexts to which the family belongs and attempt to understand the resources, the constraints, and the cultural dilemmas those multiple contexts create. Because families distill and draw selectively from the groups and ideologies to which they belong, the therapist should not assume that knowing the context is knowing the family. Consistent with the reality of shifting multiple identities, there is no list of *dos* and *don'ts* when working with various cultural groups. There is only one *do* and one *don't:* Do ask, and don't assume. Familiarity with various cultural contexts provides an avenue for raising relevant questions—the answers will be cocreated between the family and the therapist's impressions, which are likewise derived from being a witness and a participant in diverse cultural contexts and borderlands.

Further Postmodern Constructs for MECA

A postmodern definition of culture embodies social construction-ism and is contextualist and perspectivist. As it is further described in this section, although MECA incorporates systemic dimensions, it goes much beyond cultural stereotypes by offering a both/and view, and a knowing and not-knowing stance.

Beyond Cultural Stereotypes

The MECA framework is anchored in several concepts. First is the need to move beyond cultural stereotypes, particularly those based on a single dimension such as ethnicity. In a pluralistic society like the United States, persons are multicultural rather than belonging to a single ethnic group that can be summarized easily by a single or even a hyphenated label. In attempting to provide culturally attuned psychotherapy, professionals face the dilemma of acquiring sufficient cultural literacy and competence to understand and to respect the cultural beliefs of the client and yet not fall prey to stereotypical evaluations that rob clients of their individual histories and choices.

Both/And Stances

I have wrestled with the dilemma of presenting some generalizations that might be useful for those interested in multicultural psychotherapy or supervision and the challenge to reflect continuous cultural transforma-tions, new cultural blends, and cultural inconsistencies. It seems best to maintain a both/and position between making generalizations that describe some culture-specific aspect of a collective identity (e.g., "He is displaying Latino-style *machismo (not familismo)*" while recognizing similarities with other groups (e.g., "His bravado may not be dissimilar to public displays of preferred masculinities in other patriarchal societies"). Yet, it is also very important to honor subcultural and individual differences by probing personal interpretations or exceptions in the therapeutic and supervisory conversation. In an article focused on changing constructions of *machismo*, or male dominance (Falicov, 2012), I described the intricacies of applying widespread, often prejudiced, cultural and social stereotypes incorporated not only by therapists and supervisors but also by the clients themselves in defensive or accepting fashions. In that context, I described the therapeutic uses of starting conversations with the stereotype itself but deconstructing with clients fixed views by adding complexity and areas of exception and not fitting the stereotype as a way of expanding the range of personal and cultural views. Similarly in supervision, a supervisor can either refer to a widespread cultural stereotype, such as *machismo*, that the supervisee offers or recognize that it is part of the dominant outside culture and appraise more fully the cultural and personal influences for each client as a way of constructing a better developed assessment and more positive alternatives for change.

Knowing and Not-Knowing Stances

Knowing and not-knowing stances in therapy and in supervision are necessary when embracing multidimensionality. The ethnic-focused position, which requires knowing as many details about particular cultures as possible can be contrasted to a not-knowing stance in therapy. Not-knowing approaches are based on curiosity and encourage a dialogue that takes into account all meanings—cultural and personal—as they emerge in the therapeutic situation (Anderson & Goolishian, 1992; Dyche & Zayas, 1995; Lappin, 1983; Sue et al., 1998). In my opinion, the both/and approach, which combines a not-knowing stance with information about specific cultures that is relevant to the conduct of therapy, can provide the most beneficial means of working with diverse clients and client families. The following example illustrates how a supervisor applies these ideas about both/and and knowing and not-knowing in action during the live supervision of a supervisee who represents the "universal" institutionalized culture for the treatment of psychosis and the supervisor guides the situation to incorporate a cultural lens.

In a supervisory role, behind the one-way mirror, I witnessed an emerging power struggle between a supervisee at a well-known training institution and a Puerto Rican family, whom I shall call Bernal. The therapist, convinced that this was a family resistant to treatment, insisted that the father's delusions should be treated with psychotropic medication, claiming that otherwise treatment would not work. But the family politely refused pharmacotherapy.

From a knowing position, I suspected that the family's "resistance" was due to a cultural difference, although I did not know what it was exactly. With this in mind, I suggested to the therapist that she ask the family if they had other health or religious resources that might be helpful. This is a question that supervisors could regularly suggest to supervisees as a way to explore culture. The wife said she thought her husband would get better because prayer would help him. The supervisee slightly curved her shoulders, indicating incredulity about the usefulness of prayer. I could not, of course, question the therapist about this invalidating gesture at this moment, so I reserved this observation for a later private meeting. I intervened at this moment by suggesting to the supervisee that she adopt a curious stance by asking the family, "How does prayer work?" To this, the mother replied that she met twice a week with her friends to pray at a local storefront church, and all of their prayers together swelled up to a powerful, luminous energy that could counteract the dark forces that had overtaken her husband's psyche. The family believed in the power of the gradual accumulation of these positive forces through prayer, and they felt that medication would drastically interfere with this process.

A supervisor with general knowledge of cultural details, attuned to the possibility that religion may be playing a role in the family's resistance to a universal medical cure for delusions, encouraged the supervisee to inquire about the family's religious resources. Yet, the supervisor also incorporated a not-knowing approach by demonstrating curiosity about the cultural or personal particulars of prayer practices. The family, conscious of differences with the dominant culture views, might not have volunteered their prayer practice. The ethnic-focused supervisor may have stopped at a simple respect for the family's cultural solution. The MECA supervisor and supervisee, always incorporating a not-knowing, curious stance, revealed how prayer works in this particular subculture of religion.

Weaving back and forth between these stances—one informed by cultural guesses and the other guided by curiosity—the supervisor can help the supervisee to clarify the family's fears that medication would preclude their prayers from working. The supervisor can then guide the therapist to ask the client family to better define what kind of help they needed and were willing to accept from the clinic.

In such a both/and position, supervisor and supervisee must be comfortable with an ever-present "double discourse"—an ability to see the universal human similarities that unite people beyond color, class, ethnicity, and gender, while recognizing and respecting culture-specific differences that exist because of color, class, ethnicity, and gender. This double discourse may be explicit or implicit, foreground or background, expanding or shrinking the cultural emphasis. It may come about from some basic knowledge about cultural differences or from a curious and respectful not-knowing stance, depending on the demands of the particular clinical case. This both/and position also includes at all times a particularist view that recognizes and respects the uniqueness and idiosyncrasies of each family's story and choices.

Two Major Constructs About Difference

The MECA framework encompasses two contructs: (a) a *cultural diversity* practice that respects cultural preferences among clients and critically examines existing theories and techniques used in psychotherapy and (b) a *social justice* practice that focuses on the effects of power differentials (due to gender, economic, and racial inequities) on individual and family well-being and on the relationship between clients and therapists (see Exhibit 2.3).

Over the past two decades, the number of articles and books focused on cultural diversity and social justice has been increasing in the psychotherapy literature (Crethar, Torres Rivera, & Nash, 2008; Falicov, 1983, 1995, 1998, 2003; Kosutic & McDowell, 2008; McGoldrick et al., 1999; Sluzki, 2001; Turner, Wieling, & Allen, 2004). The more traditional approach about cultural competence has been to learn ethnic-specific behaviors for various cultural groups and to make room or increase tolerance for variability in values or behaviors from the dominant culture norms and expectations. The newer approach presented here may create tensions for those schooled in the more traditional approach, as the new development requires a much broader and complex definition of *culture* that includes a multiplicity of contexts, that is, social class, race, migration experiences, gender, occupation, and political ideology, as well as ethnicity. Further, self-reflection about the culture of the

EXHIBIT 2.3
Multidimensional Ecological Comparative Approach Constructs:
Cultural Diversity and Social Justice

Cultural diversity	Social justice
Meaning and belief differences tied to the following:	Power differences tied to the following:
• Ethnicity	• Gender
• Religion	• Race
• Nationality	• Social class
• Profession	• Minority status
• Political ideology	
Clinical practice	Clinical practice
• Curiosity and respect	• Empowerment
• Culture-specific adaptations	• Cultural resistance
• Transformations of theory (attachment, individuation)	• Social action
	• Legitimize local knowledge

Note. From *Latino Families in Therapy* (2nd ed., p. 30), by C. J. Falicov, 2014, New York, NY: Guilford Press. Reprinted with permission.

observer is needed to acknowledge that the observed is not "the other" that can be described objectively.

Even though there has been a progression from a belief that cultural diversity alone was part of multiculturalism without including social justice issues to a much greater awareness of the need to include the sociopolitical contextual stressors for clients, often these two constructs are still conflated. However, they have different implications for therapeutic use with individuals, couples, and families.

A Cultural Diversity Lens

Clients' beliefs or behaviors that are part of a cultural meaning system other than the one in which the therapist has been raised and has personal experience of or, alternatively, has been schooled in, could unintentionally be judged as dysfunctional, or at least problematic. To avoid confusing other cultural ways with dysfunction, a supervisor must help the therapist to incorporate a critically questioning attitude toward the Euro-American biases inherent in most professional training. The supervisor must also encourage the therapist's examination of his or her sociocultural background. This means accepting that many theories and interventions stem from local cultural niches other than the client's, and therefore, they cannot be the standard by which individuals and families can be evaluated. Instead, a practice based on curiosity and respect for cultural diversity explores the healing resources within the client's culture and develops a stance of empathic "sociological imagination" (Dyche & Zayas, 1995; Lappin, 1983; Wright Mills, 1959).

When therapist and supervisor attend to issues of race, ethnicity, social class, gender, religion, or sexual orientation, critical questions are raised about the customary assumptions of mainstream psychotherapy, such as issues of attachment, individuation, or hierarchies in individual and family life. This critical awareness on the part of the therapist and the supervisor may lead to important transformations or accommodations of taken-for-granted therapy concepts and techniques (Gergen, Gulerce, Lock, & Misra, 1996; Sampson, 1993; Taylor & Gutmann, 1994).

A Sociopolitical or Social Justice Lens

In the clinical arena, a social justice position directs the attention to life conditions, power differentials, and prejudice that limit social and economic opportunities, promote internalized racism, and affect psychological development and mental health for those who are poor or marginalized (Aldarondo, 2007; Burnes & Singh, 2010). Without a lens that includes social inequities, cultural preferences may be used as explanations for economic failure, domestic violence, or poor school performance, whereas the larger negative effects of poverty and social discrimination are downplayed (Montalvo & Gutierrez, 1983).

A sociopolitical lens is not limited to impoverished clients. For example, in the past, a case of anorexia nervosa was viewed as "idiosyncratically" linked to an "overinvolved" mother and a "peripheral" father or to an adolescent's fears of her own sexuality, without acknowledgment of the social demand for the gender specialization of each parent and the social pressures for thinness in young women. Narrative therapists consider sociopolitical discourses to be central in treatment of many clients, including those with eating disorders (Freedman & Coombs, 1996; Madsen, 2007; Maisel, Epston, & Bordan, 2004; White, 1993). A social justice practice connects mental health issues with experiences of social oppression and aims to empower families in their interactions with larger systems and cultural discourses, including those in the psychotherapy field (Hardy & Laszloffy, 1994; Korin, 1994). Laszloffy and Hardy (2000) described ways in which racism can infiltrate treatment and offer skills and strategies for addressing racism.

Lewis (2010) proposed a developmental progression in social justice training beginning with individual focus to stressing institutional change. At the level of psychotherapy change for individuals and families, interactional justice rather than procedural or distributive justice is the most important to focus on during supervision of clients. The first act of interactional justice is that the therapist treats all clients with dignity and respect. In the case of the minority client, the exploration of unfair treatment in the individual's life and how the client has responded to these experiences of injustice is another meaningful act of interactional justice.

Supervisors can suggest that therapists begin social justice inquiries early, along with obtaining the historical facts, the cultural genogram, the presenting problems, or concerns that brought the client to therapy. This timing creates a context for acknowledging that injustices are a part of life for many people, and it may provide alternative ways for client and therapist to conceptualize the client's predicament. If supervisees gain a better understanding of how injustice has affected clients' lives and help them become better prepared to deal with present and future injustices, the treatment has been at least partially an act of social justice—this is usually called *empowerment*.

THE KEY GENERIC ECOSYSTEMIC DOMAINS

The MECA framework offers a way of thinking about domains of similarities and differences that are relevant to therapeutic practice. The generic ecosystemic domains, namely, migration/acculturation, ecological context, family organization, and family life cycle (see Figure 2.2), can be applied to

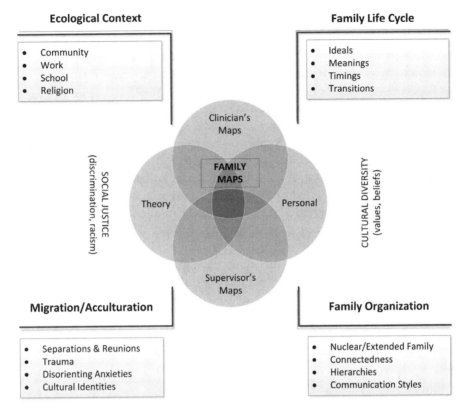

Ecological Context

- Community
- Work
- School
- Religion

Family Life Cycle

- Ideals
- Meanings
- Timings
- Transitions

SOCIAL JUSTICE (discrimination, racism)

CULTURAL DIVERSITY (values, beliefs)

Clinician's Maps

FAMILY MAPS

Theory

Personal

Supervisor's Maps

Migration/Acculturation

- Separations & Reunions
- Trauma
- Disorienting Anxieties
- Cultural Identities

Family Organization

- Nuclear/Extended Family
- Connectedness
- Hierarchies
- Communication Styles

Figure 2.2. The four generic domains of the multidimensional ecological comparative approach framework. From *Latino Families in Therapy* (2nd ed., p. 38), by C. J. Falicov, 2014, New York, NY: Guilford Press. Copyright 2014 by Guilford Press. Reprinted with permission.

the study of diverse cultural groups, incorporating cultural diversity and social justice lenses. Although a postmodern position of not-knowing and curiosity is maintained, the four dimensions can be thought as systemic domains. For example, family organization and family life cycle are a knowledge base about structure, function, and process that many systemic therapists have been schooled in and incorporate in their thinking, regardless of what their therapeutic orientation is. In MECA, the basic ideas that relationships are organized or patterned and that human beings undergo developmental processes of change are reaffirmed, but the specific content and timing of these events are not seen as universal but rather as culturally and sociopolitically diverse. Rather than learning the special characteristics of separate and distinct groups by using a different set of categories for each group, the systemic dimensions used allow for a comparative approach that often captures the common ground as well as differences among groups, hence the term *comparative* in MECA. In each of the four dimensions, namely, migration/acculturation, ecological context, family organization, and family life cycle, a supervisor must consider the multiple cultural contexts (race, social class, religion, occupation, language) in which the client, the therapist, and the supervisor are embedded.

The Journey of Migration and Culture Change

The first key generic domain—the journey of migration and culture change—attends to diversity in when, why, and how a family came to migrate. All immigrants to the United States share many psychosocial issues with other immigrant groups precipitated by the migration experience and acculturative stress. Migration may have significant mental health reverberations for the internal and external workings of individuals and families over several generations. A *psychology of migration* includes individual symptoms ranging from somatization to nightmares or family over- and underinvolvement caused by separations and reunions. A number of clinical issues are tied to such premigration experiences as coaxed migrations or traumatic crossings. Other clinical issues, from cultural gender gaps between husbands and wives to intergenerational conflicts between parents and children, emerge over time for many immigrant groups (Falicov, 1998, 2012; see also Chapter 5, this volume).

Ecological Context

The second generic domain—ecological context—examines diversity in where and how the client lives and fits in the broader sociopolitical environment. To take this into consideration, it is necessary to consider the client's total ecological field, including the racial, ethnic, class, religious, and educational communities in which the person lives; the living and working conditions; and the involvement with schools and social agencies. This domain sensitizes therapists to the *psychology of marginalization*, those psychosocial and mental health consequences of marginalized status; discrimination due to race, poverty, and documented or undocumented status; and other forms of powerlessness, underrepresentation, lack of entitlement, and access to resources. A client whose community support networks resemble that of the native village may ascribe very different meanings to depression than a client who is isolated in a strange and unwelcoming new environment. A supervisor can help the therapist phrase these ecological explorations early on and also identify social and community programs that can expand the boundaries of therapy for minority clients much beyond the private hour.

The constellation of beliefs about health, illness, religion, spirituality, and magic are relevant for understanding the client's preferred avenues and attitudes toward mainstream health care, psychotherapy, and complementary folk medicine (Falicov, 2009). Beliefs about personal responsibility and cultural styles of coping with adversity are of particular importance not only for immigrant and underserved clients but also for clients with chronic disabilities. This information is part of a *psychology of coping and healing*, but it is included under exploration of the ecological context because often the spiritual and health resources provided by priests, church congregations, and folk healers are part of the immediate neighborhood and network setting.

Family Organization

The third generic domain—family organization—considers diversity in family structure and in the values connected to different family arrangements. Many ethnic and poor families tend to share a preference for collectivistic, sociocentric family arrangements that encourage parent–child involvement and parental respect throughout life. This is in contrast to nuclear family arrangements that favor the strength of nonblood relationships such as husband–wife (Falicov, 2006). Many interactions are affected by this differential preference, such as connectedness and separateness; gender and generational hierarchies; or styles of communication and conflict resolution among family members and outsiders. Individuals and families in rapid cultural transformation often experience conflict and confusion over family models, obligations, and loyalties. It is common for immigrant and poor clients to need help in balancing affectional and pragmatic attachments to the family of origin and current loyalties to the family of procreation. These contradictions and dilemmas can be subsumed under a *psychology of cultural organizational transition*.

Family Life Cycle

The fourth generic domain—family life cycle—encompasses the dimension of time and focuses on diversity in how natural developmental stages and transitions are culturally patterned. Although the sequence of developmental events has universal biological aspects, many more are embedded in a cultural and ecological fabric: the timing of stages and transitions, the constructions of age-appropriate behavior, various growth mechanisms, and life-cycle rituals and rites, to name a few. It is valuable for therapists to understand similarities and differences between themselves and their clients, shaped in part by nationality, social class, or religion, regarding life-cycle values and experiences. These are noteworthy for therapists—and their supervisors—who were trained to assess function and dysfunction based on Euro-American life-cycle perspectives and developmental norms. A therapist may mistakenly assume a developmental individuation delay or dysfunctional attachment in, for instance, a 25-year-old married Guatemalan man who stops by his mother's to have a delicious *taquito* or *pastelito* and ask her opinions on many life issues. The impact of migration and transnational connections needs to be considered, too, because new values may coexist with traditions that complicate evaluations of developmental expectations (Falicov, 2011). This information can be considered part of a *psychology of cultural developmental transition*.

In short, the journey of migration and culture change, the patterned space of ecological context, the shapes of family organization before and after migration, and the temporal transitions of the family life cycle must always be present in the multicultural therapist's mind under the guidance of the supervisor. Each participant in the therapeutic encounter and the supervision encounter brings with them a unique cultural map that can be conceptualized in terms of MECA. In the next section, I describe how to include MECA maps in the process of supervision.

USING MECA TO COMPARE CULTURAL MAPS IN THE FIRST AND SECOND SUPERVISION SESSIONS

Awareness of MECA maps empowers therapists and supervisors to work with individuals and families of different ecological niches. It raises consciousness about professional and personal biases, and underscores the "partial perspectives" and "situated knowledge" that color our cultural observations (Haraway, 1991) and ultimately influence therapeutic interventions. It is helpful to include in the supervision contract a provision for making the steps outlined in this section part of the tasks planned for the first and second supervision sessions.

Examining Overlapping Maps

By examining these overlapping maps, areas of dissonance and consonance between family and therapist, as well as the richness of multiple contexts and cultural borderlands, are revealed. For example, family and therapist may have different ethnic backgrounds and religions but similar education and social class; they may all have experienced prejudice and marginalization because of race, gender, or political ideology, or experienced relocation or migration; or they may share developmental niches, perhaps as parents of adolescents. This multidimensional, comparative approach builds cultural bridges of connectedness between family, therapist, and supervisor. When there are areas of clear difference, the comparative approach stimulates interest in learning about the experiences and worldviews of others, and this attitude can forge new mutual understanding and respect.

Examining Ecological Niche and Cultural Borderlands for Therapist and Supervisor

The process of examining the ecological niche and cultural borderlands for therapist and supervisor should take place during the initial supervisory session. MECA provides a framework for introducing conversations about diversity and social justice in one's personal life, which are generally awkward or difficult to broach.

Examining Self-Location Regarding Culture in Therapy

To introduce a conversation about the place of cultural diversity and social justice in therapy, the supervisor can ask the supervisee to reflect on his or her own position relative to the spectrum of choice, from a universalist to a multidimensional comparative one. The supervisor follows by locating himself or herself in the spectrum of positions about culture and therapy. Therapist and supervisor jot down various cultural and sociopolitical contexts that comprise each one's ecological context.

Comparing Ecological Niches and Cultural Borderlands of Clients and Therapist

This exercise is followed by therapist and supervisor jotting down the ecological niche and cultural borderlands of the individual or family being seen in therapy. Cultural genograms also provide an alternative way to tap cultural variables in the therapeutic and the supervisory setting (Halevy, 1998; Hardy & Laszloffy, 1994). New inquiries could be broached, addressing issues of prejudice, stereotyped preconceptions, and possible countertransference with diverse clients.

Helping Supervisee Use MECA With Clients

To help the therapist navigate the client's external and internal cultural landscape, a quick perusal of the four MECA domains (migration, ecological context, family organization, and family life cycle) should happen during the second supervisory session. This facilitates decisions about what areas should be the focus of the therapeutic conversation and the extent to which these areas are connected to the presenting issues or symptoms. Exploring the family's migration history and acculturation, and its ecological resources or constraints, including religious and health supports as well as encounters with prejudice and discrimination, will help locate both therapist and client in the family's external cultural landscape. Conversations about culturally diverse values, particularly those related to family organization and life-cycle markers and processes, help a therapist enter the family's internal cultural landscape.

The therapist might note similarities and differences between the dominant cultural discourse, her own cultural background and preferences, and the client's cultural narrative, while attending in a both/and fashion to possible dilemmas and enrichments brought about by this meeting of cultures and ideologies. Among these, salient contrasts are collectivism and individualism, hierarchies and egalitarianism, and communicative directness and indirectness. Fundamental discussions center on client, therapist, and supervisor social locations and experiences of privilege and oppression (Hernández, 2008; Watts-Jones, 2010). Explorations of these and other similarities and differences in the supervisory hour should be conducted over time with respect, curiosity, and collaboration.

In sum, the many complexities of addressing multicultural encounters in supervision (Christiansen et al., 2011) could be aided by using the MECA definition of culture; by using the construct of ecological niche and cultural borderlands for the triad (client, therapist, supervisor) because such an analysis of their encounter portrays the complexity of multicultural locations; and by exploring possible overlaps, points of connectedness, and points of differences. Furthermore, the four dimensions of MECA (migration, ecological context, family organization and family life cycle) could also be incorporated in these comparisons.

STRUCTURING CONTENT AND PROCESS IN MULTICULTURAL SUPERVISION

Multicultural supervision involves several aspects that make it a didactic, descriptive, self-reflective, and experiential process (Burnes & Singh, 2010). The integration of MECA into diversity supervision competence as defined by Falender and Shafranske (2004, 2012; see also Chapter 1, this volume) can be summarized as follows:

1. Didactic aspects of multiculturalism include informative and appreciative knowledge, including a comprehensive contextual definition of culture, ecological niche, and cultural borderlands, and an examination of cultural diversity and social justice concepts, such as exploration of privilege and oppression. Supervisor suggests general readings and elective readings to apply concepts from literature to client cases, followed by

suggesting specific readings chosen to enlighten each client's issues and possible treatment course.

2. Supervisor and supervisee engage in self-examination by using ecological niche list and accompanying cultural borderlands to gain awareness of their own personal and professional history, attitudes, preconceptions, and professional and personal biases, which include ethnic and racial prejudices.

3. Assessment of a client's culture and social location by using MECA dimensions and MECA maps (see Figure 2.2) as tools to compare the therapist's and (supervisor's) maps with the client's maps with a view to integrating cultural dimensions and social justice concerns with client's presenting problems.

4. Collaborative periodic examination of the supervisory–supervisee system (self-esteem building; validation, criticism, points of connectedness, and points of cleavages).

Similarities and differences between therapists and clients and between therapists and supervisors are at the core of assessing culturally based client behavior and creating culturally attuned interventions. A process for deconstructing these similarities and differences is outlined in Figure 2.3.

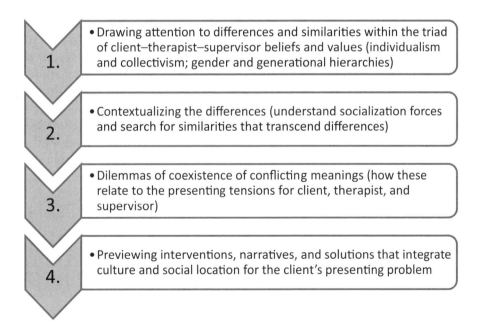

1. • Drawing attention to differences and similarities within the triad of client–therapist–supervisor beliefs and values (individualism and collectivism; gender and generational hierarchies)

2. • Contextualizing the differences (understand socialization forces and search for similarities that transcend differences)

3. • Dilemmas of coexistence of conflicting meanings (how these relate to the presenting tensions for client, therapist, and supervisor)

4. • Previewing interventions, narratives, and solutions that integrate culture and social location for the client's presenting problem

Figure 2.3. Deconstructing cultural and sociopolitical issues in supervision.

Supervisors face a complex, multilayered task that requires thoughtful consideration of culture and context for the therapeutic system encompassing the client and the therapist in various clinical settings that may have cultures of their own, such as a hospital, a school, a mental health center, or an independent practice. By examining the diversity of contexts, the supervisor can identify and clarify similarities and differences between client, therapist, and supervisor. For example, client and therapist may have different ethnicities and religions but share educational level and social class status. They may have both faced prejudice because of race or political ideology, or they may belong to a cohort that witnessed the same historical events or ideological shifts. Examining cultural matches between therapist and supervisor along cultural and sociopolitical dimensions encourages better understanding of each other's perspectives. A by-product of the supervisor taking the lead in this mutual sharing of cultural and race perspectives is that it may enhance the supervisee's perception of cultural competence and therefore confidence in the supervisor (Inman, 2006).

As discussed in Chapter 1, supervisors rarely take the initiative to discuss issues of race, ethnicity, gender, sexual orientation, social class, or religion. It is the position of the authors in this book that supervisors must take responsibility for (a) creating an environment early on in which these issues are openly dealt with; (b) creating an atmosphere of respect for cultural diversity and acknowledgment of the sociopolitical perspectives that single out groups for differential, unequal, and discriminatory treatment; and (c) addressing these issues appropriately (Estrada, Frame, & Williams, 2004).

By introducing cultural diversity and social justice in the supervision and by offering a continuous structure of awareness for comparative conversation, MECA helps to overcome common obstacles and inhibitions to address cultural and sociopolitical issues in therapy and in supervision. The methodology presented in this chapter also helps therapists to preview interventions, narratives, and possible solutions that integrate culture and social location for the client's presenting problem. The chapters in this book reflect the philosophy that culture and social justice should not be separated from the identities of any of the parties involved in the therapeutic system and need to be discussed not as an academic, add-on exercise but as an integral part of understanding a client's predicaments, strengths, and possible solutions.

REFERENCES

Aldarondo, E. (2007). *Advancing social justice through clinical practice*. Mahwah, NJ: Erlbaum.

Anderson, H., & Goolishian, H. (1992). The client is the expert: A not-knowing approach to therapy. In S. McNamee & K. J. Gergen (Eds.), *Therapy as social construction* (pp. 25–39). London, England: Sage.

Anzaldúa, G. (1987). *Borderlands/la frontera: The new mestiza.* San Francisco, CA: Spinsters/Aunt Lute.

Aponte, H., Powell, F. D., Brooks, S., Watson, M. F., Litzke, C., Lawless, J. & Johnson, E. (2009). Training the person of the therapist in an academic setting. *Journal of Marital and Family Therapy, 35,* 370–380. doi: 10.1111/j.1752-0606.2009.00123.x

Bateson, M. C. (1994). *Peripheral visions: Learning along the way.* New York, NY: HarperCollins.

Bruner, E. M. (1986). Ethnography as narrative. In V. W. Turner & E. M. Bruner (Eds.), *The anthropology of experience* (pp. 139–158). Urbana: University of Illinois Press.

Burnes, T. R., & Singh, A. A. (2010). Integrating social justice training into the practicum experience for psychology trainees: Starting earlier. *Training and Education in Professional Psychology, 4,* 153–162. doi:10.1037/a0019385

Burton, L. M., Winn, D.-M., Stevenson, H., & Clark, S. L. (2004). Working with African-American clients: Considering the "homeplace" in marriage and family therapy practices. *Journal of Marital and Family Therapy, 30,* 397–410. doi:10.1111/j.1752-0606.2004.tb01251.x

Christiansen, A. T., Thomas, V., Kafescioglu, N., Karakurt, G., Lowe, W., Smith, W., & Wittenborn, A. (2011). Multicultural supervision: Lessons learned about an ongoing struggle. *Journal of Marital and Family Therapy, 37,* 109–119. doi:10.1111/j.1752-0606.2009.00138.x

Crethar, H. C., Torres Rivera, E., & Nash, S. (2008). In search of common threads: Linking multicultural, feminist, and social justice counseling paradigms. *Journal of Counseling and Development, 86,* 269–278. doi:10.1002/j.1556-6678.2008.tb00509.x

Dyche, L., & Zayas, L. H. (1995). The value of curiosity and naïveté for the cross-cultural psychotherapist. *Family Process, 34,* 389–399. doi:10.1111/j.1545-5300.1995.00389.x

Estrada, D., Frame, M. W., & Williams, C. B. (2004). Cross-cultural supervision: Guiding the conversation toward race and ethnicity. *Journal of Multicultural Counseling and Development, 32,* 307–319.

Falender, C. A., & Shafranske, E. P. (2004). *Clinical supervision: A competency-based approach.* Washington, DC: American Psychological Association. doi:10.1037/10806-000

Falender, C. A., & Shafranske, E. P. (2007). Competence in competency-based supervision practice: Construct and application. *Professional Psychology: Research and Practice, 38,* 232–240. doi:10.1037/0735-7028.38.3.232

Falender, C. A., & Shafranske, E. P. (Eds.). (2008). *Casebook for clinical supervision: A competency-based approach.* Washington, DC: American Psychological Association. doi:10.1037/11792-000

Falender, C. A., & Shafranske, E. P. (2012). *Getting the most out of clinical training and supervision: A guide for practicum students and interns.* Washington, DC: American Psychological Association. doi:10.1037/13487-000

Falicov, C. J. (Ed.). (1983). *Cultural perspectives in family therapy*. Rockville, MD: Aspen.

Falicov, C. J. (1988). Learning to think culturally. In H. A. Liddle, D. C. Breunlin, & R. C. Schwartz (Eds.), *Handbook of family therapy training and supervision* (pp. 335–357). New York, NY: Guilford Press.

Falicov, C. J. (1995). Training to think culturally: A multidimensional comparative framework. *Family Process, 34*, 373–388. doi:10.1111/j.1545-5300.1995.00373.x

Falicov, C. J. (1998). *Latino families in therapy: A guide to multicultural practice*. New York, NY: Guilford Press.

Falicov, C. J. (2003). Culture in family therapy: New variations on a fundamental theme. In T. Sexton, G. Weeks, & M. Robbins (Eds.), *Handbook of family therapy: Theory, research and practice* (pp. 33–55). New York, NY: Brunner-Routledge.

Falicov, C. J. (2006). Family organization: The safety net of close and extended kin. In R. Smith & R. E. Montilla (Eds.), *Counseling and family therapy with Latino populations* (pp. 41–62). New York, NY: Routledge.

Falicov, C. J. (2009). Religion and spiritual traditions in immigrant families; Significance for Latino health and mental health. In F. Walsh (Ed.), *Spiritual resources in family therapy* (pp. 156–173). New York, NY: Guilford Press.

Falicov, C. J. (2010). Changing constructions of machismo for Latino men in therapy: "The devil never sleeps". *Family Process, 49*, 309–329. doi:10.1111/j.1545-5300.2010.01325.x

Falicov, C. J. (2011). Migration and the life cycle. In M. McGoldrick, B. Carter, & N. Garcia-Preto (Eds.), *The expanded family life cycle: Individual, family, and social perspectives* (4th ed., pp. 336–347). Upper Saddle River, NJ: Prentice Hall.

Falicov, C. J. (2012). Immigrant family processes. In F. Walsh (Ed.), *Normal family processes* (4th ed., 297–323). New York, NY: Guilford Press.

Falicov, C. J. (2014). *Latino families in therapy* (2nd ed.). New York, NY: Guilford Press.

Fancher, R. T. (1995). *Cultures of healing: Correcting the image of American mental health care*. New York, NY: Freeman. doi:10.1097/00005053-199509000-00010

Foster, R. (1998). The clinician's cultural countertransference: The psychodynamics of culturally competent practice. *Clinical Social Work Journal, 26*, 253–270. doi:10.1023/A:1022867910329

Freedman, J., & Coombs, G. (1996). *Narrative therapy: The social construction of preferred realities*. New York, NY: W. W. Norton.

Friedman, E. J. (1994). Sensitivity to contextual variables: A legitimate learning objective for all supervisors? *Supervision Bulletin, 7*, 4–7.

Gergen, K. J., Gulerce, A., Lock, A., & Misra, G. (1996). Psychological science in cultural context. *American Psychologist, 51*, 496–503. doi:10.1037/0003-066X.51.5.496

Halevy, J. (1998). A genogram with an attitude. *Journal of Marital and Family Therapy, 24*, 233–242. doi:10.1111/j.1752-0606.1998.tb01079.x

Haraway, D. (1991). *Simians, cyborgs, and women: The reinvention of nature.* New York, NY: Routledge.

Hardy, K., & Laszloffy, T. (1994). Deconstructing race in family therapy. *Journal of Feminist Family Therapy, 5*(3/4), 5–33. doi:10.1300/J086v05n03_02

Hernández, P. (2008). The cultural context model in clinical supervision. *Training and Education in Professional Psychology, 2,* 10–17. doi:10.1037/1931-3918.2.1.10

Howard, G. S. (1991). Culture tales: A narrative approach to thinking, cross-cultural psychology and psychotherapy. *American Psychologist, 46,* 187–197. doi:10.1037/0003-066X.46.3.187

Inman, A. G. (2006). Supervisor multicultural competence and its relation to supervisory process and outcome. *Journal of Marital and Family Therapy, 32,* 73–85. doi:10.1111/j.1752-0606.2006.tb01589.x

Juarez, J. A., Marvel, K., Brezinski, K. L., Glazner, C., Towbin, M. M., & Lawton, S. (2006). Bridging the gap: A curriculum to teach residents cultural humility. *Family Medicine, 38,* 97–102.

Korin, E. C. (1994). Social inequalities and therapeutic relationships: Applying Freire's ideas to clinical practice. *Journal of Feminist Family Therapy, 5*(3/4), 75–98. doi:10.1300/J086v05n03_04

Kosutic, I., & McDowell, T. (2008). Diversity and social justice issues in family therapy literature: A decade review. *Journal of Feminist Family Therapy, 20,* 142–165. doi:10.1080/08952830802023292

Lappin, J. (1983). On becoming a culturally conscious family therapist. In C. J. Falicov (Ed.), *Cultural perspectives in family therapy* (pp. 122–135). Rockville, MD: Aspen Systems. doi:10.1037/e467472004-001

La Roche, M. J. (1999). Culture, transference, and countertransference among Latinos. *Psychotherapy: Theory, Research, Practice, Training, 36,* 389–397. doi:10.1037/h0087808

Laszloffy, T. A., & Hardy, K. V. (2000). Uncommon strategies for a common problem: Addressing racism in family therapy. *Family Process, 39,* 35–50. doi:10.1111/j.1545-5300.2000.39106.x

Lawless, J. J. (2008). Transforming a racist legacy. In M. McGoldrick & K. V. Hardy (Eds.), *Re-visioning family therapy: Race, culture and gender in clinical practice* (2nd ed.; pp. 191–196). New York, NY: Guilford Press.

Lewis, B. (2010). Social justice in practicum training: Competencies and development implications. *Training and Education in Professional Psychology, 4,* 145–152. doi:10.1037/a0017383

Madsen, W. C. (2007). *Collaborative therapy with multi-stressed families* (2nd ed.). New York, NY: Guilford Press.

Maisel, R., Epston, D., & Bordan, A. (2004) *Biting the hand that starves you.* New York, NY: Norton.

McGoldrick, M., Almeida, R., Preto, N. G., Bibb, A., Sutton, C., Hudak, J., & Hines, P. M. (1999). Efforts to incorporate social justice perspectives into a family training program. *Journal of Marital and Family Therapy, 25*, 191–209. doi:10.1111/j.1752-0606.1999.tb01122.x

McGoldrick, M., Giordano, J., & Garcia-Preto, N. (Eds.). (2005). *Ethnicity and family therapy* (2nd ed.). New York, NY: Guilford Press.

Montalvo, B., & Gutierrez, M. (1983). A perspective for the use of the cultural dimension in family therapy. In C. J. Falicov (Ed.), *Cultural perspectives in family therapy* (pp. 15–30). Rockville, MD: Aspen Systems. doi:10.1037/e446792004-001

Rosaldo, R. (1989). *Culture and truth: The remaking of social analysis.* Boston, MA: Beacon Press.

Rust, G., Kondwani, K., Martinez, R., Dansie, R., Wong, W., Fry-Johnson, Y., . . . Strothers, H. (2006). A crash-course in cultural competence. *Ethnicity & Disease, 16*, 29–36.

Sampson, E. E. (1993). Identity politics: Challenges to psychology's understanding. *American Psychologist, 48*, 1219–1230. doi:10.1037/0003-066X.48.12.1219

Sluzki, C. (1982). The Latin lover revisited. In M. McGoldrick, J. K. Pearce, & J. Giordano (Eds.), *Ethnicity and family therapy* (pp. 492–498). New York, NY: Guilford Press.

Sluzki, C. E. (2001). All those in favor of saving the planet, please raise your hand: A comment about "Family therapy saves the planet." *Journal of Marital and Family Therapy, 27*, 13–15. doi:10.1111/j.1752-0606.2001.tb01133.x

Sue, D. W., Carter, R. T., Casas, J. M., Fouad, N. A., Ivey, A. E., Jensen, M., . . . Vazquez-Nutall, E. (1998). *Multicultural counseling competencies: Individual and organizational development.* Thousand Oaks, CA: Sage.

Taylor, C., & Gutmann, A. (Eds.). (1994). *Multiculturalism: Examining the politics of recognition.* Princeton, NJ: Princeton University Press.

Tervalon, M., & Murray-García, J. (1998). Cultural humility versus cultural competence: A critical distinction in defining physician training outcomes in multicultural education. *Journal of Health Care for the Poor and Underserved, 9*, 117–125. doi:10.1353/hpu.2010.0233

Turner, W. L., Wieling, E., & Allen, W. D. (2004). Developing culturally effective family-based research programs: Implications for family therapists. *Journal of Marital and Family Therapy, 30*, 257–270. doi:10.1111/j.1752-0606.2004.tb01239.x

Von Bertalanffy, L. (1968). *General systems theory.* New York, NY: George Braziller.

Watts-Jones, T. D. (2010). Location of self: Opening the door to dialogue on intersectionality in the therapy process. *Family Process, 49*, 405–420. doi:10.1111/j.1545-5300.2010.01330.x

White, M. (1993). Deconstruction and therapy. In S. Gilligan & R. Price (Eds.), *Therapeutic conversations* (pp. 22–61). New York, NY: Norton.

Wright Mills, C. (1959). *The sociological imagination.* London, England: Oxford University Press.

3

WOMEN, CULTURE, AND SOCIAL JUSTICE: SUPERVISION ACROSS THE INTERSECTIONS

NATALIE PORTER

As someone raised in the Roman Catholic tradition, my experiences in supervision at times are eerily reminiscent of a confessional booth: "Bless me because I have sinned; in my last session, I committed the therapy sin of _____." I note the sense of shame and anticipated rebuff that sometimes accompanies the student's admission. The sin of self-disclosure is one frequently confessed, head bowed, eyes lowered, voice tentative: "My client asked me if I had children, and I told her that I did [did not]"; "My African American adolescent client asked me if I voted for Obama, and I shared that I did . . . but I immediately felt terrible"; "The Mexican parents of my client asked me [a Jewish therapist] if I celebrated Christmas and was visiting my family over the holidays. I didn't know what to say, so I just smiled and didn't answer."

As I hear these accounts, I am struck by the students' beliefs that self-disclosure must almost never occur and that breaking this commandment

http://dx.doi.org/10.1037/14370-003
Multiculturalism and Diversity in Clinical Supervision: A Competency-Based Approach, C. A. Falender, E. P. Shafranske, and C. J. Falicov (Editors)

reflects a lapse of reason or will rather than a measured response. I am also aware that in some supervisory relationships no self-disclosure seems too trivial to go unpunished. I try to imagine how any social discourse occurs when therapists in training feel constrained to disclose nothing more personal than a weather report. It also becomes clear as I explore the "occasions of sin" more fully that the supervisees do not necessarily believe they have actually "sinned." They are contrite because they believe that I, the supervisor, will consider any form of self-disclosure a sin—regardless of the context, content, intent, or outcome of the disclosure. They claim to have been taught that all disclosures are errors, although I consider it more likely that they have confused their supervisors' exploration of their behavior with disapproval. What I note is that they seem to know and hold onto rules rather than engage in a self-reflective process to analyze the dilemmas, including self-disclosure, that they encounter in therapy. They appear less able to reason through their behaviors or decisions and provide explanations that consider their roles, the context, their clients' needs, or the potential usefulness or destructiveness of any particular behavior in therapy. Whether the supervisory focus is on self-disclosure or any other area of clinical decision making, supervision has a primary mission to facilitate thoughtful, systematic reflection about the contextual and multicultural factors affecting the clinical and supervisory relationships.

The supervision I describe in this chapter is based on a gendered, multicultural, ecological, and antiracist framework. It utilizes a feminist analysis that "addresses the understanding of power and its interconnections among gender, race, culture, class, physical ability, sexual orientation, age, and anti-Semitism as well as all forms of oppression based on religion, ethnicity, and heritage" (Feminist Therapy Institute [FTI], 1999, p. 1). From this perspective, therapist conduct is informed by analyses of the role that power plays in relationships, by recognizing the limitations of a purely intrapsychic model of psychology and the need to address the "interactive effects of the client's internal and external worlds" (FTI, p. 1), and by using therapeutic practices based on knowledge about the psychology of women and girls across cultures. From this perspective, self-disclosure, for example, is neither a sin nor a virtue but the result of an informed analysis of the meaning of particular discourses within cultural, gendered, and power contexts. Further, the goal of supervision is not to lay down the rules within a hierarchical setting but to explore them across situations in a collaborative setting. This approach complements explicit competency-based approaches to clinical supervision (Falender & Shafranske, 2004, 2008; see also Chapter 1, this volume) in its emphasis on applying knowledge and skills with a deep appreciation for the attitudes and values that contribute to the contexts in which therapeutic and supervisory discourses emerge.

TAKING A GENDERED PERSPECTIVE: SETTING THE CONTEXT

Across all cultures and racial/ethnic groups, and across almost all countries, women fare worse than their male counterparts on indicators of well-being and quality of life. Nearly universal gender inequality has been documented by the United Nations (UN) Human Development Report Office (1995, 1997) on the dimensions of earned income, life expectancy, and education (Gender Development Index) and on social equality, measured by income and the proportion of women in political office and in technical, professional, management, and administrative positions (Gender Equality Measure). Similar findings have been documented via several other indices (Bardhan & Klasen, 1999; Dijkstra, 2002). Worldwide, these gender disparities place women at risk for a host of health and mental health–related outcomes. In *The Mental Health of Women: An Evidence-Based Report*, the World Health Organization ([WHO], 2000) lays out the "tremendous health burden of women that is created by gender discrimination, poverty, social position, and various forms of violence against women" (p. 5). WHO (1998) asserts that "the status and well-being of countless millions of women worldwide remain tragically low. As a result, human well-being suffers, and the prospects for future generations are dimmer" (p. 6).

The WHO (2000) report points out that by 2020, depression, which globally is twice as prevalent in women as in men, will become the second most burdensome disease in the world. Violence-related and self-inflicted injuries will place 12th and 14th, respectively (Murray & Lopez, 1996). Citing the UN data on gender inequality, the report emphasizes the necessity of addressing the sociocultural contexts of women when addressing their mental health issues:

> Public policy, including economic policy, sociocultural and environmental factors, community and social support, stressors and life events, personal behavior and skills, and availability and access to health services, are all seen to exercise a role in determining women's mental health status as do the critical roles that social and cultural factors and unequal power relations between men and women play in promoting or impeding mental health. Such inequalities create, maintain, and exacerbate exposure to risk factors that endanger women's mental health, and are most graphically illustrated in the significantly different rates of depression between men and women, poverty and its impact, and the phenomenal prevalence of violence against women. (WHO, 2000, p. 5)

Many of the concerns outlined by WHO are also reflected in the UN Commission on the Status of Women's list of global priorities (UN, 1995, 2005). They include economic issues, such as poverty and inaccessibility of material resources; workforce issues, including pay equity and treatment on the job; intimate partner violence, and childhood and adult sexual violence; the inequality of caregiving that places substantial additional burdens on women, particularly in the current global HIV/AIDS crisis; and the exclusion of women from decision-making roles. Although feminists in the United States and throughout the world have historically linked these economic and social disparities to negative mental health outcomes in women, it is noteworthy that the UN and WHO have arrived at the same conclusions after reviewing the mental health evidence available internationally.

The United States is not immune to these disparities, although the conventional wisdom of the populace appears to be that inequality has been resolved. American families have the most work–family conflict of any of the developed nations, working longer hours with fewer laws that support working families (Williams & Boushey, 2010). The impact is most felt by lower income and single-parent families, although women with higher levels of education and income must make work–family choices not forced on their spouses. For example, when compared with 30 industrialized democratic countries, only the United States lacks paid parental leave (Ray, Gornick, & Schmitt, 2008). Although the United States appears to fare relatively well on the UN's indices for women (fifth on the Gender Development Index and eighth on the Gender Equality Index), it drops to 13th on the Standardised Index of Gender Equality (SIGE), a composite scale that adjusts for a nation's affluence, a factor that has distorted the results on the UN indices (Dijkstra, 2002). In either case, there is a discrepancy of about 25% between male and female outcomes, with greater economic equality and less social equality noted. Perhaps the failure of the United States to ratify the UN Convention to Eliminate All Forms of Discrimination Against Women (UN, 1979) 30 years after its adoption by the UN and ratification by 90% of the member nations best exemplifies the continued inequality of women. In the United States, the number of women entering poverty as single mothers continues to increase (Shaver, 1998), and economic reforms such as deregulation and globalization have disproportionately hurt women by creating lower salaries and greater job instability (Loewenson, 1999), supporting the moniker given to the U.S. public policy as the most "family-hostile" in the developed world (Williams & Boushey, 2010). Depression occurs twice as frequently in women as men in the United States (Piccinelli & Homen, 1997) and 7 times more often in girls than boys (Lewinsohn, Rohde, Seeley, & Baldwin, 2001). Women experience anxiety disorders 2 to 3 times more often than men (Brown, O'Leary, & Barlow, 2001) and constitute the majority of victims of rape or intimate partner violence (Tjaden & Thoennes, 2000) and people with posttraumatic stress distorder (PTSD; Kimerling, Rellini, Kelly, Judson, & Learman, 2002; Sutherland, Bybee, & Sullivan, 1998). Clearly, the need to address women's issues and take a gendered perspective in psychology practice still exists in the United States.

This context is important for supervision, because as is often the case with other forms of oppression, even when therapists intend to provide appropriate therapy, they often lack the necessary knowledge base. Understanding and intervening in ways that always address the multiple sources of identity, inequity, and privilege that shape people's lives is essential. Two ways to approach this intersectionality are *diversity mindfulness*, which describes the importance of complex, context-based perspectives (Russo & Vaz, 2001) and the *feminist ecological framework* (Ballou, Matsumoto, & Wagner, 2002), which situates gender within the broader contexts of "multicultural, multidisciplinary, and multinational knowledge, methods, and interventions" (Vargas, Porter, & Falender, 2008, p. 122).

UNDERPINNINGS OF SUPERVISION WITH WOMEN

In 1981, WHO defined *mental health* as

> the capacity of the individual, the group, and the environment to interact with one another in ways that promote subjective well-being, the optimal development and use of mental abilities (cognitive, affective, and relational), the achievement of individual and collective goals consistent with justice and the attainment and preservation of conditions of fundamental equality. (WHO, 2000, p. 11)

This definition shares a number of attributes with the ways that feminist therapists have defined and carried out therapy with women in the United States. It takes a biopsychosocial approach that attends to social contexts and the interrelated, multilevel, multicausation factors of mental health disorders rather than focusing solely on the individual or biological level. It recognizes the need for social change, the reduction of oppression, and the promotion of equality as conditions for positive mental health outcomes. Similarly, *feminist therapy* is defined as using empirical and qualitative scholarship to address the interrelatedness of the cultural, social, political, economic, and social contexts of women's lives with the behavioral, cognitive, affective, interpersonal, intrapsychic, and spiritual dimensions of their experiences. It attends to women's multiple identities and issues of power and equality and strives for social transformation at societal as well as individual levels (Wyche & Rice, 1997). *Feminist* is differentiated from *gender* or *gendered* in that the latter terms refer to the "psychological, social, and cultural experiences and characteristics associated with . . . being female or male" (American Psychological Association [APA], 2007, p. 32) and include prescriptive and proscriptive behavioral assumptions and expectations, stereotypes, and biases.

APA (2007) adopted the *Guidelines for Psychological Practice for Girls and Women* to help psychologists to practice effectively and to minimize harm to girls and women. The guidelines underscore the complexity of treatment of women and girls given the continued social and mental disparities and the interrelatedness of their multiple identities, including age; race; ethnicity; class; sexual orientation; marital, partnership, and parental status; gender identity; ability; culture; immigration; geography; and other life experiences (Sparks & Park, 2000; Stewart & McDermott, 2004). The interrelated nature of these aspects is well documented in (a) the stressors that have been identified for girls and women, such as " interpersonal victimization and violence, unrealistic media images of girls and women, discrimination and oppression, devaluation, limited economic resources, role overload, relationship disruptions, and work inequities" (APA, 2007, p. 949); (b) the bias and error that still pervade the diagnosis of women (Caplan & Cosgrove, 2004; Marecek, 2001), especially lesbians and women of color (Hall & Greene, 2003); (c) the inappropriate diagnosis and treatment of women who have experienced trauma (Cloitre, Karestan, Gratz, & Jakupcak, 2002); and (d) the ignoring of multiple sources of trauma for women of color (Vasquez & Magraw, 2005). These guidelines provide a framework for supervision and therapy with girls and women and can be found in Exhibit 3.1.

SUPERVISORY FOUNDATIONS FROM A FEMINIST, MULTICULTURAL PERSPECTIVE

The supervisory approach described below represents the integration of feminist supervision frameworks (Porter et al., 1997) with multicultural perspectives and diversity mindfulness (Russo & Vaz, 2001), including explicit antiracism and antioppression stances. Such an approach is consistent with the multidimensional, ecological, comparative approach (see Chapter 2, this volume) in which the supervisory relationship is considered a cultural encounter. At the 1996 Boston Conference, Shaping the Future of Feminist Psychology, a definition of, and guidelines for, supervision were developed that can be summarized as

> [Supervision] strives to empower and avoid abuses of power, is informed by social context and social constructivist perspectives, is collaborative and reflexive while maintaining standards of ethics and quality, fits the unique developmental needs of each supervisee, and promotes organizational advocacy and community activism on behalf of clients and emerging therapists. (Porter, 2010, pp. 2–3)

EXHIBIT 3.1
Guidelines for Psychological Practice With Girls and Women

1. Psychologists strive to be aware of the effects of socialization, stereotyping, and unique life events on the development of girls and women across diverse cultural groups.
2. Psychologists are encouraged to recognize and utilize information about oppression, privilege, and identity development as they may affect girls and women.
3. Psychologists strive to understand the impact of bias and discrimination upon the physical and mental health of those with whom they work.
4. Psychologists strive to use gender and culturally sensitive, affirming practices in providing services to girls and women.
5. Psychologists are encouraged to recognize how their socialization, attitudes, and knowledge about gender may affect their practice with girls and women.
6. Psychologists are encouraged to employ interventions and approaches that have been found to be effective in the treatment of issues of concern to girls and women.
7. Psychologists strive to foster therapeutic relationships and practices that promote initiative, empowerment, and expanded alternatives and choices for girls and women.
8. Psychologists strive to provide appropriate, unbiased assessments and diagnoses in their work with women and girls.
9. Psychologists strive to consider the problems of girls and women in their sociopolitical context.
10. Psychologists strive to acquaint themselves with and utilize relevant mental health, education, and community resources for girls and women.
11. Psychologists are encouraged to understand and work to change institutional and systemic bias that may impact girls and women.

Note. Data from American Psychological Association, 2007.

Exhibit 3.2 delineates the necessary competencies of supervisors from this perspective.

Diversity mindfulness addresses the complexity of people's lives and contexts, comprising multilayered, dynamic, and intersecting identities (Russo & Vaz, 2001). It overlaps with the definition of *culture* "as the dynamic and active process of constructing shared meaning, as represented by shared ideas, beliefs, attitudes, values, norms, practices, language, spirituality, and symbols, with acknowledgement and consideration of positions of power, privilege, and oppression" (Vargas et al., 2008, p. 122). Identities are considered fluid, potentially changing with the social context (see Chapter 2, this volume), although gender may be central to one's identity in one situation, and ethnicity or sexual orientation may be more salient in another (Russo & Vaz, 2001). For example, an African American woman may prioritize the human rights struggle pertaining to the unjust and disproportionate incarceration of African American men (Porter, 2009) in one context and the legal system's failure to take the rapes of Black women as seriously as the rapes of White

EXHIBIT 3.2
Principles of Feminist Supervision (Porter & Vasquez, 1997)

1. Feminist supervisors are proactive in analyzing power dynamics and differentials between the supervisor and the supervisee, model the use of power in the service of the supervisee, and vigilantly avoid abuses of power.
2. Feminist supervision is based on a collaborative relationship, defined as mutually respectful, in which the supervisee's autonomy and diverse perspectives are encouraged.
3. Feminist supervisors facilitate reflexive interactions and supervisee self-examination by modeling openness, authenticity, reflexivity, and the value of life-long learning and self-examination.
4. Supervision occurs in a social context that attends to and emphasizes the diversity of women's lives and contexts.
5. Feminist supervisors attend to the social construction of gender and the role of language in maintaining a gendered society.
6. Feminist supervisors advance and model the feminist principle of advocacy and activism.
7. Feminist supervisors maintain standards that ensure their supervisees' competent and ethical practice.
8. Feminist supervisors attend to the developmental shifts occurring in the supervisory process and provide input as a function of the skill level, developmental level, or maturational level of the supervisee.
9. Feminist supervisors advocate for their supervisees and clients in the educational and training settings within which they practice.

Note. Adapted from *Shaping the Future of Feminist Psychology: Education, Research, and Practice* (p. 170), by J. Worell and N. G. Johnson (Eds.), 1997, Washington, DC: American Psychological Association. Copyright 1997 by the American Psychological Association.

women (Calderon, 2004) in another. Individuals with multiple minority statuses may experience the negative effects of oppression for each cumulatively (Moradi & Subich, 2003; Szymanski & Kashubeck-West, 2008) or in a multiplicative way with experiences of each type of oppression interacting and intensifying the overall impact (Landrine, Klonoff, Alcaraz, Scott, & Wilkins, 1995; Szymanski & Gupta, 2009). Like feminist therapy, diversity mindfulness is strength based rather than deficiency based; empowerment, social transformation, and self-determination of all groups are key priorities.

THE SUPERVISORY PROCESS

Fostering Supervisory Alliances Through Collaboration, Authenticity, and Transparent Self-Reflection

Although personally I find that there is little that I do professionally that is more enjoyable or rewarding than supervision, the endeavor is challenging. A climate must be established that fosters the necessary openness, risk taking, and self-exploration. Potentially both the supervisor and supervisee will feel vulnerable, exposed, or uncertain. The supervisor will need to model the behaviors expected from the supervisee and convey his or her two-pronged commitment to the development and growth of the supervisee and the best possible treatment for the therapy client. The supervisor must be willing to address her or his own social location relative to the supervisee and client, maintain an authentic and empathic stance toward the supervisee, and recognize and address the various dimensions of power and privilege that will influence the supervisor–therapist-supervisee–client triad (Porter, 1995). Trust is often established through the supervisor's willingness to expose his or her own process. The supervision relationship must involve a collaborative exploration of the supervisee's goals and objectives for growth and learning, with the supervisor clearly communicating his or her expectations as well. As I have suggested previously, "the willingness to openly explore difficult issues, such as one's biases in therapy, occurs in an environment of mutual trust, where the supervisor has assumed a non-punitive and respectful stance toward the supervisee's use of self-reflection" (Vargas et al., 2008, p. 131).

Analysis of Power Dynamics to Facilitate the Supervisory Alliance

Power analysis is an explicit process in feminist therapy paradigms and one that is crucial to the supervision process. First and foremost, an honest and sensitive discussion of power in the relationship lays the foundation for a meaningful supervisor–supervisee relationship. Supervisees are well aware of the power differential conveyed in the roles of supervisor and supervisee and their potential impact on the supervisee's professional success through evaluations, grades, and letters of recommendations. The tradeoff for this subordinate position is the opportunity to learn from someone with greater knowledge and experience, as well as access to the profession.

Addressing the sociocultural and constructivist aspects of power within the supervisory and therapist–client relationships is critical. Less attended to in supervision than the explicit power dynamics described above are the relative areas of power and privilege that stem from the supervisor's and supervisee's roles in society and the ways these social locations define the relationship. I have the power to define the relationship and the supervision agenda because of the power I wield as the supervisor; however, the issues I select or ignore, hear, or do not hear and consider important or not stem from another kind of power I hold as a White, middle-class woman. The agenda I control may reflect my own biases, blind spots, and privileged assumptions. I operate from a position of power that has the potential to negate or pathologize the perspectives of a supervisee or his or her client from another cultural context, because I do not consider something that is irrelevant to me as meaningful or relevant to another. The supervisor elaborating on these more nuanced aspects of power facilitates the trust and transparency essential to a supervisory alliance and earnest self-reflection. As a supervisor, I must acknowledge my own privilege, biases, and blind spots and invite the supervisee to engage in collaborative exploration.

One destructive outcome of not fostering an alliance that permits honest self-reflection is that supervisees may not learn to think critically about therapeutic practices. They decide what issues they are willing to bring to supervision and what issues to steer clear of, because the risk seems too great. When issues are avoided, supervisees are not provided with the tools to explore the "rules" of therapy and to understand their rationales, limits, and potential exceptions and the good or harm that might come from following or deviating from a rule. The discussion of power dynamics cements the sense of safety that facilitates this supervisory alliance. The relationship becomes the conduit for the learning that occurs and for the complex and nuanced exploration that must take place.

The therapeutic issue of being presented with food or small gifts from clients provides an example of a situation where the "rules" of therapy from a dominant culture perspective might conflict with the practices of other cultures. A supervisee from a particular culture may feel caught between betraying the rules of therapy or compromising a relationship with a client with different value and interactional sets. However, supervisees might be reluctant to explore these "rules" in supervision for many reasons, including their sense of vulnerability about not knowing (Adams, 2010), their reluctance to disagree with or question their supervisors or even fear of one-upping them by knowing more than their supervisors about particular cultural contexts. They may not want to expose cultural practices they perceive will be judged negatively by their supervisors, particularly if they identify with them. When a climate has been established that incorporates mutual respect, authenticity, collaborative self-reflection, and awareness of the power dynamics operating within the relationship, learning occurs. A process that encourages asking the tough questions about any topic and basing decision-making on critical thinking and attention to the bigger picture has been launched.

The students with whom I work are all serving as therapists in community-based mental health programs, in urban school settings, and in university-affiliated and public hospitals. They are working primarily with poor clients from a wide range of cultural backgrounds; many of their clients or clients' families are immigrants. Not infrequently, these clients might bring in a token gift or homemade food in appreciation, particularly around a holiday— Mexican wedding cookies, a container of gumbo, red bean candy. Some students seem undone by these offerings. In many instances, the student feels that the natural behavior would be to accept the offering graciously, but they feel they are in jeopardy for doing so. The source of tension seems to be as much about their perceptions of being in the middle, caught between the feelings of their clients and the disapproval of their supervisors. At times, the students have shared the cultural heritage or nation of origin as their client and understood the cultural meanings behind the gift. They have also (often accurately) perceived that their European American supervisors have not. At other times, European American students with clients from different cultural groups have felt that to reject the food would be to snub the client. As with the earlier example about self-disclosure, I am often struck by the absence of an articulated analysis: When and how should they accept the food? When and how should they decline? What are the issues involved in their decision making? What were the therapeutic issues involved—Why now, why this? I am also struck by how infrequently a power/privilege analysis that focuses on the therapist–client relationship is incorporated into the discussion. For example, how might clients paying relatively little for their therapy attempt to offset their one-down positions in the relationship by compensating in another fashion? How are the clients operating from the same cultural rules with their therapists that they would use with other respected helpers— physicians, clergy, teachers? How are the clients using these food gifts as a way to signify their pride in their cultures with therapists from different cultures? Although much has been written about receiving food and small gifts, as with self-disclosure, many of the students I encounter in supervision can recite a "thou shalt not" but not an analysis of their position vis-à-vis the cultural aspects of the case. Each of these events offers the supervisor a teaching moment, a rich opportunity to address not merely the specific content of an issue but the broader supervisory, cultural, and therapeutic contexts that have the capacity to generalize to other dilemmas.

The multiple identities of both supervisor and supervisee influence the ways that power plays out within the supervisory relationship. As a White woman, my privilege prevails across the ethnic spectrum, although I have felt my authority more overtly challenged by some male supervisees. As an older woman, I recognize the greater extent to which supervisees expect me to nurture, foster, and facilitate, whereas in the past they seemed to appreciate my expertise without expecting such an array of supportive behaviors. Supervisors from nondominant racial or ethnic groups commonly relate their experiences of frequently having their expertise questioned by White supervisees, especially when cultural issues are raised in supervision (Adams, 2010; Toporek & Pope-Davis, 2005). Discourse analysis of supervision tapes has found greater resistance to the direction of female supervisors (McHale & Carr, 1998). My openness to acknowledging these dynamics typically furthers the supervisory alliance.

Exploring Multicultural Issues Through a Progressive Supervisory Process

For me, supervision progresses over time from a relatively greater focus on content and clinical competencies to process issues within supervision. I attend to the interpersonal competencies described by Falender and Shafranske (2004) as central to a working alliance, "empathy, warmth, respect, clinical knowledge, and skill, as well as agreement concerning the goals and tasks of supervision" (p. 98). I find that students are more prepared to address multicultural issues than in the past because of the greater attention on these topics in graduate school, their awareness because of the settings in which supervisees are working as therapists, and the increase in the number of students who are from diverse cultural backgrounds. As the frontline therapists in clinics and schools in poverty-stricken urban neighborhoods, the supervisees witness the impact of social conditions on the lives of their clients. They quickly realize the limitations of purely individual psychological approaches and are searching for ways to be effective with children, adolescents, families, and adults struggling with poverty, violence, discrimination, adaptation to new cultures, or substance abuse. More than in the past, it is easier to lay out expectations pertaining to diversity.

I begin with the initial session, where we both, supervisor and supervisee, lay out our goals and objectives for supervision and explore our philosophies pertaining to therapy, supervision, and change, our working styles, and our strengths and weaknesses as learners and facilitators of learning. I explicitly address how supervision will incorporate an ecological approach, a commitment to social justice, and antiracism. I emphasize that incorporating these goals into the learning process and the therapy process for the client, occurs slowly and systematically with plenty of opportunity for multiple perspectives and discussion. I attempt to embed these goals within those that have been initiated by the supervisee, and I am keenly aware of not overwhelming or overpowering the student at this point. This conversation provides the opportunity for each of us to disclose relevant aspects of our own social location and the relative bases of power with respect to one another. In the past, this dialogue would have required a strong alliance before taking place. Now I find that this exchange is part of establishing the alliance, because it is an anticipated aspect of supervision from the perspective of the student, particularly students who view themselves in the margins: ethnically diverse students; women; lesbian, bisexual, transgendered, or queer students; and those with visible disabilities. Students from these backgrounds want to know where I stand, even if they do not feel able to ask. My addressing these issues is one way of addressing the power dynamics between us. Even students with greater social privilege appear to welcome this initial conversation, as it explicitly frames expectations that remain too ambiguous or unclear in much of their supervision. They, too, are working with clients from diverse backgrounds and settings and welcome the opportunity to gain in competence and knowledge in working with them. Ironically, research suggests that multicultural issues are addressed the least with White supervisees, regardless of whether they are working with White supervisors or supervisors from racial/ethnic minority groups. White supervisor–supervisee dyads spend the least time talking about multicultural issues; dyads in which both members are from racial/ethnic minority groups spend the most time. White supervisors spend more time discussing these issues with racial/ethnic minority supervisees than racial/ethnic supervisors do with White supervisees. Overall, White supervisors spend less time discussing multicultural issues than do racial/ethnic minority supervisors and feel less competent at doing so (Hird, Tao, & Gloria, 2004). The needs of White supervisees to learn about multicultural issues clearly should become a greater priority. Although there is not the same data, I would anticipate that the same dyadic patterns would occur with gender, disability, sexual orientation, and so on. Those individuals with the least life experience or personal knowledge about a group may be receiving the least training or information about that group from their supervisors.

I have previously outlined a stage model of addressing gendered and multicultural issues within supervision, which is sufficiently flexible to reflect the knowledge, experience, and openness of the supervisee (Porter, 1995). Over time, supervision moves from a more didactic approach that focuses on the client's "problem" to the development of abilities of self-reflection and monitoring one's own biases. In the first stage, supervisees are lead to explore the intersections of clients' presenting psychological concerns with their contexts (gender, race/ethnicity, sexual orientation) as presented in research, scholarship, and literature. This procedure allows supervisees to gain fundamental information and some task competence. Given the considerable amount of knowledge that one needs to acquire about any group, phenomenon, or psychological condition, this learning process continues throughout supervision. Over time, and as the supervisees have more firsthand experience with their clients, supervision opens up the discussion of the clients' social locations to include the manifestations, origins, and impacts of specific oppressions at the societal level as well as the individual level. As the therapist adopts a broader understanding of the social, economic, and cultural forces contributing to clients' functioning, resilience, strengths, and adaptations, supervision begins to explore more directly the supervisees' (and supervisor's) misconceptions, biases, privilege, and prejudices, particularly as they are manifested in the therapy and in supervision. At the last state, supervision is broadened to explore and plan ways that community engagement and social and collective action could further the gains of individual therapy and promote personal well-being for the client as well as enhance supervisee understanding and effectiveness (Porter, 1995).

Additional Models to Aid in Collaborative Self-Reflection

Two other methods of supervision that promote systematic reflection and analysis involve using an adaptation of Freirian empowerment education dialogue (Shaffer, 1991) and a feminist ethical decision-making process (Hill, Glaser, & Harden, 1998). Both work effectively within individual or group supervision settings. The reflection format based on Freire's empowerment for critical consciousness has been helpful in helping supervisees and students draw connections between their own experiences and the sociopolitical and cultural contexts of others through a questioning process that promotes self-reflection and action. By moving from witnessing and describing an event or problem, to relating the problem to one's own and the experiences of others, to attempting to analyze the causes and sources of the problem, to empowering oneself to address the problem, supervisees learn firsthand ways to evaluate their own political and social contexts, including privilege or oppression, and develop methods to enact change (Porter & Yahne, 1995). In ethical decision-making, supervisors and supervisees (a) start with a dilemma; (b) identify the conflicts, parties to the conflict, feelings, values, anxieties, and biases of all; (c) propose solutions; (d) select a solution after it is put through the same analysis outlined in the second step; (e) review the solution for bias, power issues, congruence with values, style, client's needs, and wishes; (f) implement the solution; and (g) evaluate and analyze the outcome (Hill et al., 1998). These tools provide structured ways to address situations that typically feel ambiguous and unknowable for supervisees. Through engaging in this process with supervisees, they begin to understand that most dilemmas are approached through a reasoning process rather than via a checklist of *dos* and *don'ts*. Although it is still anxiety provoking when they recognize that the outcomes are only as good as the inputs, they develop a sense of self-efficacy as they master these processes.

SUPERVISION CASE ILLUSTRATION: TOO AMERICAN TO BE MIDDLE EASTERN AND TOO MIDDLE EASTERN TO BE AMERICAN

This supervision took place in a community-based clinic in an urban city. The student, Elie, was in her third predoctoral practicum experience. I served as an ancillary supervisor and was not involved in providing direct services at the clinic, although I was affiliated with the program through an administrative role. Elie had requested me for supervision because she thought that a gendered perspective was missing from other supervision experiences, both past and present. I replaced a supervisor who had moved midyear to another city. Elie made contact with me after I had served as a group case consultant for another student's case in the same agency.

Elie was of Lebanese Catholic descent, born in the United States to parents who had immigrated here as young adults. She grew up in a suburb that was part of a large metropolitan area in a comfortable, middle-class neighborhood. Because Elie selected me for my feminist and multicultural sensibilities, the initial supervision sessions were fairly straightforward. She defined her interest in knowing more about feminist and multicultural views of therapy and was seeking the opportunity to discuss these issues more fully in supervision. She thought that her attempts to work within cultural frameworks had been subtly rebuffed at the clinic. For example, when working with other Middle Eastern women as clients, she felt that the social discourse they expected at the beginning of sessions was discouraged by her previous supervisor, who felt it set a tone that was too familiar for a therapeutic context. Elie felt caught in the middle between what she considered to be polite Middle Eastern behavior and "good" therapy. She also thought that supervisors either glossed over or did not realize the obstacles, as a Catholic woman, in her establishing relationships with Middle Eastern Islamic women. Elie also wanted to explore how to approach gender issues sensitively with women from cultural contexts that were more overtly male dominated than in contemporary U.S. culture. She feared that she would be ineffective in addressing gendered topics, such as intimate partner violence in therapy with many immigrant women, for example, because she would be seen as acculturated and "too American"—that is, out of touch with other cultural contexts. Another goal for Elie was learning to integrate feminist therapy principles within traditional therapy frameworks.

The initial case that Elie brought to supervision had been ongoing for approximately six sessions with the previous supervisor. The client, Daya, had lived in the United States for 5 years, moving here to marry an American university professor she had met in India while he was conducting doctoral dissertation research. They had communicated for almost 2 years after his return to the United States, and she married and joined him after he had secured a position. She and her husband had been married for 6 years and had two children, both born in the United States. Daya had been trained and employed as a dentist in India but could not get a license here. She began to work as an assistant in a dental office after she was granted a green card almost 3 years ago, but the expense of day care made work impractical, and she gave it up. Daya had not anticipated being unable to be licensed and would have liked to attend a dental program in the United States but also agreed that her husband was right in discouraging her from such an expensive and time-consuming endeavor.

Daya sought therapy because she felt she was not doing all she should as a wife and mother. She described herself as procrastinating, resulting in being unable to follow through on many social commitments with her husband, not having dinner ready on time, not following through with errands such as taking his suits to the dry cleaners, and not keeping the house clean. She found herself "wasting" an inordinate amount of time on her day off, rather than attending to household chores such as cleaning or paying the bills. Her husband was in the lab at the university most of the time, although he made it home most days for dinner and would read to and bathe the children those evenings. He would often need to return to the lab in the evenings. Other family duties fell mostly to Daya. She was putting dinner on the table later each evening, preferring to read or play with her children. A crisis had occurred when she had failed to ready the guest bedroom for her in-laws by clearing out the children's playroom and had not prepared dinner for their arrival, rushing to get pizza instead.

The therapy to date had used a straightforward cognitive behavior therapy approach that the client and Daya had collaboratively agreed upon: identifying self-defeating behaviors, using feeling and thought records, altering behavioral contingencies, activity scheduling and time management, and disputing self-talk. Daya appeared eager to make changes and invigorated by each session but had rarely followed through on the homework. Little had changed at home, although Daya was reluctant to say so because she did not want to "fail" the therapist too.

Elie recognized that she was not addressing cultural and gender issues that she considered key to Daya's behavior and resistance to treatment. She had been reluctant to raise issues that the supervisor had not considered relevant, and she did not know how to initiate discussion of them with a client who seemed intent on conveying that she alone was the problem. Although Elie was frustrated with Daya, she was angry at Daya's spouse, whom she blamed for not taking on more responsibilities or allowing Daya to go to dental school. Elie was aware that there were differences in the acculturation levels between her and Daya and wanted to be sure that she was not projecting her feelings onto the client.

In discussing this case, it was important within supervision to examine the myriad ways in which the supervisor (me), supervisee–therapist (Elie), and client (Daya) differed in our ethnic identities, cultural practices and values, immigration, insider–outsider status within the United States, work–family values, and worldviews. Elie and I had to reflect on the ways that our distinct worldviews might facilitate or interfere with Daya's exploration of her priorities on her own terms. We specifically discussed the impact of a number of ecological factors, such as immigration, cultural and personal isolation, diminished expectations and self-efficacy, on Daya's functioning and on our perceptions of her.

As we explored these topics, I agreed with Elie that it was crucial that Daya lead the way in therapy. We concurred that shifting from the purely individual focus that had characterized the previous sessions to incorporate a broader cultural level would open up new avenues for exploration. I recommended that Elie research the specific cultural issues relevant to Indian immigrant women and develop a list of all of the potentially relevant cultural and gender issues based on her research. I asked her to only include items that were linked to evidence rather than suppositions about cultural contexts. Table 3.1 lists some of the items. In supervision we explored each of the issues—including the effects of immigration, isolation, loss of a professional identity and loss of status, and the value Daya placed on her role within her family. We examined how our own priorities might be different from those of Daya and from each other's.

Elie's concern that she not impose her more acculturated biases onto Daya was legitimate. I suggested that she step back from her assumptions and ask Daya to reflect on her life in India compared with life in the United States—what were the elements that were important to her? Daya identified family, friends, and an active life within a broader community as the most salient components; her career as a dentist was lower on the list. Elie was surprised by this ordering and relieved that she had not pushed her own agenda. Therapy shifted to finding ways to develop outlets that complemented Daya's familial identity while supplying more personal supports, such as encouraging more social connections with an Indian community. I supported Elie's disclosing to Daya ways her family had sought community after immigrating. Therapy first shifted to enhancing Daya's social repertoire: volunteering in the classroom, seeking Indian women friends, educating her children about Indian culture. Thought records shifted from monitoring procrastination to framing self-care as family care—essential rather than selfish. As Elie became less isolated, the "procrastination" dropped away. As she developed more supports, she described feeling more empowered. She became more able to negotiate more ably with her spouse, who seemed to welcome these changes, particularly raising the children in a richer bicultural context. Daya began to volunteer and then obtained a part-time position in a domestic violence shelter.

Supervision addressed some of Elie's personal reactivity, that is, countertransference, such as her sadness and respect when she realized for the first time the difficulties her mother had faced upon immigrating. She identified her anger at the marginalization of people of color in the United States and her press to push Daya to confront her spouse, even if Daya was not

TABLE 3.1
Culture and Gender Issues Specific to Client

Issue	Cultural influence	Gender influence	Individual influence
Immigration	Immigrant with no support system in country; some language embarrassment	As a woman in the home, fewer opportunities for developing outside outlets	Isolation and few adult contacts might lead to depression
Motherhood	Indian idealized mother role may preempt other views of self/needs	Idealization of mother role in U.S. culture may also preempt other views/needs	Guilt/shame at not getting all needs met from role as wife/mother may lead to difficulty recognizing conflict—may deny and avoid rather than identify own needs
Professional identity	Had a career in India with little outlet in U.S. for achievement outside of family	Outside achievement devalued relative to that of spouse; inequity in caretaking responsibilities	Lacks sources of identity or self-esteem outside of family, diminished power inside family
Autonomy	Autonomy may be less important from an Indian perspective than from a Western perspective; more of a relational than independent identity	Double message about autonomy for women—supposed to achieve but also must subordinate goals for others; expressing autonomy seen as unfeminine	Resists rather than expresses autonomy
Power	Diminished power relative to others (including family members) because of minority/immigrant status	Diminished power relative to others (including family members) because of gender status and lack of income	Powerlessness and sense of entrapment may lead to depression

prepared to do so, particularly on issues that turned out to be Elie's priorities rather than Daya's. We discussed her own struggles with marginalization as a woman of color, both within her own culture and from the dominant culture. One issue that emerged frequently in the supervision was how much Elie had internalized rigid therapy rules. She was uncomfortable when Daya brought her a traditional Indian sweet one session or when Daya had solicited information about her own cultural experiences. We revisited Hill et al.'s (1998) problem-solving method, which confirmed that Elie had sound judgment and critical thinking skills; however, an appropriate level of self-confidence to match her skills seemed missing. We laid out a process to assist Elie to find and trust her therapeutic voice—and not adhere to my prescriptions or another supervisor's proscriptions. We examined how Elie's discomfort might represent her own feelings of powerlessness and need to pass, for even after she had the capacity to analyze these situations, she felt subversive. We also explored the ways that resistance occurs in the face of oppression and unacknowledged power differentials. Throughout the supervision, I modeled my own willingness to explore my own biases, privilege, and assumptions as part of the process. When I thought it important to explore an aspect of Elie's reactivity, I would sometimes initiate the conversation by disclosing my own reaction. I might say, "I noticed how impatient I felt that Daya did not . . . and I wondered what you were feeling." When supervision ended, we evaluated the experience specifically using the guidelines of feminist supervision as a framework. We each reflected on and shared perceptions of our own strengths and areas for improvement as well as each other's.

CONCLUSION: ADVOCACY IS ESSENTIAL

In the graduate-level supervision classes I teach, a uniform refrain of the students is that supervisors too rarely raise multicultural, gender, or other diversity issues. The students of color comment that when ethnic/racial issues are raised with them, it is as if they, the students, do or should have all the answers. From students across the years I have gleaned that when diversity issues are raised, it seems to be because of an intense client characteristic, for instance, gang membership, severe physical disability, or being transgendered. An analysis of the social inequities for female clients is almost completely ignored even by female supervisors and even for presenting problems emblematic of gender inequities, such as anorexia, bulimia, intimate partner violence, and sexual violence. When they are raised, diversity issues are rarely integrated with therapy theory or application; these topics represent two separate discourses. Even less frequent seems to be the presentation of evidence (whether a specific knowledge-based or evidence-based therapy application for specific client characteristics) rather than broad generalizations that at times border on stereotyping (e.g. Mexican machismo, Chinese adherence to Confucianism). Rarely is there an attempt to address solutions beyond individually oriented ideas of psychopathology or treatment. For example, supervisees who work in schools beleaguered by violence and crime describe the pervasive PTSD of their clients, many of whom are repeatedly victimized taking the bus or walking to school. Nonetheless, the focus of the treatment typically remains at the level of the individual traumatized student but does not address the context of the violence or the daily re-traumatizing or triggering of past trauma as explanations for current behavior or diagnoses. Supervision does not include advocacy for clients' well-being beyond the therapy room. Supervisors seem demoralized, and supervisees become demoralized; school personnel are overwhelmed, and students continue to be victimized.

The reluctance to address these highly complex and emotionally charged issues, particularly with little ongoing education or social support, is understandable. Many of us as supervisors have had insufficient exposure to real information around the multitude of diversity issues. We work in contexts in which we are addressing the concomitants of abject poverty with psychological tools. We have too few resources and too many people who need our services. Supervision almost seems a luxury. We fear the shame of not knowing (Adams, 2010) and the powerlessness of the deteriorating social conditions outstripping our solutions. To become effective, we will have to integrate social with psychological solutions. Diversity will have to be seen as the core of our treatment, not as an add-on. We will each need to make commitments to our own education and training. We may need to develop our own consultation and support groups as supervisors.

REFERENCES

Adams, D. M. (2010). Multicultural pedagogy in the supervision and education of psychotherapists. *Women & Therapy, 33*, 42–54. doi:10.1080/02703140903404713

American Psychological Association. (2007). Guidelines for practice with girls and women. *American Psychologist, 62*, 949–979. Retrieved from http://www.apa.org/practice/guidelines/girls-and-women.pdf

Ballou, M., Matsumoto, A., Wagner, M. (2002) Feminist ecological theory. In M. Ballou & L. Brown, (Eds.), *Mental health and disorders: Feminist perspectives* (pp. 99–114). New York, NY: Guilford Press.

Bardhan, K., & Klasen, S. (1999). *On UNDP's revisions to the gender-related development index.* Retrieved from http://hdr.undp.org/en/reports/global/hdr1999/papers/undp-revisions-gender-related.pdf

Brown, T. A., O'Leary, T. A., & Barlow, D. H. (2001). Generalized anxiety disorder. In D. H. Barlow (Ed.), *Clinical handbook of psychological disorders* (3rd ed., pp. 154–208). New York, NY: Guilford Press.

Calderon, L. A. (2004). *Rape, racism, and victim advocacy.* Retrieved from http://www.blackcommentator.com/98/98_calderon_rape_racism.html

Caplan, P. J., & Cosgrove, L. (Eds.). (2004). *Bias in psychiatric diagnosis.* Lanham, MD: Aronson.

Cloitre, M. K., Karestan, C., Gratz, K. L., & Jakupcak, M. (2002). Differential diagnosis of PTSD in women. In R. Kimerling, P. & J. Wolfe (Eds.), *Gender and PTSD* (pp. 117–149). New York, NY: Guilford Press.

Dijkstra, A. G. (2002). Revising UNDP's GDI and GEM: Towards an alternative. *Social Indicators Research, 57*, 301–338. doi:10.1023/A:1014726207604

Falender, C. A., & Shafranske, E. P. (2004). Alliance in therapeutic and supervisory relationships. In C. A. Falender & E. P. Shafranske (Eds.), *Clinical supervision: A competency-based approach* (pp. 95–114). Washington, DC: American Psychological Association. doi:10.1037/10806-005

Falender, C. A., & Shafranske, E. P. (2008). Best practices of supervision. In C. A. Falender & E. P. Shafranske (Eds.), *Casebook for clinical supervision: A competency-based approach* (pp. 3–15). Washington, DC: American Psychological Association.

Feminist Therapy Institute. (1999). *Feminist therapy code of ethics.* Retrieved from http://feminist-therapy-institute.org/ethics.htm

Hall, R. L., & Greene, B. (2003). African American families. In L. B. Silverstein & T. J. Goodrich (Eds.), *Feminist family therapy: Empowerment in social context* (pp. 107–120). Washington, DC: American Psychological Association. doi:10.1037/10615-008

Hill, M., Glaser, K., & Harden, J. (1998). A feminist model for ethical decision making. *Women & Therapy, 21*, 101–121. doi:10.1300/J015v21n03_10

Hird, J. S., Tao, K. W., & Gloria, A. M. (2004). Examining supervisors' multicultural competence in racially similar and different supervision dyads. *The Clinical Supervisor, 23*, 107–122. doi:10.1300/J001v23n02_07

Kimerling, R., Rellini, A., Kelly, V., Judson, P. L., & Learman, L. A. (2002). Gender differences in victim and crime characteristics of sexual assaults. *Journal of Interpersonal Violence, 17*, 526–532. doi:10.1177/0886260502017005003

Landrine, H., Klonoff, E. A., Alcaraz, R., Scott, J., & Wilkins, P. (1995). Multiple variables in discrimination. In B. Lott & D. Maluso (Eds.), *The social psychology of interpersonal discrimination* (pp. 183–224). New York, NY: Guilford Press.

Lewinsohn, P. M., Rohde, P., Seeley, J. R., & Baldwin, C. L. (2001). Gender differences in suicide from adolescence to adulthood. *Journal of the American Academy of Child & Adolescent Psychiatry, 40*, 427–434. doi:10.1097/00004583-200104000-00011

Loewenson, R. H. (1999). Women's occupational health in globalization and development. *American Journal of Industrial Medicine, 36*, 34–42. doi:10.1002/(SICI)1097-0274(199907)36:1<34::AID-AJIM5>3.0.CO;2-F

Marecek, J. (2001). Disorderly constructs: Feminist frameworks for clinical psychology. In R. K. Unger (Ed.), *Handbook of the psychology of women and gender* (pp. 303–316). Hoboken, NJ: Wiley.

McHale, E., & Carr, A. (1998). The effect of supervisor and therapist trainee gender on supervision discourse. *Journal of Family Therapy, 20*, 395–411. doi:10.1111/1467-6427.00095

Moradi, B., & Subich, L. M. (2003). A concomitant examination of the relations of perceived racist and sexist events to psychological distress for African American women. *The Counseling Psychologist, 31,* 451–469. doi:10.1177/0011000003031004007

Murray, J. L., & Lopez, A. D. (1996). *The global burden of disease: A comprehensive assessment of mortality and disability from diseases, injuries, and risk factors in 1990 and projected to 2020: Summary.* Boston, MA: Harvard School of Public Health, World Health Organization. Retrieved from http://www.who.int/healthinfo/nationalburdenofdiseasemanual.pdf

Piccinelli, M., & Homen, F. G. (1997). *Gender differences in the epidemiology of affective disorders and schizophrenia.* Geneva, Switzerland: World Health Organization.

Porter, N. (1995). Integrating antiracist, feminist, and multicultural perspectives in psychotherapy: A developmental supervision mode. In H. Landrine (Ed.), *Handbook of cultural diversity in the psychology of women* (pp. 163–176). Washington, DC: American Psychological Association.

Porter, N. (2009). Racial and ethnic disparities in criminal justice: Criminal justice or economic servitude. In J. Lau Chin (Ed.), *Diversity in mind and in action: Vol. 3. Social justice matters* (pp. 163–179). Santa Barbara, CA: Praeger/ABC-CLIO.

Porter, N. (2010). Feminist and multicultural underpinnings to supervision: An overview. *Women & Therapy, 33,* 1–7. doi:10.1080/02703140903404622

Porter, N., & Vasquez, M. (1997). Covision: Feminist supervision, process, and collaboration. In J. Worell & N. G. Johnson (Eds.), *Shaping the future of feminist psychology: Education, research, and practice* (pp. 155–171). Washington, DC: American Psychological Association. doi: 10.1037/10245-007

Porter, N., & Yahne, C. (1995). Feminist ethics and advocacy in the training of family therapists. *Journal of Feminist Family Therapy, 6,* 29–47. doi:10.1300/J086v06n03_03

Ray, R., Gornick, C., & Schmitt, J. (2008)., *Parental leave policies in 21 countries: Assessing generosity and gender equality.* Retrieved from http://www.cepr.net/documents/publications/parental_2008_09.pdf

Russo, N. F., & Vaz, K. (2001). Addressing diversity in the decade of behavior: Focus on women of color. *Psychology of Women Quarterly, 25,* 280–294. doi:10.1111/1471-6402.00029

Shaffer, R. (1991). Beyond the dispensary: On giving community balance to primary health care. Retrieved from http://www.amoshealth.org/wp-content/uploads/2012/07/Beyond-The-Dispensary-by-Roy-Shaffer-Book.pdf

Shaver, S. (1998). Poverty, gender, and sole parenthood. In R. Fincher & J. Nieuwenhuysen (Eds.), *Australian poverty then and now* (pp. 259–276). Melbourne, Australia: Melbourne University Press.

Sparks, E. E., & Park, A. H. (2000). The integration of feminism and multiculturalism: Ethical dilemmas at the border. In M. M. Brabeck (Ed.), *Practicing feminist ethics in psychology* (pp. 203–224). Washington, DC: American Psychological Association.

Stewart, A. J., & McDermott, C. (2004). Gender in psychology. *Annual Review of Psychology, 55,* 519–544. doi:10.1146/annurev.psych.55.090902.141537

Sutherland, C., Bybee, D., & Sullivan, C. (1998). The long-term effects of battering on women's health. *Women's Health, 4,* 41–70.

Szymanski, D. M., & Gupta, A. (2009). Examining the relationship between multiple internalized oppressions and African American lesbian, gay, bisexual, and questioning persons' self-esteem and psychological distress. *Journal of Counseling Psychology, 56,* 110–118. doi:10.1037/a0013317

Szymanski, D. M., & Kashubeck-West, S. (2008). Mediators of the relationship between internalized oppressions and lesbian and bisexual women's psychological distress. *The Counseling Psychologist, 36,* 575–594. doi:10.1177/0011000007309490

Tjaden, P., & Thoennes, N. (2000). Prevalence and consequences of male-to-female and female-to-male intimate partner violence as measured by the National Violence Against Women Survey. *Violence Against Women, 6,* 142–161. doi:10.1177/10778010022181769

Toporek, R. L., & Pope-Davis, D. B. (2005). Exploring the relationships between multicultural training, racial attitudes, and attributions of poverty among graduate counseling trainees. *Cultural Diversity & Ethnic Minority Psychology, 11,* 259–271. doi:10.1037/1099-9809.11.3.259

United Nations. (1979). *Convention on the elimination of all forms of discrimination against women,* Retrieved from http://www.un.org/womenwatch/daw/cedaw/history.htm

United Nations. (1995). *Beijing declaration and platform of action.* Geneva, Switzerland: UN Publications. Retrieved from http://www.un.org/womenwatch/daw/beijing/platform/

United Nations. (2005). *Ten-year review and appraisal of the implementation of the Beijing declaration and platform for action and the outcome of the twenty-third special session of the General Assembly held during the forty-ninth session of the CSW.* Retrieved from http://www.un.org/womenwatch/daw/Review/english/49sess.htm

United Nations Human Development Report Office. (1995). *Human development report.* New York, NY: Oxford University Press. Retrieved from http://hdr.undp.org/en/reports/global/hdr1995/

United Nations Human Development Report Office. (1997). *Human development report.* New York, NY: Oxford University Press. Retrieved from http://hdr.undp.org/en/reports/global/hdr1997/

Vargas, L. A., Porter, N., & Falender, C. A. (2008). Supervision, culture, and context. In C. A. Falender & E. P. Shafranske (Eds.), *Casebook for clinical supervision: A competency-based approach* (pp. 121–136). Washington, DC: American Psychological Association. doi:10.1037/11792-006

Vasquez, H., & Magraw, S. (2005). Building relationships across privilege: Becoming an ally in the therapeutic relationship. In M. P. Mirkin, K. L. Suyemoto, & B. F.

Okun (Eds.), *Psychotherapy with women: Exploring diverse contexts and identities* (pp. 64–83). NY: Guilford Press.

Williams, J. C., & Boushey, H. (2010). *The three faces of work–family conflict: The poor, the professionals, and the missing middle*. Retrieved from http://www.american-progress.org/issues/2010/01/pdf/threefaces.pdf

World Health Organization. (1998). *The World Health Report, 1998. Executive summary*. Geneva. Retrieved from http://www.who.int/whr/1998/en/index.html

World Health Organization. (2000). *The World Health Report, 2000. Executive summary*. Geneva. Retrieved from http://www.who.int/whr/2000/en/index.html

Wyche, K. F., & Rice, J. F. (1997). Feminist therapy: From dialogue to tenets. Covision: Feminist supervision, process, and collaboration. In J. Worell & N. G. Johnson (Eds.), *Shaping the future of feminist psychology: Education, research, and practice* (pp. 57–71). Washington, DC: American Psychological Association. doi:10.1037/10245-003

4

COMPASSIONATE CONFRONTATION AND EMPATHIC EXPLORATION: THE INTEGRATION OF RACE-RELATED NARRATIVES IN CLINICAL SUPERVISION

SHELLY P. HARRELL

Racial groups, based as they are on obvious physical characteristics, however flawed the categorization process, draw lines between those who are "me" or "like-me" and those who are "not-me" or "unlike-me." (Altman, 2000, p. 590)

Racial group designations remain a critical variable to consider in interpersonal relations generally, and in psychotherapy relationships more particularly (T. N. Brown, 2003; Parker & Lynn, 2002; West, 2001; Williams & Jackson, 2005). Supervision and training can help to enhance the ability of therapists to meaningfully consider race-related issues in the treatment of diverse populations. Both interracial and intraracial dynamics may directly affect the supervisory relationship, as well as the development and course of the supervisory alliance. The description of the supervision approach presented here emerges from a large body of theory and empirical research indicating that racial group categorizations have a powerful influence on both internal and interpersonal experience, as well as on behavior (Tummala-Narra, 2004). The approach draws upon a method of working with cultural meaning systems

The author acknowledges graduate student research assistants Claudia Pena, Goni Hary Bissell, and Jayonna Bolds Cox for their assistance in the preparation of this chapter and the valuable initial collaboration with Jessica Henderson Daniel.

http://dx.doi.org/10.1037/14370-004

Multiculturalism and Diversity in Clinical Supervision: A Competency-Based Approach, C. A. Falender, E. P. Shafranske, and C. J. Falicov (Editors)

offered by Falicov (2003), which consists of naming, exploring contexts and experiences, reframing, and introducing future considerations. Similarly, the three steps for integrating race narratives into clinical supervision include (a) the elicitation and disclosure of race narratives, (b) the deconstruction and unpacking of race narratives for meanings and emotions, and (c) an exploration of the clinical implications of race narratives with particular attention to developing race-related multicultural competence.

The use of a narrative approach can help supervisees gain access to negative or unwanted feelings through connecting clinical or supervision material to their own stories about race, race relations, and racism. One of the central goals of the supervision approach is to facilitate a process that invites material experienced as unspeakable or unacceptable, a common characteristic of race-related issues, to be brought into awareness and discussion in both supervision and psychotherapy as appropriate.

Race is a problematic construct, and clarification regarding how the term is used here is important. Race is conceptualized here as a pseudobiological social construction that divides human beings into groups based on the phenotypic expression of skin color, facial features, hair texture, and body shape (Harrell & Sloan-Pena, 2006). Although the biological basis for dividing humans into distinct racial groups has been discredited (Smedley & Smedley, 2005), perceived and assigned racial group membership continues to have profound sociopolitical and interpersonal implications with respect to everyday life experiences, power, and privilege.

Racial group categorization represents a complex sociopolitical and psychosocial variable that is a powerful correlate of quality of life and that impacts the nature of daily life experiences (Altman, 2000). The research literature has found that ascribed racial group membership will be one of the first interpersonal stimuli processed, actively and/or passively, in interpersonal encounters (Plant, Butz, & Tatakovsky, 2008; Wilson, Lindsey, & Schooler, 2000). In addition, recent research suggests that phenotypic preferences can be observed within the first 6 months of life (Baron & Banaji, 2006). Empirical studies conducted in psychology and related fields have consistently documented the impact of racial categorizations on perception, facial recognition, selective attention, memory, implicit cognitive processes, stereotypes, prejudice, interpersonal behavior, and task performance (Hutchings & Haddock, 2008). Although some of these impacts are normative and largely automatic, they occur in the context of the enduring and inescapable ideology of White superiority. As this dominant ideology imposes meaning on racial group categorizations and associated psychological processes, racial prejudice and discrimination inevitably result. This process contributes to the development and maintenance of race-related social and economic asymmetries, including racial disparities in health and health care

(Williams & Jackson, 2005) and in education, employment, lending, home ownership, and criminal justice.

Darker skinned racial and ethnic groups, including African Americans, Native Americans, Southeast Asians, Pacific Islanders, and some groups of Latinos (e.g., Mexican, Puerto Rican, Central American), fare significantly worse than Whites on multiple societal indicators (Associated Press, 2006). These ongoing racial disparities occur in the historical context of multiple collective traumas perpetrated against non-White racial groups in the United States (e.g., African slavery; the Japanese internment; Native American displacement and genocide; exploitation of Chinese laborers; colonialism imposed on native Mexicans, Puerto Ricans, and Hawaiians) and coexist with a national identity centered in the idea of "liberty and justice for all." This uneasy coexistence, the enduring presence of racism alongside values of equality and freedom (as seen in the popular election and subsequent vilification of Barack Obama, the first African American president of the United States; Guinote, Willis, & Martellotta, 2010; Payne et al., 2010; Schmidt & Nosek, 2010), speaks to the complexity and collective ambivalence around race, its meaning, and its effects.

Grounded in ecological theory and informed by existing empirical research in psychology on race-related constructs (e.g., racism, racial socialization, interracial interaction, racial identity), the focus of this chapter is on the presentation of a method for navigating the experiential and sociopolitical minefields of race within the clinical supervision process. An emphasis on the socially constructed nature of race through a narrative approach provides an opportunity to explore people's stories about race and how their identity, perceptions, emotional reactions, behavior, and interpersonal interactions are affected by race-related narratives. I have found it useful to describe the method as being directed by two core guiding principles: *compassionate confrontation* and *empathic exploration* (Harrell & Bissell, 2009). Both supervisor and supervisee are tasked with confronting and exploring emotionally charged subject matter while maintaining an atmosphere of compassion and empathy for the anxiety, pain, ambivalence, and anger that can accompany the topic of race. These discussions can trigger strong affective and defensive reactions. Successful race-related dialogues require the ability to tolerate (a) the processing of unacknowledged or undiscovered material related to race-related feelings and experiences and (b) feelings of uncertainty and unfamiliarity related to "the other" (Tummala-Narra, 2009). The act of nonjudgmentally giving supervisees space to share their race-related narratives provides an in vivo experience of strengthening interpersonal relationships. The importance of developing a clear and comprehensive approach to racial issues in clinical supervision is particularly critical given the almost inevitable experience of anxiety when race-related topics are raised in open discussion (Trawalter & Richeson, 2008).

CONCEPTUAL AND EMPIRICAL GROUNDING

Several bodies of conceptual and empirical work have informed the process described here. Literature on the psychological significance of narratives and a general constructivist methodology are central to the race-related narratives supervision approach (Collins & Arthur, 2007; Polkinghorne, 1988; Tummala-Narra, 2004). Empirical research in social psychology and social cognition that illuminates the complexity of processes involved in racial attitudes and interracial interactions on topics such as contemporary expressions of racism (e.g., aversive racism; Dovidio, Gaertner, Kawakami, & Hodson, 2002), implicit prejudice and stereotypes (Wilson et al., 2000), and intergroup relations (Devine, 2001) has provided strong experimental support. Conceptual foundations have come from the growing body of theory and research in multicultural psychology, including the existing work on multicultural supervision (Daniel, Roysircar, Abeles, & Boyd, 2004). It is interesting to note that writings from the psychoanalytic tradition on the role of race and racism in psychotherapy have contributed critical perspectives on the psychological meaning of race, how racial dynamics are internalized, and how these dynamics affect the psychotherapy relationship (Altman, 2000; Hamer 2002, 2006; Leary, 1997; Suchet, 2004). Finally, the interdisciplinary framework of critical race theory provides the central pedagogical position. Its basic tenets include (a) race as a social construction and racism as endemic to American life; (b) racism as maintaining the status quo of racial stratification; (c) the necessity of challenging the dominant social ideology of color-blindness and meritocracy; (d) racial stratification influences on racial identity; (e) an insistence on analysis of cultural, historical, and sociopolitical contexts; (f) the legitimacy and primacy of the lived experience of people of color in any analysis; and (g) the significance of within-group heterogeneity (Crenshaw, Gotanda, Peller, & Thomas,1995; Delgado, 2000; Harrell & Pezeshkian, 2008).

Although informed by these multiple bodies of work, it is ecological systems theory that provides the foundational frame for working effectively with race-related issues in supervision through its insistence on multiple levels of analysis (e.g., individual, microsystem, community, organizational, macrosystem; Harrell & Gallardo, 2008). Falicov's (2003) multidimensional-ecosystemic comparative approach (MECA) is an especially useful framework that helps to ground an approach to race and supervision in the ecological context. It is based on the fundamental assumption that we are all multicultural beings whose lives are impacted by the sociocultural and sociopolitical context (Falicov, 1995, 2003). Two ideas that emerge from MECA are particularly instructive.

First, the construct of *ecological niche*, the space where people's multiple cultural locations intersect, is an important way of describing a client, therapist, and supervisor. Racial categorizations are inextricably tied to other core identity dimensions such that interpersonal interactions, ascribed characteristics, and cognitive–emotional associations are differentially influenced by different ecological niches. For example, the race-related dynamics between a 48-year-old Caucasian, atheist, high socioeconomic status (SES) trainee and a racially Asian client may be very different than with a recently immigrated 23-year-old dark-skinned, Muslim, Thai male client living at a low SES and with a third generation, 52-year-old White-skinned, Japanese, Christian female living at a high SES. The specific ecological niche of race–ethnicity–gender–age–religion–SES is particularly important to consider when exploring the influence of racial categorization on perception, behavior, and relationships.

Second, these multiple cultural locations and identities speak to the significance of considering intragroup variability and challenging any assumption that people who are ascribed the same racial group categorization also share the same cultural values or worldview. Ecological considerations such as (a) familial and community racial socialization processes, (b) the racial composition of socialization contexts, (c) experiences of racial discrimination, and (d) the amount of interpersonal contact with persons of a different ascribed race all contribute to variability on psychological variables such as racial identity and acculturation (Spencer, Dupree, & Hartmann, 1997). These constructs likely influence the nature of both interracial and intraracial encounters and race-related discussions (Jernigan, Green, Helms, Perez-Gauldron, & Henze, 2010). For example, a supervisory dyad that shares the same racial group membership may still be problematic if the supervisor and supervisee are at different or conflicting racial identity statuses (Jernigan et al., 2010). Assumed similarities also pose challenges for the trainee in the expectations of being understood and possible assumptions of experiential commonalities and a minimization of differences that are experienced. The construct of racial identity (for both Whites and people of color) is foundational for understanding the dynamics of interracial and intraracial encounters. Racial identity involves the salience of race, degree of racial group identification, meanings and beliefs about race, as well as the evaluative and affective judgments about race. Racial identity research has produced findings that suggest both direct and indirect relationships with indices of psychological well-being (Sellers, Caldwell, Schmeelk-Cone, & Zimmerman, 2003). The social construct of race can be represented quite differently in terms of identity and meaning for individuals within the same racial group categorization. It is critical to avoid the assumption that it is only cross-race encounters where race-related multicultural competencies are relevant.

On a related note, conflictual interpersonal interactions between Whites and people of color can be triggered by differences in the salience and meaning of race to personal identity. The construct of race is a more salient aspect of identity for visible racial–ethnic groups because of the life experiences, interpersonal encounters, and structural White privilege that can serve as frequent reminders that they are "the other" (Altman, 2000; Boatright-Horowitz & Seoung, 2009; Boyd, 2008; Hamer, 2002, 2006; Tatum, 2000). Therefore, clients, therapists, and supervisors whose phenotypic characteristics differ from White may notice race-related issues, as well as attribute more importance to racial issues than their White counterparts. Racial issues may be more experientially salient for people of color in supervision and therapy dyads (e.g., therapist–client, supervisor–supervisee), which has the potential to create tension and misunderstandings. In addition, the idea of color-blindness is likely to have a more positive and desirable connotation for Whites as it facilitates an ability to ward off the anxiety that the topic of race can trigger. Part of exercising White privilege is being able to choose to minimize racial issues and affirm color-blindness as the correct way to approach issues of race. This is often accompanied with positive intentions but can have the potential effect of silencing, pathologizing, and creating an invalidating atmosphere when race-based experiences are shared. This privilege is reinforced by social distance and the relative racial homogeneity in the composition of our social contexts within neighborhoods, schools, places of worship, friendship and social groups with respect to race, ethnicity, and social class (Plant et al., 2008). In addition, significant reactivity in the form of defensiveness and denial can manifest for Whites who claim color-blindness or who romanticize and idealize interactions and relationships with people of color, as well as for visible racial/ethnic group individuals who struggle with internalized racism, which can provide the temporary anxiety-reducing benefit of minimizing race and racism.

Race-related multicultural competence for both therapists and supervisors requires ongoing reflective practice, given the multiple layers of sociopolitical, interpersonal, and intrapersonal meaning of race in the United States. This is further complicated by the current situation in many training contexts, where supervisors have had limited multicultural training, less interracial social experience, fewer open discussions about race, and can be less informed about current theory and research than their supervisees (M. T. Brown & Landrum-Brown, 1995; Tummala-Narra, 2004).

RACE-RELATED MULTICULTURAL COMPETENCIES IN THERAPY AND SUPERVISION

Specific race-related multicultural competencies can be identified and organized into the classic multicultural competence domains of awareness, knowledge, and skills (American Psychological Association [APA], 2003; Arredondo et al., 1996; Collins & Arthur, 2007). These will be expanded here for the purpose of clarity and labeled *attitudes, values, and awareness* (AVA); *knowledge of theory and research* (KTR); and *interpersonal and professional skills* (IPS) (see Table 4.1). Adequate levels of achievement in each of these competency domains is a prerequisite for supervisors to be able to effectively train and evaluate supervisees in the area of race-related multicultural competence. It may be helpful to distinguish the different emphases of race-related versus ethnicity-related competencies. Multicultural competencies associated with the diversity dimension of ethnicity focus on the particular ethnocultural group's ancestry, history, values, preferences, customs, worldview, and so on. Multicultural competencies associated with race have a different emphasis such that issues of power, privilege, racism, and ingroup/outgroup dynamics are more central to the awareness, knowledge, and skills required. Both aspects of multicultural competence are important and should be distinguished in supervision.

Attitudes, Values, and Awareness

There are two general goals for competency in this area: (a) the development of a strong personal awareness of the role and meaning of race and racial content and (b) the cultivation of a set of professional attitudes and values related to racial material. Achieving these goals provides the foundation for the ongoing acquisition of an ever-evolving set of knowledge and skills necessary to work competently with race-related clinical material. Eleven specific AVA competencies can be identified and are presented in Table 4.1. Five of these can be considered core competencies. The most important starting point on this dimension is the competency of *racial self-awareness*, understanding self and personal identity in the context of societal racial stratification. Another central attitudinal competency is *race-related empathy*, the feeling of compassion for the harm that racism has done, and continues to do, in people's lives. A third attitudinal competency is *respect for different race-related experiences*, valuing the life experiences and social perceptions of people with phenotypic expression different from one's own, particularly when those experiences and perceptions are unfamiliar. The fourth core AVA competency is *awareness of racial bias, stereotypes, and prejudices*, the ability to identify and process one's own racial stereotypes and prejudice. These four attitudinal competencies are foundational and should be considered necessary for race-related multicultural competence. Additional AVA competencies include self-awareness of thoughts, needs, and internal processes during interracial and intraracial encounters; self-awareness of interpersonal behavior in both interracial and intraracial interactions; awareness of power and privilege dynamics in one's own relationships; awareness of ways that one colludes with the maintenance of racism and White privilege; awareness

TABLE 4.1
Race-Related Multicultural Competencies

Attitudes, values, and awareness	Knowledge of theory and research	Interpersonal and professional skills
• *Racial self-awareness* • *Race-related empathy* • *Respect for different race-related experiences* • *Awareness of racial biases, stereotypes, and prejudices* • Attitude of openness to learning about and discussing race-related issues • Self-awareness of thoughts, needs, and internal processes during interracial and intraracial encounters • Awareness of interpersonal behavior in both interracial and intraracial interpersonal interactions • Awareness of attitudes and opinions on race-related topics • Awareness of race-related power and privilege dynamics in own relationships • Values the exploration of the relationship of race to psychological experience • Awareness of collusion with White privilege and the maintenance of racism	• *Racial identity theory* • *Racial socialization* • *White privilege* • *Racism-related stress and mental health* • *Internalized racism and colorism* • *Intraracial heterogeneity, intersectionality, and multiple identities* • Aversive and contemporary racism, implicit prejudice and stereotypes, ingroup bias • Intergroup conflict and conflict resolution • Prejudice reduction and antiracism strategies • Critical race theory • Liberation psychology • Ecological levels of analysis and ecological theory • History of race in psychology and psychotherapy • Neuroscience of racial perceptions and interracial interactions	• *Expresses authenticity and genuineness in interracial interactions* • *Creates a safe environment for and demonstrates openness during race-related discussions* • *Can identify and manage difference dynamics in professional relationships* • *Recognizes the impact of one's own race-related issues on professional and clinical relationships* • *Integrates race-related considerations into case conceptualization* • Possesses ability to recognize and process the influence of race on the therapeutic alliance • Possesses ability to process and recover from race-related ruptures in the therapeutic relationship • Integrates race-related inquiries during intake process • Incorporates race-related content into psychological interventions as appropriate • Integrates attention to resilience, strengths, positive development in the context of racism or race-related stress • Has ability to process client's overtly expressed racism

Note. Italicized text indicates competencies that are foundational and necessary for race-related multicultural competence.

of attitudes and opinions on race-related topics; an attitude of openness to learning about and discussing race-related issues; and valuing the exploration of the relationship of race to psychological experience.

Knowledge of Theory and Research

The theory and research on race within the field of psychology is large and diverse. However, there are particular bodies of work that can enhance the level of competence and sophistication with which race-related considerations are integrated into professional activities. Table 4.1 presents 14 specific areas of theory and research that compose the KTR competencies. Six of these should be considered necessary and foundational to effectively work with racial issues and diverse racial-ethnic groups. The six areas of theory and research that comprise the core KTR competencies include racial identity; racial socialization; racism-related stress; internalized racism; White privilege; and the study of aversive racism, implicit prejudice, and ingroup bias within the social cognition literature (Boyd, 2008; Burgess, van Ryn, Dovidio, & Saha, 2007; Dovidio, 2001; Dovidio et al., 2002). Additional areas of theory and research that will enhance multicultural practice relevant to the construct of race include the following: intraracial heterogeneity, intergroup conflict, prejudice reduction and antiracism strategies, critical race theory, liberation psychology, neuroscience of race, history of race in psychology, and ecological theory (Adams, 2009; Burgess et al., 2007; Comas-Díaz & Jacobsen, 1991).

Interpersonal and Professional Skills

Identifying and managing the dynamics of difference within therapeutic and supervisory relationships represents a critical area of skill for all dimensions of diversity. However, because of the visible markers of race, racial differences are likely to be influential in the "like-me" and "not-like-me" processing of both the therapist and client, as well as the supervisor and supervisee. Consequently, interpersonal interactions and behaviors will necessarily be affected by the racial baggage of the people involved. With this in mind, the 11 IPS competencies include authenticity and genuineness in interracial interactions, demonstration of empathy when experiences of racism are reported, the ability to cocreate a safe and open environment for discussion of race-related content, recognizing and attending to the specific impact of one's own race-related issues on the content and process of interactions, recognizing and processing the influence of the client's race-related experiences and perceptions on the therapeutic alliance, ability to work through and recover from race-related ruptures in the therapeutic relationship, inclusion of race-related inquiries during the intake process, integrating race-related considerations into case formulation, incorporation of racial content into psychotherapy interventions, and the ability to process any overt expressions of racism (see Table 4.1).

THE SUPERVISION APPROACH: USING RACE NARRATIVES AS AN ORGANIZING FRAMEWORK

The development of race-related multicultural competence is facilitated by a process that is able to incorporate attention to the emotional, cognitive, and contextual issues related to managing the dynamics and issues related to race and racism. It is critical for therapists to be able to be fully "present" in the room with the client. Strategies to reduce the race fog that prevents the therapist from being present with themselves and with the client are important. Research suggests that people are better able to manage emotions when they have a coherent narrative about their lives (McAdams, 2006). Working through emotional reactivity and reducing cognitive dissonance are two important goals that can be achieved through processing our narratives (Burgess et al., 2007; Wilson et al., 2000). A *race narrative* is a story that people have involving the construct of race, attributes of racial groups, race relations, and/or racism (Harrell & Bissell, 2009). Each person has multiple race narratives that emerge from a variety of life contexts. Personal, familial, cultural, collective, and dominant societal narratives all have strong influences on people's meaning systems, memory, identity, values, relationship, and community (Rappaport, 1995). Social constructivist narrative theory suggests that people's stories are not only created by their lives but simultaneously contribute to creating their lives (McAdams, 2006). The narratives that people hear and those that they author are influenced strongly by the dynamics of power and privilege. Some narratives are silenced, whereas others are amplified. People have differential access to some narratives because of their sociocultural locations. The sociopolitical nature of narrative constructions is profound, making understanding deconstructions of diverse race narratives particularly critical in the process of unmasking the influence of race in clinical supervision and the psychotherapeutic process. In addition, one of the cornerstones of narrative practice is an emphasis on the individual separating the "problem" from the "self" (Hays, Chang, & Havice, 2008). A narrative-centered process can facilitate an understanding that an issue can be constructed in a variety of ways and that the stories people tell about the issue reflect something about themselves. Processing issues of race and racism through this lens can facilitate empowerment and provides a method to work through racial issues without engaging in the "blame and shame game."

I propose here that a narrative approach facilitates the integration of the cognitive, affective, and behavioral elements through the use of story. Tummala-Narra (2009) suggested that it is the tendency to separate the cognitive and affective aspects of racial issues that make race a particularly challenging issue to discuss and contends that both cognitive and emotional insight is necessary. She further suggested that mental health professionals need to direct more attention to affective and interpersonal processes in issues of race and racism that arise in treatment and supervision. Working with narratives can deepen the processing of race- and racism-related content in supervision in the service of building clinical and multicultural competence. The approach can be organized into four general phases: Laying the groundwork (Phase I), Timing and opportunity (Phase II), Implementation of the three-step supervision strategy (Phase III), and Evaluation (Phase IV).

Phase I: Laying the Groundwork

Before describing and illustrating the three supervision processes in more depth, it is important to discuss the conditions necessary for the race narrative approach to be effective. These include the preparation and competence of the supervisor, the establishment of multicultural competence as part of the supervisory agreement, and the creation of an open and emotionally safe supervision atmosphere. Ideally, some groundwork has been laid from the beginning of the supervisory relationship regarding expectations of supervision generally, the challenges of processing diversity-related clinical material (e.g., discomfort, minimization, marginalization), and acknowledgment of the power differentials in the supervisory relationship. It is important to note that a strong and positive supervisory alliance is both a condition for, and an outcome of, processing racial and other multicultural content. A solid supervisory alliance is a prerequisite to doing this work in a manner that has depth and meaning. At the same time, lack of attention to important racial and multicultural dynamics can block or interfere with the development of a strong supervisory alliance. As the supervisory relationship deepens, the ability to process race-related content will be enhanced. As race-related content is more meaningfully processed, the supervisory relationship will deepen. These processes occur simultaneously and work together over time to create an optimal space for learning, for clinical development, and for deepening the way in which multicultural competence is demonstrated in the care of the client.

Difference is the one of the fundamental dynamics operating at the intersection of diversity and psychotherapy (Greene, 2008). Supervisor alertness to signals that race-related differences are affecting the supervisory or therapeutic relationship can help inform the integration of race narratives into the supervision process. Harrell (1995) identified five common strategies (the Five Ds of Difference) that are manifested in everyday interactions in the service of managing the discomfort, anxiety, and other various internal experiences associated with difference experiences. These strategies continuously operate in interracial encounters and include denial, distancing, defensiveness, devaluing, and discovery. The *denial* strategy involves a selective focus on sameness that minimizes the existence or significance of differences and allows dimensions of diversity to be overlooked. The *defensiveness* strategy involves externalizing negative actions and feelings in order to maintain one's sense of self as an ally of marginalized or stigmatized communities. The *devaluing* strategy involves the often unacknowledged dynamics of power and privilege and functions to maintain the status quo with respect to normality, superiority, and status hierarchies. The *distancing* strategy involves physical, intellectual, and/or emotional separation from diverse communities and can provide protection from meaningful connection to the painful experiences of oppressed groups. Ultimately, these first four approaches to difference can create tensions as they define for others what is acceptable or important enough to consider. Finally, the *discovery* strategy involves embracing diversity challenges and approaching them as opportunities for learning and growth. Differences are seen, acknowledged, and explored in relationship to self and to the larger sociopolitical context. Awareness of these dynamics can serve as an organizing frame for supervisors to assess the appropriate time for integration of the race-related narrative approach to more deeply process issues of race.

Phase II: Timing and Opportunity

There are multiple issues related to client care, treatment strategies, and therapist development, as well as numerous moments of an observed psychotherapy session that can be explored in any given supervision meeting. An important issue, then, is when a supervisor should pay particular attention to race-related issues and dynamics. Certainly, when the supervisee brings race-related content to supervision, the supervisor can incorporate race narratives into the processing of that content. However, opportunities arise through various stimulus issues that occur in supervision related to client content, client conceptualization and treatment planning, in-session therapy behaviors, therapeutic alliance issues, and/or supervision process issues.

A synthesis of the literature on multicultural issues in psychotherapy and supervision (Adams, 2009; Collins & Arthur, 2007; Gloria, Hird, & Tao, 2008; Jernigan et al., 2010; Tummala-Narra, 2009) resulted in the identification of 10 indicators of a potential need to pay specific attention to race-related multicultural competence and/or racial dynamics in supervision. Table 4.2 presents common race-related issues that can manifest in supervision, as well as

TABLE 4.2
Indicators Suggesting Attention Is Needed to Race-Related Content or Dynamics

Indicator	Description	Example
1. Gaps in self-awareness	Race and privilege are unexplored areas of identity and experience	"I don't really think of myself in terms of race."
2. Reactivity	Strong emotional reaction to racial material that may be expressed as defensiveness	"I feel like you are attacking me."
3. Minimization or devaluing the significance of race	Race-related content and/or process is dismissed as irrelevant or unimportant	"There are so many other more significant things going on here."
4. Interpersonal dynamics	Anxiety, lack of empathy, distancing, and/or aggression manifested in interpersonal interactions	"I feel like he is making too big of a deal out of this."
5. Unfamiliarity, inexperience and lack of knowledge	Limited knowledge of, and life experience with, people from diverse racial categorizations	"I've never really talked to anyone who is like this person before."
6. Oversimplification or superficiality	Making broad generalizations about race and racial issues without critical analysis; lack of sophistication in understanding racial dynamics	"African Americans make too much of a big deal out of racism."
7. Invisibility of race	Absence of race as a consideration or topic for exploration, particularly when racial content is obvious	"I didn't even see race as a difference between us because I identify so much with her as a woman."
8. Guilt, shame, or internalized racism	Self- or group-deprecating remarks and sentiments	"White people have just done so much damage to people of color." (White person speaking)
9. Context minimization error ("blaming the victim")	Attributing race-related issues to problems or pathology of groups and individuals	"They just want to come over here and take advantage of handouts."
10. Naive, idealizing	Expressions of color-blindness, sentiments that racism is gone, and/or romanticizing of interracial interactions	"I get along with everybody. Like MLK said, It's better not to even see race."

examples of verbalizations that reflect the issue. These can be experienced as microaggressions (Jernigan et al., 2010; Tummala-Narra, 2004, 2009) by the trainee and/or the supervisor and can accumulate to such an extent as to affect the supervision. Alertness to the expression of these issues is a way of assessing whether the quality of supervision and/or treatment would benefit from increased attention to race and culture.

A brief example illustrates the potentially negative impact that an avoidance of discussing race-related content can have on the supervisory relationship. A 32-year-old female African American trainee at a local homeless shelter had been seeing an African American male client under the supervision of a 54-year-old White male Jewish psychologist. When discussing this case, the trainee experienced the supervisor as frequently making comments about race that he seemed to feel were appropriate but that she felt were offensive. During one meeting, the supervisor, attempting to explore the intraracial dynamics in the therapeutic relationship, stated, "It's clear that the client thinks you are an 'Oreo.'" During my consultation with this trainee, she disclosed that she felt like he was trying to show his multicultural competence and seemed to really want her to like him and think he was "cool." However, the statement, and the broader context of his interactions with the trainee, reinforced her feeling that the supervisor had unexamined racial stereotypes and assumptions about African Americans and thus could not be trusted. The supervisee recognized that she shut down to exploring any potential countertransference issues to her client in supervision and maintained a distanced posture with the supervisor. Consequently, at midyear evaluation, she received low ratings on "reflective practice." The rupture to the supervisory relationship may be linked possibly to the manifestation of the supervisor's anxiety regarding the difference between himself and the supervisee (by trying too hard), as well as expressions of oversimplification and superficiality (see Point 6, Table 4.2) when discussing African Americans. In this example, the supervisor apparently neglected to examine his own potential contribution to the rupture in the supervisory relationship, and he did not process it with the student; the result was a negative evaluation of the supervisee. In addition, the supervisee's management of her own race-related anxiety through distancing behaviors prevented her from bringing up her concerns directly with the supervisor. Unfortunately, the lack of exploration of racial dynamics contributed to the deterioration of the supervisory relationship over time. By the time the student reached out to consult with me, the relationship was nearly beyond repair. The supervisory relationship as well as the trainee's clinical work and development may have benefitted from early identification of the interracial and intraracial dynamics that surfaced and the opportunity to process these dynamics.

Phase III: Implementing the Three-Step Supervision Strategy

The supervision strategy recommended here requires that either the supervisor or the trainee initiate a discussion of race-related content or process. Once the supervisee has opened the door to discussion of racial issues, or once the supervisor has seen an opportunity to more deeply process racial content, the strategy of working with race-related narratives can be helpful in providing a systematic supervision approach. The three steps for incorporating the race narratives approach will be described, and an illustrative example from a supervision session will be presented for each step. Table 4.3 summarizes the three steps.

TABLE 4.3
Three Steps of Incorporating Race Narratives Into Clinical Supervision

Step	Description	Illustrative intervention
1. Elicitation and disclosure	Invitation to share personal, family, cultural, or dominant social narratives related to the construct of race; supervisee (and sometimes supervisor) disclosure and description of narratives associated with the stimulus issue or event	"I'm thinking it would be a good idea to pause for a moment and focus in on what happened in the session when_____. I'd like to invite you to take a moment to try to connect any personal experiences involving race that are associated with _____."
2. Deconstruction and analysis	Exploration of the narrative with respect to the supervisee's internal experience, multicultural issues (e.g., power and privilege, identity, bias), and impact of these on the therapy and/or supervisory process	"I'm wondering if you notice any similarities between your thoughts and feelings associated with your experience and what happened in the session." "Let's explore a bit more about your experience with respect to the role of race in your sense of self and identity as it may have been reflected in your work with this client."
3. Reconstruction and integration	Facilitation of the supervisee's process of integrating self variables, client variables, and contextual variables (and possibly supervisor variables) to form a coherent narrative of the therapy or supervisory event or issue and the supervisee's developmental process	"Let's take a step back now and look at what happened in the session in the context of some of what we just processed." "How might you describe your process from the session to now with respect to the theme of race"?

Step 1: Elicitation and Disclosure

The first step in the process involves eliciting relevant narratives by inviting the supervisee to process the stimulus issue more deeply. The goal is to uncover and share the narratives associated with the stimulus issue. The principle of compassionate confrontation should operate strongly here. Invitations to process race-related material may be met with socially desirable, superficial, or defensive responses. The skill of the supervisor in normalizing reactivity to the topic of race, acknowledging the emotionally charged nature of racial issues, and gently pushing the supervisee to begin making connections will have an effect on the quality of the disclosure. I have found it useful to be explicit about the clinical value of the process and the connection to clinical skill development. I have also found it useful, particularly for beginning therapists, to provide an "I wonder" statement that can help the supervisee connect to a potentially central theme such as avoidance of conflict, minimization, maintenance of self-image, overidentification with client, and so on (e.g., "I wonder whether you've had any experiences where you might have felt that race was being overly emphasized or someone was playing the race card"). Relevant narratives can also be identified by inviting the supervisee to share what stands out for him or her about what he or she has heard, observed, or been told related to the particular issue. This can help to elicit family, cultural, and dominant social narratives that have been internalized and interact with personal narratives to influence reactions and behavior in the therapeutic context. As the supervisee begins to make connections to his or her own experiences and observations, the supervisor should assist the supervisee in structuring the disclosure as a story, with a beginning, middle, and end. This can be accomplished by asking questions such as, "What happened before that?" "Why do you think it happened that way?" or "What is your understanding of how that ended up?" During this step, it is important for the supervisor to provide encouraging, validating, and reflective comments to maintain an atmosphere of safety and compassion. It may sometimes be appropriate for the supervisor to briefly share elements of his or her own narrative to model the process or help the supervisee make connections. The following excerpt is an example of the elicitation-process. The trainee therapist is a 33-year-old, upper middle class, White American woman of Greek ancestry; the client is a 32-year-old, working class, African American woman whose parents were born in Belize; and the supervisor is a 46-year-old, upper middle class, African American woman. The therapy took place at a university-based community clinic in a large urban area.

> *Supervisor:* Thank you so much for sharing some of what came up for you in that session. Let's pause for a moment and explore your impatience with your client's job searching process. Where do you think that's coming from for you?

Supervisee:	I feel like she's not doing enough, like she's just wants to take the easy way out. I guess I'm disappointed in her.
Supervisor:	What's "the easy way out" mean?
Supervisee:	I don't know, like go on welfare or something, like giving up. I mean I like her so much and I thought she was different.
Supervisor:	Different from what?
Supervisee:	[Uncomfortable laugh] I don't think I know what you mean.
Supervisor:	You said you thought your client was different, so I was just wondering different from what?
Supervisee:	[Silence] I don't know.
Supervisor:	It seems like you may have thought about something that you are hesitant to say. I just want to invite you to explore it, as it may have important implications for your work with this client.
Supervisee:	[Puts her hands over her face] I just caught myself. I'm so embarrassed. I guess I put her in some category of being different from other Black people. This reminds me of something we talked about in the cross-cultural class in the first year, how we can hold on to negative stereotypes even if we have close relationships with people of that group. I mean on an intellectual level I know everybody has stereotypes, and I know that includes me. But . . . I don't know . . . I feel like I have done a lot of thinking about White privilege and challenging my assumptions.
Supervisor:	I know racial issues can be hard stuff to explore, but I'm thinking it's really important to your treatment with her. It was very courageous of you to say this out loud. Is it OK with you if we go a little deeper into what you just recognized about your stereotyping?
Supervisee:	Sure . . . but I don't want you to hate me. [Uncomfortable laugh]
Supervisor:	I promise I won't hate you . . . but I am wondering how this makes you feel about yourself. Race is such a sensitive issue and can bring up a lot for people. What do you think?
Supervisee:	I just want to crawl out of my skin right now, I feel so embarrassed. I mean I really like you and really like my client, and I feel like I have done good work with her. I guess maybe I hope my client doesn't hate me too! I just want her to know that I'm not one of "those" White people.

Supervisor:	It seems like you have some ideas about White people and Black people that may be connected to your life experiences or observations. Do your feelings now remind you of any other situations?
Supervisee:	Hmmmm . . . I don't know if this fits but it makes me think about when I was in elementary school and the only girl that would be friends with me was an African American girl. There weren't many African Americans in my school. Other kids teased me because I brought weird Greek food for lunch, and they said the food smelled funny and I smelled funny. They teased her too because she wore her hair in like these like five or six short braids with ribbons and these round hair ornaments that looked like marbles or something. Anyway, we decided that we didn't like White people and that they were kind of rude and stupid.
Supervisor:	Wow. That's powerful stuff. How did this situation turn out?
Supervisee:	Well, my friend Candace and I pretty much kept to ourselves socially. It didn't help that we were both, like, "the smart kids." We were like each other's refuge, even through junior high school. Both of us were rather socially awkward. It's not like we stopped liking each other or being friends, it's just that we went to different high schools and kind of lost touch.
Supervisor:	If I can ask, what did your family think of your friendship?
Supervisee:	Well, they always wanted me to make some more friends. It's not that they didn't like her; I just think they didn't want me to be the target of discrimination because of my association with her. I mean, Candace spent a lot of time at my house and I spent a lot of time at her house too. They were nice to her because she was my friend, but they sometimes put down Black people as a whole. And I hated that. I hated when they would say something negative about Black people. They weren't, like, racist but I do think they had some stereotypes about Black people that were negative.

The supervisor recognizes that there is something going on that needs to be examined. The trainee is initially hesitant to disclose, but the supervisor pushes gently. The disclosure of the personal narrative involving her childhood friend, and the family narrative about African Americans brought some important issues to the forefront relevant to what was triggered for the trainee in working with an African American client.

If time is an issue, as in a supervision group, the supervisor can proceed to facilitate the trainee processing the implications for her work with her client. However, the issues are very complex, sensitive, and tempting to move away from. Engaging in Steps 2 and 3 of the supervision process can yield greater awareness, learning, and therapeutic implications.

Step 2: Deconstruction and Analysis

The second step involves a process of deconstructing the narrative by facilitating connections to the supervisee's internal experience and exploring race-related issues embedded in the narrative (e.g., identity, stigma, privilege). The process of deconstruction may be particularly challenging as it may bring up feelings such as fear, shame, guilt, and anger. The principle of empathic exploration can provide grounding for the supervisor as he or she guides the trainee therapist through the deconstruction process. This step includes identifying the origins of the narrative, associations with the narrative, unpacking the meaning of the narrative, and exploring how it has affected in-session reactions and behaviors as well as the development of the therapeutic alliance. It is sometimes helpful to frame exploration of the narrative's meaning in terms of takeaways, or lessons, to emphasize the active process of constructing meaning and laying the groundwork for reconstructing the narrative and meaning-making in the last step. The supervisor can assist the trainee in identifying both the general and specific triggers for the activation of the narrative in the clinical situation. This step helps to heighten the supervisee's self-awareness and ability to anticipate and identify triggers related to client characteristics, issues, and behavior. The deconstruction process also contributes to helping the supervisee develop the reflective practice skills necessary for developing metacompetence related to race and other multicultural issues. The following excerpt is an example of the deconstruction step.

> *Supervisor:* So let's continue to look at how your relationship with your client and how your reaction to your client relates to your own experiences with African Americans, particularly your friend Candace. What I have heard so far in your personal narrative about your experience with your friend Candace, you said you didn't want me or your client to think of you as one of "those" White people.

> *Supervisee:* Wow! So many things are coming together for me now. I mean I knew I wanted Candace to like me, and I knew that I feel a special connection to African American women and that had something to do with Candace. But what is really hitting me now is how as a child I didn't really think about myself as White, and I think it was really hard for me when around high school I realized the world saw me as a White girl.

Supervisor: And maybe Candace started seeing you as a White girl too?

Supervisee: And I remember not really understanding why we weren't as close as we got older. I thought I might have done or said something to offend her and maybe she thought that I was like the White girls that were so mean. And it was especially hard for me because I never felt like I fit in with the White girls at my high school or college . . . or even now . . . but I know that women of color don't see me as one of them.

Supervisor: What would it have meant if you had said something to offend Candace?

Supervisee: I don't know.

Supervisor: I wonder if you ever worried that you had done something to put distance between you and Candace?

Supervisee: I can't stand that thought! I hate the idea that, maybe, in Candace's eyes, I was a White girl.

Supervisor: There are a lot of layers here in your associations with your narrative about Candace . . . I'm hearing some possible shame, some racial identity issues that you might look at, and other things. What are your thoughts?

Supervisee: I agree. It's so strange . . . I really wasn't thinking about this stuff but it clearly is part of what is going on with me. I really need to think about how it all affects how I am with African American women.

Supervisor: It seems that a trigger may have been when you felt some frustration with the client regarding her job situation.

Supervisee: Yeah . . . I just felt like I wanted her to take more responsibility with this whole job thing. I don't want her to be an unemployed African American woman. Maybe I so much didn't want her to fit a stereotype that it became more about my reaction than about her experience with looking for a job. Now I feel bad that I wasn't present and did not empathize with what she is going through!

Supervisor: [Smiles] And what makes you think you are so different from all of us other therapists who are sometimes not as present with our clients' experience as we wish to be?

Supervisee: [Laughs] Or like somehow I'm immune from having stereotypes or getting lost of my own stuff! OK . . . I get it. This is part of my struggle. . . . I have to be less reactive to having a negative thought about an African American woman. Wow!

Step 3: Reconstruction and Integration

The final step in the process is guided by the idea that intentional meaning-making of race-related narratives can reduce race-related anxiety and result in therapist behaviors that are productive in the management and incorporation of race-related content. The process of reconstructing the psychotherapy or supervision narrative that (a) incorporates a reflective normalization of race-related issues, (b) integrates insights from the deconstruction process, and (c) is consistent with values and self-image can contribute to both personal and professional growth and development. Both compassionate confrontation and empathic exploration are important guiding principles. Identifying the connection between supervisee narratives and therapeutic behavior and the therapist–client alliance requires compassion for the shame or embarrassment or fear of judgment likely experienced by the supervisee related to issues of race, while pushing the supervisee to reflect meaningfully on the racial dynamics involved. Expressing appreciation and gratitude for disclosures and risk taking, as well as ensuring confidentiality of the content shared, is important. The supervisee is likely to come away with a positive experience if the supervisor assists the trainee in identifying learning and insights related to both general clinical competence and multicultural competence. The supervisee's ability to effectively consider and integrate therapist variables, client variables, and contextual variables so that a coherent story of the therapeutic event can be told is the ultimate goal. During this phase, the supervisor also facilitates the exploration of the issues raised in the context of implications for clinical practice with respect to ongoing self-assessment and development of increased metacompetence. Discussions of clinical follow-up, consideration of the implications for ongoing work with the current client and future clients, and monitoring of the impact on the supervisory relationship are also strongly recommended. The following excerpt from a supervision meeting illustrates the implementation of this phase of the process.

> *Supervisor:* So, given what we have been discussing, how are you understanding what is happening in the therapy with you and your client? Let's start with the context of the treatment and the therapist–client relationship generally.
>
> *Supervisee:* Mmmm . . . Well, we've been working on her depression and ways to help her be less depressed. Recently, we have been talking a lot about her being unemployed and how that feels.
>
> *Supervisor:* And the therapeutic relationship?
>
> *Supervisee:* I feel like we have a strong relationship. We've been working together for almost 6 months. She comes regularly and seems to trust me. I think we've done really good work. She's

less depressed now. But the last couple of sessions it has felt different somehow, like we aren't as connected . . . It has been more superficial, and I felt like we weren't really getting anywhere. And I have felt frustrated with her for the first time since she started therapy.

Supervisor: And so how do you understand your frustration with your client from the perspective of the racial dynamics?

Supervisee: Well, I generally feel a connection with African American women, and I think that has something to do with my friendship with Candace growing up. It's sort of embarrassing to admit, but I like that women of color seem to accept me. I guess I'm sort of proud of it. I feel like it has helped me build a strong relationship with my client. But I feel like my experience with Candace has also contributed to maybe me being overinvested in that whole thing and that I got wrapped up in who I wanted to be and who I wanted her to be. It's like I got distracted from really listening to what her experience is.

Supervisor: So your friendship with Candace contributed to some strengths you bring to developing relationships with African American women but also may have created some blind spots.

Supervisee: Yeah, I always thought it was just positive . . . but, like, I'm realizing that I guess my ego is involved too.

Supervisor: So what do you think this means for your work with your client?

Supervisee: I'm definitely going to be more aware of how my needs might sometimes prevent me from being empathic with her struggles. Do you think I should bring any of this up with her?

Supervisor: What do you think?

Supervisee: I don't know. I mean what would I say?

Supervisor: I'm thinking it would be useful to look at the DVDs of your last two sessions and see what you observe in terms of the process. This might give you some ideas about how you might want to follow-up.

Phase IV: Evaluation

Consistent with a competency-based approach, evaluation should be guided by observation of indicators of professional behaviors, expressed attitudes, and demonstrated knowledge of the supervisee on the race-related multicultural competencies identified earlier. In addition, the achievement of metacompetence, that is, the ability to assess self-assess areas of relatively stronger or weaker competence (Falender & Shafranske, 2007), is particularly important for issues of race-related multicultural competence. In this context, metacompetence involves ongoing reflective practice related to race, interracial interactions, racial issues, and racial identity. With respect to formal evaluation, Table 4.1 provides specific competencies that can be incorporated into both a self-assessment process with the trainee and oral and/or written feedback. However, evaluation and self-assessment of race-related knowledge, skills, and attitudes are complicated by the emotionality that may be associated with race. Social desirability and the motivation to appear nonracist or color-blind may interfere with the identification and remediation of race-related competencies that need further development. Supervisors and supervisees may collude to avoid race-related metacompetence conversations to guard against perceptions of being racist, naive, having a chip on one's shoulder, "playing the race card," and other unwanted attributes. Because of these dynamics, it may be particularly challenging for supervisors to provide feedback to trainees who do not demonstrate expected levels of the competencies listed in Table 4.1. Supervisors should seek consultation from colleagues who have expertise in multicultural issues to process ways to deal with challenging race-related dynamics with trainees. Institutional support can be provided through consultation groups for supervisors that focus on multicultural issues and challenges in supervision.

CONCLUDING REMARKS

The central purpose of integrating race narratives into supervision is to facilitate the meaningful consideration of race-related material in the process of therapy, supervision, and professional relationships more generally. To that end, it is my experience that there is significant value in the approach described here. Exploring race narratives provides an opportunity to go beyond identification of racial differences and similarities and more deeply understand the meaning of race that has emerged from each person's multiple cultural locations and life experiences. Compassionate confrontation of race-related issues that emerge in clinical development and practice creates a safe space in supervision for processing content that may be experienced as dangerous and threatening. Empathic exploration of the emergent race narratives allows the supervisee to experience an ally in the sometimes painful process of looking directly at multicultural and sociopolitical dynamics that may be inhibiting effective therapy with clients. Supervisees get in vivo training in the process of reflective practice, which is an essential competency for professional psychology (Fouad et al., 2009). However, supervisors should be mindful of some of the inevitable challenges of implementing this approach.

One of the central challenges for supervisors integrating racial material into the supervision process is the sensitivity and defensiveness that frequently come with the subject matter. When race is spoken about, it is often in racially homogeneous settings or within groups of like-minded others so that it is common to have increased anxiety when talking about race "in mixed company" (Tatum, 1992; Tummala-Narra, 2009). Many supervisors and supervisees will be unaccustomed to open discussions on the subject of race as it applies to their own internal and interpersonal process and may have never previously explored or discussed their own race narratives. The trainee's stories about interracial and intraracial encounters and relationships, racial identity development, beliefs about race and racial groups, and experiences and understandings of racism are going to strongly influence their willingness to process race-related content, their assessment of the value of spending supervision time on the process, the depth and authenticity of their disclosures, and the effect on clinical practice.

The strengths and limitations of the approach will be strongly influenced by the supervisor's metacompetence relevant to multicultural content generally and race-related content in particular. Supervisors must be familiar enough with the multicultural competence literature to accurately assess their own limitations and gaps in knowledge and skills. One of the biggest barriers to facilitating supervisee multicultural competence is the reluctance and/or inability of supervisors to identify race-related material and bring the issues to the supervisee's attention. Fostering the willingness and readiness of both the supervisor and supervisee to process sensitive racial issues requires an atmosphere of trust and safety, openness to the possible emergence of unexpected memories or unforeseen vulnerabilities, and most important, the prior establishment of a supervisory agreement that includes personal exploration of sensitive topics. The exploration of race narratives with a supervisee requires that the supervisor has engaged in, and continues to engage in, the process of examining his or her own race narratives, including racial identity, racism, privilege, interracial encounters and relationships, and beliefs about race and racial groups. Supervisors should be aware that processing race-related narratives may trigger unanticipated reactions and potentially expose the supervisor's own vulnerability around these issues. The quantity and quality of the supervisor's previous experience discussing race in both professional and personal contexts also influence the implementation of the supervision approach described here. Effective supervision and evaluation of supervisees on the racial dimension of multicultural competence is not possible without the ongoing reflective practice and self-assessment of the supervisor.

REFERENCES

Adams, D. (2009). Multicultural pedagogy in the supervision and education of psychotherapists. *Women & Therapy, 33*, 42–54. doi:10.1080/02703140903404713

Altman, N. (2000). Black and White thinking: A psychoanalyst reconsiders race. *Psychoanalytic Dialogues, 10*, 589–605. doi:10.1080/10481881009348569

American Psychological Association. (2003). Guidelines on multicultural education, training, research, practice, and organizational change for psychologists. *American Psychologist, 58*, 377–402. doi:10.1037/0003-066X.58.5.377

Arredondo, P., Toporek, R., Brown, S. P., Jones, J., Locke, D., Sanchez, J., & Stadler, H. (1996). Operationalization of the multicultural counseling competencies. *Journal of Multicultural Counseling and Development, 24*, 42–78. doi:10.1002/j.2161-1912.1996.tb00288.x

Associated Press. (November 14, 2006). *Census report: Broad racial disparities persist—differences in income, education, home ownership continue, data finds*. Retrieved from http://www.msnbc.msn.com/id/15704759/

Baron, A. S., & Banaji, M. R. (2006). Development of implicit attitudes: Evidence of race evaluations from ages 6 and 10 and adulthood. *Psychological Science, 17*, 53–58. doi:10.1111/j.1467-9280.2005.01664.x

Boatright-Horowitz, S. L., & Seoung, S. (2009). Teaching White privilege to White students can mean saying good-bye to positive student evaluations. *American Psychologist, 64*, 574–575. doi:10.1037/a0016593

Boyd, D. (2008). Autoethnography as a tool for transformative learning about White privilege. *Journal of Transformative Education, 6*, 212–225. doi:10.1177/1541344608326899

Brown, M. T., & Landrum-Brown, J. (1995). Counselor supervision: Cross-cultural perspectives. In J. G. Ponterotto, J. M. Casas, L. A. Suzuki, & C. M. Alexander (Eds.), *Handbook of multicultural counseling* (pp. 263–286). Thousand Oaks, CA: Sage.

Brown, T. N. (2003). Critical race theory speaks to the sociology of mental health: Mental health problems produced by racial stratification. *Journal of Health and Social Behavior, 44*, 292–301. doi:10.2307/1519780

Burgess, D., van Ryn, M., Dovidio, J., & Saha, S. (2007). Reducing racial bias among health care providers: Lessons from social–cognitive psychology. *Journal of General Internal Medicine, 22*, 882–887. doi:10.1007/s11606-007-0160-1

Collins, S., & Arthur, N. (2007). A framework for enhancing multicultural counselling competence. *Canadian Journal of Counselling, 41*, 31–49.

Comas-Díaz, L., & Jacobsen, F. M. (1991). Ethnocultural transference and countertransference in the therapeutic dyad. *American Journal of Orthopsychiatry, 61*, 392–402. doi:10.1037/h0079267

Crenshaw, K., Gotanda, N., Peller, G., & Thomas, K. (Eds.). (1995). *Critical race theory: The key writings that formed the movement*. New York, NY: The New Press.

Daniel, J. H., Roysircar, G., Abeles, N., & Boyd, C. (2004). Individual and cultural diversity competency: Focus on the therapist. *Journal of Clinical Psychology, 60*, 755–770. doi:10.1002/jclp.20014

Delgado, R. (2000). *Critical race theory: The cutting edge*. Philadelphia, PA: Temple University.

Devine, P. G. (2001). Implicit prejudice and stereotyping: How automatic are they? Introduction to the special section. *Journal of Personality and Social Psychology, 81*, 757–759. doi:10.1037/0022-3514.81.5.757

Dovidio, J. F. (2001). On the nature of contemporary prejudice: The third wave. *Journal of Social Issues, 57*, 829–849. doi:10.1111/0022-4537.00244

Dovidio, J. F., Gaertner, S. L., Kawakami, K., & Hodson, G. (2002). Why can't we just get along? Interpersonal biases and interracial distrust. *Cultural Diversity & Ethnic Minority Psychology, 8*, 88–102. doi:10.1037/1099-9809.8.2.88

Falender, C. A., & Shafranske, E. P. (2007). Competence in competency-based supervision practice: Construct and application. *Professional Psychology: Research and Practice, 38*, 232–240. doi:10.1037/0735-7028.38.3.232

Falicov, C. J. (1995). Training to think culturally: A multidimensional comparative framework. *Family Process, 34*, 373–388. doi:10.1111/j.1545-5300.1995.00373.x

Falicov, C. J. (2003). Culture and family therapy: New variations on a fundamental theme. In T. R. Sexton, G. L. Weeks, & M. S. Robbins (Eds.), *Handbook of family therapy* (pp. 41–53). New York, NY: Routledge.

Fouad, N. A., Grus, C. L., Hatcher, R. L., Kaslow, N. J., Hutchings, P. S., Madson, M., . . . & Crossman, R. E. (2009). Competency benchmarks: A developmental model for understanding and measuring competence in professional psychology. *Training and Education in Professional Psychology, 3*(4, Suppl.), S5—S26. doi:10.1037/a0015832

Gloria, A. M., Hird, J. S., Tao, K. W. (2008). Self-reported multicultural competence of White predoctoral intern supervisors. *Training and Education in Professional Psychology, 2*, 129–136. doi:10.1037/1931-3918.2.3.129

Greene, B. (2008). How difference makes a difference. In J. C. Muran (Ed.), *Dialogues on difference: Studies of diversity in the therapeutic relationship* (pp. 47–63). Washington, DC: American Psychological Association.

Guinote, A., Willis, G.B., & Martellotta, C. (2010). Social power increases implicit prejudice. *Journal of Experimental Social Psychology, 46*, 299–307. doi: 10.1016/j.jesp.2009.11.012

Hamer, F. M. (2002). Guards at the gate: Race, resistance, and psychic reality. *Journal of the American Psychoanalytic Association, 50*, 1119–1236. doi:10.1177/000306 51020500041301

Hamer, F. M. (2006). Racism as a transference state. *The Psychoanalytic Quarterly, 75*, 197–214. doi:10.1002/j.2167-4086.2006.tb00037.x

Harrell, S. P. (1995, August). *Dynamics of difference: Personal and sociocultural dimensions of intergroup relations*. Paper presented at the 103rd Annual Convention of the American Psychological Association. New York, NY.

Harrell, S. P., & Bissell, G.H. (2009, December). *Pathways to culturally-syntonic practice: Integrating diversity narratives into clinical supervision.* Continuing education workshop presented at Loyola Marymount University, Los Angeles, CA.

Harrell, S. P., & Gallardo, M. (2008). Sociopolitical and community dynamics in the development of a multicultural worldview. In J. A. Asamen, G. Berry, & M. Ellis (Eds.), *Child development, multiculturalism, and the media* (pp. 113–128). Thousand Oaks, CA: Sage. doi:10.4135/9781412982771.n8

Harrell, S. P., & Pezeshkian, A. (2008). Critical race theory. In F. T. L. Leong (Ed.), *Handbook of counseling: Vol. 3. Cross-cultural counseling* (pp. 1072–1079). Thousand Oaks, CA: Sage.

Harrell, S. P., & Sloan-Pena, G. (2006). Racism and discrimination. In Y. Jackson (Ed.), *Encyclopedia of multicultural psychology* (pp. 396–402). Thousand Oaks, CA: Sage. doi:10.4135/9781412952668.n176

Hays, D. G., Chang, C. Y., & Havice, P. (2008). White racial identity statuses as predictors of White privilege awareness. *The Journal of Humanistic Counseling, Education and Development, 47*, 234–246. doi:10.1002/j.2161-1939.2008.tb00060.x

Hutchings, P. B., & Haddock, G. (2008). Look Black in anger: The role of implicit prejudice in the categorization and perceived emotional intensity of racially ambiguous faces. *Journal of Experimental Psychology, 44*, 1418–1420. doi: 10.1016/j.jesp.2008.05.002

Jernigan, M. M., Green, C. E., Helms, J. E., Perez-Gualdron, L., & Henze, K. (2010). An examination of people of color supervision dyads: Racial identity matters as much as race. *Training and Education in Professional Psychology, 4*, 62–73. doi:10.1037/a0018110

Leary, K. (1997). Race, self-disclosure, and "forbidden talk": Race and ethnicity in contemporary clinical practice. *The Psychoanalytic Quarterly, 66*, 163–189.

McAdams, D. (2006). The problem of narrative coherence. *Journal of Constructivist Psychology, 19*, 109–125. doi:10.1080/10720530500508720

Parker, L., & Lynn, M. (2002). What's race got to do with it? Critical race theory's conflicts with and connections to qualitative research methodology and epistemology. *Qualitative Inquiry, 8*, 7–22. doi:10.1177/107780040200800102

Payne, B. K., Krosnick, J. A., Pasek, J., Lelkes, Y., Akhtar, O., & Tompson, T. (2010). Implicit and explicit prejudice in the 2008 American presidential election. *Journal of Experimental Social Psychology, 46*, 367–374. doi: 10.1016/j.jesp.2009.11.001

Plant, E. A., Butz, D. A., & Tartakovsky, M. (2008). Interethnic interactions: Expectancies, emotions, and behavioral intentions. *Group Processes & Intergroup Relations, 11*, 555–574. doi:10.1177/1368430208095827

Polkinghorne, D. (1988). *Narrative knowing and the human sciences.* Albany: State University of New York.

Rappaport, J. (1995). Empowerment meets narrative: Listening to stories and creating settings. *American Journal of Community Psychology, 23*, 795–807. doi:10.1007/BF02506992

Schmidt, K., & Nosek, B.A. (2010). Implicit (and explicit) racial attitudes barely changed during Barack Obama's presidential campaign and early presidency. *Journal of Experimental Social Psychology, 46*, 308–314. doi: 10.1016/j.jesp.2009.12.003

Sellers, R. M., Caldwell, C. H., Schmeelk-Cone, K. H., & Zimmerman, M. A. (2003). Racial identity, racial discrimination, perceived stress and psychological distress among African American young adults. *Journal of Health and Social Behavior, 44*, 302–317. doi:10.2307/1519781

Smedley, A., & Smedley, B. D. (2005). Race as biology is fiction, racism as a social problem is real: Anthropological and historical perspectives in the social construction of race. *American Psychologist, 60*, 16–26. doi:10.1037/0003-066X.60.1.16

Spencer, M. B., Dupree, D., & Hartmann, T. (1997). A phenomenological variant of ecological systems theory (PVEST): A self-organization perspective in context. *Development and Psychopathology, 9*, 817–833. doi:10.1017/S0954579497001454

Suchet, M. (2004). A relational encounter with race. *Psychoanalytic Dialogues, 14*, 423–438.

Tatum, B. D. (1992). Talking about race, learning about racism: The application of racial identity development theory in the classroom. *Harvard Educational Review, 62*, 1–24.

Tatum, B. D. (2000). The complexity of identity: "Who am I?" In M. Adams, W. J. Blumenfeld, R. Castaneda, H. Hackman, M. L. Peters, & X. Zuniga (Eds.), *Readings for diversity and social justice: An anthology on racism, anti-Semitism, sexism, heterosexism, ableism, and classism* (pp. 9–15). New York, NY: Routledge.

Trawalter, S., & Richeson, J.A. (2008). Let's talk about race, baby! When Whites' and Blacks' interracial contact experiences diverge. *Journal of Experimental Social Psychology, 44*, 1214-1217. doi:10.1016/j.jesp.2008.03.013

Tummala-Narra, P. (2004). Dynamics of race and culture in the supervisory encounter. *Psychoanalytic Psychology, 21*, 300–311. doi:10.1037/0736-9735.21.2.300

Tummala-Narra, P. (2009). Teaching on diversity: The mutual influence of students and instructors. *Psychoanalytic Psychology, 26*, 322–334. doi:10.1037/a0016444

West, C. (2001). *Race matters* (2nd ed.). Boston, MA: Beacon.

Williams, D. R., & Jackson, P. B. (2005). Social sources of racial disparities in health. *Health Affairs, 24*, 325–334. doi:10.1377/hlthaff.24.2.325

Wilson, T. D., Lindsey, S., & Schooler, T. Y. (2000). A model of dual attitudes. *Psychological Review, 107*, 101–126. doi:10.1037/0033-295X.107.1.101

5

IMMIGRANT CLIENTS, SUPERVISEES, AND SUPERVISORS

CELIA J. FALICOV

Increasing attention is being paid in clinical training and supervision to the idea that applied psychological practice (both practice itself and the mainstream theoretical concepts that underlie clinical technique) is culture bound and needs to be questioned and modified when dealing with clients of other cultures. These concerns have led to descriptions of cultural differences and of multicultural competencies that guide therapists in developing or selecting culturally appropriate interventions.

One foundational premise in this effort (and central to this text) is that multiple cultural identities contribute to a person's experience and shape the challenges they face, as well as influence their approach to problem-solving (see Chapters 1 and 2, this volume). This perspective not only encourages consideration of all aspects of cultural identity but also focuses on the

Portions of this chapter are adapted from Chapter 3 of *Latino Families in Therapy, Second Edition*, by C. J. Falicov, 2014, New York, NY: Guilford Press. Copyright 2014 by Guilford Press. Adapted with permission.

http://dx.doi.org/10.1037/14370-005
Multiculturalism and Diversity in Clinical Supervision: A Competency-Based Approach, C. A. Falender, E. P. Shafranske, and C. J. Falicov (Editors)

inevitable interaction between all the sources that influence meaning and behavior. Although most clinicians and supervisors would likely endorse this premise, it is challenging to actually put this perspective into practice. Some cultural identities often seem to be placed in the background, minimized, or subsumed under other cultural influences. Such is the case for immigration. In spite of advances in the field, the focus on incorporating culture has sometimes resulted in subsuming under culture the considerable long-term effects of migration stresses that can occur independently as a phenomenon per se, or in conjunction with encounters with cultural difference. This chapter takes up immigration as a multicultural feature that exerts influence independently and in interaction with other identities, such as ethnicity.

MIGRATION AS A UNIQUE INDIVIDUAL AND CULTURAL INFLUENCE

The issue of migration is usually taken into consideration when cultural and language changes are discussed in supervision. Nevertheless, migration appears more as an inevitable background and less as a forefront concern of therapists and supervisors. Such an approach delimits careful consideration of the complex and important experiences that occur in migration and the potential longstanding impacts on clients and families. Recently, the American Psychological Association Presidential Task Force on Immigration (2012) focused on this important issue with the goal to provide psychological researchers, practitioners, educators and graduate students with an understanding of the psychological processes of immigration and derive evidence-informed recommendations for the provision of mental health services to immigrants. Consonant with these goals, this chapter aims to provide supervisees and supervisors with specific competencies necessary for clinical practice with immigrant clients. As discussed in Chapter 2, the multidimensional ecological comparative approach (MECA) framework provides an approach to consider immigration processes. I believe it is important to move premigration, migration, and postmigration experiences to the foreground of assessment and treatment because of their complex, specific, and far-reaching psychosocial disruptions at the cognitive, affective, and social behavioral levels. These disruptions start in the country of origin and often continue through the lifetime of the immigrant and the generations that follow. To be sure, migration is not a uniform experience. It varies with class, race, gender, age at migration, nationality, and proximity to country of origin, among other variables (see Falicov, 2012). In spite of these numerous differences, similar processes of migration are often found across groups. Contemporary developments, such as advances in global communication, are allowing immigrants to interact in multiple ways with their countries of origin simultaneously with the adoptive cultures. This adds to the complexity of immigration, which needs to be attended to within the framework of cultural awareness and sensitivity.

Migration inflicts many stresses on individuals and families. Families often must undergo painful separations from loved ones. Traumatic events may have taken place before, during, and after the migration. The effects of migration may affect several generations of the family. Although immigrant stories often portray losses and challenges, there are also gains to be had and many triumphs to celebrate (Falicov, 2012, 2014). It is important for supervisors and therapists to develop a strength-based view of migration effects instead of only considering losses and deficits. Migration generates short-term and long-term relational stresses and struggles but often marshals resources and strengths for those undergoing the experience, regardless of their cultural backgrounds. To capture these strengths, the concepts and practices of relational resilience advanced by Walsh (2006) greatly enhance work with immigrants.

MECA moves away from a purely ethnic-focused position that lists and describes value differences. Rather, it enlarges the concept of culture to encompass many dimensions derived from each person's location in multiple contexts, such as nationality, social class, race, gender, religion, occupation, and migration background, among others that compose each person's ecological niche. The integration of social locations and exclusions is an important part of the model that requires a social justice conceptualization and practice along with cultural diversity issues. We turn now to a discussion of specific competencies.

LEARNING MIGRATION-SPECIFIC COMPETENCIES

A large interdisciplinary field of migration studies exists that focuses exclusively on immigrants, but most psychologists and other mental health professionals have limited participation in this field. In the present chapter, I draw upon this body of work to describe migration issues and outline migration-specific competencies that supervisors and therapists need to develop to conduct effective clinical work with immigrants. Although these competencies apply primarily to work with economic immigrants, they are also helpful in working with other types of immigrants, including refugees, who also requires advanced competencies in trauma work. In Chapter 2, I made a distinction between cultural competence and cultural humility. I should add here that I offer competencies as thoughts and practices collected over many years of work with immigrants but I consider humility, curiosity, respect, and flexibility as the necessary bases for building competence. To address the treatment needs of immigrants, and the training of therapists and supervisors for this type of work, I propose seven migration-specific competencies, which the rest of this chapter describes in depth.

1. *Learning training and supervision tools.* Several instruments are helpful aids to the process of supervision: (a) to coconstruct with family members a migration narrative; (b) a genoecogram (GEg), which combines a family genogram with an ecomap; (c) MECAmaps (see Chapter 2, this volume, and Falicov, 2014); and (d) MECAgenograms (see Falicov, 2014).

2. *Identifying migration relational stresses and strengths.* Some stresses and strengths include coaxed and unprepared migrations, marital polarizations, life-cycle pile-up, trauma and separations–reunifications, and learning to apply relevant practice ideas.

3. *Selecting therapist's roles according with the pattern observed.* These observations fall into cultural patterns, situational stress patterns, problematic patterns of cultural transition, and transcultural dysfunctional patterns.

4. *Selecting practice ideas according to the client's stage in the migration/acculturation (MA) process.* Each stage in the trajectory of migration for the various generations may profit from various perspectives in the therapist's interaction with the client.

5. *Engaging in self-reflection about MA by supervisor and supervisee.* This reflection involves personal historical lives and professional competence dimensions. Differences in the relationship between supervisee and supervisor and clients must be acknowledged and their impact on treatment explored. MECAmaps are a helpful tool for these comparisons.

6. *Becoming aware of possible errors of cultural assessment and treatment.* Become aware of these both with clients and in the supervisor–supervisee relationship.

7. *Integrating migration as a complex process in interaction with other MECA domains.* Migration issues need to be integrated with ecological context, family organization, and the family life cycle. The MECAgenogram provides a tool to depict the interaction of the four dimensions.

These seven competencies and their practice ideas can be acquired through didactic, exploratory, descriptive, self-reflective, and practice experiences and processes. To supplement the limited knowledge that most supervisors and supervisees have about migration processes and increase their experiential connection, I suggest that supervisors and supervisees turn to specific fictional readings, documentaries and movies that depict the immigrant's plight, preferably in conjunction with a clinical case that bears similarities.

Migration-Specific Competency 1: Learning Training and Supervision Tools—Migration Narratives, Genoecograms, MECAmaps, and MECAgenograms

Characteristics of a Migration Narrative

A *migration narrative* is a tool that I have found helpful for work with immigrant individuals and families (Falicov, 2014). It emerges from supportive inquiries whereby the individual client or family reconstructs the migration journey. The process of leaving one's home country and encountering a new one constitutes an overlapping of situational events, developmental changes, and existential tasks that render a phenomenology of migration. This subjective experience can best be understood and shaped by the family members through an invitation to tell their own migration story. The construction of such a narrative in a therapeutic setting reveals the personal meanings of migration events and processes for each family and for individual family members. Although it is not always possible to obtain a linear account, it is useful to cover information related to the motivations; premigration events; entry experience; and the process of settlement, including future plans.

Therapists can begin by asking who is in the family here and in their home countries by using a conventional genogram in which the family here and the family back home are circled. This is extremely important because, unless asked, families will often mention only the family members present but not those who remain in the country of origin. A genogram is the most expedient, least tension-filled manner to inquire about migration separations and reunifications. In addition to age and gender of all individuals, it is useful to ask how long each individual has been here, who immigrated first and who was left behind or came later, and who is yet to be reunited. While addressing questions about the premigration and entry experience, it is important to explore the motivations behind the move, who first thought of the idea, the sense of responsibility of the people who initiated the process, their hopes and regrets, their choice points, the ordeals they went through to get here, the attachments to those family members who stayed and those who had already left, and the reception by those who may already have been here.

Questions about how family members are learning the new language and culture can provide an avenue to tap interpersonal strengths and supports, as well as conflicts or injustices. Migration narratives may also include a close look at the emergence of spontaneous rituals and the persistence and evolving new shapes of cultural rituals from routine family interactions (dinners or prayers) to celebrations of birthdays, holidays, and rites of passage, as well as the old and new meanings various family members associate with them. Migration narratives should include where the individual or family are positioned in relation to their cultural rituals, that is, over- or under-ritualized.

Questions need to be included about the emotional reactions of those left behind, particularly members of the nuclear family, together with the current long-distance interactions with them and the hopes of reunification.

In securing a migration narrative, it is best not to get bogged down by contradictions about dates, places, or events about the time or place of entry. The family's vagueness may be an attempt to conceal their unauthorized entry or status, the extent of their hardships back home, or the traumatic effects of the migration journey. The therapist's reading of the client's emotional response to these questions, plus collaborative input from the family, should determine how far to go and when to stop the process of narration. For some clients, it may be too soon and too painful to review the experience of physical, social, and cultural uprooting; for others, it may prove cathartic (Falicov, 2014).

Characteristics of a Genoecogram

Several assessment graphic instruments are adaptable for use with immigrants. Family therapists of various orientations have used a basic genogram to gather historical and relational data for clients (McGoldrick, Gerson, & Schellenberger, 1999). Over time, this standard genogram has been found to present significant limitations to depict diversity in families. For example, Watts-Jones (1997) proposed an African American genogram that takes into account the fact that many African American families define family in a larger social and functional way than the mainstream definition of family as a biological entity. This type of genogram is helpful for work with immigrant families that, through a combination of cultural tradition and socioeconomic necessity, have incorporated within the safety net of close kin a large number of relatives and nonrelatives who may be living under the same roof (Falicov, 2014).

Culture-centered genograms have been proposed both as a clinical ethnic-oriented instrument (Thomas, 1998) and as a training aid by Hardy and Laszloffy (1995). The latter authors emphasize sources of pride and of shame in their ethnic- and race-focused genograms, opening up reflection about areas of pride in one's race and heritage and areas of internalized shame stemming from experiences with oppression. Adding issues of migration, social class, and acculturation enlarges the usefulness of this type of genogram for immigrants, many of whom are people of color. Santiago-Rivera, Arredondo, and Gallardo-Cooper (2002) added to the culture centered genogram information about immigration date, language usage, frequency of contact with native country, and bicultural characteristics. Keiley et al. (2002) suggested using cultural genograms in a self-reflexive way to help trainees become more aware of their cultural background and more attuned to similar cultural inquiries with clients. More recently, McGoldrick, Gerson, and Petry (2008) attempted to use genograms to symbolize community and culture.

An *ecomap* (Hartman, 1995) is a tool that visually organizes the social and institutional world in which the client's life is embedded. Ecomaps are used as companions to genograms to depict social and institutional connections for family members. Along similar lines of inclusion of social or cultural dimensions in graphic form, some authors have proposed *culturagrams* (Congress, 2004), which are basically ecomaps that include reasons for relocation, legal immigration status, and cultural family values. *The community genogram* (Rigazio-DiGilio, Ivey, Kunkler-Peck, & Grady, 2005) is close to an ecomap in which clients depict their community of origin and current community. It is a free-form activity that clients can construct by themselves or with the therapist's assistance, encouraging client's creativity and personal voice.

Recently, the notion of a *critical genogram* (CritG) has been introduced as a training tool. It explores a therapist's social ecologies and promotes critical consciousness, that is, understanding the influence of social and institutional systems on individual and family dynamics (Kosutic et al., 2009). The CritG focuses on intersecting forms of oppression (sexism, classism, racism) and making visible power differentials between dominant and oppressed groups.

My own preference is to use a GEg, a tool I devised that integrates a family genogram and an ecomap. The family genogram, with its classic symbols, is at the center of the diagram surrounded by ecomaps that depict the family in either past or present, or both, in its community context, that is, extended family, peer group, workgroups, housing, neighborhood, school, church, and health systems in one, rather than two, diagrams. Thus, the GEg, unlike all the preceding tools, combines a genogram and an ecomap in the same diagram. It is a parsimonious information tool and an invaluable way to join with a family and to engage children and adolescents in finding out about the parents' lives. Furthermore, it gives youth a unique opportunity to reveal more about their own communities and contexts than they may habitually do. Often, the generations find out a lot about each other that had never been discussed before.

Like culture-centered genograms, a GEg includes information about immigration date, language usage, frequency of contact with native country and bicultural characteristics along with an opportunity to discuss individual stories of struggle and triumph (Santiago-Rivera et al., 2002). These stories can provide past and present positive role models that can shape identity and worldviews. With the GEg, it is possible to incorporate other tools, such as the strength-based culture-specific technique of *cuento therapy* (Costantino, Malgady, & Rogler, 1986), by asking questions about positive role models in the family, in the community, in the nation, or in fictional characters of the culture of origin or the culture of adoption.

In constructing the GEg, I prefer to start by asking first what past and present issues are important for clients. Like Rigazio-DiGilio et al. (2005),

I encourage clients to add to the genogram that we already have created on a large piece of paper their own free-form depictions of their community of origin and their current communities of belonging, including positive and negative influences of individuals or institutions.

I suggest that clients create fitting symbols for their relationships with institutions and with individuals in their family, community, and institutions, symbols that can depict strengths and risks in the relationships. This search is quite fascinating, more fun and accurate than imposing my symbols. My clients have chosen to draw a flower (for a beautiful influence) or a stone (for a heavy burden) around a person or a place. Some clients have chosen wings (new attachments) and roots (old attachments), or also wings (angelic) and horns (devilish) for significant persons and places. One client chose to draw a Pandora's box (for unpredictable neighbors that she could not trust) and a golden box (for her medical clinic, where she felt she could trust everybody completely). An older sister wrote "Despair" for a brother in jail and "Hope" for a brother in school.

A GEg can also include inquiries about spontaneous rituals of connection (phone calls, remittances, visits) with the family in the country of origin, memory rituals (reminiscing about the past with offspring and friends) recreation of ethnic spaces and social networks spaces and cultural rituals (language usage, life cycle rituals, religious festivities; Falicov, 2002, 2012). If possible, it is helpful to provide continuity and connections, to have the large paper that depicts the GEg hanging on a wall or sitting on a table at every family therapy session, and of course the supervisee can also bring it to supervision.

Characteristics of MECAmaps and MECAgenograms

In Chapter 2, I described the various domains of the MECA framework and noted that through the use of a MECAmap, the therapist, supervisor, and family can reflect and compare their experiences in the areas of MA, ecological context (EC), family organization (FO), and family life cycle (FLC). A MECAgenogram is similar to a MECAmap, but it depicts the family genogram at the center, whereas the four MECA domains of MA, EC, FO and FLC are filled with the specific data on those domains for each family (see Figure 5.1).

The best way for supervisees to learn these instruments (MECAmaps and MECAgenograms) is to first apply them to themselves. Likewise, supervisors are better equipped to guide supervisees in this process if they have become familiar with the rationale and procedures for these instruments and have applied them to their own life experiences. The supervisee can collect information with one or more of these instruments to bring to supervision sessions as the basis for relating the migration history and also to detect possible sources of relational and acculturative stresses and strengths.

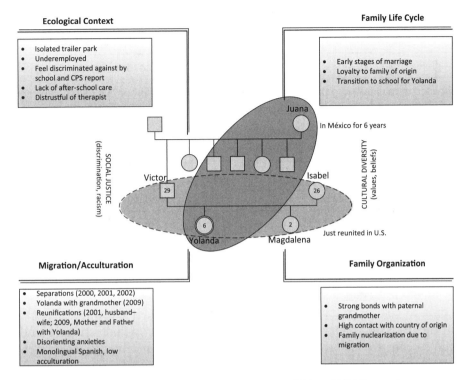

Ecological Context

- Isolated trailer park
- Underemployed
- Feel discriminated against by school and CPS report
- Lack of after-school care
- Distrustful of therapist

Family Life Cycle

- Early stages of marriage
- Loyalty to family of origin
- Transition to school for Yolanda

SOCIAL JUSTICE (discrimination, racism)

CULTURAL DIVERSITY (values, beliefs)

Juana

In México for 6 years

Victor 29

Isabel 26

Yolanda 6

Magdalena 2

Just reunited in U.S.

Migration/Acculturation

- Separations (2000, 2001, 2002)
- Yolanda with grandmother (2009)
- Reunifications (2001, husband–wife; 2009, Mother and Father with Yolanda)
- Disorienting anxieties
- Monolingual Spanish, low acculturation

Family Organization

- Strong bonds with paternal grandmother
- High contact with country of origin
- Family nuclearization due to migration

Figure 5.1. The Díaz Ortiz family MECAgenogram. CPS = Child Protective Services. From *Latino Families in Therapy* (2nd ed., p. 41), by C. J. Falicov, 2014, New York, NY: Guilford Press. Copyright 2014 by Guilford Press. Reprinted with permission.

Migration-Specific Competency 2: Identifying Migration Relational Stresses and Strengths, and Their Corresponding Practice Ideas

It is important for supervisees to learn to inquire about relational stresses because these are a nearly inevitable and often transient aspect of migration. Several migration relational stresses that may bring immigrants to therapy are life-cycle transitions pile-ups, coaxed migrations, ambivalent or unprepared migrations, traumatic passages, separations, and reunifications. I have suggested several strength-based practice ideas to work with these stressful patterns (see Exhibit 5.1).

Here, I only briefly refer to these patterns; for a more detailed exposition of relational stresses, practice ideas, and case illustrations, see Falicov (2014). Supervisors can introduce these patterns didactically or identify them when they appear in the clinical case.

EXHIBIT 5.1
Migration Relational Stresses, Strengths, and Practice Ideas

Migration relational stress		Practice ideas/interventions
Coaxed or reluctant migrations	➡	"As-if" preparations rebalancing contracts
Ambivalent or unprepared migrations	➡	Obtain community supports
Martial polarizations (to stay/to go back)	➡	Oscillation rituals (odd days/ even days)
Life-cycle pile-up intersections (divorce, death, illness)	➡	Healing rituals
Traumatic passages	➡	Testimony rituals
Separations and reunifications	➡	Therapies of globalization

Note. From *Latino Families in Therapy* (2nd ed., p. 103), by C. J. Falicov, 2014, New York, NY: Guilford Press. Copyright 2014 by Guilford Press. Adapted with permission.

Coaxed or Reluctant Migrations

Often there is a subtle, gendered or generational line between voluntary and coaxed migrations. Many immigrants are not equal participants in the decision to migrate. Coaxed participants may include children and adolescents, the elderly who come to join their adult children, or women in asymmetrical marriages who reluctantly follow their husbands. These individuals may experience more difficulties in adjustment than those who actively choose to migrate. When it is possible to distinguish leader from follower, the party responsible for initiating the migration may need to exert compensatory efforts to help make the reluctant immigrant's situation more emotionally comfortable.

Redressing the injustice taps strengths and restoration of agency for both leader and follower. A suggested intervention is a *rebalancing migration contract*; this is a contracted, conditional option to return home. Although the migration has already taken place, the newly devised contract can still create a trial period for everyone. This new migration contract may involve empowering agency in the coaxed partner to dismantle the present arrangement and create an as-if scenario of questions, thoughts, and expression of needs that should have taken place before the migration. It also involves clear-cut efforts on the initiator of the migration to support the follower's needs and redress possible injustices committed in the decision to migrate.

Ambivalent or Unprepared Migrations

Ambivalent and unprepared migrations share some similarities with coaxed migrations. Many older immigrants experience life-cycle stresses such as illness, old age, or the loss of a spouse connected to the decision to migrate. This last stress often creates confusion or ambivalence over readiness to migrate, even if it is for the joyful purpose of joining their adult children. A suggested intervention is obtaining community support for the new immigrant, a practice that acknowledges that an unprepared new immigrant usually lacks a supportive network. Therapists may need to explore community resources, such as church and neighborhood associations, and provide support by keeping expectations about cultural and language adaptation at a minimal level of demand.

Life-Cycle Transition Pile-Ups

Like all families, immigrant families undergo major life-cycle changes such as birth, leaving home, illness, and death. When nonambiguous, irretrievable losses occur in the life of an immigrant family—perhaps the death of a relative back home—the uncertainty of the old goodbyes accentuates migration loss. The immigrant family may experience the appearance of other ambiguous losses, such as a teenager leaving home or a spouse separating and divorcing, as more stressful than if they had occurred in a context that did not involve migrations (Falicov, 2002, 2010).

Family transitions that involve members of the family who have stayed behind in the country of origin may be particularly stressful. Many immigrants postpone visiting an aging parent for lack of money or time. When a death occurs, they may feel profound regret at not having made the effort to see more frequently their parent, sibling, or friend. There may be worry about not being present to help other family members and unbearable loneliness at not participating in communal grieving. Creating one's own commemoratory rituals that recreate past cultural and personal sources of strength, while communicating with the family at long distance, may have healing effects.

Immigration as Trauma

Although many stressors accompany migration, not all stressors precipitate trauma. The possibility that migration involves trauma has been less explored for economic immigrants than it has been for refugees (Falicov, 2002). There is increased interest in the compounding, overlapping effects of trauma with migration stressors at various stages of migration: premigration events, during transit, and at settlement (Foster, 2001).

If deemed clinically appropriate, the migration narrative may include details of the crossing, transportation, and entry, as these stages may have involved trauma. Even people who have been in this country for several years may be suffering its effects, as reactions may be delayed or protracted. The narrative tool called *testimonio* (testimony) involves a first-person oral or written (perhaps dictated to the therapist or to a supportive family member) account focused on validating personal experiences of loss, trauma, and abuse

(Weine, Dzubur Kulenovic, Pavkovic, & Gibbons, 1998). Then client and therapist together look for the appropriate ways to let the story be known to others. Testimony is an avenue for reworking the painful experiences but also for regaining the strengths accorded by dignity and respect (Aron, 1992).

Separations and Reunifications

Migration always involves separation. However, the nature of separation and reunification has changed in different historical periods. Poverty and global labor opportunities has given rise to transnational families that undergo short- and long-term separations between parents, particularly mothers, and children or adolescents, with potential serious consequences, such as behavior and school problems, depression and family fragmentation (Falicov, 2007). A number of concepts and techniques can be subsumed under the general rubric of transnational therapies to be implemented during separation and reunification. These approaches offer specific practice ideas (catching-up life narratives, making meaning out of the separation, repairing family bonds) that may help repair bonds and counteract deficit views of these experiences (Falicov, 2014). Supervisors and supervisees should reflect on their own preconceptions regarding voluntary family separations as these attitudes impact the therapeutic relationship.

Migration-Specific Competency 3: Selecting the Therapist's Role According to Pattern Observed

Taking into account the family's cultural preferences and present social context is crucial to understanding the family's predicament and helping supervisees to construct their therapeutic role. In my experience with immigrant clients, I have found a number of presenting patterns, that is, cultural patterns, situational stress patterns, problematic patterns of cultural transition, and transcultural dysfunctional patterns (see Exhibit 5.2), that can be linked to corresponding therapist roles. Each one of these therapeutic roles presents practice resources and constraints. When working with a supervisee, I help her or him to distinguish among the four patterns in Exhibit 5.2 and

EXHIBIT 5.2
Pattern Definition and Selection of the Therapist's Role

A.	Cultural pattern: Being a cultural observer
B.	Situational stress: Being a social intermediary
C.	Problematic patterns of cultural transition: Being a cultural or family mediator
D.	Transcultural dysfunctional patterns: Being a therapist

Note. From *Latino Families in Therapy* (2nd ed., p. 94), by C. J. Falicov, 2014, New York, NY: Guilford Press. Copyright 2014 by Guilford Press. Adapted with permission.

discuss what types of interventions would fit best the presenting issues. As we progress, I also warn the supervisee about possible pitfalls or errors in each role taken (see Competency 6).

Cultural Patterns: Being a Cultural Observer

Cultural patterns include cultural belief systems, developmental expectations, and family roles and rules. For example, a 5-year-old child sitting on his mother's lap or a 3-year-old child drinking out of her bottle, although not in line with Euro American expectations, are not patterns in need of change. These child-rearing practices are consonant with collective and interdependent ideals that many immigrant families bring with them. To cite another example, cultural variations in preferred physical distance are often observable. An office that has a couch that comfortably seats three Latino or Middle Eastern family members accommodates only two Euro American family members. To judge the Turkish or the Mexican family as overinvolved or overprotective would be to conceptualize as dysfunctional patterns that are cultural and that should be respected as such. These patterns generally do not require intervention on the part of the therapist, who becomes a cultural observer, much like an anthropologist entering a new culture. This is not to imply that all cultural patterns are harmless or above critical consideration or that they do not present ethical dilemmas that may need to be addressed, but generally, a therapist will not see an immigrant family unless one of the following patterns is also present.

Situational Stress Patterns: Being a Social Intermediary

Situational stress patterns occur at the interface between the immigrant family and society. They include problems of social isolation and lack of knowledge about social or community resources. It is often difficult to distinguish the multiple situational problems created by poverty from those caused by migration. In the case of immigrants, there may also be acculturative stress or dissonance between the normative expectations of the home and those of the school, the peer group, or institutions.

If these stresses impair the family's ability to cope with external demands, then the supervisor can help the therapist become a social intermediary or matchmaker between the family and the community. The therapist can mobilize the family to use existing family, social, or church networks or can facilitate the building of new reciprocal relationships in the community. As a social intermediary, the therapist may sometimes need to assume an active role as a link between the family and appropriate institutional or neighborhood resources. The supervisor should elicit from the therapist simple explanations and solutions first, before searching for complex and purely psychological aspects. The following example illustrates points relevant to a situational stress pattern and its management in therapy and in supervision.

> Mrs. R, an older woman, was referred to a mental health center by a priest. She had been seeing him because she was depressed and irritable and had been losing weight. A GEg revealed that Mrs. R was in an isolated situation within the ethnic neighborhood. She had migrated from Mexico eight years before to live with her two sons and an older single daughter. Two years ago, the sons had moved to a nearby city in search of better jobs, and Mrs. R had remained with her daughter, who spoke no English and did not work.
>
> The therapist, an empathic early-career professional Latina, was advised by the Latina supervisor to inquire about possible causes for the symptom by asking, "Are you losing weight because you have lost your appetite?" Mrs. R quipped, "No, I've lost my teeth, not my appetite! That's what irks me!" Indeed, Mrs. R had almost no teeth left in her mouth. Apparently, her conversations with the priest (an American who had learned to speak Spanish during a South American mission) had centered on the emotional losses of migration and the isolation she had suffered recently as the cause of her "anxious depression" without considering the practical issues.
>
> Using the GEg provided by the supervisor, the supervisee obtained more concrete information. Mrs. R had no medical insurance and had no financial resources to use a private dentist. Mrs. R's situational stress pattern required a social intermediary to help find dental care. A university dental clinic agreed to have her seen by supervised dentistry practicum students. This required a long trip to another part of the city to an institution that had no Spanish-speaking personnel. Empathic and proactive, the therapist was aware of Mrs. R's fears to venture into new environments and reassured her that solutions could be found.
>
> Searching for sources of practical help in the GEg, the next step was for the therapist to help Mrs. R to enlist the cooperation of a bilingual neighbor, Rose, to accompany her to her appointments at the dental clinic. Rose was willing to do it. To reciprocate (and with only a hint on the therapist's part), Mrs. R began to do some babysitting for Rose's young baby.

The supervisor had encouraged the therapist to shift from an internal psychological lens to a social adaptation lens in viewing the problem. However, supervisors need to encourage therapists to reflect about their reactions to the role of social intermediary, particularly with ethnic minority trainees who might feel that they are being relegated to a less deep approach to therapy. Mrs. R's therapist somewhat coyly confessed to feeling like "a social worker" intervening in the external circumstances of clients rather than their deeper inner lives. A discussion about this common dichotomous perception about therapy and psychosocial empowerment, using a social–economic justice lens ensued, from which both therapist and supervisor emerged with renewed clarity about the importance and dignity of adopting a social intermediary role when working with underserved immigrant clients.

Problematic Patterns of Cultural Transition: Being a Cultural Mediator or a Family Intermediary

Problematic patterns of cultural transition are interactional patterns reflecting organizational changes that initially helped to accomplish the immigrant's objectives, but eventually became rigid and hampered some aspect of the individual or family's functioning. For instance, leaving a child behind under the care of a grandmother may be an expedient decision, but it may lock mother, grandmother, and child in a negative triangle that developed during the separation and may require intervention at the time of reunification.

Normal developmental stresses, such as the developmental transition of becoming independent and leaving home, can become more problematic when immigrant parents have developed dependencies on their more acculturated children to be intermediaries with the larger culture and may find it difficult to work out a gradual separation. Difficulties of separation/individuation may become more apparent at life-cycle transitions such as marriage, terminal illness, or death (Falicov, 1997).

Some studies indicate that the stresses of acculturation and parent–child cultural dissonance may play a major role in the occurrence of suicide attempts in Latina teens (Smokowski & Bacallao, 2011; Zayas, 2011), who also tend to suffer much stricter controls than their brothers. In Asian families, both boys and girls attempt suicide in similar numbers following incidents of parent–child cultural conflict (Lau, Jernewall, Zane, & Myers, 2002), presumably because restrictions are applied equally regardless of gender.

To deal with these types of generational and gender problems, the supervisor works with the therapist to assume the role of cultural mediator or a family intermediary. In this role, the therapist can relabel the present problematic pattern as a stress of cultural transition. A supervisor can help a therapist to find the best way to ask family members to reflect about culturally based behavior toward one another, how to justify conflict, how to encourage compromise and negotiation, and how to correct or ameliorate structural imbalances that have resulted from the migration and cultural transition. The case of Javier and his parents discussed under Competency 4 illustrates these issues.

Transcultural Dysfunctional Patterns: Being a Clinician

Dysfunctional family patterns may be aggravated by migration and acculturative stress, but often they belong to categories of universal, or at least transnational, human problems. A limited range of repetitive and rigid behaviors, developmental impasses, hierarchical imbalances, or interpersonal boundary problems are characteristics of dysfunctional individuals and families probably found everywhere, tied to chronic depression, psychosis, or affective disorders. Immigrant families, like other families, come to therapy with problems of this nature, although the content, meanings, and coping strategies may be organized around culture-specific issues. There are also a number of culture-specific syndromes that have their own cultural interpretations and cures (Falicov, 2014).

When therapists are confronted with dysfunctional behavior that transcends cultural patterns, generic or mainstream, techniques of clinical work can be helpful, tempered by accommodating therapeutic goals to fit cultural definitions. There are situations for which therapists may see a connection between a presenting pattern and a cultural preference but is not aware that sometimes culture may mask or camouflage other family processes that could be problematic.

In the following case, the focus on the child at the expense of the marital relationship, the self-sacrifice of the mother, and the extreme closeness between the mother and the child all had a culturally plausible quality, but the degree, the length of time, and rigidity of these behaviors and the consequences for family members were clearly beyond normative expectations.

> Frank G, Jr., 9 years old, was referred to an outpatient clinic by Children's Hospital for night terrors and multiple fears. The supervisee obtained the following information illustrated in a MECAgenogram. Mrs. G was born and raised in Guatemala. She remained at home through her 20s and was intensely and ambivalently attached to her mother. Her mother did not want her to leave home as an adult for fear that she might get sexually involved with somebody while away in school. Sometime in her 30s, she met Mr. G, an older single man. However, she felt she could not marry him until her mother died. After her mother's death she married Mr. G at age 41 and went to live with him in the United States. Mr. G came from a poor Honduran family. Early in his life he was a street boy, successfully coping but remaining suspicious of others. Their initial marital adjustment went smoothly until Frank, Jr. was born. Mother and son became a close dyad that excluded the father.
>
> This family's first attempts to get help with Frank, Jr.'s extreme fears started when he entered kindergarten. After seeking treatment at several agencies, mother and son were hospitalized and placed under heavy sedation during a mutual psychotic episode when Frank, Jr. was 6 years old. At that time, the psychiatrists felt this was a hopeless case and advised sending the boy to live with relatives. The parents complied even though mother said separation from the boy was like death to her. After some time, however, Mrs. G began to recover, and the relationship with her husband improved until the relatives reported that Frank, Jr. was having nightmares. Mother went to fetch the boy and brought him home, where he again displaced father. Subsequently, Frank, Jr. developed ter-

rors about going anywhere alone, including to the bathroom. Mother and boy constituted an undifferentiated unit.

Although cultural patterns, primarily those of family organization and family life cycle, were entertained, neither the supervisor nor the therapist fell prey to the cultural mask of close family relationships or culturally normative mother–son attachment. The pattern in this family appeared to be one of symbiotic oppressive embrace that left no room for individual autonomy. The therapist and the supervisor worked to develop a multilevel interdisciplinary treatment plan that involved the use of medication for mother and son and working collaboratively with school personnel to keep Frank, Jr. in school as much as possible. Couple therapy was also recommended, including individual and family sessions. The internal workings of the individuals and the family unit were more relevant to the treatment plan than issues of migration, cultural diversity, or social justice.

Migration-Specific Competency 4: Selecting Practices According to the Client's Stage in the Migration/Acculturation Process

There are certain regularities in the experiences of cultural transition for each succeeding generation of an immigrant family. Comparisons of the family patterns of the first, second, and third generation have consistently illuminated acculturation and assimilation changes (Falicov, 2014; Landale & Oropesa, 2007).[1] The therapist's roles described for Competency 3 roughly apply also to the various stages in the acculturation process from first through third generation. However, in Competency 4, the applications of therapist's roles or positions and accompanying actions are more extensive, as the number of issues and possible interventions are more articulated for each generation. Migration and culture do appear in every stage, but they acquire different forms and intensities, and the therapist can explore a number of strategies and roles, as shown in Exhibit 5.3.

Because families comprise two or three generations, it is important to be able to understand the issues of each. The following case illustrates interactional patterns prompted by cultural transition (as well as some cultural and situational patterns) and the various components of the role of the therapist as cultural family intermediary, balancing the generational hierarchies and acting as a cultural philosopher.

Javier, a 16-year-old boy, was referred to the counseling intern at his school for persistent truancy. The counselor, who was a third-generation

---

[1]*First generation* refers to foreign immigrants born to parents who were not U.S. citizens. *Second generation* refers to native U.S.-born persons of immigrant parent(s), and *third-generation* persons are native U.S. born of native U.S.-born parentage.

EXHIBIT 5.3
Practice Ideas by Stages of Migration

First stage: Social intermediary	Second stage: Cultural or family intermediary	Third stage: Cultural integrator
• Explore spontaneous rituals (old and new) • Advocate/culture broker • Linking/facilitator • Crisis intervention • Help restore ecological order	• Narrative of ambiguous loss/frozen state • Include trauma • Deal with boundary ambiguity • Balance gender and generation hierarchies • Cultural philosopher	• Revive or diffuse rituals • Increase flexibility • Values clarification • Issues of cultural identity

man of half-Portuguese background, brought for supervision the following narrative. Nine years ago, Javier's family, consisting of mother, father, and four younger siblings, had moved from Tijuana, Mexico, to San Diego, California, to better their economic situation. Javier was bilingual and served as the family interpreter in their dealings with outside institutions, but he preferred to speak English and was clearly more acculturated than his parents. The father began the session by complaining bitterly about Javier's unruly behavior, his insufficient help to his mother, and his lack of respect toward his parents. The mother appeared to agree with her husband's views about Javier, although she protested that she did not need much help around the house. Whenever the father escalated pressures for compliance, Javier would become more rebellious, threatening to leave school to find a job. Because of Javier's higher degree of acculturation, he had more power in the outside world than did his parents—a position that could easily upset family hierarchies.

The MECAgenogram revealed that the father had hoped to set up his own small business as a car mechanic after migration, but he had not succeeded and was supporting the family precariously with occasional small jobs. Although he valued his competence and honesty (he proudly displayed a very old letter of recommendation from a client in his original community, which he always carried with him), he refused to go to work in a company under an American foreman. In his view, "they [Americans] don't respect us Mexicans, and when you turn around they exploit you." It was clear that the father's employment potential was affected by experiences of discrimination. It seemed also likely that the lack of fulfillment of the breadwinner role debilitated his leadership position in the family. The dilemma was how to approach a discussion of this subject without undermining him further.

I suggested to the therapist that he reflect about the congruence and differences of his MECA theoretical and personal maps with the maps of the family and its members. He focused on cultural diversity in family organization and in family life-cycle patterns as the two areas most problematic for his therapeutic alliance. He tended to downplay the sociopolitical aspects evident in migration and ecological context dissonances between the son and the father's experience. Being a young male, removed from the immigrant experience by two generations, the counselor felt a much greater identification with the predicament of the second-generation late adolescent immigrant wanting the freedom to prove himself in the work world. Thus, the counselor had little empathy or liking for a father whom he saw as rigid and authoritarian toward the son and paternalistic towards the wife. The supervisee was tempted to challenge Javier's father on those counts, but his self-reflection regarding his own social location and cultural similarities and differences between the client family and his family of origin motivated him to turn to supervision for guidance.

I asked the supervisee if he could imagine the various consequences of challenging the father's position and, more precisely, how confrontation would lead to positive new relational developments in the strained, hierarchically imbalanced relationship between father and son. Wisely, the supervisee concluded that most likely he would risk the therapeutic alliance at this early point because the father might feel that he was siding with the son. Instead, we settled for the idea that the father needed to be recognized and praised first. We thought of how to praise the father's contributions to the family, because it seemed likely that his rigid stance toward the son and his protectiveness toward his wife stemmed in part from feeling diminished in his traditional family masculine role but also from being discriminated on the basis of skin color and immigrant status in the host country.

I pointed out to the supervisee that there is evidence of a correlation between an authoritarian stance and compromised self-worth due to social injustices in studies of Mexican men (Hondagneu-Sotelo & Meissner, 1997). The therapist decided to express his admiration for the father's integrity. He had remained honest in a business where there is so much dishonesty and had maintained his pride in his ethnic identity in spite of the financial difficulties it had occasioned him. The therapist then asked him whether his family appreciated him and could write a letter of recommendation for him like his client had done. Father was visibly moved and said he did not know.

Hearing about this interaction prompted me to praise the therapist for the generosity of his intervention. I also asked him if he might find an opportunity to reframe the son's opposition as showing care and concern for the family. Perhaps the son had tried to grow up and be practical in a rather American way, but the values of loyalty and solidarity, in contrast to American values of individualism or "selfishness," had been obviously successfully inculcated by the parents. The conflict between the parents and Javier was thus labeled as an understandable "cultural transition misunderstanding" that often occurs between immigrant parents and their children because of apparent value differences. The therapist, prompted by the supervisor, cited his own family as one in which those types of misunderstandings occurred; this empathic disclosure led to a philosophical discussion about the pros and cons of each value system (see the role of cultural philosopher in Exhibit 5.3).

The therapeutic and supervisory processes involved learning to appreciate the different viewpoints in a positive light as a necessary step to being a cultural family intermediary; creating bridges; emphasizing similarities in personal strengths; and narrowing the cultural gap between father and son, and even between the therapist and the family, as well as between the therapist and supervisor. It was also necessary to decrease the son's power position while encouraging his right to autonomy in certain areas but supporting the parent's authority in other areas. Assuming the role of social intermediary, the therapist worked with the parents with a focus on removing emotional and practical roadblocks to the employment of the father. He also enlisted the cooperation of the school's academic counselor to deal with Javier's educational future plans—a more developmentally advantageous approach than leaving school to help the family financially.

Migration-Specific Competency 5: Engaging in Self-Reflection About Migration/Acculturation by Supervisor and Supervisee

In Chapter 2, this volume, I discuss the importance of deconstructing cultural and sociopolitical issues for therapists and suggest a number of steps in that direction. A significant aspect of supervisee–supervisor interaction is to discuss each person's experiences with migration and acculturation in terms of professional and personal experience with the topic. In this conversation, it is important to include values relative to the process of cultural change. A number of publications are helpful in outlining topics for reflective practices, such as beliefs systems, attitudes and skills, privilege, and ethnic countertransference (Collins, Arthur, & Wong-Wylie, 2010; Roysircar, 2004).

Although the family is the ultimate arbiter of how they prefer to negotiate cultural change, therapists and supervisors bring to the cultural encounter with clients their own values, concerns and experiences, both personal and professional, regarding inevitable choices of therapy that shape the process of cultural change. Therapy can be seen as an arena for increasing cultural adaptation, affirming ethnicity, dealing with cultural dilemmas, or working toward biculturalism. The models for cultural change presented in Exhibit 5.4 help organize these discussions.

I engage supervisees in a discussion of these issues, drawing from them their preferences and manifesting mine. I may extol the virtues of biculturalism, both in terms of the research that demonstrates its advantages, for example, for the relationship between parents and adolescents (Smokowski & Bacallao, 2011) and my own biases toward this focus for work with individuals, couples, and families. I summarized in Chapter 2 of this volume the literature on the advantages of developing a bicultural identity for minority

EXHIBIT 5.4
Cultural Change Models in Therapy and Supervision

Models		Therapist and supervisor focus
Acculturation	➡	Adaptation
Culturalist	➡	Ethnic Reaffirmation
Alteration	➡	Cultural Dilemmas
Hybrid Blend	➡	Biculturalism

Note. From *Latino Families in Therapy* (2nd ed., p. 156), by C. J. Falicov, 2014, New York, NY: Guilford Press. Copyright 2014 by Guilford Press. Adapted with permission.

therapists, that is, an identity that honors their ethnic group and integrates it with a professional identity anchored in the mainstream culture. This entails a process of understanding one's own positions regarding cultural diversity, social justice, and allegiances to cultural and social change. This process is aimed at empowering supervisees, including dealing with power differentials in the supervisory relationship, which in turn prepares them for empowering clients (Porter, 1994).

These issues dovetail with another crucial consideration. Schwartz, Domenech Rodriguez, Field, Santiago-Rivera, and Arredondo (2010) called our attention to the ethical dilemmas that emerge from the current common situation that takes place when a psychotherapist in training and a client speak the same language and/or share similar culture and the supervisor does not. The first ethical consideration is the trainee/supervisor competence in regards to language and/or culture. Language competence is crucial in trying to figure out whether a person is able to competently translate sessions to the supervisor. A psychotherapist's language competence should not be understood to imply cultural competence; for example, an Uruguayan therapist may speak the same language as a Dominican client but may have no knowledge of the client's culture or migration stresses (Castaño, Biever, González, & Anderson, 2007; Field, Korell-Chavez, & Domenech Rodriguez, 2010). On the other hand, a therapist can have plenty of experience with persons from a different culture and not be fully fluent in that language. Other ethical issues associated with language matching in the psychotherapist–client pair include addressing whether the trainee is willing to work with clients in another language and thus ensuring that they do not feel forced, and/or discriminated into doing so, as sometimes minority therapists have felt. Another fairness issue toward the psychotherapist is to separate the issue of translating consent forms, medical/legal forms, from the provision of psychotherapy.

Few supervisors have had specialized culture and language training and clinical experience to be competent in the provision of supervision to minority therapists and clients. There is an increasing number of supervisors of the same ethnic group as the supervisee, for example, Latina supervisors with Latina supervisees, but this dyadic combination does not ensure successful matches, as they require not only considerations of specialized training but also awareness of complex processes of identification on both sides, such as idealization or blurred boundaries. Field et al. (2010) developed a helpful integrative model of supervision that takes into account these complexities. It includes a multicultural supervisory model with specific competencies for supervisor and supervisee, a review of ethnic identity status for supervisor and supervisee, and integration of developmental theories of supervision. Agencies need to think carefully about models and procedures for cross-language and cross-culture supervision to ensure accurate technical translation of sessions brought for supervision and adequately addressing competence of supervisor and supervisee regarding cultural and context issues.

Migration-Specific Competency 6: Becoming Aware of Possible Errors of Cultural Assessment and Treatment With Clients and in the Supervisor–Supervisee Relationship

It is possible for therapist and for supervisors to fall into four errors based on biases when observing a cultural pattern. Common errors are listed in Exhibit 5.5.

In earlier writings, I outlined two common errors in cross-cultural work, ethnocentrism, and ethnic stereotyping (Falicov, 1983). An *ethnocentric* position minimizes the existence of cultural differences. Falling prey to ethnocentrism is to judge a culturally different pattern with the lenses of one's one culture as representing universality. I labeled this error with the Greek letter alpha. This universalistic view could cause clinicians to overlook important culture and context differences, particularly when they differ from mainstream theories and applications. Often, difference is confused with pathology.

EXHIBIT 5.5
Errors in Assessment by Therapist and/or Supervisor

Ethnocentrism (universalists)	• Reductionism to universal processes
Ethnic stereotyping (culturalists)	• Reductionism to culture-specific preconceptions
Ecological rescuing	• Excessive reviewing
	• Excessive curiosity
	• Disempowering helpfulness
Interpersonal siding	• One individual
	• A family subsystem
	• Induction by gender or by generation

Note. From *Latino Families in Therapy* (2nd ed., p. 99), by C. J. Falicov, 2014, New York, NY: Guilford Press. Copyright 2014 by Guilford Press. Adapted with permission.

The opposite error, which I labeled with the Greek letter beta, is *ethnic stereotyping*. This error maximizes cultural differences. It stems from broad, quick generalizations about ethnic-specific preconceptions that give the therapist and/or supervisor a false sense of confidence in their cultural competence. This culturalist view does not make room for the variety of patterns present in all cultures, some functional, others dysfunctional. It is possible, for example, to err by accepting any level of interdependence as within the normative expectations of collectivistic cultures when in fact that level may be exaggerated. The case example of Frank, Jr.'s, family in Competency 2 in this chapter illustrates the potential for pitfalls of ethnic stereotyping and so does the later example of Victor Díaz Ortiz in Competency 7. Ethnocentrism and ethnic stereotyping may lead the therapist to form precipitous conclusions and to omit necessary therapeutic action.

A third error is *ecological rescuing*. It occurs when a therapist unwittingly becomes over involved and sets out to rescue a first- or second-generation family member from obstacles in the larger society, without an awareness of the disempowering effects of excessive helpfulness. Even in the role of social intermediary, care should be taken to empower family members to take initiative in making positive adaptations. A case illustration is provided by Mrs. R in Competency 2.

A fourth error is *interpersonal siding*, either with an individual or a family subsystem, usually on the basis of common gender or generation with the therapist. The case of Javier in Competency 4 illustrates this potential error. Migration and cultural competencies require constant vigilance regarding these possible pitfalls inherent in cross-cultural work.

Migration-Specific Competency 7: Integrating Migration as a Complex Process in Interaction With Other MECA Domains—Ecological Context, Family Organization, and Family Life Cycle

Migration is one domain of the MECA model, along with ecological context, family organization and family life cycle. The course of therapy and supervision includes an examination of the migration and cultural maps of therapist, supervisor, and clients. These maps integrate the four domains, which are closely interrelated (see Chapter 2, this volume). In this chapter, I describe one case and include the family, supervisor, and therapist maps, along with practice ideas that take into account the interaction of domains and the various players in the therapeutic and supervisory contexts. The MECAgenogram, which fills the four areas with specific content for each family, facilitates a rapid visualization of important issues for the family, as well as comparisons with therapist and supervisors' maps, as described in the MECAmaps in Chapter 2.

ILLUSTRATED APPLICATION OF MECA DOMAINS

The following de-identified case illustrates the complex features that are often encountered by supervisees. The Díaz Ortiz family is composed of a 26-year-old mother, Isabel, a 29-year-old father, Victor, and two children, 6-year-old Yolanda and 2-year-old Magdalena. The presenting problem was that the father, Victor, had been accused of hitting Yolanda and was reported for investigation to Child Protective Services (CPS) by school authorities. Because the evidence was inconclusive, CPS referred the family for counseling at a local mental health center. There, the Díaz Ortizes were seen by a therapist in training whom I supervised. Victor was articulate and vocal about how upset he was by the school intervention and referral to CPS. He was indignant at what he considered a violation of his rights and the intrusion of strangers into his family life. He did not deny hitting Yolanda but justified it as a reaction to his, and his wife's, frustration with the girl's frequent whining and refusal to eat "her mother's food." His wife, Isabel, was quiet and appeared to tacitly support Víctor's position.

Migration

Seven years ago, Mr. and Mrs. Díaz Ortiz migrated from a small town near San Luis de Potosí, Central Mexico, to San Marcos, California, a small town north of San Diego, in search of a better economic future. A migration narrative revealed that Victor had initially come to California on his own and felt encouraged to have found small construction and gardening jobs, He returned to Mexico to marry Isabel. He poignantly described to her how comfortable the couches seemed to be in America and how the TV programs advertised many wonderful household appliances that could be bought in easy installments. Isabel, who was only 19, came back with him to the United States and worked as a maid the first year but became pregnant soon after. The couple was concerned that, without the help of their extended family, they would be unable to manage financially and emotionally once the new baby arrived. They returned to Mexico, where they lived with Victor's family for 10 months. But their economic situation became worse, spawning a desire to return to the United States. For practical and economic reasons, Victor urged Isabel to leave their baby, Yolanda, in Mexico with Juana, her paternal grandmother. Isabel was uncomfortable with this idea, but Victor argued that without the responsibility of caring for Yolanda, his wife could continue to work in the United States. Victor also feared that because Isabel was so young and did not speak any English, she would not be able to handle any emergency involving Yolanda in this country. With intense pressure from Victor (and Victor's mother), Isabel finally acquiesced. The arrangement was a common one from the standpoint of Mexican culture—children remain behind with extended family during the initial stages of migration and are reunited at a later date. Four years later, when the couple was expecting another child, Isabel decided she would stop working and bring Yolanda to San Diego. The grandmother resisted. Yolanda resisted. The girl and the grandmother prevailed (with a little help from Victor, who continued to favor his mother's wishes over his wife's). Another year passed, and as the time approached for Yolanda to start elementary school, Isabel renewed her campaign to fetch her daughter. Arguing that her child would get a better education in the United States, Isabel's choice prevailed.

The family came in contact with the mental health system 4 months after Yolanda's own migration and reentry into the Díaz Ortiz family. As soon as the child arrived from Mexico, she began throwing tantrums during mealtimes. She disliked many foods and often refused to eat. She also resisted calling her parents "mother" and "father," for she had learned to call her grandmother "mother" and believed her parents to be her siblings. Among the therapist's first hypotheses—which she related to her supervisor—was that Yolanda must be missing the flavors of her grandmother's home-cooked Mexican food. This assumption turned out to be incorrect. On the contrary, Isabel was a superb Mexican cook, whereas the grandmother had indulged Yolanda's sweet tooth with commercial candy.

Ecological Context

The therapist was asked by the supervisor to inquire about the present ecological context. The therapist obtained the following information.

The Díaz Ortiz family lived in an isolated trailer park on the outskirts of San Diego with a few Latino neighbors and other working-class families. Given their precarious economic position, Isabel's wish to stay home was not possible. She found a job at a factory that had a nursery to care for her youngest, Magdalena. But Isabel and Victor had trouble finding after-school child care for Yolanda. Both parents were working, and neither was able to pick up Yolanda at 5 p.m. Victor was angry at the indifference of school authorities, who told him there was a long waiting list for after-school care and that he had applied too late. The couple said in therapy that they suspected discrimination because of language difficulties and their race. In fact, they felt the school wanted to get rid of them. The report to CPS confirmed to the Díaz Ortizes that school authorities "had it in for them." Unfamiliar with American laws, they believed that a child abuse allegation was a ploy to invade their privacy, to close doors on them, and to send them back to Mexico. This fearful response can be observed in other immigrants, including those who are documented. Feeling scared, isolated, ashamed, and unaccustomed to ask for institutional help, the Díaz Ortiz family felt they had nowhere to turn.

Family Organization

When asked about the meaning of his decision to leave his daughter in Mexico, Victor Díaz responded, "There is no greater love than a mother's love, blood of her blood." At first he confused the therapist and me with what we thought to be a contradiction—he had worked hard to convince the child's mother, his wife, to leave Yolanda behind. The mother he was referring to, however, was not his wife but his own mother. For Victor, the direct bloodline was between his mother and his daughter, without recognition of his wife. His allegiances and definition of mother (perhaps with a capital M) revolved around his own mother, not Isabel. By virtue of his Mexican ethnicity and his Roman Catholic upbringing, his family had been organized such that loyalty to intergenerational bonds, particularly between mother and son, was stressed over marital allegiance.

Isabel understood the guilt and distress Victor felt leaving his mother to come to the United States. She explained empathically that Victor was worried his mother would *morir de tristeza* (die of sadness) had he refused to leave Yolanda with her. This strong intergenerational bond typifies many extended family arrangements in which family connectedness is valued over individuation and interdependence is better accepted than autonomy. This extended family lifestyle promotes a high reliance on the family network for support rather than on help from institutions.

After a few years alone in this country, however, and perhaps because Isabel was working outside the home, the Díaz Ortizes' conception of family was slowly transforming into a higher acculturation arrangement that focused more on the husband–wife tie and on more egalitarian views. Migration had made them rely more on each other rather than on an extended family network for emotional and practical support.

Family Life Cycle

For the Díaz Ortiz family, migration precipitated a dramatic change in family organization. This change intersected with the normative life-cycle transitions of early marriage, creating a troubling combination of stressors. Victor and Isabel, as a young couple, were still steeped in family of origin norms when they married and left Mexico. A sense of responsibility toward their families and guilt for leaving tormented them, creating a need for parental approval. This was especially true for Victor, who was the prime initiator of the migration. Had they stayed in Mexico, it is likely that both Victor and Isabel would have remained tied to their families of origin even after marriage. Greater autonomy and personal authority would have come when the couple was older. Victor's loyalty to his mother would have been manifested by paying visits several times a week, helping out financially, and bringing the baby to visit her grandmother on weekends. Leaving the child behind at the time of migration may have ensured some continuity of presence, a symbolic offering of family loyalty, in spite of the distance and the separation.

As it is the case for many families, migration truncated a stage of the life cycle that is shared collaboratively or conflictually, but almost always together, by the three generations in the country of origin. Both young parents, but more so Isabel, attempted to retrieve Yolanda during developmental transitions, such as the pregnancy and birth of the second child. Isabel was unsuccessful for several reasons: lack of support from her husband and the forcefulness of his attachment to his mother, with which his wife empathized; Isabel's own initial guilt and ambivalence about leaving extended family for a second time after the failed attempt to return home; practical and economic limitations; and the grandmother's and the child's own resistance. At a later point in the life cycle, two natural developmental transitions legitimized Isabel's renewed attempts to reunite with Yolanda: First, the birth of another baby had already consolidated the Díaz Ortiz as a family unit and established Isabel as even more of a mother than before; second, the forthcoming entrance to primary school for Yolanda supported the immigrant's dream for their nuclear and extended family—education and a better future for their offspring in a new country.

The Therapist's Maps and the Supervisor's Maps

Before considering the therapeutic/supervisory process in detail, let's look at the therapist's maps, which include her perspectives of the four key domains, her interaction with the family, and hypotheses she began to formulate, based on the unique interaction of what she and the family both brought to the therapy encounter. Because it is the interactive dyad of therapist–supervisor that collaborates in both the therapy and the supervision process, self-awareness about migration and culture is also important for the supervisor.

The therapist was a 24-year-old social work trainee, a first-generation Mexican American whose parents had migrated about 30 years earlier and had raised six children before her in California. Her Spanish was laborious but acceptable. She was definitely more comfortable speaking English. She understood the values that shape family life for Mexicans and for Americans but had incorporated the mental health model in which she had been trained, namely, that which values the mother—child bond in the nuclear family, autonomy over interdependence, and symmetry over complementarity in the relationships between men and women and those between parents and adult children.

Out of her worldview, the therapist had developed three psychological hypotheses. First, the parents and Yolanda were insufficiently bonded with each other, given the history of separation at a critical developmental time.

It is not surprising that the therapist was critical of this separation. Second, the father had a "pathological" attachment to his own mother and lacked empathy for his wife. Third, the wife was subservient to her husband and needed to become more assertive. As constructions, they were legitimate guesses and could certainly become part of a conversation with the family. Yet, they were all deficit based and carried considerable judgmental weight. In addition, they lacked a comparative analysis of cultural similarities and dissonances between the family and the therapeutic culture represented by the therapist and the supervisor.

The first hypothesis seemed to be the most promising place to start because it involved the three family members and even the new sibling. It also had the most positive, blame-free emotional tone and could be easily linked to the separation–reunification pattern that manifested in Yolanda's eating problems and her parents' polarized, punitive, and protective reactions. The other two constructions were based, at least in part, on ethnic stereotypes (and the therapist's personal feelings) about Mexican men's relationships to their mothers and wives, and the women's reactive or complementary responses. These two hypotheses were charged with considerable irritation and disapproval, manifest in the supervisee's judgmental attitude toward Victor.

In my role as supervisor, I revealed my own migration narrative and my understanding, both personal and professional, of Mexican collectivistic settings. I understood that leaving children behind has become a common practice of economic immigrants in globalized world (Falicov, 2007, 2014). I also understood the importance of intergenerational relationships throughout one's lifetime. In supervision, I encouraged the supervisee to practice her sociological imagination about this family's culturally patterned life (particularly in terms of their family organization, life-cycle expectations, and ecological context) had they remained in their native village. The supervisee was also asked to imagine the nuclear and extended families' state of mind then, and now, based on the couple's migration narrative. This imaginative stance opened up an avenue for a more flexible, more empathic, more curious, and less critical view of the two young parents. We could also then discuss which patterns seemed best suited to various roles for the therapist—being a cultural observer, a social intermediary, a family cultural intermediary, or a therapeutic agent—and how to integrate these roles at different times or aspects of the therapeutic process.

The Therapy Process

The therapist was probably initially seen by the parents as in cahoots with the school officials, aiming to find fault so as to "get rid of them." Feeling defensive and suspicious, the parents united to fight off the "invaders"— Victor challenged the young therapist, asking her why and how she expected them to disclose so much personal information when she was unwilling to reveal anything about herself. The "attack" was an uncharacteristic deviation from customary cultural politeness: The family was probably reacting to a perceived threat. The therapist worried that an impasse had been reached. How could she make a useful appraisal of the family situation given what felt like a standoff? The therapist told me about the family's feelings of isolation, anger, and vulnerability, and requested that I meet with them. She felt overwhelmed by the task of accurately evaluating the presenting problem, particularly because the family appeared to be uncooperative. Under circumstances of a therapist feeling overwhelmed by a client, I usually agree to do an interview together because I believe that considerable training and supervision take place through modeling and observing a more experienced therapist at work. I also feel the ethical mandate to help both the family and the therapist, so that treatment can continue effectively.

Practice Idea: Being a Social Intermediary and a Cultural Intermediary— Exploring and Clarifying Feelings Related to Discrimination

When we all met, I expressed my understanding of the Díaz Ortizes' outrage and fear of discrimination. I praised them for their indignation as a demonstration of resistance to oppression. But I also told them that it was important to clarify information regarding the child abuse laws of CPS, stressing that these applied to people of all ethnicities, races, and social classes. I gave examples of American parents who were undergoing severe scrutiny from CPS, cases in which children would most likely be removed from the home. Hearing this, and learning about the state's interpretation of "the best interest of the child," Isabel and Victor visibly relaxed their guard. This cultural information enabled them to be more open about our inquiries and to taking the steps necessary to comply with the legal requirements and accept our role of social intermediaries in this processes. These steps included attending parenting classes and family therapy sessions geared to help Yolanda's integration in the family.

Practice Idea: Exploring the Meaning of Physical Discipline

The therapist reported that she explored the history of physical abuse for each parent and for Yolanda. As it turned out, the physical discipline was the first time the father had intervened forcefully on his wife's behalf against the whining child. Neither parent had a history of being hit as children, except for some occasional light spanking. As therapist and supervisor, we were also concerned about Mr. Díaz's anger, and we wondered if Mrs. Díaz, and perhaps even Yolanda, could be concealing the extent of the physical abuse for various reasons, for example, to protect the family against outsiders who might discriminate against them or deport them. Such concealment might also result from intimidation into silence by the possibility of Victor's retaliation.

Practice Idea: Creating Safety for Disclosure in Individual Sessions

The therapist explored possible abuse by interviewing each family member separately, and although the private sessions did not unearth new information, they gave the wife and child a chance to freely share their concerns. Individual sessions also improved the relationship between each parent and the therapist, who later used the information she had gathered to comment on many positive aspects of the family: their care for and interest in one another, their pride in their family, and their desire to do what was right for all members. The therapist was clearly able to shift from a deficit-based to a strength-based perspective.

Practice Idea: Reframe Physical Discipline as Family Reunification Stress

The therapist had developed more empathy for the family's reunification challenges. I suggested then that she could regard and label the parents' problems with Yolanda, the school, and child protection authorities as "issues of family reunification" and "cultural transition." The therapist openly supported Victor's attempts to help Isabel get Yolanda to eat while disapproving of the means he used. Using a cognitive approach, both parents were helped to co-develop, list on a blackboard, and discuss other possible reasons for Yolanda's eating problems and to move away from feeling that Yolanda was simply "bad" or "spoiled" by the grandmother. The therapist helped the parents expand on alternative explanations, for example, that Yolanda could be *nerviosa* (nervous) and upset, reacting to the trauma of recent migration, which included the loss of many familiar faces, places, and objects, but especially her grandmother.

Practice Idea: Recognizing Child's Migration Stress

Yolanda was undergoing her own unrecognized trauma of recent migration and despondency over the separation from her beloved grandmother. The parents were not at all aware of the child's inner state and lacked empathy for the child's suffering, losses, and culture shock. Indeed, an eating disorder could be seen in part as a somatization for psychological stress, a connection that is culturally congruent (stomach problems caused by stress) and that the parents could easily understand. As the therapist's empathy with the predicament of each family member increased, so did Yolanda's parents became more sympathetic toward their daughter's losses and confusion. In addition, Isabel began to disentangle her relationship with Yolanda from a web of rivalry with her mother-in-law.

Practice Idea: Identifying Movement Toward Family Nuclearization

Though he handled them poorly, the husband had good intentions to help his wife establish her influence over their daughter because, as he put it, "She [Yolanda] is ours now." The therapist, supported by the supervisor, underlined this positive shift in the husband's ability to empathize and support his wife, even at the risk of disappointing his own mother. This movement toward a stronger parental alliance could be construed as a move toward a husband–wife model of family organization.

Practice Idea: Family Empowerment in the New Ecological Context

The Díaz Ortiz family faced another common dilemma of minority parents. The state orders most families to take parenting classes after they have had encounters with CPS, but the therapist could find only English-speaking classes where Victor and Isabel lived. It was surprising, but Mr. Díaz became interested in turning this upsetting experience into a useful cause. He figured that other Spanish-speaking parents were unaware of state child protection laws and the psychological reasons behind them. Victor and Isabel asked us to find a Spanish-speaking expert to begin a group with other parents. They offered to help develop this group by inviting parents they met at work or at their trailer park.

The supervisee volunteered to facilitate the group, which met at a local church. The family's and therapist's empowerment came from understanding the components of their ecological niches and the potential resources of family and community that could emerge from this difficult experience within the family and with outside agencies. The supervisor also felt gratified that both cultural diversity and social justice variables were integrated in the assessment and treatment approach with this immigrant family.

CONCLUSION

This chapter presented seven migration-specific competencies for supervisors and supervisees designed to equip them to work effectively with immigrant individuals and families. These competencies cover conceptual issues about clients and about the interaction between supervisee and supervisor, practice ideas, and tools that help in assessment and treatment. Possible biases or errors inherent in this work are also included. The integration of migration issues with ecological context, family organization, and family life cycle is discussed and illustrated with case examples centered around possible stresses and strengths that immigrant clients present in therapy. The argument is made that supervisors and supervisees need to gain specific skills and self-reflective practices regarding cultural diversity and social justice issues to prepare themselves to attend to the needs of the growing population of immigrant clients.

REFERENCES

American Psychological Association, Presidential Task Force on Immigration. (2012). *Crossroads: The psychology of immigration in the new century.* Retrieved from http://www.apa.org/topics/immigration/report.aspx

Aron, A. (1992). Testimonio: A bridge between psychotherapy and sociotherapy. In E. Cole, O. Espin, & E. D. Rothblum (Eds.), *Refugee women and their mental health: Shattered societies, shattered lives* (pp. 173–189). Binghamton, NY: Haworth. doi:10.1300/J015V13N03_01

Castaño, M. T., Biever, J. L., González, C. G., & Anderson, K. B. (2007). Challenges of Providing Mental Health Services in Spanish. *Professional Psychology: Research and Practice, 38,* 667–673. doi:10.1037/0735-7028.38.6.667

Collins, S., Arthur, N., & Wong-Wylie, G. (2010). Enhancing reflective practice in multicultural counseling through cultural auditing. *Journal of Counseling & Development, 88,* 340–347. doi:10.1002/j.1556-6678.2010.tb00031.x

Congress, E. P. (2004). Cultural and ethical issues in working with culturally diverse patients and their families: The use of the culturagram to promote cultural competent practice in health care settings. *Social Work in Health Care, 39,* 249–262. doi:10.1300/J010v39n03_03

Costantino, G., Malgady, R., & Rogler, L. H. (1986). Cuento therapy: A culturally sensitive modality for Puerto Rican children. *Journal of Consulting and Clinical Psychology, 54,* 639–645. doi:10.1037/0022-006X.54.5.639

Falicov, C. J. (1983). Introduction. In C. J. Falicov (Ed.), *Cultural perspectives in family therapy* (pp. xiii–xix). Rockville, MD: Aspen Systems.

Falicov, C. J. (1997). So they don't need me anymore: Weaving migration, illness, and coping. In S. Daniel, J. Hepworth, & W. Doherty (Eds.), *Stories about medical family therapy* (pp. 48–57). New York, NY: Basic Books.

Falicov, C. J. (2002). Ambiguous loss: Risk and resilience in Latino immigrant families. In M. Suarez-Orozco (Ed.), *Latinos: Remaking America* (pp. 274–288). Berkeley: University of California Press.

Falicov, C. J. (2007). Working with transnational immigrants: Expanding meanings of family, community, and culture. *Family Process, 46,* 157–171. doi:10.1111/j.1545-5300.2007.00201.x

Falicov, C. J. (2010). Migration and the life cycle. In M. McGoldrick, B. Carter, & N. Garcia-Preto (Eds.), *The expanded family life cycle: Individual, family, and social perspectives* (4th ed., pp. 336–347). Upper Saddle River, NJ: Prentice Hall.

Falicov, C. J. (2012). Immigrant family processes: A multidimensional framework (MECA). In F. Walsh (Ed.), *Normal family processes* (pp. 297–323). New York, NY: Guilford Press.

Falicov, C. J. (2014). *Latino families in therapy* (2nd ed.). New York, NY: Guilford Press.

Field, L. D., Chavez-Korell, S., & Domenech Rodriguez, M. M. (2010). No hay rosas sin espinas: Conceptualizing Latina–Latina supervision from a multicultural developmental supervisory model. *Training and Education in Professional Psychology, 4*, 47–54. doi:10.1037/a0018521

Foster, R. P. (2001). When immigration is trauma: Guidelines for the individual and family clinician. *American Journal of Orthopsychiatry, 71*, 153–170. doi:10.1037/0002-9432.71.2.153

Hardy, K., & Laszloffy, T. (1995). The cultural genogram: Key in training culturally competent family therapists. *Journal of Marriage and Family Therapy, 21*, 227–237. doi:10.1111/j.1752-0606.1995.tb00158.x

Hartman, A. (1995). Diagrammatic assessment of family relationships. *Families in Society, 76*, 111–122.

Hondagneu-Sotelo, P., & Meissner, M. A. (1997). Gender displays and men's power: The "new man" and the Mexican immigrant man. In M. M. Gergen & S. N. Davis (Eds.), *Toward a new psychology of gender: A reader* (pp. 503–520). New York, NY: Routledge.

Keiley, M. K., Dolbin, M., Hill, J., Karupassawamy, N., Liu, T., Natrajan, R., . . . Robinson, P. (2002). The cultural genogram: Experiences within a marriage and family therapy program. *Journal of Marital and Family Therapy, 28*, 165–178. doi:10.1111/j.1752-0606.2002.tb00354.x

Kosutic, I., Garcia, M., Graves, T., Barnett, F., Hall, J., Haley, E., . . . Kaiser, B. (2009). The critical genogram: A tool for promoting critical consciousness. *Journal of Feminist Family Therapy, 21*, 151–176. doi:10.1080/08952830903079037

Landale, N. S., & Oropesa, R. S. (2007). Hispanic families: Stability and change. *Annual Review of Sociology, 33*, 381–405. doi:10.1146/annurev.soc.33.040406.131655

Lau, A. S., Jernewall, N. M., Zane, N., & Myers, H. F. (2002). Correlates of suicidal behaviors among Asian-American outpatient youths. *Cultural Diversity & Ethnic Minority Psychology, 8*, 199–213. doi:10.1037/1099-9809.8.3.199

McGoldrick, M., Gerson, R., & Petry, S. (2008). *Genograms: Assessment and Intervention* (3rd ed.). New York, NY: Norton Professional Books.

McGoldrick, M., Gerson, R., & Schellenberger, S. (1999). *Genograms in family assessment*. New York, NY: Norton.

Porter, N. (1994). Empowering supervisees to empower others: A culturally responsive supervision model. *Hispanic Journal of Behavioral Sciences, 16*, 43–56. doi:10.1177/07399863940161004

Rigazio-DiGilio, S. A., Ivey, A. E., Kunkler-Peck, K. P., & Grady, L.T. (2005) *Community genograms: Using individual, family, and cultural narratives with clients.* New York, NY: Teachers College Press.

Roysircar, G. (2004). Cultural self-awareness assessment: Practice examples from psychology training. *Professional Psychology: Research and Practice, 35*, 658–666. doi:10.1037/0735-7028.35.6.658

Santiago-Rivera, A. L., Arredondo, P., & Gallardo-Cooper, M. (2002). *Counseling Latinos and la familia: A practical guide.* Thousand Oaks, CA: Sage.

Schwartz, A., Domenech Rodriguez, M. M., Field, L. D., Santiago-Rivera, A. L., & Arredondo, P. (2010). Cultural and linguistic competence: Welcome challenges from successful diversification. *Professional Psychology: Research and Practice, 41*, 210–220. doi:10.1037/a0019447

Smokowski, P. R., & Bacallao, M. (2011). *Becoming bicultural: Risk, resilience and Latino youth.* New York, NY: New York University Press.

Thomas, A. J. (1998). Understanding culture and worldview in family systems: Use of the multicultural genogram. *The Family Journal, 6*, 24–32. doi:10.1177/1066480798061005

Walsh, F. (2006). *Strengthening family resilience* (2nd ed.). New York, NY: Guilford Press.

Watts-Jones, D. (1997). Toward an African American genogram. *Family Process, 36*, 375–383. doi:10.1111/j.1545-5300.1997.00375.x

Weine, S. M., Dzubur Kulenovic, A. D., Pavkovic, I., & Gibbons, R. (1998). Testimony psychotherapy in Bosnian refugees: A pilot study. *American Journal of Psychiatry, 155*, 1720–1726.

Zayas, L. H. (2011). *Latinas attempting suicide: When cultures, families and daughters collide.* New York, NY: Oxford University Press. doi:10.1093/acprof:oso/9780199734726.001.0001

6

CONSIDERING SOCIAL CLASS AND SOCIOECONOMIC STATUS IN THE CONTEXT OF MULTIPLE IDENTITIES: AN INTEGRATIVE CLINICAL SUPERVISION APPROACH

NADYA A. FOUAD AND SHANNON CHAVEZ-KORELL

This chapter addresses the much neglected issue of socioeconomic status (SES) and social class differences, how these play out in the supervision process, and how SES and class interact with the various cultural and sociopolitical identities present within the supervisory triad (client, supervisee, and supervisor). Our supervision approach is integrative in nature, incorporating the multisystemic ecological comparative approach (MECA; Falicov, 1998; see also Chapter 2, this volume) as the framework for conceptualizing multicultural similarities and differences across the supervisory triad, coupled with a competency-based approach to supervision (Falender & Shafranske, 2004; Fouad et al., 2009; see also Chapter 1, this volume) for identifying the knowledge, skills, and values associated with the appreciation of social class and SES. Often the assumptions in supervision, and in training in general, are that all individuals involved are of the same social class and that they

http://dx.doi.org/10.1037/14370-006

Multiculturalism and Diversity in Clinical Supervision: A Competency-Based Approach, C. A. Falender, E. P. Shafranske, and C. J. Falicov (Editors)

share the same worldview. Although others in this book (e.g., Chapters 3 and 5) discuss worldview differences as related to race, gender, and so on, we focus here on how social class may shape worldview and how that affects supervision.

Social class is the income, wealth, and resources that individuals have, often stratified across groups (Fouad & Brown, 2000). Thus, individuals in the United States are thought of as belonging to lower class, working-class, middle class, upper middle class, or upper class groups. Each social class group has its own particular way of viewing the world that is in keeping with its members' ability to access resources and benefits. Those with more resources have the privilege of using those resources, often to accrue more income and benefits, and those with fewer resources often have less power to influence their acquisition of wealth, in addition to other human features such as health, security, safety, and so on. The relative resources around social class have come into sharp focus with the effects of the most recent U.S. recession. In 2010, slightly more than 15% (46 million) of U.S. residents were found to live in poverty, the highest rate in the 52 years the poverty rate has been calculated (U.S. Census Bureau, 2011). The poverty rate is the number of families of four falling below an annual income of $22,314. Although the poverty rate has increased, the incomes of those in the middle class have decreased and the incomes of those in the top earning brackets (more than $181,000) have increased (U.S. Census Bureau, 2011). This income inequality, coupled with increasing rates of health insurance, has led to a shrinking middle class. The income disparities are particularly stark for racial/ethnic minority group members. Whereas the overall poverty rate is 15.1%, it is 26.7% for Hispanic/Latinos and 27.5% for African Americans, and Hispanic/Latinos and African Americans are much more likely to not have health insurance (31% and 21%, respectively), adding to income inequality (U.S. Census Bureau, 2011).

Liu (2012) argued that social class categories do not accurately capture the subjective experiences of social class. Subjective experiences of social class may come into focus in supervision, as the supervisor and supervisee may view clients' problems, resources, and opportunities to implement suggestions in very different ways. Consider a working-class trainee who has an upper class supervisor and is conducting therapy with a working-class client who is struggling with unemployment. The supervisor may express frustration that the trainee is not implementing suggestions for career development activities to help the client find appropriate training for future employment. The trainee may not be implementing the suggestions because she or he feels that the immediate issue for the client is paying rent and buying food. Both responses are shaped by the individuals' social class worldviews. Neither is wrong, and both may be very appropriate activities for the client, but this example helps to illustrate how social class may influence supervision. In this chapter, we provide an overview of social class, with a particular focus on power and privilege aspects as they are magnified when one or more members of the supervisory triad are of a different SES and/or social class group. We also emphasize social justice and the role of clinicians (supervisors and supervisees) as social change agents.

SOCIOECONOMIC STATUS AND SOCIAL CLASS

Race, ethnicity, gender, and social class are considered to be among the most influential contextual influences in an individual's life and help to shape his or her worldview. Although gender, race, and ethnicity often help to define the way that children are socialized from an early age, social class is often defined as individuals gain a perception of themselves in relation to others. However, race and social class are often unclearly defined and conceptualized, and authors frequently either use one as a proxy for the other construct or use measures that confound the two (Fouad & Brown, 2000). One of the reasons is that race is often a social stratification variable, with majority culture individuals viewing racial/ethnic minority individuals as part of a lower social class, regardless of that individual's actual social class level. Several racial identity models have theorized how individuals belonging to particular minority groups differ from others' worldviews in addition to other features (e.g., Cross, 1971; Helms, 1984; Ruiz, 1990). Parts of those models incorporate how much the racial/ethnic minority accepts and endorses the social stratification of the dominant culture.

Defining Social Class

Thus, social class is a critically important variable to capture in both research and practice, but an important problem arises when trying to conceptualize and define social class. SES has been used to measure social class and is often operationalized as one's level of resources (Gallo & Matthews, 2003). This often includes income, education, and occupation. Yet, social class may be seen to comprise more than simply these three factors. Brown, Fukunaga, Umemoto, and Wicker (1996) posited that social class is composed of economic resources, prestige, and power. Clearly, their definition goes beyond income, education, and occupation and captures the comprehensive nature of this construct. Liu and Ali (2008) suggested that social class has come to denote social status as well as access to resources. They noted, however, that organizing individuals into varying groups according to social class (e.g., middle class, working class) does not provide any information on the psychological experiences of class or the effects of classism on individuals' lives (which is of particular importance when working with clients).

The American Psychological Association's (2007) *Report of the APA Task Force on Socioeconomic Status* argues that it is also important for psychologists to understand how individual experiences and perspectives help to shape social class. The report summarizes a large body of literature that documents the effects of lower access to material resources: higher rates of depression, lower rates of achievement, and lower levels of many indices of physical and mental health. Fouad and Brown (2000) reviewed social class indices related to education, work, health, and parenting, finding empirical support for disparities across social class levels. Social class also helps to shape access to resources, including educational resources, and in this way is hypothesized to influence level of occupational attainment and aspirations (Blustein et al., 2002).

Differential Status Identity

Whereas both race and social status constitute important features of one's cultural context, it is necessary to construct an integrative framework to investigate the influence of race and social class. To do so, Fouad and Brown (2000) developed the construct of differential status identity (DSI) to conceptualize how individuals perceive themselves and how they believe others perceive them. According to Fouad and Brown (2000), DSI is the

> identity derived from social standing differences from the ordinant group. The theory incorporates the psychological and psychosocial dimensions of race and social class that are social and behaviorally salient and that differentiate individuals and their in-groups from members of out-groups. (p. 387)

DSI is hypothesized to develop as people compare themselves with members of a perceived ordinant group with respect to social variables of prestige, economics, and power. *Ordinant groups* are social groups with the highest social standing; thus, these groups possess more economic resources, power, and prestige than do other groups in society. These groups are the bases in which other groups are hierarchically ordered. The DSI construct takes into account the dynamic influences of multiple social stratification variables on the development of personal identity and psychosocial outcomes. Therefore, it is hypothesized to represent a more comprehensive descriptor than race, gender, or class alone. The concept of DSI can be a functional framework to understand the impact of cultural orientation variables independent and interdependent self-construals, individualism and collectivism, racial identity, ethnic identity, racial salience, acculturation and racism and discrimination. DSI may thus provide utility for psychologists examining the role of social stratification in identity formation and psychological development.

The concept of DSI incorporates several factors, including economic, prestige, and power factors, in conceptualizing how individuals perceive themselves in social standing. *Economic factors* include those that illustrate how an individual participates in the production of goods and services, the resources that influence that participation, and the resources consequential to that participation (Fouad & Brown, 2000). These include economic security and choice, amount of control over material and human resources, and indices of affluence. *Prestige factors* demonstrate how much individuals and the groups to which they belong to are valued and prized in society. These factors include occupational prestige; status; an evaluation of racial, ethnic, and religious groups; consumption behavior; and group participation. Finally, *power factors* illustrate the ability of the individual to determine societal ideas and include indicators of amount and types of control over the nature and distribution of social values (Fouad & Brown, 2000). Economic, prestige, and power factors all play a role in DSI and thus should be incorporated in the conceptualization of this construct.

Social Class Worldview Model

Liu (2002; Liu & Ali, 2008) developed a social class worldview model that focuses on an individual's subjective perspective rather on that individual's interactions with the outside world. Liu and Ali (2008) proposed that individuals form perceptions of themselves and that those "self-perceptions do more to define their social class than the objective conditions in which they live" (p. 167). They suggested that individuals live in economic cultures that provide them with different types of capital (e.g., relationships, skills). Economic cultures impose demands on and set expectations for the individual. The individual views that economic culture through his or her social class worldview, which has developed as a result of socialization messages from family, neighborhood, and community.

DEVELOPING SOCIOECONOMIC STATUS AND SOCIAL CLASS COMPETENCIES

A primary goal of supervision is to foster supervisees' professional competence, which is inclusive of both clinical and multicultural competence, as clinical competence cannot be attained without multicultural awareness, knowledge, and skills (Kaslow et al., 2004; Sue, Arredondo, & McDavis, 1992). Thus, the supervisor is responsible for assessing and facilitating the supervisee's understanding of multicultural issues, including SES and social class, in interpersonal and therapeutic processes (Constantine, Fuertes,

Roysircar, & Kindaichi, 2008). The supervisor observes, evaluates, offers feedback, facilitates supervisee self-assessment, and assists supervisees in gaining knowledge and skills by instruction, modeling, and problem solving (Falender & Shafranske, 2004). Supervision provides an ideal opportunity and relationship for the supervisee to engage in honest self-reflection and open discussion about social class and how it intersects with a number of cultural and sociopolitical factors present in the supervision triad.

The competency benchmarks (Fouad et al., 2009) are a useful framework for grounding meaningful discourse on the influence of SES and social class in the supervision triad. Using a competency-based approach, eight functional competency domains (i.e., assessment/diagnosis/conceptualization, intervention, consultation, research/evaluation, supervision, teaching, advocacy, and management/administration) intersect with seven foundational competency domains (i.e., reflective practice/self-assessment, scientific knowledge and methods, relationships, ethical and legal standards/policy issues, individual and cultural diversity, professionalism, and interdisciplinary systems). Purposefully discussing the intersection of these domains in relationship to SES and social class lays the groundwork for a meaningful discourse. Individual and cultural diversity, a foundational competency with delineated benchmarks (Fouad et al., 2009, p. S13), should be specifically evaluated in regard to supervisee's awareness, sensitivity, and skills in working with clients, groups, and communities who represent various SESs and social classes.

Supervision processes of "culturally responsive supervisors include supervisors' awareness of their cultural identities and values [including SES and differential statuses across supervisor, supervisee, client], openness, vulnerability and self-disclosure, attending to and exploring cultural factors, and providing opportunities for multicultural engagement" (Constantine et al., 2008, p. 113). Asking questions and encouraging supervisees to explore their own SES and social class through self-reflection and self-assessment can help to increase supervisees' awareness and knowledge of social class issues. When appropriate, supervisors may also disclose how social class has influenced their own clinical or supervisory work. Sample questions to help facilitate this discussion include: What are SES and social class? How do you identify in regards to SES and social class? How do you see my own SES as different from (or similar to) yours? How do your SES and social class influence your worldview, value system, and clinical work? How do SES and social class intersect with other facets of identity? How does SES and social class influence the competency-based domains identified in the competency benchmarks?

Multicultural dialogue, exploration, and consideration in the supervisory dyad serve as a model for the supervisee to raise culture-related concerns (Miville, Rosa, & Constantine, 2005). Supervisors model how to incorporate SES and social class issues into clinical work by discussing them in the context of how they influence the supervisor–supervisee dyad. The supervisor may also disclose and offer reflections on their own SES and social class, what it means to them, how it has changed and/or remained the same over time, factors influencing these changes, how it intersects with other facets of their identity, and how social class and SES influence their value system and worldview.

The supervisor challenges the supervisee to be inclusive of SES and social class factors in conceptualizing client treatment plans, assessments, diagnosis, and interventions. The supervisor asks the supervisee to consider how the client's SES and social class influence his or her presenting concerns. The supervisor uses the here-and-now as a tool for immediacy and relational modeling. The supervisor is aware of parallel processes and transference/countertransference and uses these as clinical tools when appropriate.

The competency benchmarks (Fouad et al., 2009) can be used as a guide in thinking about how social class and other multicultural and contextual understandings are integrated into the functional competency domains of treatment (i.e., assessment/diagnosis/conceptualization, intervention, consultation, and advocacy). The supervisor and supervisee can discuss each of the functional domains in relationship to client cases and consider how SES and social class, in the context of other cultural and sociopolitical factors, influence the client's presenting concerns, assessment, appropriate interventions, the supervisee's response, and so on.

The supervisor can refer to the competency benchmarks specific to individual and cultural diversity (Fouad et al., 2009, pp. S13–S14) as a tool for evaluating the supervisee's understanding and integration of social class issues into his or her clinical work. To do this, he or she would begin with Benchmark D, applications based on individual and cultural context, as all of the other individual and cultural diversity competency benchmarks (i.e., Benchmarks A, B, and C) are predicated upon Benchmark D. Working backward (D: Application based on individual and cultural context, C: Interaction of self and others as shaped by individual and cultural diversity and context, B: Others as shaped by individual and cultural diversity and context, and A: Self as shaped by individual and cultural diversity and context) through the competency benchmarks established for individual and cultural diversity, the supervisor is able to evaluate the supervisee's sensitivity, knowledge, skills, and attitudes regarding social class and SES based on the behavioral anchors identified in each section (Fouad et al., 2009).

Insensitivity, misinformation, bias, or prejudice expressed by the supervisee should be immediately addressed in supervision. The supervisor engages the supervisee in a dialogue, which can be guided by the competency benchmarks for individual and cultural diversity (specifically Benchmarks A and B) with reflection on the supervisee's awareness, attitudes, knowledge, and skills. The supervisor facilitates this discussion in a sensitive way that encourages the supervisee to be introspective and ultimately reconsider their insensitivity. The dialogue also includes consideration about how the supervisee's biases influence the quality of care rendered to clients. Misinformation about SES and social class should be challenged by the supervisor and corrected; quality resources (e.g., articles, books, immersion opportunities) could be recommended by the supervisor to assist the supervisee in gaining knowledge about social class and SES. The supervisor's attention and sensitivity to social class and SES issues in supervision model for the supervisee the attention and consideration that social class and SES must be given in the latter's clinical work.

STRENGTHS AND LIMITATIONS

The supervision approach presented here has strengths and weaknesses that should be considered. Its primary strength is that the clinical and multicultural training needs of the supervisee are taken into account, as are the clinical needs and cultural context of the client and the clinical and cultural context of the supervisor. In addition, established models, research, and professional competency benchmarks are incorporated to facilitate increased awareness, knowledge, and skills of supervisees while offering competency benchmarks to guide supervisors in training and evaluation of supervisees. This supervision approach, integrating the competency-based benchmarks (Falender & Shafranske, 2004; Fouad et al., 2009) with the MECA, conceptually captures the complexity and multifaceted nature of the supervisory triad. An added strength is that this approach is testable, as the constructs of the model are well established in the supervision literature, thereby making it research ready.

The primary limitation of this approach is that a positive growth-oriented learning experience for the supervisee is almost entirely dependent on the supervisor's level of development, in his or her clinical professional development and in his or her cultural identity development. This may be ameliorated if the supervisor adopts a more collaborative approach in supervision, drawing on curiosity and appropriately seeking input from the supervisee and client, ensuring that this is done while still meeting his or her clinical and training needs. It is also critical for supervisors to seek out growth-oriented consultation. A second limitation of this approach is that it is strictly theoretical, although influenced by existing supervision research; it needs to be researched to provide a more solid understanding of how these clinical and multicultural dynamics interact across the supervisory triad.

AN EXAMPLE OF THE APPROACH

Context of Supervision

The following session takes place during the supervision of a predoctoral intern at a university counseling center located in the northeast region of the United States. The supervisor has more than 25 years of experience as a clinician and supervisor but no formal training in supervision. The supervisor grew up in an upper-middle-class household, as the child of immigrants who came to the United States from different countries to work as professors. Both sets of grandparents were wealthy. She is comfortable talking about social class and other facets of cultural identity and expects supervisees to discuss their clients' cultural and sociopolitical contexts. The supervisee is a Latina who grew up in a working-class home and is the first in her extended family to attend college. The supervisee's professional competence is at, or exceeds, the readiness for internship benchmarks (Fouad et al., 2009). She has well-developed competencies in individual and cultural diversity.

The supervisor and supervisee are discussing the supervisee's client. The client is from a working-class background and is a first-generation college student. He is White with a strong Italian American ethnic identity, and is currently working at a local community center in the neighborhood he grew up in. The client's presenting concern is depression. He attributes his depression to financial problems and poor academic performance exacerbated by his difficulty concentrating and lack of energy. During the course of therapy, the client has gained employment at a local community center. Recent therapy sessions have often focused on the personal meaning the client has gained from his work at the community center; there is often deep process regarding personal, emotional, and political issues he struggles with as a result of this position. He talked about his work at the community center as being meaningful for multiple reasons; one reason was because he had attended this same community center when he was young. The following supervision follows a session toward the end of treatment when the client was clearly reporting decreased depressive symptoms and was gaining clarity about situational factors contributing to his depression.

Supervision goals follow a competency-based approach and MECA. Supervisors encourage supervisees to be aware of themselves and others as cultural beings (including social class as part of their identity) and to consider the intersections of cultural and sociopolitical contexts. There is sensitivity to power differentials and awareness of "how people are denied access or excluded from certain settings" (Falicov, 2003, p. 40) and how this in turn influences their experiences, values, and worldview. Supervisors also want supervisees to increase their knowledge about various cultural dimensions and strive to help supervisees further develop their clinical skills and attain clinical competence.

Processes in this approach include use of questions to help raise awareness and encourage critical thinking and self-reflection. Other processes used in this supervision session example include the supervisor's facilitation of a multicultural dialogue with the supervisee, supervisor disclosure, encouragement of the supervisee to elaborate on conceptualizations that include consideration of SES and social class, use of the here-and-now, and awareness of transference and countertransference. The use of these supervision processes depends on the level of competence of the supervisee; the supervisor should assess the competency level of the supervisee and challenge only as is helpful for that level of development. The supervisee in this supervision case example meets the readiness for internship benchmarks (Fouad et al., 2009) and is approaching readiness for practice. In this supervisory dyad, the supervisor models critical thinking and self-reflection, provides challenges to help the supervisee become "unstuck" by pointing out inconsistencies, and asks difficult questions. The supervisor facilitates/navigates the difficult dialogue, thus modeling for the supervisee, who in turn is better prepared to do this with her client. Supervisors need to be comfortable with their own identity as cultural beings and need to have reflected on the development of their various cultural identities and subjective social class worldview. Finally, supervision needs to be multifaceted, acknowledging the many layers of identity that each supervisee brings to supervision and how those identities may be more or less salient in various clinical situations.

(noticeable)

Supervision Session Example

Supervisee: My client continues to talk about his work at the community center, and the role he is serving as a mentor/big brother. His own mentor/big brother played a really important role in his [client's] life because he strongly encouraged him [client] to be a community activist. Sadly, his big brother ended up being shot and killed during an altercation between White ethnic rival groups a few years ago. But he [client] credits his experiences at this community center during his teen years for the reason he has strong community commitment and pride. He feels a calling to step up and take on a community leadership role. During our recent session, the client was trying to describe to me a historical marker near the community center. He was having difficulty describing its location, but I knew exactly what he was talking about. I told him, "I know exactly the place you are referring to." Appearing surprised, he said, "How do you know this area?" And I said, "I know what you are talking about because I live in that neighborhood too." And he said, "Oh you do!? Where do you live?" And I said, "I live by Johnny's Food Market." And he said, "Oh I know exactly where you live—you really do live in my hood." At that time, this shared neighborhood experience seemed to serve as a positive connection between us. It felt like a newly established common ground between us. Later in the session, the client was talking about how difficult it was for him and his friends to remain living in his neighborhood. He was saying, "It's really weird because the neighborhood, over the generations, is slowly crumbling and the commitment between the families and to one another is breaking down. Me and my friends, we're dedicated to the neighborhood, and we're doing all this service there, but at the same time I'm very aware that I can't stay in this neighborhood." And then I said, "Why is that?" And he just stared at me hard and finally said, "Because you live there, Ms.!" Even telling you now [supervisee to supervisor], I can feel my cheeks get flushed because I know exactly what he's talking about . . . it's the gentrification of neighborhoods and he sees me as being a part of that, and I don't want to be. In that moment, I'm thinking about how I'm a first-generation college student, Latina, from a working-poor background from the barrio . . . and my family still lives paycheck to paycheck in the barrio! I've just moved barrios as far as I'm concerned! I felt this strong need to say all of this to him [client] . . . to make sure he knows who I really am . . . but I didn't because I knew that was my stuff. [Supervisee is self-aware about the personal reaction the client is triggering for her. She is mindful of her client's transference and her own countertransference. She is made aware of the incongruence between how she perceives herself and is perceived by others (DSI)]. And here I have a White man telling me that I'm kicking him out of his neighborhood. I don't feel I've been able to take advantage of the social class privilege he's talking about. . . . I'm still moving into that social class. [The supervisee is discussing the salience of her various cultural identities and particularly social class, which she thought she shared with the client.]

Supervisor: He ascribed it to you before you were ready to ascribe it to yourself. [The supervisor points out the conflict between the supervisee's subjective social class worldview and the social class ascribed to her by her client (DSI). The supervisor is also reflecting on the intentionality of the supervisee's disclosure about living in the same neighborhood as the client. The supervisee described the disclosure as bridging in establishing common ground with the client but it also seemed to be an unplanned disclosure.]

Supervisee: Exactly! And I wasn't prepared to defend it [the social class ascribed to the supervisee by the client] because it doesn't represent me either [DSI]. And so for the first time, I was really perplexed about the whole thing. [Supervisee had not considered how her SES had slowly changed over the recent years and increased her social privilege and access to resources (social class).]. In the moment I felt this need to detach myself [from the supervisee's emotional reaction] because I knew that wouldn't have been productive for him—my emotional response was about me [evidence of supervisee's self-reflection and awareness]. I knew that if I'd said, "Oh, I'm not [part of the social class ascribed to the supervisee by the client] . . . " to disown the privilege . . . that wasn't the point that he was making. He was talking about what I represent in general [people with socioeconomic power and privilege, which can be used to leverage desired resources such as housing], and he's right!

Supervisor: Yeah, although I also have a reaction that your struggle with the privilege prevented you from talking to him about what that privilege means to him. Why does he have to leave because he's going to college? [The supervisor identifies the supervisee's struggle and the clinical implications of this struggle. The supervisor challenges the supervisee to self-reflect and consider the clinical implications for the client.]

Supervisee: So he's soon to be the people he's talking about.

Supervisor: Exactly. So why does he have to leave because people like you are moving in? What if he becomes people like you? [The supervisor asks a difficult question to encourage the supervisee to realize the clinical implications of her struggle with her identity.]

Supervisee: I didn't go there at all.

Supervisor: No, because you realized what that meant for you.

Supervisee: That was the first time in my entire life that all of a sudden it was like this slap in the face that I represent a group that I don't even want to own myself. [The supervisee demonstrates an increased awareness and engaging in self-reflection about her social class changes.]

Supervisor: Was it realizing that this moves you away from your family? [The supervisor is encouraging self-reflection to raise self-awareness as would be consistent with the MECA. The dialogue is also influenced by the supervisor's level of development in interacting with the supervisee's level of identity development. The supervisor believes that the supervisee is ready to engage in this level of self-reflection.]

Supervisee: Well, I don't think it is moving away from my family because my family knows where I'm coming from [regarding the working-class background of supervisee], but to think that at a community level I don't represent where I'm coming from is really hard for me. I feel that with his comment I was left to defend a group that doesn't represent me and that I don't want to represent [DSI].

Supervisor: I also go to that unfair homogeneity.

Supervisee: Yeah, and thinking about the intersections of our work in terms of identity; the fact that he's White and I'm Latina and then even the gender piece. [Supervisees' awareness of intersections of identity and sociopolitical contexts as described in the MECA.]

Supervisor: But does he see that? [The supervisor is speaking about the clinical implications of the supervisee's self-reflection.]

Supervisee: Yes, we've talked before about some of the differences we bring into our work. We never talked about SES because I felt like this was shared common ground until this comment.

Supervisor: If he had said that to me I wouldn't have had any offense. My reaction as a therapist to that comment would have been, "What does that mean for you that you can't live there if people like me move in?" But you didn't go there, and I think you would have normally gone there. [The supervisor is pointing out that the supervisee's struggle with subjective social class worldview may have prevented her from her normal therapeutic responses.]

Supervisee: I didn't go there because I felt I knew exactly what he meant.

Supervisor: But you might not have.

Supervisee: Wow, good point! I am also feeling a little self-conscious wondering how you were taking it when I said I don't want to be a part of this group—your [social class] group. I wonder if you're taking offense. [The supervisee is evidencing her ability to process her feelings with the supervisor about the differences in their social class.]

Supervisor: But you're now a part of my group.

Supervisee: Maybe at a surface level. I don't have that social class background of knowing. This is new for me. I feel like it's a foreign experience for me on a regular basis in terms of not knowing how to behave or social expectations on a regular basis. So I'm not a part of this group. Maybe more recently I've moved into it through my education leading to increased income, but it's doesn't reflect my worldview or my values. It might be income, but that is the extent. [The supervisee is articulating her subjective social class worldview.]

Supervisor: Or the occupation. But not sense of self?

Supervisee: No.

Supervisor: So there's incongruence between how you are perceived and how you feel. Do you think this misperception occurs with most people? [The supervisor is encouraging the supervisee to realize how clients view her social class and how this may influence subjective social class worldview.]

Supervisee: I don't know, because it depends to some degree on the type of engagement because to me there is a cultural norm around social class. There is a cultural norm regarding engagement, the ways we interact, and things we say with one another. I experience it with other students; there is a way we engage with one another that confirms our shared social class background and experiences.

Supervisor: Seriously?

Supervisee: Yes.

Supervisor: So how does that play out with us? [The supervisor is bringing their own differences in social class into the supervision process, using this as a model for the supervisee to discuss social class with her clients.]

Supervisee: Well, we don't have that same [social class] background or that same type of engagement around shared social class experience. It's not a connecting piece for us.

Supervisor: So the question is, "Is there a disconnect?" [The supervisor is demonstrating her comfort with her role in inviting an open discussion about their social class differences and how it might affect supervision.]

Supervisee: I don't know if there is a disconnect, but I know there is not a connect. It [social class] is not a common ground that we share. So when I bridge to you in supervision around something I'm struggling with, it [social class] is not a bridge I go to for common ground with you.

Supervisor:	So in supervision is that a barrier that I'm not going to understand or that I don't immediately understand? Like, I didn't have that same immediate reaction to your client.
Supervisee:	In that moment [referring to the session with her client], it felt like a pie-in-the-face moment. It felt insulting. But it felt insulting in that it was something that was so far off my own radar of awareness. And so . . . I wasn't even . . . it might sound naïve, but my identity is so connected to being a first-generation college student struggling financially, from a poor family and a poor community. So for him to say I represent this other [upper SES] group, it felt like . . . it was unowned privilege that I had not thought about because I didn't really feel I had that privilege. I'm still getting paid very little; I still cannot capitalize on that privilege. It was a slap in the face—probably more of a slap in the face than a pie in the face. A slap in the face because it was a wake-up call and at the same time kind of a shameful experience.
Supervisor:	So if you go back to the difference between our social classes, then how does it intersect with our supervision? I mean are there things that you feel you can't talk about? Does it feel like there is a barrier? I'm wondering if I move through the world with unexamined privilege that sets up a barrier. [The supervisor brings the discussion of social class differences into the here-and-now, bringing the focus back to the supervisory relationship. Supervisor reflects on her own power and privilege, inviting feedback on unexamined privilege. Again, the supervisor provides modeling for the supervisee.]
Supervisee:	When I think about our engagement . . . how do we connect with one another? When I connect with you, social class definitely is not one of those ways. I don't feel like that [social class] is something we share. We share common ground in regards to our profession, gender, ethnic minority status . . . it's these other shared realms where we connect. Social class is just not one of those things we connect on. But it's so hard sometimes for me to tease apart what's my Latina background and what's SES. So maybe social class is a part of our supervision by not being one of the connecting facets we share in supervision. It is clearly a part of what we each bring to the table.

Evaluation and Outcomes

Outcomes of this approach include supervisees who are ready for entry to practice as defined by the individual and cultural diversity competence

(Fouad et al., 2009). They are able to independently monitor and apply knowledge of self and others as cultural beings in assessment, treatment, and consultation. This includes the ability to continuously monitor and improve their clinical effectiveness. Competent professionals are able to initiate supervision around issues of diversity. They are also able to articulate how their own cultural identity (including social class) interacts with the cultural identity of others, both their supervisors and their clients. Finally, they are able to apply that knowledge in their clinical work. The critically important outcome for clients is that this approach helps to ensure that clients receive clinically and culturally competent services from their clinicians, which safeguards against early termination, results in appropriate treatment intervention and adaptation, and ultimately improves treatment outcomes for clients. Finally, outcomes of this approach for supervisors include an ongoing commitment to personal growth, enhancement of self-awareness and knowledge, and further refining of skills that can bolster personal well-being and enrich the quality of professional services rendered to clients, supervisees, trainees, and colleagues.

REFERENCES

American Psychological Association. (2007). *Report of the APA Task Force on Socioeconomic Status*. Retrieved from http://www.apa.org/pi/ses/resources/publications/index.aspx

Blustein, D. L., Chaves, A. P., Diemer, M. A., Gallagher, L. A., Marshall, K. G., Sirin, S., & Bhati, K. S. (2002). Voices of the forgotten half: The role of social class in the school-to-work transition. *Journal of Counseling Psychology, 49*, 311–323. doi:10.1037/0022-0167.49.3.311

Brown, M. T., Fukunaga, C., Umemoto, D., & Wicker, L. (1996). Annual review, 1990–1996: Social class, work, and retirement behavior. *Journal of Vocational Behavior, 49*, 159–189. doi:10.1006/jvbe.1996.0039

Constantine, M. G., Fuertes, J. N., Roysircar, G., & Kindaichi, M. M. (2008). Multicultural competence: Clinical practice, training and supervision, and research. In B. Walsh (Ed.), *Biennial review of counseling psychology* (Vol. 1, pp. 97–127). New York, NY: Taylor & Francis.

Cross, W. E., Jr. (1971). The Negro-to-Black conversion experience. *Black World, 20*, 13–27.

Falender, C. A., & Shafranske, E. P. (2004). *Clinical supervision: A competency-based approach*. Washington, DC: American Psychological Association. doi:10.1037/10806-000

Falicov, C. J. (1998). The cultural meaning of family triangles. In M. McGoldrick (Ed.), *Re-visioning family therapy: Race, culture, and gender in clinical practice* (pp. 37–49). New York, NY: Guilford Press.

Falicov, C. J. (2003). Culture in family therapy: New variations on a fundamental theme. In T. Sexton, G. Weeks, & M. Robbins (Eds.), *Handbook of family therapy: Theory, research, and practice* (pp. 37–55). New York, NY: Brunner-Routledge.

Fouad, N. A., & Brown, M. T. (2000). Role of race and social class in development: Implications for counseling psychology. In S. D. Brown & R. W. Lent (Eds.), *Handbook of counseling psychology* (pp. 379–408). New York, NY: Wiley.

Fouad, N. A., Grus, C. L., Hatcher, R. L., Kaslow, N. J., Hutchings, P. S., Madson, M. B., . . . Crossman, R. E. (2009). Competency benchmarks: A model for understanding and measuring competence in professional psychology across training levels. *Training and Education in Professional Psychology, 3*(4 Suppl.), S5–S26. doi:10.1037/a0015832

Gallo, L. C., & Matthews, K. A. (2003). Understanding the association between socioeconomic status and physical health: Do negative emotions play a role? *Psychological Bulletin, 129,* 10–51. doi:10.1037/0033-2909.129.1.10

Helms, J. E. (1984). Toward a theoretical explanation of the effects of race on counseling: A Black and White model. *The Counseling Psychologist, 12,* 153–165. doi:10.1177/0011000084124013

Kaslow, N. J., Borden, K. A., Collins, F. L., Jr., Forrest, L., Illfelder-Kaye, J., Nelson, P., . . . Wilmuth, M. E.(2004). Competencies conference: Future directions in education and credentialing in professional psychology. *Journal of Clinical Psychology, 60,* 699–712. doi:10.1002/jclp.20016

Liu, W. M. (2002). The social class–related experiences of men: Integrating theory and practice. *Professional Psychology: Research and Practice, 33,* 355–360. doi:10.1037/0735-7028.33.4.355

Liu, W. M. (2012). Developing a social class and classism consciousness. In E. M. Altmaier & J.-I. C. Hansen (Eds.), *Oxford library of psychology. The Oxford handbook of counseling psychology* (pp. 326–345). New York, NY: Oxford University Press.

Liu, W. M., & Ali, S. R. (2008). Social class and classism: Understanding the psychological impact of poverty and inequality. In S. D. Brown & R. W. Lent (Eds.), *Handbook of counseling psychology* (4th ed.; pp. 159–175). Hoboken, NJ: Wiley.

Miville, M. L., Rosa, D., & Constantine, M. G. (2005). Building multicultural competence in clinical supervision. In M. G. Constantine & D. W. Sue (Eds.), *Strategies for building multicultural competence in mental health and educational settings* (pp. 192–211). Hoboken, NJ: Wiley.

Ruiz, A. S. (1990). Ethnic identity: Crisis and resolution. *Journal of Multicultural Counseling and Development, 18,* 29–40. doi:10.1002/j.2161-1912.1990.tb00434.x

Sue, D. W., Arredondo, P., & McDavis, R. J. (1992). Multicultural competencies and standards: A call to the profession. *Journal of Multicultural Counseling and Development, 20,* 64–88. doi:10.1002/j.2161-1912.1992.tb00563.x

U.S. Census Bureau. (2011). *American fact finder 2.* Retrieved from http://factfinder2.census.gov/faces/nav/jsf/pages/index.html

7

SUPERVISION AND DISABILITIES

JENNIFER A. ERICKSON CORNISH
AND SAMANTHA PELICAN MONSON

Approximately 50 million (one in five) people in the United States currently live with a disability (American Psychological Association [APA]'s, 2011, *Guidelines for Assessment of and Intervention With Persons With Disabilities*; hereinafter, APA *Guidelines for Assessment*). In addition to being personally affected, individuals may experience disability as a caregiver, a parent, or a child of someone with a disability (Cornish, Gorgens, & Monson, 2008). Because the numbers of people with disabilities are expected to increase as the populace ages and health risks such as obesity affect greater numbers of younger people (Alley & Chang, 2007), it is likely that psychologists and other mental health professionals will increasingly be presented with opportunities to provide psychotherapy to people with disabilities (Olkin, 2002) and/or those affected secondarily. Disability issues have only recently begun to be recognized as a multicultural issue (Palombi, 2008), yet persons with disabilities constitute a large minority group in the United States, second

http://dx.doi.org/10.1037/14370-007
Multiculturalism and Diversity in Clinical Supervision: A Competency-Based Approach, C. A. Falender, E. P. Shafranske, and C. J. Falicov (Editors)

only to combined ethnic groups (U.S. Census, 2003). Psychologists should therefore take into consideration the role of disability when exploring a client's multicultural identities, as well as reflect on the impacts of other cultural dimensions on the client's experience of disability.

For the purposes of this chapter, *disability* may be considered an evolving concept including "physical, mental, intellectual or sensory impairments that, in the face of various negative attitudes or physical obstacles, may prevent those persons from participating fully in society" (United Nations Enable, 2006, "Defining Disability" section, paragraph 1). Of persons living with functional impairments in the United States, 21.2 million have a condition that limits basic physical activities; 12.4 million have a physical, mental, or emotional condition causing difficulty in learning, remembering, or concentrating; 9.3 million have a sensory disability involving sight or hearing; and 6.8 million have a physical, mental, or emotional condition resulting in difficulty with dressing, bathing, or getting around inside the home. Of those ages 16 and older, 18.2 million live with a condition that makes it difficult to go outside the home to shop or visit a doctor, and 21.3 million live with a condition that affects their ability to work (U.S. Census, 2003). In addition, more than 26% of Americans ages 18 and older meet the diagnostic criteria for mental illness each year (Kessler, Chiu, Demler, Merikangas, & Walters, 2005).

Clearly, mental health professionals need appropriate training and supervision to be competent providers of services to persons with disabilities. However, "most graduates of counseling programs do not possess competencies to provide services to clients with disabilities" (Smart & Smart, 2006, p. 36), and the number of academic classes on disability within psychology programs actually decreased from 1989 to 1999 (Olkin, 2002). Given these limitations, many psychologists may be "unprepared to provide clients with disabilities with professionally and ethically sound services" (APA, 2011a, p. 43) and "most able-bodied therapists are doing cross-cultural counseling with clients with disabilities without requisite training" (Olkin, 2002, p. 132). Although graduate education and training appears to be lacking, some excellent resources exist for practitioners wishing to learn more about disability issues (e.g., Mackelprang & Salsgiver, 1999; Olkin, 1999, 2005), and the Association on Higher Education and Disability (see http://www.ahead. org) has resources for educators related to accommodations. Of particular note, APA's (2011a) recently published *Guidelines for Assessment* provides recommendations to help psychologists "conceptualize and implement more effective, fair, and ethical psychological assessments and interventions with persons with disabilities" (p. 43). These guidelines form the basis of ethical, responsive practice; however, attention to disability issues specifically related to supervision remains lacking in the literature (Falender & Shafranske, 2004). As Olkin (2008) pointed out, most supervisors may not "know what we don't know about disability" (p. 492) and may be "teaching what we are still learning" (p. 493).

Obviously, before supervising in the area of disabilities, supervisors should be able to apply basic supervision theories (e.g., competency based, developmental, evidence based) and techniques (e.g., Bernard & Goodyear, 2009). Given the apparent lack of attention to disabilities in training, supervisors should not expect themselves to be perfect; in fact, taking a stance of humility and openness is essential to developing or enhancing competence. Our hope is that supervisors will become increasingly able to identify their own limitations and to seek further education and training to become competent supervisors with regard to disability issues.

This chapter summarizes competency areas (knowledge, skills, and attitudes/values) necessary to work with persons with disabilities, dispels common misconceptions, and highlights areas of particular concern for supervision. To illustrate these concepts, we present two supervision vignettes, including verbatim dialogue and associated commentary from supervision sessions. Finally, we give recommendations for supervisors, as well as for the field in general.

COMPETENCY

Competencies specific to supervision were defined by Falender et al. (2004), and empirical support for these was provided by Rings, Genuchi, Hall, Angelo, and Erickson Cornish (2009). Also, supervision competencies are included in APA's (2011b) *Revised Benchmark Competencies*. In addition, multicultural supervision competencies have been described by Falender and Shafranske (2004), among others. Although competency ensures that "a professional is capable (i.e., has the knowledge, skills, and values) to practice the profession safely and effectively" (Rodolfa et al., 2005, p. 349), what knowledge, skills, and values and attitudes are necessary for supervisors to possess related to disability issues?

Basic knowledge necessary to supervise disability issues should include understanding and proficient use of the Americans With Disabilities Act (ADA; 1990) and the ADA Amendments Act (2008). Supervisors should be familiar with models specific to conceptualizing ableness and disability (e.g., moral, medical, grief, minority, and wellness models; see, e.g., Jones, 1996; Olkin, 1999; Prilleltensky & Prilleltensky, 2003). Consideration of the unique implications associated with specific types of disability (e.g., congenital/ early onset, traumatic, emergent, psychiatric) is important, as are developmental issues such as dating, sex, pregnancy, childbirth, and parenting (e.g., DeLoach, 1994). Identity issues (e.g., Gliedman & Roth, 1980) should include understanding of multiple minority statuses (e.g., age, ethnicity, gender, immigration, language, race, religion/spirituality, sexual orientation, size, social class) and the overarching themes of oppression and privilege (e.g., Sue & Sue, 2008). Supervisors should also feel comfortable considering ethical issues when working with these populations (e.g., Cornish et al., 2008). Finally, it is important to stay timely with current issues, such as the impact of injury or newly acquired disability on returning soldiers from the Afghan and Iraqi wars.

Skills pertinent to supervising in the area of disability issues must include a focus on the supervisory and therapeutic relationships and parallel process. When one, two, or three members of the triad live with disabilities, balancing appropriate attention (yet not over-attention) on the effect of the disabilities on the relationships is crucial. For instance, a supervisor with a physical disability supervising a student with a learning disability treating a client with an emotional disability presents unique challenges in terms of adequate consideration of what each brings to the triad and how that impacts both the supervision and the therapy. Because of the often highly emotional reactions toward disability issues, it is the responsibility of the supervisor to raise these issues, including transference and countertransference, and to help the supervisee feel safe discussing them (e.g., Borg, 2005). Supervisors must also have the skills to aid the supervisee in adapting assessments, diagnostic tools, interventions, consultations, and referrals to incorporate disability issues. Presenting didactic information and setting appropriate boundaries are also important supervisory skills. Because so few supervisors have been trained with regard to disability issues, ongoing consultation is essential. Finally, attention must be paid to disability disclosure, any needed logistical modifications, and power differentials.

Values and attitudes held by supervisors should include an affirming approach toward disability issues, respect and compassion for everyone in the supervisory triad, and constant vigilance against stereotyping, and over or underestimating abilities. Valuing empowerment, particularly in the face of oppression and discrimination, is necessary. Modeling ongoing self-reflection and self-awareness is also essential.

COMMON MISCONCEPTIONS

Misconceptions with regard to supervision around disability issues are often likely to occur, leading to ruptures and strains in the supervisory relationship, and even potentially negatively affecting the client. One example is focusing solely on disability in the supervision or the treatment when, for instance, the supervisee has other concerns or the client has other presenting problems. Focusing exclusively on disability (similar to diagnostic over-shadowing) without taking into consideration other contextual factors is a disservice to the client. This point was well made in the APA (2011a) *Guidelines for Assessment*: "Above and beyond their *disability* experiences, persons with disabilities have their own *life* experiences and, like everyone else, their own personal characteristics, histories, and life contexts" (p. 43). Therefore, failure to integrate disability into other aspects of identity, or to focus solely on disabilities at the expense of multiple identities, is another common problem. Similarly, it is important to consider how different cultural, religious, and underrepresented groups may attribute different causes or meanings to disability (APA, 2011a).

The assumption of ability, particularly when invisible disabilities are present, or viewing disabilities solely as disabilities rather than unique cultural strengths (e.g., Deaf culture; Williams & Abeles, 2004) are additional misconceptions. In addition to misconceptions, supervisees and supervisors may be ill-prepared or unfamiliar with issues involved with appropriate use of language (e.g., derogatory terms, person-first or disability-first attributions), full range of disabilities, accommodations appropriate in psychological testing and assessment, and issues related to health promotion. Trainees and supervisors may wonder about the limitations imposed by their personal experiences of ableness and disability. For example, is it necessary for a supervisor or supervisee to live with a disability to understand clients with disabilities? Abels (2008) argued that having a disability may or may not help but that it does not lead to automatic competency. Olkin (1999) asserted that able-bodied supervisors need both direct training and supervised clinical experience in conducting therapy with individuals with disabilities before providing supervision on such issues.

Taking a disabilities-affirming approach to supervision has both strengths and weaknesses from the point of view of the supervisee. Most supervisees can be expected to embrace such a model, but as with introducing any type of multiculturalism into supervision, discomfort and even resistance may be anticipated as well. How these reactions are handled by the supervisor impacts the ongoing supervisory relationship as well as the supervisee's comfort in discussing disability issues in the future. The supervisor's initiating proactive discussion about discomfort and resistance as expected parts of learning may decrease the supervisee's anxiety about saying the wrong thing or not knowing enough. The supervisor's judiciously disclosing their own past mistakes in working with disability issues may increase the supervisee's comfort in sharing their own potential mistakes and may enable relaxation of any self-expectations around being perfect when newly dealing with these issues. Finally, the supervisor's use of formative evaluation procedures when the supervisee's learning curve is still steep may enable the supervisee to see incremental growth in this area, as well as reduce fear of a negative summative evaluation being permanently placed in a record while she or he is still actively learning.

SUPERVISION AREAS OF CONCERN

A particular concern with supervision in the area of disabilities is when the developmental level of the supervisee with respect to disability issues exceeds that of the supervisor (e.g., Ancis & Ladany, 2001). Not knowing what we don't know (*metacompetence*; Olkin, 2008) and failing to provide accommodations for any member of the supervisory triad are also concerning. Turning supervision into psychotherapy can be a problem, particularly when authority differentials are ignored or misused. Finally, although this chapter focuses on individual supervision, providing supervision in a group format leads to additional challenges because of the number of participants and the potential impact of group process issues.

Two supervision vignettes follow, illustrating how challenges associated with disability issues can be handled. As with any multicultural supervisory context, each relationship and interaction bears unique features. Therefore, these examples are meant to provide a rough framework and stimulus for discussion, rather than a script.

Supervision Vignette 1: Disability Discrimination

Disability issues are often made more complicated by being interwoven with one another. The following is an excerpt from a point in an ongoing supervisory process when two disability issues arise simultaneously. In this example, the client, a Caucasian woman in her early 20s with a chronic endocrine disease and depressive symptoms shares a story of probable discrimination with the supervisee, a Latina female clinical psychology doctoral student in her late 20s not living with a disability. The conversation is between the supervisee and her supervisor, a Caucasian woman in her early 50s not living with a disability, during a practicum in a community mental health center. The supervision pair had previously discussed multicultural issues within a trusting and supportive relationship but had not specifically considered disability issues with this client. The supervisee had identified a likely injustice immediately upon hearing it, but she did not label it as such with the client because she was not confident in her appraisal of the situation and she thought the client did not consider herself disabled. The incident in question was the client's experience of being asked by a professor to repeat a class after missing 1 week out of the semester because she had been in the hospital.

The client had immediately obliged, seemingly without thought of accommodations she could have requested instead. The transcript begins with the supervisee soliciting her supervisor's expertise and expressing her confusion about how to proceed. The supervisor, aware of the emerging parallel process, models empowerment for the supervisee before explicitly discussing it and then demonstrating use of consultation.

Supervisee: Sitting there, it was so hard for me to hear how she'd been treated. It just screamed of the type of discrimination and unfairness that I know people with disabilities face.

Supervisor: Wow, it sounds like it was a tough session for you. [The supervisor validates the supervisee's emotions and notes internally that the supervisee may have had her own experiences with discrimination based on her ethnicity.]

Supervisee: Yeah, it was. I was pretty mad about what had happened to her. But then I started second-guessing myself. I mean, if she didn't feel discriminated against, was she? Am I making too much of it?

Supervisor: Good questions. What do you think? [The supervisor begins modeling empowerment for the supervisee by soliciting her ideas.]

Supervisee: Well, I'm just thinking about how much training I've had about multicultural therapy. On one hand, I feel like I'm attuned to issues that may come up for clients in their lives or in the therapy room. But on the other hand, I worry that I may see things that aren't actually there. What if I apply generalizations where they don't actually fit? Or what if my judgment is being clouded by my excitement to use my knowledge?

Supervisor: It seems like you've already spent a lot of time thinking about this case.

Supervisee: Yes, I have. I really want to do the right thing. But I'm not sure what that is. Do you think I should bring up the possibility of discrimination with her?

Supervisor: It seems like there's another issue that needs to be considered before you make that decision. Your client doesn't consider herself disabled, correct? [The supervisor helps the supervisee prioritize the disability issues present (i.e., possible discrimination and disability identity), safeguarding client-centered therapy.]

Supervisee: Well, I'm not entirely sure. She's never specifically said either way. However, I assume that she doesn't, based on the way she talks about her disease.

Supervisor:	So that impacts how you proceed, right?
Supervisee:	Yes, it certainly does. I don't want her to be overwhelmed by me saying, "Hey, you're disabled, AND it sounds like you've been discriminated against." That might be a lot to take in all at once.
Supervisor:	I agree. So how do you think you might present all of this to her? Actually, backing up even further, *do* you think you should present all or part of this to her? [The supervisor reminds the supervisee that the presence of discrimination does not mandate an intervention, as much as the supervisee might wish to protect her client.]
Supervisee:	I definitely feel like I need to bring it up. I feel like it's my responsibility as her therapist to make sure she knows she has rights and that they might have been violated. I actually think it might be validating for her to hear that her experience was as wrong as it felt to her.
Supervisor:	OK.
Supervisee:	So, I guess what I'm thinking is that I need to have a specific conversation with her about the fact that her disease is covered under the Americans With Disabilities Act. Maybe that's how I could bring both issues up with her. I could ask whether she knows that and go from there.
Supervisor:	What if she doesn't even know what the Americans With Disabilities Act is? [The supervisor points out that the client's disability knowledge may be lacking, and the supervisee may be required to provide some education.]
Supervisee:	Hmmm . . . I hadn't considered that. Well, I will just have to take it slowly and educate her along the way.
Supervisor:	Depending on how much she knows, it might be a lot for her to take in. You already mentioned that, when we started talking about this. So what do you think you want to do about that? [The supervisor reminds the supervisee to attend to the client's disability identity and knowledge.]
Supervisee:	I think it will be really important to be client-centered in the way I have this conversation with her. I'll need to be attuned to how she's receiving the information and be prepared to shift my approach accordingly.
Supervisor:	I agree, and what about this conversation might feel similar to the experience she recently had. [The supervisor

raises the issue of parallel process in the therapy. Aware of a potential parallel process in the supervision also, the supervisor models empowerment over disenfranchisement throughout the discussion.]

Supervisee: Hmmm . . . I'm not really sure what you mean.

Supervisor: Well, she just had an experience where she was told what to do, without being given any choice, and it had everything to do with her disease. You're about to tell her that her disease is covered by the Americans With Disabilities Act and that she was likely a victim of discrimination. Do you see any room for parallel process? [Even basic clinical concepts may appear complicated in the presence of disability issues, so the supervisor willingly provides clarification.]

Supervisee: Now that you put it that way, yeah! She might feel bossed around by me or disempowered.

Supervisor: Exactly. So what could you do about that? [The supervisor continues modeling empowerment.]

Supervisee: I could name her as the expert on her disease and present the information like she can choose to do with it what she wishes. She can put energy into deciding whether she feels disabled or not. She can pursue the discrimination or not. It's up to her.

Supervisor: You might even be able to use those exact words with her. To your second point, what if she wants to pursue the discrimination? [Suggesting that the using phrases already rehearsed in supervision might increase the supervisee's comfort with the anticipated conversation.]

Supervisee: I have no idea. I've never done that before.

Supervisor: Neither have I, actually. So we'll be learning about that together. [The supervisor models acknowledging limitations.] I think we should look into it before you meet with her, so you can be prepared with the information, in case she wants it. You could start with www.ada.gov, and I have a colleague who has a disability who also might be able to enlighten us. [The supervisor models use of written and in-person consultation.] He's published on disability issues, and I've talked with him about them before, so I know he's comfortable serving as an expert in this area. [The supervisor models accessing experts who are clearly willing to serve this purpose, instead of drafting someone with a disability into the role without their consent.] Could I introduce the two of you? [The supervisor provides the student with the opportunity to increase her comfort with discrimination discussions.]

Supervisee: Sure, that sounds great. I'll do the Internet research right away, and you can let me know the plan for us talking with your colleague.

In this supervision session, the supervisee is empowered to develop her own plan for discussing the client's disability status and possible experience of discrimination, much like the empowerment the supervisor hopes the client will feel during the upcoming therapy session with the supervisee. The supervisor models this potential parallel process before explicitly discussing its relevance to the client's situation with the supervisee. The supervisor ensures that the supervisee considers the client's experience of being viewed by her therapist as a person with a disability, especially because the client may not even consider herself a person with a disability. The supervisor also raises the importance of consultation, using both written materials and colleague collaboration. Consultation in this case holds a double purpose. First, the student is encouraged to increase her knowledge about the disability issue that came up in therapy. Second, the student is given the opportunity to have her attitude about the disability issue that came up in therapy modified through experiential activities. Specifically, researching written materials on discrimination could increase the student's empathy for the process of responding to such an incident, and talking with an individual who has a disability could improve the student's comfort with discussions of discrimination. It is important that the supervisor made clear the colleague's willingness to serve as an expert, thereby not perpetuating a reluctant-spokesperson effect. Supervisory interactions like this enable supervisees to learn the process of sorting out disability issues instead of being handed a prescriptive plan.

Further considerations for this supervision might include additional information or clarification from the supervisee on whether the client shared with her professor that her chronic illness led to missing class, and if she did, whether she might have invoked the ADA and/or whether the professor should have been knowledgeable about that and initiated a discussion accordingly. It would also have been useful for the supervisor to give further guidance about when clients may or may not consider themselves to be living with a disability or when there are differing attributions about the existence of a disability. Further, the cultural similarities and differences between the supervision triad (supervisor–supervisee–client) would bear consideration, particularly related to the impacts of multiple cultural identities.

Supervision Vignette 2: Supervision or Therapy?

Although it is always essential for a supervisor to provide supervision and not psychotherapy when countertransference threatens to disrupt the supervisee–client relationship, this is particularly critical when disability issues are present. However, toeing this invisible line can be extremely difficult. In this excerpt, the client is a Caucasian man in his early 30s with hypochondriasis and anxious symptoms, and the supervisee is a Caucasian man clinical psychology doctoral intern in his early 20s who sustained a spinal cord injury in childhood and walks using forearm crutches. The client and supervisee have been engaged in weekly therapy at a Veterans Affairs outpatient mental health clinic for several months with the goal of reducing the client's anxiety about his health. The supervisor, an African American man in his early 40s not living with a disability, and supervisee have discussed the supervisee's disability before, but not in the context of therapy with this particular client. The transcript begins with the supervisee venting his frustration about the client's limited progress since starting therapy. Although the supervisor immediately thinks the supervisee's attitudes about his own disability are impacting his frustration with the client, the supervisor waits to raise this until he hears it in the content of the supervisee's presentation.

> *Supervisee:* I've spent hours and hours with this client, and he's in exactly the same place as when we started. It feels like all he does is complain; if it's not his headaches potentially indicating a tumor, it's his chest pain likely from a serious heart condition. He just doesn't quit. At first I had no trouble empathizing with him, but it's getting harder. Why can't he see that he *has* his health, instead of constantly looking for it?

> *Supervisor:* I really appreciate your honesty. While I think it's important that we discuss your treatment planning and interventions, I also think we need to talk about this significant reaction you're having to him. What do you think? [Although the supervisor suspects that the supervisee may be envious that the client "*has* his good health," he does not make this interpretation. He wants it confirmed in what the supervisee says, first.]

> *Supervisee:* Well, I'm not sure what more there is to say. I'm frustrated. That's pretty much it. I see him again tomorrow, and I really want to make sure I shouldn't be doing things differently with him.

> *Supervisor:* Hmmm . . . I see your point. But regardless of your treatment plan and interventions, do you think you might get

too annoyed with him to listen? It sounds like he's pretty difficult to be with right now.

Supervisee: Yeah, he is. I'd like to think I could control my emotions with him, but it couldn't hurt to talk about it, I guess.

Supervisor: OK, so when's the last time you felt this way about a client?

Supervisee: Hmmm . . . that's a good question. I can't actually think of any time I've felt this way before. It's unlike me to feel so frustrated. Usually I'm pretty understanding, regardless of what clients bring into the room.

Supervisor: Interesting; what feels different about how things are going with this client? [Aware of the potential for the supervision to shift toward therapy, the supervisor focuses on the supervisee–client interaction—instead of the intrapsychic processes of the supervisee.]

Supervisee: Well, I've never seen a client with hypochondriasis before. I mean, I've read a lot about it, but it's different to be treating someone with this diagnosis.

Supervisor: "Different" how?

Supervisee: Different in that the main focus of our sessions is him talking about diseases he doesn't have. When he talks about his anxiety about his symptoms, I have no problem empathizing. But I seem to lose him when he starts talking about the diseases he might have. It's like he's borrowing trouble. I almost get the feeling that he would be relieved if he was diagnosed with one of the diseases, that it would be validating in some way. How many people want to be sick? It seems like a pretty unusual problem to have. Most people who are actually sick would be envious of a guy like him, a guy with a clean bill of health.

Supervisor: It sounds like you've really pinpointed where the empathic rupture occurs. You've got him at his symptoms, and you've lost him at his feared diseases. [Although the supervisor wonders if "most people" in the supervisee's comment actually referred to the supervisee, he did not pursue it. He is still not sure that the supervisee's disability is impacting the countertransference, and he does not want the supervision to become psychotherapy to explore that possibility.]

Supervisee: Exactly. You know, I feel a little awkward bringing this up, but I've been thinking about how I'm not sick but how I am disabled. It's not the same thing, but somehow it feels relevant. I feel with him similarly to how I feel when someone illegally parks in a handicap parking space.

Supervisor: I'm glad you brought this up. Before you did, I was wondering about it myself. Your reaction seems totally understandable, and I appreciate you being so self-aware and honest with me about it. [The supervisor validates the supervisee's experience and makes clear that it is safe to discuss disability issues.]

Supervisee: No problem. I'm glad you don't think I'm way off base.

Supervisor: Not at all. I feel like there's a lot we could talk about here, but I'm very aware of our context, which is supervision and not therapy. Therefore, the way I've handled this with other supervisees who've struggled with similar issues is to really focus on the way the therapy, including the therapeutic alliance, is being affected or might be affected. How does that sound to you? [The supervisor establishes a clear supervision boundary and offers a suggestion for how the countertransference might be handled within this framework. Additionally, the supervisor normalizes the supervisee's experience and, at the same time, reminds the supervisee that he has experience supervising individuals with disabilities.]

Supervisee: That sounds great.

Supervisor: So as you feel yourself getting frustrated, like when you see someone in a handicap parking spot who shouldn't be there, do you notice anything changing about the therapy? [The supervisor uses the supervisee's words and briefly refers to the countertransference before structuring the discussion with a question.]

Supervisee: Hmmm . . . I haven't really thought about that. I guess I try to move things along, not changing the subject, but pushing us forward on the subject.

Supervisor: Can you give me an example?

Supervisee: Sure. Last session, he was talking about how much time he spends doing Internet research on his symptoms, trying to figure out which disease he has. He went on and on about all of the websites he uses, and when he was finished, all I could think to do was to point out how positive it was that he hadn't found anything, that it might be a good sign. I don't think what I said was bad, but I think he felt cut off. He wanted to talk more about his search, and I wanted us to move on from the search.

Supervisor: Wow, great self-observation! So what might you do differently next time something like this happens? [The supervisor emphasizes the value of the supervisee's insight.]

Supervisee: Maybe I'll really attend to where the client is and make sure I stay there. When I feel an inkling of frustration, I'll make note of it and hyperfocus on the client's agenda.

Supervisor: Sounds like a reasonable plan. Do you think it could ever be useful for you to share your frustration with the client? [The supervisor suggests that the countertransference could be helpful, not just harmful. However, as this self-disclosure is tied to the supervisee's disability, the supervisor gives full decision-making power to the supervisee.]

Supervisee: Wow, probably not. I never talk about anything having to do with my disability with my clients, unless they directly ask, of course.

Supervisor: It sounds like you've sorted out what's best for you in terms of self-disclosure about your disability, and there's really not a right or wrong answer. I just wanted to make sure you're thinking about it, and to let you know that we can discuss it further if you think it would be helpful. [The supervisor shows respect for the supervisee's decision about self-disclosure but leaves an opening for future discussion.]

Supervisee: OK, good to know. I'll keep that in mind.

During this supervision session, the supervisor is faced with the challenging dilemma of how to support the supervisee without shifting from supervision to therapy. Although the supervisor considers early on that that supervisee's disability is impacting his countertransference, the supervisor waits to hear this from the supervisee. The supervisor remains focused on the therapeutic interaction instead of the supervisee's intrapsychic processes, both before and after the supervisee raises the relevance of his disability. The supervisor creates an affirming supervision environment by validating and normalizing the supervisee's reaction, and then the supervisor proposes a plan for assuring that their discussion stays within the parameters of supervision and not therapy. The supervisor supports the supervisee in creating a plan for addressing the countertransference during therapy and suggests that it can even be used therapeutically. Here, the supervisor may also be drawing on his experiences as an African American male and his consequent empathic abilities. As self-disclosure of this countertransference is directly linked with the supervisee's disability, the supervisor emphasizes the student's right to self-disclose or not, leaving open the possibility of future discussion. If nothing else, a supervision interaction like this hopefully leaves a student with the impression that discussion of disability issues in supervision is valuable and that they potentially have both positive and negative implications for a therapeutic process.

Additionally, it could be useful for the supervisor to tease out the countertransference/envy of the supervisee with a disability toward the presumably "healthy" client. It might also be useful to normalize the response of the supervisee further in that any therapist might be triggered, irritated, or annoyed by the hypochondriac client's obsessive self-focus (including an able-bodied therapist). In other words, the supervisee's reaction might be viewed as fairly typical, without invoking a deficit comparison, which could be seen as pathologizing. The supervisor correctly lets the supervisee choose if, when, and how to share his frustration with the client, but it is important to add that this does not require the therapist to reveal his own disability or personal comparison. It could have been refreshing for the supervisor to entertain the possibility that the supervisee's reaction had nothing to do with his disability and to make more of an effort to separate the total therapist from a single label of disability.

SUMMARY AND RECOMMENDATIONS

The prevalence of disabilities ensures that mental health professionals will have the opportunity to work with clients with disabilities or with clients secondarily impacted by disabilities, and this phenomenon is only expected to increase as the population ages. Therefore, mental health professionals must be prepared not only to provide treatment for these individuals but also to offer supervision to the new generations of mental health professionals on the relevant issues. It is unfortunate that training on disability competence is currently lacking (Olkin, 2002), as is its presence in the professional literature (Falender & Shafranske, 2004) and body of empirical research; this deficit is even more pronounced for supervision.

Supervision competencies in the area of disability include knowledge of the ADA and ADA Amendments Act, models of ableness, specific types of disability, developmental and identity issues, multiple minority statuses and associated oppression, unique ethical considerations, and relevant current events. Additionally, required supervisory skills include focusing on relationships within the supervisory triad and parallel process, appropriately attending (not over-attending) to disability, creating a safe environment for supervisees to discuss their emotional reactions, supporting the supervisee in making necessary adaptations to clinical tools, presenting didactic information, setting boundaries, exploring disclosure issues, using consultation, arranging for logistical accommodations, and addressing power differentials. Finally, essential supervisory values and attitudes include an affirming approach toward disability issues, respect and compassion for the members of the supervisory triad, vigilance against prejudice, empowering in the face of oppression, and valuing of self-awareness.

There is a tremendous risk of misconceptions about disability negatively affecting the supervisory process. This can be ameliorated through heightened awareness of the most common misperceptions, which include the need to have a disability to provide disability supervision, the exemption of supervisors with disabilities from disability training, the assumption of ability, the failure to consider multiple identities, and equating disabilities solely with deficits.

Certain supervisory situations in the presence of disability issues require additional caution before proceeding. These include the developmental level of the supervisee exceeding that of the supervisor, a supervisor's ignorance of his or her own blind spots, failure to provide necessary accommodations for any member of the supervisory triad, and tendencies toward turning supervision into therapy. In addition, group supervision brings other challenges. Again, consultation should be considered to ensure a proper course of action.

Providing supervision in the presence of disability issues is a privilege that should not be undertaken casually. It is recommended that disability-focused training and clinical supervision be sought to increase knowledge, improve skills, and hone values and attitudes. Although this should occur regardless of disability status, potential supervisors who are able-bodied would also benefit from increased exposure to the disability community to address misconceptions they may hold. Throughout the supervision process, challenges should merit additional consultation with an expert. As with any multicultural supervisory framework, the extra effort expended pales in comparison with the rewards of engaging in the process.

REFERENCES

Abels, A. (2008). Putting disability ethics into practice. *Professional Psychology, Research and Practice, 39*, 495–497.

Alley, D. E., & Chang, V. W. (2007). The changing relationship of obesity and disability, 1988–2004. *JAMA, 298*, 2020–2027. doi:10.1001/jama.298.17.2020

American Psychological Association. (2011a). *Guidelines for assessment of and intervention with persons with disabilities*. Retrieved from http://www.apa.org/pi/disability/resources/assessment-disabilities.aspx

American Psychological Association. (2011b). *Revised benchmarks competencies*. Retrieved from http://apa.org/ed/graduate/benchmarks-evaluation-system.aspx

Americans With Disabilities Act. (1990). Retrieved from: http://www.ada.gov/

Americans With Disabilities Act Amendments Act of 2008. Retrieved from http://www.ada.gov/

Ancis, J. R., & Ladany, N. (2001). A multicultural framework for counselor supervision. In L. J. Bradley & N. Ladany (Eds.), *Counselor supervision: Principles, process, and practice* (3rd ed., pp. 63–90). Philadelphia, PA: Brunner-Routledge.

Bernard, J. M., & Goodyear, R. K. (2009). *Fundamentals of clinical supervision* (4th ed.). Boston, MA: Pearson Education.

Borg, M. B. (2005). "Superblind": Supervising a blind therapist with a blind analysand in a community mental health setting. *Psychoanalytic Psychology, 22,* 32–48. doi:10.1037/0736-9735.22.1.32

Cornish, J. A. E., Gorgens, K. A., & Monson, S. P. (2008). Toward ethical practice with people who have disabilities. *Professional Psychology: Research and Practice, 39,* 488–497. doi:10.1037/a0013092

DeLoach, C. (1994). Attitudes toward disability: Impact on sexual development and forging of intimate relationships. *Journal of Applied Rehabilitation Counseling, 25,* 18–25.

Falender, C. A., Cornish, J. A. E., Goodyear, R., Hatcher, R., Kaslow, N. J., Leventhal, G., . . . Grus, C. (2004). Defining competencies in psychology supervision: A consensus statement. *Journal of Clinical Psychology, 60,* 771–785. doi:10.1002/jclp.20013

Falender, C. A., & Shafranske, E. P. (2004). *Clinical supervision: A competency-based approach.* Washington, DC: American Psychological Association.

Gliedman, J., & Roth, W. (1980). *The unexpected minority: Handicapped children in America.* New York, NY: Harcourt Brace Jovanovich. doi:10.1097/00004356-198012000-00030

Jones, S. R. (1996). Toward inclusive theory: Disability as social construction. *NASPA Journal, 33,* 347–352.

Kessler, R. C., Chiu, W. T., Demler, O., Merikangas, K. R. & Walters, E. E. (2005). Prevalence, severity, and comorbidity of 12-month DSM–IV disorders in the National Comorbidity Survey Replication (NCS-R). *Archives of General Psychiatry, 62,* 617–627. doi:10.1001/archpsyc.62.6.617

Mackelprang, R., & Salsgiver, R. (1999). *Disability: A diversity model approach in human service practice.* Belmont, CA: Brooks/Cole.

Olkin, R. (1999). *What psychotherapists should know about disability.* New York, NY: Guilford Press.

Olkin, R. (2002). Could you hold the door for me? Including disability in diversity. *Cultural Diversity & Ethnic Minority Psychology, 8,* 130–137. doi:10.1037/1099-9809.8.2.130

Olkin, R. (2005). *Disability-affirmative therapy: A beginner's guide* [Video]. (Available from Emicrotraining.com)

Olkin, R. (2008). Social warrior or unwitting bigot? *Professional Psychology: Research and Practice, 39,* 492–493.

Palombi, B. (2008). Focus on disability: It's about time. *Professional Psychology: Research and Practice, 39,* 494–495.

Prilleltensky, I., & Prilleltensky, O. (2003). Synergies for wellness and liberation in counseling psychology. *The Counseling Psychologist, 31,* 273–281. doi:10.1177/0011000003031003002

Rings, J. A., Genuchi, M. C., Hall, M. D., Angelo, M. A. & Erickson Cornish, J. A. (2009). Is there consensus among predoctoral internship training directors regarding clinical supervision competencies? A descriptive analysis. *Training and Education in Professional Psychology, 3,* 140–147. doi:10.1037/a0015054

Rodolfa, E., Bent, R., Eisman, E., Nelson, P., Rehm, L., & Ritchie, P. (2005). A cube model for competency development: Implications for psychology educators and regulators. *Professional Psychology: Research and Practice, 36,* 347–354. doi:10.1037/0735-7028.36.4.347

Smart, J. F., & Smart, D. W. (2006). Models of disability: Implications for the counseling profession. *Journal of Counseling & Development, 84,* 29–40. doi:10.1002/j.1556-6678.2006.tb00377.x

Sue, D. W., & Sue, D. (2008). *Counseling the culturally diverse: Theory and practice* (5th ed.). Hoboken, NJ: Wiley.

United Nations Enable. (2006, December 13). *Convention on the rights of persons with disabilities.* Retrieved from http://www.un.org/disabilities/default.asp?id=223

U.S. Census. (2003). *Disability status: 2000.* Retrieved November 5, 2007, from http://www.census.gov/prod/2003pubs/c2kbr-17.pdf

Williams, C. R., & Abeles, N. (2004). Issues and implications of deaf culture in therapy. *Professional Psychology: Research and Practice, 35,* 643–648. doi:10.1037/0735-7028.35.6.643

8

ADDRESSING RELIGIOUSNESS AND SPIRITUALITY AS CLINICALLY RELEVANT CULTURAL FEATURES IN SUPERVISION

EDWARD P. SHAFRANSKE

Among the cultural identities that shape personal experience, religion and spirituality (R/S) stand out as particularly important. Integral to the worldviews or global meanings people create, R/S informs daily strivings and interpretations of events (Park, 2005; Park, Edmondson, & Hale-Smith, 2013); involves ways of thinking that influence beliefs, values, attitudes, morals, and standards for behavior; often is a source of comfort in times of distress and hardship (Gall & Guirguis-Younger, 2013; Pargament, 1997); and offers a possible spectrum of solutions to life's problems. For many (if not most) people, R/S is essential to their lives and contributes significantly to their sense of purpose, life satisfaction and health, as well as serves as a potent source of cultural identity, affiliation, and loyalty. It is striking, therefore, that R/S, although covered to some extent in graduate education (Schafer, Handal, Brawer, & Ubinger, 2011), is so often neglected (Shafranske & Cummings,

http://dx.doi.org/10.1037/14370-008
Multiculturalism and Diversity in Clinical Supervision: A Competency-Based Approach, C. A. Falender, E. P. Shafranske, and C. J. Falicov (Editors)

2013). Hathaway (2013) concluded that most graduate training contexts for professional psychologists are not providing systematic training aimed to prepare clinicians to practice competently at an entry level when encountering religious and spiritual issues. In light of this situation, supervisors may find it necessary not only to supervise specific R/S issues emergent in treatment but also to introduce the clinical relevance of R/S more generally. This chapter discusses ethics and the knowledge, skills, and attitudes/values that inform a culturally sensitive and competency-based approach to address R/S in clinical supervision.

THE ETHICAL IMPERATIVE

Taking into consideration the religious and spiritual backgrounds of clients is not only clinically useful, it is ethically required. The American Psychological Association (APA; 2010), consistent with other professional mental health organizations (e.g., American Counseling Association, 2005; American Psychiatric Association, 1989), requires in its code of conduct awareness and respect for

> cultural, individual and role differences, including those based on . . . religion . . . and [requires psychologists to] consider these factors when working with members of such groups [and to] try to eliminate the effect on their work of biases based on those factors. (p. 1063)

Complementing this policy, APA adopted in 2008 a resolution that acknowledges the roles of R/S and contemporary psychology in addressing the human condition and concluded that R/S "can promote beliefs, attitudes, values, and behaviors that can dramatically impact human life in ways that are either enhancing or diminishing of the well-being of individuals or groups." The resolution further

> encourages all psychologists to act to eliminate discrimination based on or derived from religion and spirituality . . . [and] encourages actions that promote religious and spiritual tolerance, liberty, and respect, in all arenas in which psychologists work and practice, and in society at large.

These policies, as well as the principles put forth in APA's (2002) *Guidelines for Multicultural Education, Training, Research, Practice, and Organizational Change for Psychologists*, provide a foundation on which R/S may be addressed in psychological treatment and clinical supervision.

Supervisors play a crucial role in modeling attention to R/S as clinically relevant, guiding processes aimed to enhance supervisee self-awareness and in encouraging appropriate inquiry and integration of R/S in treatment. Adopting an *intentional orientation* (Shafranske, 2013) ensures that supervision (and psychological treatment) adequately addresses the contributions of R/S to the client's worldview and offers a comprehensive and holistic approach to psychological practice attuned to the R/S values and preferences of clients (Shafranske & Sperry, 2005).

ATTITUDES AND VALUES

To understand the client, particularly with respect to his or her R/S beliefs, attributions, and practices, supervisees and supervisors must be fully committed to a stance of respect and openness. Taking such a stance does not require explicit or tacit agreement with the client's spiritual perspectives; rather, it requires respect for the client's right to hold his or her own beliefs and genuine interest in understanding another's perspective. Supervision provides the primary means by which trainees are supported in their attempts to grasp the ways in which clients make sense of their lives and learn how to assess the psychological impacts of R/S on mental health and coping. Somewhat paradoxically, this begins with a focus on the supervisee rather than on the client. Trainees must first develop an awareness of the beliefs, assumptions, and biases that inform their stance towards R/S (Leach, Aten, Boyer, Strain, & Bradshaw, 2010; Wiggins, 2009). Such a task is not easy because the worldviews, or "world hypotheses," we hold are "so intimate and pervasive," it is difficult to look at them "from a distance" (Pepper, 1942/1972, p. 2). This introspective process is an important and necessary first step because failure to acknowledge one's ontological, existential, or faith commitments forecloses the ability to see how such personal beliefs affect one's understanding of the client's worldview and the meanings associated with his or her psychological difficulties.

This is also important given the likely differences in personal faith commitments and R/S practices of most supervisees (and their supervisors) and the clients they serve. Survey research has consistently found that psychologists are in many ways less religious than most Americans; for example, less than half of psychologists report religion to be "very important" or "fairly important" compared with almost 90% in U.S. polls conducted by Gallup (Shafranske & Cummings, 2013). Such differences may affect a supervisee's (and supervisor's) appreciation of the importance of R/S for a client. In addition to personal preferences, trainees will likely be influenced by the dominant values and epistemological perspectives held within the profession. An argument can be made that psychology as a discipline is neither neutral nor absent values; rather, it is inherently, a value-laden enterprise. For example, personality theories are embedded with assumptions about human nature, the good life, and health (Yarhouse & Johnson, 2013), and psychotherapies have underlying metaphysical systems and epistemological foundations.[1] Psychology frames its truth claims under the mantle of empiricism; however, some critics have argued that there is pervasive implicit bias against theism in psychology (Slife & Reber, 2009).

On a related note, psychologists are the least religious among the professorate (e.g., 50% do not believe in God), which would seemingly influence the value they place on R/S in their professional, as well as personal, lives. The intellectual and academic climate in which R/S is presented to psychology graduate students may minimize the importance religious faith or spirituality holds for most people and limit exposure to the scientific underpinnings found in the psychological study of R/S (L. J. Miller, 2012; Pargament, Exline, & Jones, 2013; Pargament, Mahoney, & Shafranske, 2013). Nevertheless, there appears to be support among clinical and counseling psychologists for inclusion of R/S in multicultural training (Crook-Lyon et al., 2012), and more than 75% of respondents to a survey of APA leaders, particularly those with a clinical focus, agreed that R/S are important to consider when providing professional services (McMinn, Hathaway, Woods, & Snow, 2009). These observations point to some sources of influence that likely affect the supervisee's worldview and consequently impact consideration of client R/S.

Clinical supervision provides a context for thoughtful reflection on the beliefs and assumptions, derived from personal and professional sources, that influence appreciation of the contributions of R/S to the client's worldview. The simple act of drawing attention to R/S models sensitivity to this dimension of multicultural identity and underscores that cultural diversity includes diversity of thought and belief (i.e., metaphysics and epistemology) as well as values and decision making (i.e., ethics; Vargas, personal communication). Supervisors can further enhance supervisee development by implementing the following recommendations:

1. Explicitly include in the supervision contract identification of R/S as one of the identities and influences to be considered in the development of multicultural competence.
2. Include in trainee orientation activities or didactic training individual reflection and group discussion of R/S as a multicultural feature, including what Bartoli (2007) referred to as "conceptual inheritance," using prompts such as those listed below.
   a. In what ways, if at all, were the roles of R/S in mental health or in clinical practice discussed in your graduate program or in previous clinical training?

[1]The author appreciates comments offered by Luis Vargas, PhD, regarding the philosophical and metaphysical underpinnings of psychology and R/S, which informed this discussion.

b. When R/S was discussed, what was the context and with what tone? Were examples of R/S chosen that in general presented positive, negative, or neutral impacts on mental health?

c. Does psychology or science provide the best answers to questions regarding human meaning or fulfillment? In general, what messages did you receive regarding the relevance of R/S in clinical practice?

d. Reflect on your own current personal beliefs about the nature and purpose of human life and reflect on the influence of R/S over your life span. How do your own views of R/S reflect the general ways you look at problems and solutions to them (increasing awareness of the therapist's own therapist's worldview)? Note: Due to the highly personal nature of an activity, any invitation to disclose must be voluntary and noncoercive and a climate of respect must be established. The use of spiritual and religious genograms and ecomaps (Hodge, 2013) are effective tools for self-reflection.

e. Reflect on your stance toward R/S. Would you characterize your perspective as rejectionist (R/S as illusion and offers limited, no, or negative value), exclusivist (R/S reflects reality, although only within the limits of the exclusivist's worldview), constructivist (R/S is not related to absolute reality but rather reflects the ability of persons to construct meaning within a given sociocultural context), or pluralist (recognizes the existence of a transcendent reality reflected in R/S traditions) (adapted from Zinnbauer & Pargament, 2000), or in what other way might you characterize your stance? What reactions have you had when working with a client who holds a different orientation to R/S? How did you address those reactions personally and in supervision? Do you think that the client was aware of the differences between his or her worldview and your R/S beliefs? What impact did R/S differences have on the therapeutic relationship and on treatment?

3. Inquire about the R/S backgrounds of clients presented in supervision, encourage reflection and discussion of the supervisee's personal and professional reactions to the client's R/S beliefs, affiliations, and practices. Discussion of R/S and its interwoven role in relationship to what might be viewed as more secular manifestations of the presenting problems and solutions to them promotes awareness of the relationship between R/S and other cultural identities rather than as an isolated feature of

identity. Such inquiry should be directed to the clinical issues presented in the case.

4. Model and encourage supervisees to draw on the resources of the psychology of R/S (Note: Clinical resources are presented in the References section), and consider appropriate consultation with and referral to R/S professionals (e.g., chaplains, ministers, rabbis, priests, imams).

5. Include considerations of R/S when discussing clinical issues; for example, present disclosure of personal religious beliefs as a possible boundary crossing when discussing ethics or discuss the use of positive religious coping when assessing client strengths.

In addition to establishing R/S as an area of clinical and supervisory interest, supervisors have the responsibility to ensure that supervisees are demonstrating appropriate respect for client autonomy and do not impose their personal R/S beliefs, values and assumptions (including non-belief or agnosticism) on the client. Pargament (2007) identified types of therapist attitudes and behaviors that pose not only problems, but are dangerous to client welfare. Spiritual intolerance, which takes the forms of rejectionism and exclusivism, is likely to create a misalliance and constitute serious boundary problems on the part of the clinician. Blatant, antagonistic statements towards a client's beliefs constitute serious lapses of judgment, professionalism, and ethics and are probably quite rare (particularly since the supervisee's conduct is being monitored). However, more subtle forms of rejectionism, such as challenging (rather than inquiring about) religious truth claims, e.g., "Well, do you have any proof that God really exists?" or holding a prima facie assumption that R/S leads to neurotic guilt, also may damage the alliance and foreclose any clinically meaningful consideration of R/S in treatment. Spiritual exclusivism reflects the clinician's assumption that "there is one single absolute truth and a best way to approach it" (Pargament, 2007, p. 188). A supervisee holding such an absolutist perspective may violate a critical professional boundary and impose their personal beliefs by subtly disputing, disregarding or attempting to influence the client. Such behavior is damaging and unethical. Although challenges may occur when supervisees work with clients whose R/S beliefs and practices differ from their own, complex personal, professional, ethical, and even constitutional issues arise when a supervisee holds an R/S faith commitment, which he or she believes precludes providing services to particular clients, affirming particular lifestyles, or treating particular conditions (Behnke, 2012; Forrest, 2012).[2] Supervisors hold first responsibility to the

---

[2]In addition to ethical and professional issues, political initiatives and legislation involving "conscience laws" add to the complexity of preparing trainees to develop competence in providing psychological services to all clients while respecting the trainee's R/S beliefs and values.

client and must ensure that appropriate care is provided as well as protect the client from discrimination; at the same time, supervisees must develop competence to serve diverse clients and to learn how to professionally manage tensions that ensue from differences between personal beliefs and values and professional values and ethics. Central to this issue is mutual respect and tolerance for the supervisee's and client's beliefs and values in the context of assuring client welfare, and the development of supervisee clinical competence, which includes "dynamic worldview inclusivity" (Bieschke & Mintz, 2012) and upholds the values of the profession.

Supervision addressing the R/S dimension of professional practice is founded on respect and tolerance and is facilitated by providing a context for supervisees to examine the ways in which their own beliefs and values influence their understanding of the client. Further, trainees learn to manage the inevitable tensions that arise when differences in worldviews exist and their personal reactions result in misalliances or impair the ability to appropriately address the role of religion or spirituality in the client's difficulties or as resources to enhance their functioning.

KNOWLEDGE

Supervision provides a context in which to incorporate the applied psychology of R/S in clinical practice. In this section, we highlight domains of knowledge that are important when considering R/S as a multicultural factor that influences mental health and treatment; we also provide recommendations for supervision practice. Pargament (2007) identified spiritual illiteracy to be a common problem, given the limited exposure to R/S provided in graduate psychology training; for example, in a survey of directors of clinical training in the United States and Canada, only 13% reported that they offered a course in R/S (Brawer, Handal, Fabricatore, Roberts, & Wajda-Johnson, 2002). Our discussion begins with what is meant by R/S.

Religion and Spirituality

A consensus does not exist among scholars or the public as to precise meanings of R/S, rather a plurality of perspectives appears (Hill et al., 2000; Zinnbauer & Pargament, 2005; Zinnbauer et al., 1997). However, studies have found that people differentiate religion and spirituality; the term *religion* is commonly associated with institution-based affiliation, involving predefined beliefs and rituals, and *spirituality* connotes an individualized, experientially-based approach. Setting the definitional issue aside, R/S are best understood as multidimensional, multilevel constructs, serving multiple purposes and having multiple consequences (Pargament, Mahoney, Exline, Jones, & Shafranske, 2013). Also, although the majority of Americans report belief in God and identify with a religious tradition, there is wide variability in involvement. For example, more than 80% of U.S. adults maintain a religious identity, preference, or affinity with some religious tradition; however, between 50% and 60% are actually members of a religious congregation, and less than one third attend religious services at least once per week (Gallup, 2012). Such statistics do not fully capture personal R/S involvement or its importance; for example, 85% of Americans reported in a Gallup (2003) poll that because of their faith, they have meaning and purpose in their lives.

It is important that supervisees develop an awareness of the role and importance R/S has for many of their clients as well as to the diverse nature of R/S involvement and practices. Gaining some familiarity with the psychology of R/S, as well as with demographic trends, fosters recognition of the relevance of R/S as a multicultural and clinical variable. Supervisors also can guide trainees to avoid rigidly dichotomizing religion as institutional and spirituality as individual, which fails to take into account that "spirituality always unfolds within a larger field of religious, institutional, and cultural forces" (Pargament, 2013, p. 267). Similarly, efforts should be taken to avoid any simplistic, reductionistic (and biased) appraisal that spirituality is good and religion is bad, because both forms offer benefits and impose limitations.

Religion, Spirituality, and Culture

R/S do not exist in a vacuum; rather "the specific language of spirituality is guided by one's ethnicity and culture" (Cervantes & Parham, 2005, p. 72) and involves not only values and beliefs but also ways of thinking about and seeing the world, one's personal epistemology. For example, R/S pathways are shaped by cultural features such as individualism and collectivism, materialism and prosperity, and political climate (Loewenthal, 2013). In collectivist subcultures, spiritual experience is fostered through ritual and social relationships whereas individualistic subcultures emphasize individual encounters with the sacred or God. In a reciprocal manner, R/S also influences cultural attitudes, such as viewpoints on marriage or homosexuality. R/S impacts a host of multicultural identities, such as gender, age, ableness, ethnicity, and sexual orientation, and the interaction of these factors in turn impacts R/S. Therefore, supervisees should be encouraged to look beyond simple one-directional and one-dimensional impacts of R/S on the client and consider more broadly and contextually the mutual and bidirectional influences between R/S and culture.

Religious identity also serves to maintain social identity and affiliation in immigrant communities. Religious involvement provides a hub of social interaction, support, and continuity, and for many people religious rituals and celebrations maintain the essential connection to their cultural homeland. R/S also contributes to cultural resilience and promotes coping to past and present trauma and oppression (Comas-Díaz, 2012). As Comas-Díaz (2012) described,

> Many ethnic minorities commit to a colored spirituality in order to repair an oppressed mentality and reformulate a fractured identity. As a result a colored spirituality attempts to heal soul wounds through the rescue and affirmation of individuals' ethnocultural and indigenous roots . . . [and offers] opportunities for hope and redemption . . . Grounded in a collectivist worldview, a colored spirituality helps people of color to deepen their existential sense of meaning and purpose in life. Consequently, the spirit world is omnipresent among most people of color. (p. 199)

Supervision provides a context to develop appreciation for the dynamic interactions between R/S and other cultural dimensions. This task is not an academic one but requires thoughtful consideration of the confluence of factors that influence the client's worldview, attributions, coping, and health.

Religion, Spirituality, and Mental Health

A number of comprehensive reviews of the empirical literature (Koenig, 2004, 2008; Koenig, King, & Carson, 2012; Masters & Hooker, 2012) have identified clinically relevant associations between R/S and mental health, and in many cultures spiritual or religious concerns are believed to be related to illness or psychosocial distress (Fukuyama & Sevig, 1999). Religious involvement appears on the whole to be associated with better mental health (Pargament, Mahoney, Shafranske, Exline, & Jones, 2013); however, religious struggles and certain R/S beliefs (e.g., belief that one was abandoned by God) can create serious problems and endanger health (Plante & Thoresen, 2012). Supervisors should familiarize supervisees with this literature and correct any misassumptions about the impacts of R/S on health. Important distinctions need to be made between general research findings and the actual function and impact of R/S on the client.

Religion, Spirituality, and Coping

One important function of R/S is providing a context of meaning and spiritual pathways through which coping with life challenging events (i.e., trauma, injury, job loss) is enhanced (Pargament, 1997, 2007). R/S beliefs, attributions, and practices supply the means to conserve the sacred, support coping, and offer hope and acceptance. Supervisees will likely draw upon their own use of R/S (and its effectiveness) in their initial appraisal of the client's use of religious coping. Supervisors should examine with the supervisee the influences that inform his or her tacit support or rejection of the R/S attributions or practices that the client is drawing upon. The following conclusions from the literature should inform the supervisory discussion and therapy process (Shafranske, 2013):

1. Religious coping is often turned to when facing extreme, life-challenging circumstances, particularly, when psychological and other resources are exhausted.
2. The efficacy of religious coping is associated with the extent to which R/S is internalized, intrinsically motivated, well integrated, and based on a secure relationship with God. It may be further enhanced when situated within a faith community congruent with the client's essential beliefs and commitments.
3. There are advantages and disadvantages to even the most controversial forms of religion, and the use of religious coping is highly contextual, based on the severity of the stressor and subjective experience, as well as on situational factors, such as the culture's valuation of religion (Gebauer, Sedikides, & Neberich, 2012).
4. Use of R/S resources does not always lead to healthy adjustment. For example, the use of negative religious coping is associated with poorer outcomes and spiritual struggles may negatively impact emotional well-being and adjustment.

Once again, it is important to assess the contributions of R/S to coping in relation to the host of cultural, systemic, and individual values and factors that influence adjustment. Gall and Guirguis-Younger (2013) concluded, "It is clear that understanding the cultural contexts of religious and spiritual coping is essential to grasping its meaning and function across religious traditions, ages, gender, social role, and ethnicity" (p. 358).

Supervisors can enhance the supervisee's knowledge and thereby integrate a science-informed approach to professional practice supervisors by implementing the following recommendations:

1. Develop familiarity with the theoretical and empirical literature integral to the applied psychology of R/S.
2. Model and encourage supervisees to draw on the clinical applied literature when considering the role of R/S. Monitor and bring to the supervisee's attention assumptions not supported in the literature, which may suggest bias.
3. Examine with the supervisee the impacts of their personal beliefs and experiences on their understanding of the client or willingness to draw on the scientific literature.

4. Include in the training clinic library resources that present theory and empirical research in the applied psychology of R/S (see references) and draw attention to reports such as *U.S. Religious Landscape Survey* (Pew Research Center's Forum on Religion & Public Life, 2008) and *The Spiritual Life of College Students: A National Study of College Students' Search for Meaning and Purpose* (Higher Education Research Institute, 2004) to obtain an understanding of general trends in American spirituality.

SKILLS

By drawing attention to the role of personal values and encouraging the development of a clinical understanding that draws on the scientific literature, supervisors set the stage to assist the supervisee to develop skill in implementing evidence-based practice. With the adoption by the APA of evidence-based professional practice as the standard, psychologists are duty-bound to integrate "the best available research with clinical expertise in the context of patient characteristics, culture, and preferences" (APA Presidential Task Force on Evidence-Based Practice, 2006, p. 273). Attention to client R/S is consistent with the mandate to consider patient characteristics and culture. Minimally supervision should have the objective of ensuring the provision of spiritually conscious care (in contrast to spiritually avoidant care). Saunders, Miller, and Bright (2010) defined *spiritually conscious care* as

> an approach that assesses SRBT [spiritual and religious beliefs and practices] in a respectful and sensitive manner to determine its general importance to a patient, but also to assess the influence, if any, of SRBP on the presenting problem and the potential of SRBP as a resource to help recovery. [It] entails explicitly evaluating these issues during the formal evaluation of the intake phase of treatment, and remaining open to their emergence and potential influence as treatment progresses. (p. 359)

Collaborating with the client to consider the potential of R/S as a resource in treatment invites inclusion of client preferences consistent with the principles of evidence-based practice. Supervisors closely monitor the intake and opening phase of treatment to ensure that R/S dimensions of the case are considered and client preferences are elicited.

Skills in Assessing Religion and Spirituality as Clinically Relevant and Inclusion of Client Preferences

A comprehensive discussion of assessment procedures is beyond the scope of this chapter; however, I make some brief comments specific to the role of supervision. The assessment and opening phase of treatment is particularly important in establishing the therapeutic alliance, collaboratively establishing goals, and arriving at a consensus about the means to achieve the goals. All supervisees should be trained to assess the level of importance R/S has for the client and involvement of R/S in the client's difficulties. Training presentations or in supervision session involving role plays can assist in developing comfort, confidence, and competence to initiate discussion of R/S with the client. Supervisees are often surprised that this can be readily accomplished by asking simple open-ended questions, such as, "I was wondering how important is religion and spirituality to you?" and then following up with inquiry about the nature of the client's religious or spiritual involvement. If R/S appears to be salient and is clinically relevant to the goals of treatment, the client should be directly asked whether he or she believes that it would be useful to discuss R/S during treatment. In this way, client preferences are elicited and informed consent to address R/S is obtained. What is important is that the supervisee inquire early in the assessment/treatment process and respond in a respectful, sensitive manner. In-depth assessment of R/S should be conducted only when salience of religion is high and is directly relevant to the client's difficulties, a therapeutic alliance has been established, and the client has expressed preference and given consent. A number of texts are available to provide guidance to the supervisee and supervisor (Hodge, 2013; Leach, Aten, Wade, & Hernandez, 2009; Pargament & Krumrei, 2009; Richards & Bergin, 2005).

Integrating Religion and Spirituality in Treatment

Supervisors can assist trainees in gaining comfort and confidence by pointing out that examining R/S beliefs and attributions is similar to examining other thoughts that shape behavior and experience associated with psychological problems. Supervisees should learn to carefully assess the use of positive and negative religious coping, drawing on Pargament's model (2007), as well as become acquainted with forms of spiritual struggle, such as anger toward God, facing moral imperfection, and offenses by members of religious groups (Exline, 2013).

Many people use R/S resources in their daily life. Clients may use resources such as prayer, mediation, spiritual reading when they are facing crisis and hardship or if they have done so in the past. Supervision provides a setting to consider the effects of such activities and how these resources, if demonstrating benefit, might be encouraged or ethically incorporated into treatment (Plante, 2009). For many supervisees (as well as supervisors and clinicians) the idea of encouraging or using a spiritual resource in treatment may seem inappropriate, if not unethical. Careful consideration of ethics is always warranted when considering direct integration of R/S resources (Barnett & Johnson, 2011; Gonsiorek, Richards, Pargament, & McMinn, 2009; Hathaway, 2011; Tjeltveit, 2012). However, it is useful to consider that for some clients R/S resources are naturally occurring, self-chosen activities, and just as a clinician might encourage a client who derives psychological benefits from jogging to continue to run, a psychologist might support the use of an R/S resource.

Models of spiritually oriented psychotherapy (Aten & Leach, 2009; L. J. Miller, 2012; Pargament, Mahoney, & Shafranske, 2013; Plante & Thoresen, 2012; Richards & Bergin, 2004, 2005; Shafranske, 2009, 2012; Shafranske & Sperry, 2005; Sperry, 2013), as well as empirically supported religiously accommodative treatments (Worthington, Hook, Davis, & McDaniel, 2011), have been developed. Implementation of these treatment approaches requires specialized training and supervision, a discussion of which is beyond the scope of this chapter.

Supervisors contribute to supervisee skill development by implementing the following recommendations:

1. Promote the supervisee's willingness and ability to engage in introspection to self-assess and to appreciate how personal beliefs, values, and worldviews affect her or his interactions with culturally and R/S diverse clients.

2. Review the knowledge, skills, and values/attitudes that are assembled to competently address client R/S as a clinically relevant variable. The supervisor should carefully assess his or her competence to supervise clinical processes involving R/S and then guide the supervisee in a process of self-assessment, attending first to attitudes and values and then focusing on knowledge and skills. Discussion should include goals for supervision, respective of addressing R/S (Aten & Hernandez, 2004).

3. Review, apply, and discuss with the supervisee the ethical principles associated with consideration of R/S in psychological treatment (e.g., APA, 2008, 2010; Gonsiorek et al., 2009; Hathaway, 2011); practice guidelines; and knowledge of, and experience in, religion-based forms of integration, which require knowledge of specific training and practice models (Tan, 2009). Consider using a decision-making process, such as that presented by Barnett and Johnson (2011).

4. Closely monitor any interventions addressing R/S and explore with the supervisee level of comfort, personal reactions, client response, impacts on alliance, and therapeutic process. Be

certain that client preferences were elicited and informed consent was obtained to address R/S in treatment.

5. Avoid boundary crossings by limiting inquiry to personal attitudes, values, and experiences that directly impact the supervisee's ability to effectively address R/S in the therapeutic relationship. Model respect for the supervisee's autonomy in respect for his or her beliefs and faith commitment, while addressing potential tensions between client and supervisee worldviews.

6. Elicit feedback about the effectiveness of supervision and consider using tools focusing specifically on spirituality, such as the Spiritual Issues in Supervision Scale (M. Miller, Korinek, & Ivey, 2006).

7. Include in the training clinic library textbooks and training materials, such as *The American Psychological Association Spirituality Video Series* (APA, 2004–2011), that present models and illustrations of spiritually oriented psychotherapy practices, including resources that present features specific to particular religions (Richards & Bergin, 2000).

8. Organize training with experts in the field (if available locally), as well as invite members of the clergy to present on common R/S challenges.

Supervision of cases involving R/S is conducted on the same principles and use similar procedures to supervision in general. However, particular attention is paid to the supervisee's level of comfort, empathy, and reactions to client R/S, therapeutic alliance, and impacts of interventions directed to R/S.

SUPERVISION CASE ILLUSTRATION

The supervisee, Laura, is a single, Caucasian female doctoral student in her mid-20s, whose primary theoretical orientation is cognitive–behavioral and who has particular interest in, and is developing competence in, empirically supported treatments for anxiety disorders, as well as dialectical behavior therapy. She sought supervision with the intent of obtaining exposure to a psychodynamic therapeutic orientation. Her openness to alternative approaches to conceptualization and treatment reflected both confidence and cognitive flexibility. She begins the session reporting on a new client, whose intake she completed the day before our supervision session. The client, Gina, is a single Hispanic woman about the same age as the supervisee, who presented with primary symptoms of depression associated with mixed feelings of guilt. The following excerpt focuses specifically on supervision interaction dealing with R/S.[3]

Supervisee: After she described how she was feeling depressed and isolated from others, particularly from men, she blurted out that the primary reason why she had come to counseling was to get help to stop her bad behavior. Before I could inquire, she said that a friend at church thought that counseling might help. I asked what behaviors did she consider to be bad and she said that she felt bad because there were times that she would touch herself, self-stimulate herself. To clarify I asked, "You mean you feel bad about masturbating?" She shook her head yes and asked somewhat plaintively if I could help her to stop. I sensed this was awkward for her, and so I asked her to share why she thought touching herself was bad rather than asking about frequency.

Supervisor: Uh-huh, so you sensed her discomfort.

Supervisee: Well, she says that she knows that it is a sin, but when she feels pent up and anxious, she will pleasure herself but then she feels guilty, sinful, and a failure—it's a downward arrow to depression. I don't know if this was right but I said to her, "I don't understand, what you are describing is perfectly natural." She replied that she knew it was natural but that didn't mean it wasn't sinful to give in to those urges. I honestly didn't know what to say.

Supervisor: Well, what comes to mind now as you are relating this to me? [This question was intended to direct attention to the supervisee's experience in the moment and to prompt self-reflection.]

Supervisee: I guess just the feeling of confusion.

Supervisor: Confusion? [Offered as a prompt]

Supervisee: I just didn't know the best way to proceed.

Supervisor: Well, let's look at this together. It seems that you initially responded by trying to normalize her behavior . . . to, in some way, relieve her of the conflict or discomfort that she was feeling in the moment, and you seemed to be somewhat confused by the nature of her conflict. [This confusion could be seen as a product of the disjunction between their worldview.]

---

[3]This case example is a composite incorporating supervisory/clinical issues from several related cases. The interactions are accurate; however, certain details (not related to R/S or the supervisory process) have been altered to protect the confidentiality of the participants.

Supervisee: Yes, I could see how upset she was and about something she shouldn't be upset about. Later she said that this happens maybe once every two or three weeks, but she feels guilty about having sinned and her friend from church repeated what the pastor had said to not give in to temptation. I don't get that something natural is seen as so sinful. I know you have an interest in religion. Does this make any sense or am I missing something?

Supervisor: Yes, I do have interest in how religion or spirituality is addressed in treatment and mental health. Well, we may be missing something, but let's start with her presentation and your reaction to it. Let me first ask about your thoughts and reactions to your client's belief that her actions are sinful.

Supervisee: Well, as I think about it, her religious perspective seems extreme and is contributing to her feelings of guilt. I'm not religious myself, so her thinking is hard to grasp.

Supervisor: It seems a situation is unfolding in which you and your client have differing perspectives. How do you feel about looking at how your attitudes may be influencing the therapeutic process?

Supervisee: Sure.

Supervisor: The intent is not to question your beliefs but just to see how your personal values are influencing how you are addressing the issues with your client. It seems from what you have said that the client holds religious views that are hard for you to understand.

Supervisee: Yes, that's right. I think masturbation is normal, and nothing is wrong with it as long as it doesn't interfere with other aspects of your life or relationships. Also, I've never seen the value in church for me; I wasn't raised in a particularly religious family.

Supervisor: Laura, I appreciate your sharing and awareness of the differences between you and your client. Let's turn to what you know about the client's religiosity.

Supervisee: Well, she put down on the intake form that she was Christian, and she confirmed that in the interview.

Supervisor: Do you know the denomination or the specific church that she attends and something about her religious history or how she became affiliated with this church?

Supervisee: No, I hadn't thought to ask and we were running out of time.

Supervisor: Well, if there is a natural opening to ask in the next session, it would be useful to get a bit more information about her how she came to be affiliated with this church, the denomination, that being, for example, Methodist, Baptist, Evangelical Protestant, and ask an open-ended question about her religious background, participation as a child, or her family's participation. Of course this isn't to be 50 questions, let her take the lead. You might, if an opportunity presents, ask how she felt about last week's session and any impact during the week. The questions about denomination may give us a sense of the normative status of her judgments about her behavior since Christian congregations vary in respect to attitudes toward sexual morality and behavior. Also, it is useful to understand the factors that may have motivated her to join this particular congregation, particularly if this church is significantly different from those she had participated in the past. Also, your motivation to normalize her behavior seems to be driven in part by your personal beliefs, so I suggest that you reflect on how you can be open to understand her perspective when it appears to be different from your own. How does that sound? Is this helpful to you?

Supervisee: Yes, I'm actually pretty interested in learning about her beliefs, although I really think that my goal is to alleviate her depression.

Supervisor: And mine, too. The approach would be to assist her to understand more fully the meaning of her conflicts, while respecting her faith commitments. So, the goal, as I see it today, is not to dispute her beliefs, which raises a number of ethical and clinical issues, but rather to support thoughtful reflection. Also, just as we need to more fully understand her spiritual history, it is important to obtain a sexual history; although, initially, let that emerge on its own, although you could ask if she always felt guilty about masturbation or sexuality. Also, we will need to better understand her cultural identification as well as other personal factors.

In the next few sessions, the therapeutic alliance was strengthened by slowing the pace of the interaction, expressing empathy, letting the client take the lead, and inviting reflection on her religious beliefs and church affiliation. Although the focus in this session initiated discussion of the role of R/S, it was important to explore the multiple cultural and contextual features that conjoined to shape the client's beliefs. For example, cultural factors of gender, age, ethnicity, and urban culture contributed alongside her religiosity.

Although full explication of the case goes beyond the scope of this narrative, it is important to note that Laura conveyed genuine interest and respect in her tone and questions and Gina described that she was drawn to the church because of her close friend's influence and because she felt like she needed to get her life back on track following a period of unfulfilling personal and sexual relationships. Over the course of time, although Gina did not change her aspiration to not engage in masturbation, she became less self-critical and condemning. Many months into treatment Gina revealed an earlier traumatic sexual incident, when she was a young teenager, which she had never shared with anyone. The focus of treatment then shifted to working through this trauma, as well as other painful events in her childhood. As the trauma work became more intense, the client became more anxious and began cancelling appointments. It was clear that the therapy was nearing an impasse, if not a crisis.

> Supervisee: Gina came to her session and she was having a very difficult time processing and containing her affect; she reported that she was considering leaving treatment and that things were getting worse rather than better.

We discussed in detail the clinical interaction and the client's self-report of emotional states and behaviors outside of session. It was clear that we needed to bolster the collaboration, instill hope, and fortify her resources. We consulted with an expert in posttraumatic stress disorder, which confirmed the general exposure-focused approach that we were employing as well as using techniques from dialectical behavior therapy.

> Supervisor: Let's review the ways in which your client counters dysregulation and can regain a sense of control. Some techniques that you have been employing have helped in the past but are less effective in managing the dysregulation in the session.

> Supervisee: [Laura summarizes the approaches that have been used.] She reports that when things really feel out of control that she prays and repeats a prayer over and over until she calms.

> Supervisor: Have you considered offering her the opportunity to pray briefly in the session?

> Supervisee: Well, no. I mean, can we do that?

> Supervisor: In my view, prayer appears to be a naturally occurring spiritual resource that Gina uses, and it appears to help her feel connected to God and safe. As we have assessed, spirituality is very important to her, and in fact, her use of religious resources seems to be increasing following her disclosure of the traumatic event. What are your thoughts as I raise the

possibility? [When considering the use of an R/S resource, it is important to not only bring into supervision the scientific literature and the client's values and preferences (and to obtain explicit informed consent) but also to engage the supervisee in his or her own values and reactions regarding the use of such an intervention.]

Supervisee: Well, I would do anything to help her, but as you know I'm not religious. Would I have to be religious to pray?

Supervisor: While you would not need to be religious and I'm not suggesting you change your beliefs, it would be important that you respect the authenticity of the experience for her.

Supervisee: I do respect her; she has a lot of integrity.

We further discussed the nature of prayer, the ethical issues involved, and I asked her to read some additional material on explicit integration and the spiritual pathways. We made the decision to introduce the offer of incorporating a minute of prayer at the beginning of the session with the understanding that Laura will participate in silence; also, she will elicit feedback from the client at the end of the session about her experience of beginning with prayer. The client was surprised by Laura's suggestion, given her assumption that her therapist was not a Christian, but appreciated her offer and agreed that prayer was often the only thing that got her through difficulty times, because in prayer she could call upon God to protect her. In the next session, Gina began with a heartfelt prayer for safety, wept for a moment, and seemed to calm, and the session proceeded. Although it is difficult to assess the impact of this intervention, it did appear to bolster the therapeutic alliance and therapy progressed. Gina did not pray often in session, but when she did, she appeared to find strength and resolve. Laura's genuine concern, empathy, and therapeutic skill, as well as her developing sensitivity to her client's R/S involvement, conveyed respect and facilitated Gina's exploration of the role of R/S in her life.

COMMENTARY

This excerpt drawn from supervision sessions illustrates many of the concepts discussed in the chapter. First of all, crucial to the effectiveness of the supervision was attention to differences in the R/S commitments between the client and supervisee. The supervisee's openness to examine the influence of her personal beliefs, her empathy, and her fundamental respect for her client established the conditions for a therapeutic alliance to form and sustain. After obtaining information about the client's religious affiliation (free-standing, Evangelical congregation), Laura was better able to understand the normative, culture-specific beliefs that Gina endorsed, as well as to explore with her client how holding these beliefs played a role in dealing with her psychological conflicts involving sexuality. Developing an understanding of spiritual pathways, religious coping, and R/S resources provided the necessary, theoretically sound understanding to incorporate an R/S resource into treatment, mindful of ethics and with the client's consent. This case also illustrates how evidence-based practice may be implemented, taking into consideration scientific literature, clinician and supervisor expertise, and patient characteristics, culture, and preferences.

REFLECTIVE PRACTICE

Self-reflection and self-assessment are essential to ethical practice and the development of competence (Falender & Shafranske, 2007). The development of self-reflective practice is critically important in clinical supervision, which aspires to fully implement multicultural perspectives. I close with four questions, adapted from Gonsiorek et al. (2009, p. 238), to stimulate metacompetence when conducting supervision of cases involving R/S:

1. Do I have the ability to ensure the creation of a spiritually safe and affirming therapeutic environment for the client?
2. Do I have the ability to ensure that an effective religious and spiritual assessment of the client will be conducted?
3. Do I have the ability to ensure that religious and spiritual interventions will be used or encouraged appropriately, if indicated, to help clients access the resources of their faith and spirituality during treatment and recover?
4. Do I have the ability to effectively consult and collaborate with and, when needed, to direct referrals to clergy and other pastoral professionals?

REFERENCES

Note: Resources that are specifically intended to assist clinicians to develop competence in the use of religion and spirituality interventions in psychological treatment are indicated by * following the reference, and such resources that are also cited in the chapter are indicated by **.

American Counseling Association. (2005). ACA code of ethics. Retrieved from http://www.ncblpc.org/Laws_and_Codes/ACA_Code_of_Ethics.pdf

American Psychiatric Association. (1989). *Guidelines regarding possible conflict between psychiatrists' religious commitments and psychiatric practice.* Washington, DC: Author.

American Psychological Association. (2002). *Guidelines for multicultural education, training, research, practice, and organizational change for psychologists.* Washington, DC: Author.

American Psychological Association. (2004–2011). *The American Psychological Association spirituality video series.* Washington, DC: Author.*

American Psychological Association. (2006). Evidence-based practice in psychology. *American Psychologist, 61,* 271–285. doi:10.1037/0003-066X.61.4.271

American Psychological Association. (2008). Resolution on religious, religion-based, and/or religion-derived prejudice. *American Psychologist, 63,* 431–434.

American Psychological Association. (2010). *Ethical principles of psychologists and code of conduct (2002; amended June 1, 2010).* Retrieved from http://www.apa.org/ethics/code/index.aspx

Aten, J. D., & Hernandez, B. (2004). Addressing religion in clinical supervision: A model. *Psychotherapy: Theory, Research, Practice, Training, 41,* 152–160. doi:10.1037/0033-3204.41.2.152

Aten, J. D., & Leach, M. M. (Eds.), (2009). *Spirituality and the therapeutic process: A comprehensive resource from intake to termination.* Washington, DC: American Psychological Association. doi:10.1037/11853-000*

Aten, J. D., McMinn, M. R., & Worthington, E. L., Jr. (2011). *Spiritually oriented interventions for counseling and psychotherapy.* Washington, DC: American Psychological Association. doi: 10.1037/12313-000*

Barnett, J. E., & Johnson, W. (2011). Integrating spirituality and religion into psychotherapy: Persistent dilemmas, ethical issues, and a proposed decision-making process. *Ethics & Behavior, 21,* 147–164. doi:10.1080/10508422.2011.551471

Bartoli, E. (2007). Religious and spiritual issues in psychotherapy practice: Training the trainer. *Psychotherapy: Theory, Research, Practice, Training, 44,* 54–65. doi:10.1037/0033-3204.44.1.54

Behnke, S. H. (2012). Constitutional claims in the context of mental health training: Religion, sexual orientation, and tensions between the first amendment and professional ethics. *Training and Education in Professional Psychology, 6,* 189–195. doi:10.1037/a0030809

Bieschke, K. J., & Mintz, L. B. (2012). Counseling psychology model training values statement addressing diversity: History, current use, and future directions. *Training and Education in Professional Psychology, 6,* 196–203. doi:10.1037/a0030810

Brawer, P. A., Handal, P. J., Fabricatore, A. N., Roberts, R., & Wajda-Johnston, V. A. (2002). Training and education in religion/spirituality within APA-accredited clinical psychology programs. *Professional Psychology: Research and Practice, 33,* 203–206. doi:10.1037/0735-7028.33.2.203

Cashwell, C. S., & Young, J. S. (2011). *Integrating spirituality and religion into counseling.* Alexandria, VA: American Counseling Association.*

Cervantes, J. M., & Parham, T. A. (2005). Toward a meaningful spirituality for people of color: Lessons for the counseling practitioner. *Cultural Diversity & Ethnic Minority Psychology, 11*, 69–81. doi:10.1037/1099-9809.11.1.69

Comas-Díaz, L. (2012). Colored spirituality: The centrality of spirit among ethnic minorities. In L. J. Miller (Ed.), *The Oxford handbook of psychology and spirituality* (pp. 197–206). New York, NY: Oxford University Press.

Crook-Lyon, R. E., O'Grady, K. A., Smith, T. B., Jensen, D. R., Golightly, T., & Potkar, K. A. (2012). Addressing religious and spiritual diversity in graduate training and multicultural education for professional psychologists. *Psychology of Religion and Spirituality, 4*, 169–181. doi:10.1037/a0026403

Exline, J. J. (2013). Religious and spiritual struggles. In K. I. Pargament, J. J. Exline, & J. W. Jones (Eds.), *APA handbook of psychology, religion, and spirituality: Vol. 1. Context, theory, and research* (pp. 459–475). Washington, DC: American Psychological Association. doi:10.1037/14045-025

Falender, C. A., & Shafranske, E. P. (2007). Competence in competency-based supervision practice: Construct and application. *Professional Psychology: Research and Practice, 38*, 232–240. doi:10.1037/0735-7028.38.3.232

Forrest, L. (2012). Educators' and trainers' responsibilities when trainees' personal beliefs collide with competent practice. *Training and Education in Professional Psychology, 6*, 187–188. doi:10.1037/a0030799

Frame, M. W. (2003). *Integrating religion and spirituality into counseling.* Pacific Grove, CA: Brooks/Cole.*

Fukuyama, M. A., & Sevig, T. D. (1999). *Integrating spirituality into multicultural counseling.* Thousand Oaks, CA: Sage.*

Gall, T., & Guirguis-Younger, M. (2013). Religious and spiritual coping: Current theory and research. In K. I. Pargament, J. J. Exline, & J. W. Jones (Eds.), *APA handbook of psychology, religion, and spirituality: Vol. 1. Context, theory, and research* (pp. 349–364). Washington, DC: American Psychological Association. doi:10.1037/14045-019

Gallup. (2012). *Religion* [Graphs and data set]. Retrieved from http://www.gallup.com/poll/1690/Religion.aspx

Gebauer, J. E., Sedikides, C., & Neberich, W. (2012). Religiosity, social self-esteem, and psychological adjustment: On the cross-cultural specificity of the psychological benefits of religiosity. *Psychological Science, 23*, 158–160.

Gonsiorek, J. C., Richards, P., Pargament, K. I., & McMinn, M. R. (2009). Ethical challenges and opportunities at the edge: Incorporating spirituality and religion into psychotherapy. *Professional Psychology: Research and Practice, 40*, 385–395. doi: 10.1037/a0016488**

Hathaway, W. L. (2011). Ethical guidelines for using spiritually oriented interventions. In J. D. Aten, M. R. McMinn, & E. L. Worthington, Jr. (Eds.), *Spiritually oriented interventions for counseling and psychotherapy* (pp. 65–81). Washington, DC: American Psychological Association. doi: 10.1037/12313-003**

Hathaway, W. L. (2013). Pathways toward graduate training in the clinical psychology of religion and spirituality: A spiritual competencies model. In K. I. Pargament, A. Mahoney, & E. P. Shafranske (Eds.), *APA handbook of psychology, religion, and spirituality: Vol. 2. An applied psychology of religion and spirituality* (pp. 635–649). Washington, DC: American Psychological Association. doi:10.1037/14046-033

Hathaway, W. L., Scott, S. Y., & Garver, S. A. (2004). Assessing religious/spiritual functioning: A neglected domain in clinical practice. *Professional Psychology: Research and Practice, 35*, 97–104. doi: 10.1037/0735-7028.35.1.97*

Higher Education Research Institute. (2004). *The spiritual life of college students: A national study of college students' search for meaning and purpose.* Retrieved from http://spirituality.ucla.edu/docs/reports/Spiritual_Life_College_Students_Full_Report.pdf

Hill, P. C., Pargament, K. I., Hood, R. R., McCullough, M. E., Swyers, J. P., Larson, D. B., & Zinnbauer, B. J. (2000). Conceptualizing religion and spirituality: Points of commonality, points of departure. *Journal for the Theory of Social Behaviour, 30*, 51–77. doi:10.1111/1468-5914.00119

Hodge, D. R. (2013). Assessing spirituality and religion in the context of counseling and psychotherapy. In K. I. Pargament, A. Mahoney, & E. P. Shafranske (Eds.), *APA handbook of psychology, religion, and spirituality: Vol. 2. An applied psychology of religion and spirituality* (pp. 93–123). Washington, DC: American Psychological Association. doi:10.1037/14046-005**

Hook, J. N., Worthington, E. L., Jr., Davis, D. E., Jennings, D., Gartner, A. L., & Hook, J. P. (2010). Empirically supported religious and spiritual therapies. *Journal of Clinical Psychology, 66*, 46–72.*

Koenig, H. G. (2004). Religion, spirituality, and medicine: Research findings and implications for Clinical Practice. *Southern Medical Journal, 97*, 1194–1200.

Koenig, H. G. (2008). *Medicine, religion, and health: Where science and spirituality meet.* West Conshohocken, PA: Templeton Foundation Press.

Koenig, H. G., King, D. E., & Carson, V. B. (2012). *Handbook of religion and health* (2nd ed.). New York, NY: Oxford University Press.

Leach, M. M., Aten, J. D., Boyer, M. C., Strain, J. D., & Bradshaw, A. K. (2010). Developing therapist self-awareness and knowledge. In M. M. Leach & J. D. Aten (Eds.), *Culture and the therapeutic process: A guide for mental health professionals* (pp. 13–36). New York, NY: Routledge/Taylor & Francis Group.

Leach, M. M., Aten, J., Wade, N., & Hernandez, B. (2009). Spirituality and the clinical intake. In J. Aten & M. M. Leach (Eds.), *Spirituality and the therapeutic process: A comprehensive resource from intake through termination* (pp. 75–92). Washington, DC: American Psychological Association.

Loewenthal, K. (2013). Religion, spirituality, and culture: Clarifying the direction of effects. In K. I. Pargament, J. J. Exline, & J. W. Jones (Eds.), *APA handbook of psychology, religion, and spirituality: Vol. 1. Context, theory, and research* (pp. 239–255). Washington, DC: American Psychological Association. doi:10.1037/14045-013

Masters, K. S., & Hooker, S. A. (2012). Religion, spirituality, and health. In L. J. Miller (Ed.), *The Oxford handbook of psychology and spirituality* (pp. 519–539). New York, NY: Oxford University Press.

McMinn, M. R., Aikins, D. C., & Lish, R. A. (2003). Basic and advanced competence in collaborating with clergy. *Professional Psychology: Research and Practice, 34*, 197–202. doi: 10.1037/0735-7028.34.2.197*

McMinn, M. R., Hathaway, W. L., Woods, S. W., & Snow, K. N. (2009). What American Psychological Association leaders have to say about psychology of religion and spirituality. *Psychology of Religion and Spirituality, 1*, 3–13. doi:10.1037/a0014991

Miller, G. A. (2003). *Incorporating spirituality in counseling and psychotherapy.* New York, NY: Wiley.*

Miller, L. J. (Ed.). (2012). *The Oxford handbook of psychology and spirituality.* New York, NY: Oxford University Press.

Miller, M., Korinek, A. W., & Ivey, D. C. (2006). Integrating spirituality into training: The Spiritual Issues in Supervision Scale. *American Journal of Family Therapy, 34*, 355–372. doi:10.1080/01926180600553811

Pargament K. I. (1997). *The psychology of religion and coping.* New York, NY: Guilford Press.**

Pargament, K. I. (2007). *Spiritually integrated psychotherapy: Understanding and addressing the sacred.* New York, NY: Guilford Press.**

Pargament, K. I. (2013). Searching for the sacred: Toward a nonreductionistic theory of spirituality. In K. I. Pargament, J. J. Exline, & J. W. Jones (Eds.), *APA handbook of psychology, religion, and spirituality: Vol. 1. Context, theory, and research* (pp. 257–273). Washington, DC: American Psychological Association. doi:10.1037/14045-014

Pargament, K. I., Exline, J. J., & Jones, J. W. (2013). *APA handbook of psychology, religion, and spirituality: Vol. 1. Context, theory, and research.* Washington, DC: American Psychological Association. doi:10.1037/14045-000

Pargament, K. I., & Krumrei, E. J. (2009). Clinical assessment of clients' spirituality. In J. D. Aten & M. M. Leach (Eds.), *Spirituality and the therapeutic process: A comprehensive resource from intake to termination* (pp. 93–120). Washington, DC: American Psychological Association. doi: 10.1037/11853-005**

Pargament, K. I., Mahoney, A., Exline, J. J., Jones, J. W., & Shafranske, E. P. (2013). Envisioning an integrative paradigm for the psychology of religion and spirituality. In K. I. Pargament, J. J. Exline, & J. W. Jones (Eds.), *APA handbook of psychology, religion, and spirituality: Vol. 1. Context, theory, and research* (pp. 3–19). Washington, DC: American Psychological Association. doi:10.1037/14045-001

Pargament, K. I., Mahoney, A., & Shafranske, E. P. (2013). *APA handbook of psychology, religion, and spirituality: Vol. 2. An applied psychology of religion and spirituality.* Washington, DC: American Psychological Association. doi:10.1037/14046-000**

Pargament, K. I., Mahoney, A., Shafranske, E. P., Exline, J. J., & Jones, J. W. (2013). From research to practice: Toward an applied psychology of religion and spirituality. In K. I. Pargament, A. Mahoney, & E. P. Shafranske (Eds.), *APA handbook of psychology, religion, and spirituality: Vol. 2. An applied psychology of religion and spirituality* (pp. 3–22). Washington, DC: American Psychological Association. doi:10.1037/14046-001

Park, C. L. (2005). Religion and meaning. In R. F. Paloutzian & C. L. Park (Eds.), *Handbook of the psychology of religion and spirituality* (pp. 295–314). New York, NY: Guilford Press.

Park, C. L., Edmondson, D., & Hale-Smith, A. (2013). Why religion? Meaning as motivation. In K. I. Pargament, J. J. Exline, & J. W. Jones (Eds.), *APA handbook of psychology, religion, and spirituality: Vol. 1. Context, theory, and research* (pp. 157–171). Washington, DC: American Psychological Association. doi:10.1037/14045-008

Pepper, S. C. (1972). *World hypotheses: A study of evidence*. Berkeley and Los Angeles, CA: University of California. (Original work published 1942)

Peteet, J., Lu, F., & Narrow, W. (Eds.). (2011). *Religious and spiritual issues in psychiatric diagnosis: A research agenda for DSM–V*. Washington, DC: American Psychiatric Publishing.*

Pew Research Center's Forum on Religion & Public Life. (2010). *U.S. religious knowledge survey*. Retrieved from http://www.pewforum.org/U-S-Religious-Knowledge-Survey-Who-Knows-What-About-Religion.aspx

Plante, T. G. (2009). *Spiritual practices in psychotherapy: Thirteen tools for enhancing psychological health*. Washington, DC: American Psychological Association.**

Plante, T. G. (2011). Addressing problematic spirituality in therapy. In J. D. Aten, M. R. McMinn, & E. L. Worthington, Jr. (Eds.), *Spiritually oriented interventions for counseling and psychotherapy* (pp. 83–106). Washington, DC: American Psychological Association. doi: 10.1037/11872-000*

Plante, T. G., & Thoresen, C. E. (2012). Spirituality, religion, and psychological counseling. In L. J. Miller (Ed.), *The Oxford handbook of psychology and spirituality* (pp. 388–409). New York, NY: Oxford University Press.

Post, B. C., & Wade, N. G. (2009). Religion and spirituality in psychotherapy: A practice-friendly review of research. *Journal of Clinical Psychology, 65*, 131–146. doi: 10.1002/jclp.20563*

Richards P. S., & Bergin, A. E. (Eds.). (2000). *Handbook of psychotherapy and religious diversity*. Washington, DC: American Psychological Association. doi: 10.1037/10347-000**

Richards, P. S., & Bergin, A. E. (Eds.). (2004). *Religion and psychotherapy: A casebook*. Washington, DC: American Psychological Association. doi: 10.1037/10652-000**

Richards, P. S., & Bergin, A. E. (2005). *A spiritual strategy for counseling and psychotherapy* (2nd ed.). Washington, DC: American Psychological Association. doi: 10.1037/11214-000**

Saunders, S. M., Miller, M. L., & Bright, M. M. (2010). Spiritually conscious psychological care. *Professional Psychology: Research and Practice, 41*, 355–362. doi: 10.1037/a0020953*

Schafer, R. M., Handal, P. J., Brawer, P. A., & Ubinger, M. (2011). Training and education in religion/spirituality within APA-accredited clinical psychology programs: 8 years later. *Journal of Religion and Health, 50*, 232–239. doi:10.1007/s10943-009-9272-8

Shafranske, E. P. (2009). Spiritually oriented psychodynamic psychotherapy. *Journal of Clinical Psychology: In Session, 65*, 147–157. doi: 10.1002/jclp.20565**

Shafranske, E. P. (2013). Addressing religiousness and spirituality. Advancing evidence-based practice. In R. Paloutzian & C. Park (Eds.), *The handbook of the psychology of religion* (2nd ed., pp. 595–616). New York, NY: Guilford Press.**

Shafranske, E. P., & Cummings, J. P. (2013). Religious and spiritual beliefs, affiliations, and practices of psychologists. In K. I. Pargament, A. Mahoney, & E. P. Shafranske (Eds.), *APA handbook of psychology, religion, and spirituality: Vol. 2. An applied psychology of religion and spirituality* (pp. 23–41). Washington, DC: American Psychological Association. doi:10.1037/14046-002

Shafranske, E. P., & Sperry, L. (2005). Addressing the spiritual dimension in psychotherapy: Introduction and overview. In L. Sperry & E. P. Shafranske (Eds.), *Spiritually oriented psychotherapy* (pp. 11–29). Washington, DC: American Psychological Association. doi:10.1037/10886-001**

Slattery, J. M., & Park, C. L. (2011). Meaning making and spiritually oriented interventions. In J. D. Aten, M. R. McMinn, & E. L. Worthington, Jr. (Eds.), *Spiritually oriented interventions for counseling and psychotherapy* (pp. 15–40). Washington, DC: American Psychological Association. doi: 10.1037/12313-001*

Slife, B. D., & Reber, J. S. (2009). Is there a pervasive implicit bias against theism in psychology? *Journal of Theoretical and Philosophical Psychology, 29*, 63–79. doi:10.1037/a0016985

Sperry, L. (2012). *Spirituality in clinical practice: Theory and practice of spiritually oriented psychotherapy* (2nd ed.). New York, NY: Routledge/Taylor & Francis.*

Sperry, L. (2013). Distinctive approaches to religion and spirituality: Pastoral counseling, spiritual direction, and spiritually integrated psychotherapy. In K. I. Pargament, A. Mahoney, & E. P. Shafranske (Eds.), *APA handbook of psychology, religion, and spirituality: Vol. 2. An applied psychology of religion and spirituality* (pp. 223–238). Washington, DC: American Psychological Association. doi:10.1037/14046-011

Sperry, L., & Shafranske, E. P. (Eds.) (2005). *Spiritually oriented psychotherapy*. Washington, DC: American Psychological Association. doi: 10.1037/10886-000*

Tan, S.-Y. (2009). Developing integration skills: The role of clinical supervision. *Journal of Psychology and Theology, 37*, 54–61.

Tjeltveit, A. C. (2012). Religion, spirituality, and mental health. In S. J. Knapp, M. C. Gottlieb, M. M. Handelsman, & L. D. VandeCreek (Eds.), *APA handbook of ethics in psychology: Vol. 1. Moral foundations and common themes* (pp. 279–294). Washington, DC: American Psychological Association. doi:10.1037/13271-010

Wiggins, M. I. (2009). Therapist self-awareness of spirituality. In J. D. Aten & M. M. Leach (Eds.), *Spirituality and the therapeutic process: A comprehensive resource from intake to termination* (pp. 53–74). Washington, DC: American Psychological Association. doi:10.1037/11853-003

Worthington, E. L., Jr., Hook, J. N., Davis, D. E., & McDaniel, M. A. (2011). Religion and spirituality. *Journal of Clinical Psychology, 67,* 204–214. doi:10.1002/jclp.20760

Yarhouse, M. A., & Johnson, V. (2013). Value and ethical issues: The interface between psychology and religion. In K. I. Pargament, A. Mahoney, & E. P. Shafranske (Eds.), *APA handbook of psychology, religion, and spirituality: Vol. 2. An applied psychology of religion and spirituality* (pp. 43–70). Washington, DC: American Psychological Association. doi:10.1037/14046-003

Zinnbauer, B. J., & Pargament, K. I. (2000). Working with the sacred: Four approaches to religious and spiritual issues in counseling. *Journal of Counseling & Development, 78,* 162–171. doi:10.1002/j.1556-6676.2000.tb02574.x

Zinnbauer, B. J., & Pargament, K. I. (2005). Religiousness and spirituality. In R. F. Paloutzian & C. L. Park (Eds.), *Handbook of the psychology of religion and spirituality* (pp. 21–42). New York, NY: Guilford Press.

Zinnbauer, B. J., Pargament, K. I., Cole, B., Rye, M. S., Butter, E. M., Belavich, T. G., . . . Kadar, J. L. (1997). Religion and spirituality: Unfuzzying the fuzzy. *Journal for the scientific study of religion, 36,* 549–564. doi:10.2307/1387689

9

A COMPREHENSIVE APPROACH TO COMPETENTLY ADDRESSING SEXUAL MINORITY ISSUES IN CLINICAL SUPERVISION

KATHLEEN J. BIESCHKE, KELLY A. BLASKO, AND SUSAN S. WOODHOUSE

The scholarship of lesbian, gay, bisexual, and transgender (LGBT) psychology is in the midst of a paradigm shift, one that recognizes the critical importance of examining sexual minority status in conjunction with gender, race, ethnicity, religion, class, disability, and other aspects of sociocultural location (Croteau, Bieschke, Fassinger, & Manning, 2008). Societal attitudes toward those who identify as a sexual minority are both rapidly shifting and widely varying (e.g., Halpert, Reinhardt, & Toohey, 2007). Yet few training programs offer in-depth training pertaining to issues of sexual minority clients (e.g., Murphy, Rawlings, & Howe, 2002), and it is likely that many clinical supervisors are unprepared to work effectively with issues pertaining to minority sexual orientations (Phillips & Fisher, 1998). The anecdotal literature is rife with stories from LGBT trainees who have encountered unaffirmative behavior from their supervisors (e.g., Croteau, Lark, Lidderdale, & Chung, 2005; Singh & Chun, 2010), and

http://dx.doi.org/10.1037/14370-009
Multiculturalism and Diversity in Clinical Supervision: A Competency-Based Approach, C. A. Falender, E. P. Shafranske, and C. J. Falicov (Editors)

such experiences are confirmed in the existing empirical literature (e.g., Burkard, Knox, Hess, & Schultz, 2009).

We begin this chapter by briefly summarizing Fassinger and Arseneau's (2007) model of identity enactment of gender-transgressive sexual minorities as one way in which to envision the contextual realities of LGBT individuals. Although all aspects of sociocultural location are important to sexual identities, we discuss religion in some detail, given the values conflicts that can ensue in training settings. We argue that only supervision that is affirmative of LGBT identities is maximally effective, and we present the integrative affirmative supervision (IAS) model (Halpert at al., 2007) as an effective approach for working with sexual minority issues in supervision. Affirmative supervision is necessary but not sufficient for competent supervision, and we integrate Falender and Shafranske's (2004) competency-based approach into our discussion of how to work effectively with sexual minority issues in supervision. We end with a detailed a case example that explicates how to provide competency-based clinical supervision (Falender & Shafranske, 2004) using both Halpert et al.'s (2007) IAS model and Fassinger and Arseneau's model of identity enactment.

MODEL OF IDENTITY ENACTMENT OF GENDER-TRANSGRESSIVE SEXUAL MINORITIES

Fassinger and Arseneau's (2007) model of identity enactment of gender-transgressive sexual minorities centralizes the contexts in which identity is enacted for sexual minorities. Further, the model highlights the extent to which sexual minorities transgress gender roles, both relative to choice of sexual partner and to gender expression. Fassinger and Arseneau proposed that understanding of sexual minorities is enhanced by consideration of three aspects of identity: (a) gender orientation (i.e., an individual's sense of self as male or female), (b) sexual orientation (i.e., an individual's sense of to whom they feel sexually and intimately attracted), and (c) cultural orientation (e.g., religion, race, ethnicity, socioeconomic status). They noted that each of these three aspects of identity interrelate and must be understood relative to temporal influences. Fassinger and Arseneau proposed that sexual minorities manifest and negotiate their identities within four developmental arenas: mental and physical health, family and relationships, education and work, and legal and political rights.

Croteau et al. (2008) noted that Fassinger and Arseneau's (2007) complex view of sexual minorities allows for wide variation in how sexual identity is formed and expressed across life experiences and social locations. Further, the model identifies gender transgression as a commonality underlying sexual minority experience, providing a useful way of considering how to best work with LGBT individuals who on the surface may seem to have little more in common than a political agenda (Bieschke, Perez, & DeBord, 2007). Another important contextual commonality binding this group together is pervasive invisibility and social stigma. Bieschke, Hardy, Fassinger, and Croteau (2008) noted, "invisible identities carry with them a host of related problems: isolation, limited resources, constrained experiences, lack of modeling, biased or inaccurate information, stereotyping, stress and compromised coping, disrupted or inauthentic interpersonal relationships, and profound silence from helping professionals" (p. 179). These authors also pointed out the necessity of attending to the role of temporal influences, given that the experiences of sexual minorities vary greatly by the historical cohort to which an individual belongs, as well as the context created by one's chronological age.

Bieschke et al. (2008) reviewed the empirical literature focused on the intersectional identities for sexual minorities. They noted that the literature base was small and tended to be conceptualized from an additive point of view (i.e., sexual minority status is centralized and then another marginalized identity is added). Certainly, the lives of sexual minorities are more complex than such an additive model suggests. Knowledge about sexual minorities is greatly enhanced by understanding the intersection of multiple identities, such as age, disability, race/ethnicity, social class, and religion.

Using Fassinger and Arseneau's (2007) model to conceptualize sexual minority issues can provide supervisors and trainees with a shared framework that will ensure a complex understanding of the lives of sexual minority individuals. Although all aspects of Fassinger and Arseneau's model are equally important, we argue that in the context of a discussion about supervision and training, it is particularly important to be aware of how religion influences the lives of sexual minorities. Perhaps more than other cultural orientation, religious identity influences the treatment sexual minorities receive, as well as how training in regard to sexual minority issues is approached (e.g., Bieschke, Paul, & Blasko, 2007). Further, the existence of religiously and culturally derived biases about sexual minority clients makes it essential to discuss whether a therapist can be competent to work effectively with LGBT clients if he or she is not affirmative of sexual minorities. We begin by presenting some information about the complex relationship many LGBT individuals have with religion and then describe in detail how values conflicts between religious and sexual identities can present particular challenges in the training setting.

RELIGION

Sexual minority individuals often experience conflicts between their religion and their sexual orientation (e.g., Beckstead & Israel, 2007; Schuck & Liddle, 2001). Evidence suggests that those individuals for whom religion is an organizing principle tend to experience more internalized homonegativity (Tozer & Hayes, 2004). Individuals with a sexual minority status often resolve conflicts between sexual orientation and religion by withdrawing from their religion or pursing religion privately (e.g., Schuck & Liddle). Further, the existing empirical evidence indicates that some individuals, particularly those who affiliate with religions that have a strong heterosexist bias and for whom religion is central to their identity, pursue conversion therapy to resolve this conflict (e.g., Shidlo & Schroeder, 2002). In such cases, conversion therapy is pursued despite evidence suggesting that it is ineffective in changing sexual orientation and has a high potential to do harm (American Psychological Association [APA], 2009). Although the path to resolution of this conflict is fraught with conflicting emotions for LGBT individuals, religion and sexual minority issues are not necessarily incompatible. Affirming faith experiences have been found to indirectly influence positive psychological health via their influence on internalized homophobia and spirituality (Lease, Horne, & Noffsinger-Frazier, 2005).

Just as the conflict between religiously derived biases and sexual identity has the potential to create values conflicts for sexual minority clients, psychologists, particularly those who are religious, also face and must personally address such conflicts. Professional ethics codes and standards explicitly express that psychologists must demonstrate respect for both religion and sexual orientation. Beckstead and Israel (2007) argued that sufficient resolution of such values conflicts is essential to the provision of competent services to sexual minority individuals, particularly given the power differential that exists between therapists and clients. Similarly, we argue that supervisors must also successfully mediate any values conflicts between religion and sexual orientation to provide competent supervision.

Perhaps not surprisingly, few issues have elicited such polarization within the training field as has the divide between sexual minority concerns and religion. In particular, trainees affiliated with religions that do not affirm minority sexual orientations feel that they are being forced to be affirmative. Alternatively, sexual minority trainees are fearful of retribution from their religious supervisors and question whether they will be perceived as unfit to become psychologists (see Croteau et al., 2005; Singh & Chun, 2010). Further complicating this issue is that both a religious and a sexual identity can be hidden on the part of clients, supervisors, and trainees. What can result is that trainees (either those who are religious or those who identify as a sexual minority) may focus more on discerning whether supervision is a safe place to discuss such conflicts rather than on skill development. It is difficult to envision how competence to work with sexual minorities can be facilitated in a climate characterized by suspiciousness and fear.

We have focused on the particular complexities of religion and sexual orientation, given their particular relevance to education and training, but we want to stress that there exists a multiplicity of ways in which understanding sexual minority issues in context is essential to the provision of effective treatment and supervision. Further, understanding how to conceptualize and approach sexual minority issues is not sufficient for the provision of competent clinical supervision of sexual minority issues. The IAS model proposed by Halpert et al. (2007) provides a useful structure for conceiving how to facilitate competence relative to sexual minority issues in the supervision setting.

INTEGRATIVE AFFIRMATIVE SUPERVISION MODEL

The IAS model (Halpert et al., 2007) draws upon a collection of existing supervision models (i.e., Bruss, Brack, Brack, Glickhauf-Hughes, & O'Leary, 1997; Buhrke, 1989; House & Holloway, 1992; Pett, 2000). It is an atheoretical model, designed to fit a wide range of supervision theories and styles. This model rests on the assumption that the supervisor is competent in regard to supervisor tasks, such as those identified by Falender and Shafranske (2004): building and maintaining the supervisory working alliance, attending to relevant legal and ethical issues, and providing both formative and summative feedback. The IAS model was developed to facilitate effective supervision with both sexual minority and heterosexual trainees. We briefly present the model, along with some commentary about existing data, and focus on how the model might be expanded to more explicitly incorporate attention to cultural context as discussed by Fassinger and Arseneau (2007).

The IAS model rests on the assumption that "all gender and sexual orientations are equally valid and respected" (Halpert et al., 2007, p. 342), and in our estimation, this serves as the foundation of affirmative supervision. Halpert et al. (2007) argued compellingly that creating a safe, respectful, and empowering supervision environment in both group and individual supervision is necessary for both heterosexual and sexual minority supervisees to effectively use supervision to develop competence. Recent empirical literature bears out the importance of affirmative supervision for trainees (Burkard et al., 2009; Harbin, Leach, & Eells, 2008; Messinger, 2007; Satterly & Dyson, 2008). We see particular value in this assumption relative to addressing the values conflicts that emerge between religion and sexual orientation.

The IAS clearly identifies the supervisor as the individual most responsible for providing a productive learning environment. Halpert et al. (2007) described three separate phases: presupervision, supervision, and advanced/continuing tasks. We describe each in turn.

Presupervision Tasks

Halpert et al. (2007) emphasized the importance of supervisor attention to skill development in the area of sexual minority issues prior to engaging with trainees within the supervisory context. It is not possible to simply avoid working with sexual minority issues because, as we have stressed, sexual minority identity can be hidden. In fact, LGBT trainees are constantly scanning their environment, searching for signs that it is safe to reveal their identity (Burkard et al., 2009). To a lesser extent, allies of sexual minorities are engaging in a similar process.

Thus, we agree with Halpert et al. (2007) that supervisors must be equipped to work with sexual minority issues prior to supervision. Specifically, Halpert et al. recommended that supervisors be knowledgeable about this population; develop self-awareness of attitudes, biases, and beliefs that impede the development of LGBT affirmation; develop an understanding of the systemic effects of heterosexism on sexual minorities; and work towards developing training environments that are affirmative. Such recommendations are consistent with models proposed by Fassinger and Arseneau (2007) and Falicov (2003), both of which encourage providers to broaden their perceptions of individuals beyond a primary identity or group, and to carefully consider how both individual and systemic factors influence how individuals behave. In addition, Singh and Chun (2010) recently described the queer people of color resilience-based model of supervision; this model focuses on how supervisors can draw upon experiences of oppression and resilience to provide both culturally competent and affirmative supervision to trainees.

Such preparation is essential, given the power dynamics in supervision and the highly charged nature of sexual identity issues. Supervisors must have resolved their own values conflicts prior to helping supervisees to do the same. In addition, supervisors will need to carefully consider how to best facilitate supervisee growth in this area, including wrestling with what constitutes competency relative to these issues. Frankly, supervisors must resolve in their own minds whether trainees can effectively provide competent services to sexual minority clients if they are not affirmative of those who identify as lesbian, gay, or bisexual.

Supervisors must also develop some understanding of the critical issues facing this population. A thorough grounding in the Fassinger and Arseneau (2007) model will facilitate a supervisor's ability to keep abreast of rapidly changing social mores in regard to this very diverse population. For example, we have discussed briefly how religion can be challenging for sexual minorities, but clearly, the situation becomes considerably more complex when one considers other sociocultural identities, such as gender, race, age, and type of religion. This complexity makes it important for supervisors to be at least modestly aware that, for example, one's racial identity can influence the expression of one's sexual orientation, that religion and sexual orientation can be in conflict, and that the experience of LGBT individuals can vary greatly by age cohort. No one can know everything, even those who themselves identify as LGBT, but one can at least have a rudimentary understanding of the complexity inherent to this population.

Finally, we strongly agree with Halpert et al. (2007) that supervisors must lead by example. Working to understand one's biases and assumptions, evidencing basic understanding of the central issues facing this population, and creating training environments where respect is evidenced for all sexual minorities all serve as a communiqué to trainees about the supervisor's competence to work with sexual minority issues (Bieschke & Mintz, 2012).

Supervision

Halpert et al. (2007) stressed the importance of, once supervision begins, attending to the creation of a supervision environment where trainees feel safe and where sexual minority issues can be explored. Further, they stressed the importance of assessing a supervisee's competencies. Finally, they delineated the importance of facilitating trainees' abilities to conceptualize and treat sexual minority clients. Israel, Gorcheva, Walther, Sulzner, and Cohen (2008) confirmed the important role supervisors play in regard to determining which LGBT clients have helpful therapeutic experiences.

Creation of an affirmative environment might consist of behaviors directed toward sexual minority supervisees as well as a wider audience. In particular, similar to the literature on multicultural supervision, evidence suggests it is the responsibility of the supervisors to bring up issues of sexual orientation within the supervisory relationship, even if it does not seem apparent that such issues are central (Falender & Shafranske, 2004; Gatmon et al., 2001). Supervisors might consider being clear about their affirmation to the community by displaying affirmative signs in their offices, such as "safe zone" stickers or small pink triangles, or using gender-neutral pronouns when asking about romantic partners. Of course, these indications of a safe environment are only effective if the supervisor has completed the tasks outlined earlier in the presupervision phase.

Existing empirical data support the central role of the supervisory relationship for sexual minority trainees. Lark and Croteau (1998) interviewed 14 sexual minority trainees about their mentoring experiences and found that safety is critical to the success of mentoring. In particular, participants noted the importance of expression of affirmation and sensitivity to level of outness. Burkard et al. (2009) examined the influence of unaffirmative and affirmative supervision events on sexual minority trainees and concluded that unaffirmative events in supervisory relationships "impede supervisee development" (p. 186) and result in "diminished client care" (p. 186). Similarly, Messinger (2007) concluded that open communication about issues pertaining to sexual minority identity is essential to facilitating student learning and client treatment in sexual minority trainees. It is interesting that in a study by Harbin et al. (2008) that focused on the influence of sexual orientation and homonegativism on supervisory style and satisfaction, the authors concluded that "homonegativism may adversely impact the process and outcomes of supervision—even when neither the supervisor nor the trainee is LGB" (p. 71). Consistent with the current literature, Halpert et al. (2007) emphasized that it is the supervisor's responsibility to facilitate the creation of an environment in which issues pertaining to LGBT clients can be discussed safely, given the highly charged nature of this discussion.

Creation of such an environment is essential, because as Burkard et al. (2009) discussed, training to work competently with sexual minorities is lacking. Further, although much of this chapter has focused on examination of biases, supervisors must also attend to the development of competent trainee clinical skills, as clarity about biases alone is not sufficient to provide adequate services (Bieschke, Paul, & Blasko, 2007; Falender & Shafranske, 2004). Supervisors must carefully balance attention to the development of clinical skills while facilitating examination of personal values relevant to this area. Regarding skill development, supervisors might find two competencies measures useful, the Sexual Orientation Counselor Competency Scale (Bidell, 2005) and the Lesbian, Gay, and Bisexual Affirmative Counseling Self-Efficacy Inventory (Dillon & Worthington, 2003). Both have respectable psychometric properties. At a minimum, supervisees should be familiar with existing resources regarding the provision of services to this population, including the most recent APA (2009) resolution as well as APA's (2000) *Guidelines for Psychotherapy With Lesbian, Gay, and Bisexual Clients.*

A trickier issue is how to work affirmatively with supervisees whose personal values conflict with those of the profession in regard to sexual orientation. Clarity about expectations regarding resolution of conflicts between personal and professional values is essential (Bieschke & Dendy, 2010). Working with trainees on resolving conflicts may be particularly difficult if the supervisor believes that only affirmative trainees can be competent. Yet, numerous recent publications suggest that trainees' affirmation of sexual minorities may not be necessary to be competent to work with such clients (e.g., APA, 2002; Bieschke & Mintz, 2012; Council of Counseling Psychology Training Program, Association of Counseling Center Training Agencies, & Society of Counseling Psychology, 2009). Rather, Bieschke and Mintz (2012) argued that trainees must be able to work competently with those who challenge their belief system and evidence "dynamic worldview inclusivity" (p. 202); that is, the ability to work effectively with those whose worldviews, values, or beliefs are diametrically opposed to their own.

What about trainers with religiously or culturally derived anti-sexual minority bias? Can such individuals be effective if not affirmative? We argue that the most effective supervision relative to sexual minority issues is that which is affirmative, and evidence from Burkard et al. (2009) is clear that nonaffirmative events in supervision push supervisees away and compromise client care. Further, given that religious identity must also be honored, is it acceptable to simply refuse to work with sexual minority clients on the basis of religion? Mintz et al. (2009) argued compellingly that although professional codes do not mandate beliefs, they are clear about the importance of providing competent services. What is less than clear is whether it is possible to provide competent services in such cases, and specific research on this area is lacking.

Relative to conceptualization, consistent with the models proposed by Falicov (2003) and Fassinger and Arseneau (2007), it is important not to focus on one identity status to the exclusion of other compelling cultural identities or presenting concerns (Mohr, Weiner, Chopp, & Wong, 2009). In particular, Halpert et al. (2007) warned against learning information from clients that the therapist should have sought out him or herself; educating the therapist places an undue burden on the client. Further, all clients (and supervisees, for that matter) are not in conflict about their sexual orientation, and if they are, the manifestation of that conflict is highly dependent on the context in which the conflict occurs (e.g., Beckstead & Israel, 2007; Fassinger & Arseneau, 2007). Finally, it is important to remember that some clients who are in conflict may seek out treatment to change sexual orientation. As per the 2009 APA resolution, it is important to note that there is no evidence to support the use of conversion therapy. Rather, supervisors are reminded that sexual minority status does not connote pathology and are encouraged to explore with supervisees how to work effectively with clients to incorporate their sexual orientation into their lives, being mindful of course, of the complications that may ensue due to intersecting identities.

Advanced and Continuing Tasks

Once a foundation has been established, supervisees and supervisors will be able to delve more quickly into complex issues, such as parallel process, countertransference/transference, and termination (Falender & Shafranske, 2004), as well as issues specific to sexual minorities. For example, Mair and Izzard (2001) and Lebolt (1999) both reported that the gay men in their studies found therapy to be particularly helpful when therapists were able to engage in discussions about sexuality. And indeed, there is some preliminary evidence to suggest that trainees are hesitant to approach such issues

(Rutter, Leech, Anderson, & Saunders, 2010). In addition, competent supervision will assist in the identification of appropriate referrals to community resources for clients with sexual minority concerns.

Ongoing, in-depth exploration of sexual minority issues seems essential if trainees are to fully explore their attitudes toward sexual orientation. Bieschke, Croteau, Lark, and Vandiver (2005) recommended that trainers challenge superficial affirmation (i.e., "it's okay to be gay") via the consideration of such topics as the social construction of sexual orientation and gender, the existence of sexual orientation along a continuum, and the importance of social advocacy. Finally, supervisors as part of an evaluation process can provide trainees with specific suggestions in regard to further training relative to sexual minority concerns. For example, sexual minority trainees may wish to discuss whether it is appropriate to come out to their clients, whereas heterosexual trainees may struggle with whether to respond to antigay bias evidenced by clients.

SUPERVISEE PERSPECTIVE

Strengths

Because the IAS model requires supervisors to do a tremendous amount of self-reflection and skill enhancement before providing supervision of sexual minority issues, supervisees are often relieved that they are not required to educate their supervisors. Many sexual minority and heterosexual supervisees have been in this position, given the appalling lack of training that occurs in regard to sexual minority issues. Further, particularly for heterosexual trainees, supervisors' self-reflection during the presupervision phase can serve as a model for how a supervisee might approach challenging beliefs, attitudes, and knowledge about LGBT-relevant issues. In addition, supervisors may have more empathy for how difficult such a journey may be, and this may provide some comfort to trainees who are struggling with the resolution of personal and professional values. Sexual minority trainees are often relieved to find an affirmative supervisor, given that it is still common for trainees to encounter supervisors who are blatantly heterosexist (see, e.g., Burkard et al., 2009). Given the attention to contextual issues per the integration of Fassinger and Arseneau's (2007) model, they are further relieved to find that this affirmation is not shallow but rather attentive to the complexities of what it means to be a sexual minority. This comprehensive approach is perceived as expanding competence to work not only with sexual minority clients but also with other clients who have marginalized or oppressed identities.

Challenges

Supervisors who truly embrace this model can cause some supervisees to be hesitant or even fearful about entering into the supervisory relationship. This is particularly true for those who are not comfortable with LGBT issues. Further intensifying this fear is the lack of clarity that exists in the profession about what constitutes competency in regard to sexual minority issues. This lack of clarity may cause trainees to question whether they will be evaluated negatively, even if they evidence honest attempts to resolve values conflicts. Clear articulation of what constitutes minimal competence seems important to establish at the outset. Even for supervisees who are aware of their biases and strive to be affirmative, establishing an ongoing conversation about such issues is essential. For example, recent research suggests that trainees, even those who perceive themselves as able to avoid their biases, are influenced by their biases when making clinical judgments of their clients (Mohr et al., 2009).

EXAMPLE OF THE APPROACH

The following is a case example that demonstrates how the IAS model is applied when differences exist in sexual orientation within the supervisory triad (i.e., supervisor, supervisee, and client). In this case, the supervisor identifies as a heterosexual female, is a long-standing ally of LGBT people, and has more than 15 years of supervisory experience. The supervisee, who identifies as lesbian, is in the first year of her doctoral program in counseling psychology and has had limited experience as a therapist. Both supervisor and supervisee are White, with middle-class European American backgrounds.

Taehyung, a Korean male, self-identifies as gay but often questions his sexual orientation because of his Christian religious beliefs. He is a second-year doctoral student in sociology program at a mid-Atlantic public university. Taehyung grew up in Korea but before his doctoral studies worked in Europe and South America for a Korean government agency. Taehyung is the only member of his family to live outside of Korea. He is struggling financially and has received limited resources from his family. At the beginning of treatment, Taehyung reported experiencing moderate depression and anxiety resulting from career indecision; social isolation; and adjusting to living in a small, rural community. Although sexual minority status was discussed during the treatment, much of the clinical focus was on his depression and anxiety as they related to his other concerns.

In this first supervision scenario, the supervisor and supervisee discuss how to develop the therapeutic working alliance, given that Taehyung is gay and the supervisee is lesbian. The question at hand is whether it would be therapeutic for the supervisee to come out as a lesbian to Taehyung. The supervisee and supervisor had an established relationship, as the former was in a multicultural class taught by the latter. The supervisee had experienced firsthand the presupervision tasks undertaken by the supervisor and observed the supervisor's comfort and knowledge concerning LGBT issues. This contributed to the supervisee's comfort in coming out to her. Although this particular segment demonstrates the supervision phase of the IAS model, it captures how the presupervision tasks of the supervisor enabled her to provide an open and affirmative environment in supervision. In this environment, the supervisee could explore her own experiences of coming out and assess whether coming out to the client is therapeutic.

Supervisee: I don't know how to effectively join with Taehyung, particularly since I know he's gay and he doesn't seem to have any idea that I'm a lesbian.

Supervisor: What makes it difficult?

Supervisee: I'm an out lesbian in this community, and he's not questioning his sexual orientation per se but rather how to connect with the gay community in this town. I don't know if I should come out to him or not. If he becomes involved with the gay community, we may run into each other.

Supervisor: Yeah, you might run into him . . . but do you have other concerns . . . like coming out to him when he isn't really talking about his sexual orientation?

Supervisee: Yeah. I'm not sure how my disclosure of my sexual orientation to him is clinically relevant . . . but a part of me wants him to know that I understand an important part of his identity.

Supervisor: Well, let's explore more about your reluctance to come out to him . . . I know you are out in other parts of your life.

Supervisee: This seems different from coming out to friends or colleagues, because I'm not in a therapeutic relationship with them. But I guess it is similar because I would be concerned how it would affect those relationships too. And if he does show ambivalence about his sexual orientation, I'm not sure how it would be helpful for him to know I'm a lesbian. I'm thinking that if I tell him it would give him room to process all the aspects of what it means for him to be gay . . . if this issue should come up.

Supervisor: Any other reasons? For example, what about your alliance with him?

Supervisee:	I'm not sure how I could tell if my coming out to him is affecting him or our relationship . . . maybe he would reject me as a therapist . . . maybe it would improve our alliance. I wouldn't want to make him uncomfortable.
Supervisor:	I'm guessing that you've had this question about coming out in other situations, and I wonder what makes this different.
Supervisee:	Maybe that I think that I want his experience of me to be that I'm affirmative . . . so how can I do that without him knowing my own sexual orientation? This is different, since usually coming out is how I do this. Also, self-disclosure in my therapeutic relationship is not something I often do with clients . . . but a part of me wants him to know that I can really understand this aspect of his identity.
Supervisor:	This is a real dilemma for you isn't it? So how can you show that you're affirmative without coming out to him?
Supervisee:	I'm not sure . . . maybe by not pathologizing his experience or struggles as a gay man . . . I don't want to discount the fact that he's gay by not talking about it at all. It would be easy to just ignore the issue and talk about other issues . . . but in a way it would give the message that therapy is not a place he can explore this and how it affects his life.
Supervisor:	I agree that it's important to create a safe environment where he can explore this part of his identity.

This example of the supervision phase of the IAS model is an instance of parallel process and evidences the importance of a strong supervisory working alliance (Falender & Shafranske, 2004). An integral part of the IAS model is for the supervisor to respectfully discuss LGBT issues in a way that is neither threatening nor critical. In this case example, the supervisee experiences the supervisor in a way that is safe and accepting. The supervisor helps the supervisee examine her assumptions related to how to provide an affirmative environment for the client. This example of affirmative supervision enabled the supervisee to think about how to provide a similar affirmative environment with her client. Yet, the supervisee discovers that coming out may not be the only way to create an affirmative environment for her client regardless of his presenting concerns.

Another important part of this therapeutic relationship is the intersection of religion and sexual orientation, which, as mentioned previously, is often difficult to navigate. The IAS model assumes that as the supervisory relationship becomes more open and affirmative, other aspects of the supervisee's identity can be explored. In this next segment, the supervisee explores with the supervisor her discomfort with her own views of religion and sexual orientation.

Supervisee: It seems like Taehyung is struggling with fitting in, given his many cultural identities. First, he's Korean in a predominantly White culture. Second, he attends a Christian church that he's not sure accepts him as a gay person. Third, he's a gay man with a desire to connect with the gay community in town. I feel like I'm one of his only main supports in his life.

Supervisor: So true . . . what do you know about his experience?

Supervisee: I think we talk mostly about his lack of connections with others in his program and the Asian community because he feels different there. He also has talked about how important his faith is to him and how important it is for him to include that in his life. We don't really talk about how these all work together . . . but when you add in his identity as a gay man I can see why he's having difficulty connecting with others . . . I'm not sure where to go from here. The only identity I think I know the most about is his identity as a gay man . . . I guess I know very little about his experience.

Supervisor: Quite a few different identities. Maybe it would be helpful to talk about your own issues around religion and sexual orientation. What are your assumptions about his experience?

Supervisee: Well, to start, I think it would be difficult to be Asian in a predominantly White community . . . and then add the gay man component . . . he could be feeling very isolated . . . see, that's why I feel a lot of pressure in my relationship with him . . . because if I don't understand his experience better, he might not get the treatment he needs.

Supervisor: I'm not sure I'm understanding what the pressure is about for you. It's interesting that you didn't really answer my question about your assumptions regarding religion and sexual orientation.

Supervisee: Yeah . . . I'm making assumptions about what his experience of being gay and Christian is like. He has been shopping around for just the right church, but he has alluded to his willingness to give up his gay identity to have a better religious community. My immediate reaction is to help him see how wrong it would be to not be himself as a gay man because of his faith in God. But I guess that's just as bad as the opposite of suggesting conversion therapy. He has not directly asked about conversion therapy, but he has talked about how his gay identity is not as important to him as having a Christian community.

Supervisor:	Let's talk more about your reactions around being Christian and gay at the same time. Do you think that is possible or not? It seems from what you have said that you don't think it is possible to have both.
Supervisee:	Yeah, I guess in my desire to be affirmative around being gay I'm not being open enough to other identities he talks about being important to him. Of course, I would never give him advice to pick one or the other, but secretly I feel I would like to protect him from rejection. I'm not sure why I feel I need to protect him.

As demonstrated in the previous segment, it can often be difficult for the supervisee to discuss sexual orientation and integrate that with other aspects of the client's identity, such as religion. Consistent with Falender and Shafranske's (2004) definition of diversity competence, the IAS model suggests that it is the responsibility of the supervisor to create the affirmative environment necessary for supervisees to discuss the integration of their own and clients' multiple cultural identities.

One phase of the IAS model is a focus on the supervision of advanced aspects in the therapy process, such as transference, countertransference, and termination processes. In this following segment, the supervisor is supportive of discussing LGBT issues as they relate to enhancing clinical skills. In this segment, the supervisor and supervisee talk about termination of the client's therapy. It demonstrates how the client thinks he has made progress concerning acceptance of being gay, even though that issue was not central to the therapy.

Supervisee:	You won't believe what he brought to therapy today! A list of positive statements that he said resulted from our work together in therapy.
Supervisor:	I've noticed a lot of uncertainty you've felt along the way.
Supervisee:	What's strange is that he included a statement about his progress related to his sexual orientation. He stated this about himself: "I will have to continue dealing with my sexual orientation since it will always appear in my life, and I will manage it well."
Supervisor:	Wow! It seems like a great way to end the work.
Supervisee:	I must say I was quite surprised by his list . . . It's weird that I didn't even realize he felt he had figured out a way to think about his sexual orientation. If I think about what we worked on in therapy, the focus was not exclusively on his sexual orientation. In fact, that was a very small part of the work.

Supervisor:	Yeah, I was thinking about that too. He seems to be telling you that he found a way to deal with his ambivalence about his sexual orientation. My guess is that your working in supervision on resolving your own doubts about whether you could be affirmative without coming out has translated into creating a safe and open environment for him to explore other issues.
Supervisee:	I guess . . . I'm just surprised that an affirmative environment really helps even when sexual orientation is not the focus of the therapy. I guess I didn't see some of the progress along the way on how he felt about being gay.

This example demonstrates how being affirmative does not mean that the issues around sexual orientation have to be the focus of the therapy. The supervisee was surprised by the client's perspective on the progress he made on sexual identity issues, because their work together was not exclusively related to his struggle around sexual orientation. Yet, the supervisee, through discussion with her supervisor, did carefully consider how best to provide an affirmative environment for this particular client.

All the preceding case examples highlight a particular phase in the IAS model. One aspect of the IAS model not illustrated in these examples is the evaluative component of supervision. Each of the examples demonstrated the power of affirmative clinical supervision. Evaluation is an aspect of supervision that can often create hesitancy on the part of the supervisee to share concerns or growing edges he or she is faced with as a therapist (Falender & Shafranske, 2004). Often, evaluation is part of the formal process of supervision but is subjective in nature. In affirmative clinical supervision, the supervisor's main responsibility is to create a safe and open supervisory environment for supervisees not only to grow clinically but also to explore their own biases and assumptions related to LGBT issues. A question a supervisee might have regarding affirmative clinical supervision is, Will I feel free to share concerns even in an affirmative environment if I know I am being evaluated? One approach to address this issue is for supervisors to reassure supervisees from the beginning that exploring biases and assumptions is a part of the learning process and can contribute to a positive evaluation.

CONCLUSION AND RECOMMENDATIONS

In this chapter, we have focused primarily on the supervisor's role in building trainee competence to work with sexual minority issues. It is also important to address the role of the training environment in creating an affirming environment. As described by Mintz and Bieschke (2009) in their introduction to a major contribution of *The Counseling Psychologist* focused on the counseling psychology model training values statement addressing diversity, it can be complex for training programs to take a multicultural perspective that is affirming of both diversity in religion and sexual identity. Nevertheless, finding ways to navigate values conflicts at the programmatic level can facilitate successful training in the context of supervision.

Inclusion of sexual minority issues in supervision is clearly a complex endeavor because client, supervisee, and supervisor all have intersecting identities that must be attended to. Moreover, each individual in the supervisory triad (supervisor, supervisee, client) is at some point in his or her own personal identity development process, regardless of sexual identity. Most supervisors may be familiar with models for conceptualizing LGBT identity and identity development (see, e.g., McCarn & Fassinger, 1996), but many are not aware of models of heterosexual identity development (see, e.g., Mohr, 2002). Knowledge about models of identity development can be used to spur self-awareness in both the supervisor and the supervisee, and it can be a helpful springboard for beginning to develop crucial supervisory and therapy skills.

One of the central recommendations that we propose is the importance of supervisors taking time to gain knowledge and self-awareness about sexual minority issues before engaging in supervision. We describe the importance of supervisors' work to resolve conflicts between their own values and being affirming. In addition, however, knowledge of both LGBT and heterosexual identity development models can help supervisors reflect on their own identity development and how their identity development status may influence what they see in clients and supervisees. Knowledge of such identity development models can be very helpful in deciding how to provide supervision that is developmentally appropriate for both LGBT and heterosexually identified supervisees. Supervisors may gain insight into why supervisees react the way they do to particular supervisory interventions. Additionally, such models may help to shed some light on how evaluation, a key part of supervision, can change over time in a developmentally appropriate way. For example, in the early years of training, there may need to be a great deal of initial support for exploration, but over time, supervisors could support efforts to negotiate and resolve conflicting values. Eventually, supervisors may (or may not) see some resolution begin to emerge. It may be helpful for supervisors to clearly articulate the expectations so as to reduce supervisee anxiety and help supervisees attain expected goals.

Throughout the chapter, we have emphasized supervisory skills that are important for supervisors to have in working with supervisees with respect to sexual minority issues. We drew on the clinical supervision competencies identified by Falender and Shafranske (2004), relative to basic skills. For the skills specific to sexual minorities, we drew on Halpert et al.'s (2007) IAS model (e.g., create a safe environment for exploration and communicating affirming attitudes; bring up and explore sexual minority issues even when they are not apparent; use Fassinger and Arseneau's, 2007, model so as to have a shared vocabulary for conceptualizing the intersection of clients' identities; use gender-neutral pronouns when asking about romantic partners). Additionally, it can be helpful for supervisors to avoid comments that support either negative or positive stereotypes about any LGBT group. Supervisors can also help to build supervisees' multicultural competency by asking them to talk about their own experiences with intersecting identities and the multiplicity of cultural factors that may be relevant to their work; such conversations can include discussions about sexual identity and religion.

It is important for supervisors to support trainees in gaining awareness about their own values and in working to resolve any conflicts between their values and an affirming stance in treatment. Further, it is important for supervisors to consider the knowledge and skills supervisees need to develop with regard to competency in working with sexual minority issues. At a minimum, supervisees should know about the APA's (2000) *Guidelines for Psychotherapy With Lesbian, Gay, and Bisexual Clients*, as well as the more recent APA (2009) resolution that outlines the empirical evidence indicating that conversion therapy does not work. Knowledge about models of identity development can help to clarify questions trainees may have (e.g., What do I do if the client feels bad about being LGBT?), as can knowledge of research on intersecting identities. This kind of knowledge can help trainees to avoid common mistakes, such as pressuring clients to come out to everyone or to leave their religion, or otherwise ignoring contextual variables. Other important clinical skills can include learning how to educate oneself so as not to burden the client, how to conceptualize cases and form treatment plans that neither overemphasize nor ignore sexual minority status, how to think about community resources that could be important, and how to think about whether to come out to clients.

Supervisor knowledge about the clinically relevant self-awareness, knowledge, and skills that trainees need to develop in supervision can be very helpful. The question remains whether supervisors can provide competent supervision without themselves being affirming. The answer is most likely that it depends; nevertheless, taking the time to resolve conflicts that may interfere with being affirming is most likely going to be very helpful to the process of supervision. Finally, a comfort with ambiguity and an ability to sit with, and think deeply about, dilemmas that emerge are likely to enhance development for both supervisors and their supervisees.

REFERENCES

American Psychological Association. (2000). Guidelines for psychotherapy with lesbian, gay, and bisexual clients. *American Psychologist, 55,* 1440–1451. doi:10.1037/0003-066X.55.12.1440

American Psychological Association. (2002). Ethical principles of psychologists and code of conduct. *American Psychologist, 57,* 1060–1073. doi:10.1037/0003-066X.57.12.1060

American Psychological Association. (2009). *Resolution on appropriate affirmative responses to sexual orientation distress and change efforts.* Retrieved from http://www.apa.org/pi/lgbc/publications/resolution-resp.html.

Beckstead, A. L., & Israel, T. (2007). Affirmative counseling and psychotherapy focused on issues related to sexual orientation conflicts. In K. J. Bieschke, R. M. Perez, & K. A. DeBord (Eds.), *Handbook of counseling and psychotherapy with lesbian, gay, bisexual, and transgender clients* (2nd ed., pp. 221–244). Washington, DC: American Psychological Association. doi:10.1037/11482-009

Bidell, M. P. (2005). The Sexual Orientation Counselor Competency Scale: Assessing attitudes, skills, and knowledge of counselors working with lesbian, gay, and bisexual clients. *Counselor Education and Supervision, 44,* 267–279. doi:10.1002/j.1556-6978.2005.tb01755.x

Bieschke, K. J., Croteau, J. M., Lark, J. S., & Vandiver, B. J. (2005). Toward a discourse of sexual orientation equity in the counseling professions. In J. M. Croteau, J. S. Lark, M. Lidderdale, & Y. B. Chung (Eds.), *Deconstructing heterosexism in the counseling professions: Multicultural narrative voices* (pp. 189–210). Thousand Oaks, CA: Sage. doi:10.4135/9781452204529.n22

Bieschke, K. J., & Dendy, A. K. (2010). Using the ethical acculturation model as a framework for attaining competence to work with clients who identify as sexual minorities. *Professional Psychology: Research and Practice, 41,* 424–434.

Bieschke, K. J., Hardy, J., Fassinger, R. F., & Croteau, J. M. (2008). Intersecting identities of gender-transgressive sexual minorities: Toward a new paradigm of affirmative psychology. *Biennial review of counseling psychology* (pp. 177–208). New York, NY: Taylor & Francis.

Bieschke, K. J., & Mintz, L. B. (2012). Counseling psychology model training values statement addressing diversity: History, current use, and future directions. *Training and Education in Professional Psychology, 6,* 196–203. doi:10.1037/a0030810

Bieschke, K. J., Paul, P. L., & Blasko, K. A. (2007). Review of empirical research focused on the experience of lesbian, gay, and bisexual clients in counseling and psychotherapy. In K. Bieschke, R. Perez, & K. DeBord (Eds.), *Handbook of counseling and psychotherapy with lesbian, gay, bisexual, and transgender clients* (2nd ed.; pp. 293–315). Washington, DC: American Psychological Association. doi:10.1037/11482-012

Bieschke, K. J., Perez, R. M., & DeBord, K. A. (2007). Introduction: The challenge of providing affirmative psychotherapy while honoring diverse contexts.

In K. Bieschke, R. Perez, & K. DeBord (Eds.), *Handbook of counseling and psychotherapy with lesbian, gay, bisexual, and transgender clients* (2nd ed., pp. 3–10). Washington, DC: American Psychological Association. doi:10.1037/11482-000

Bruss, K. V., Brack, C. J.., Brack, G., Glickhauf-Hughes, C., & O'Leary, M. (1997). A developmental model for supervising therapists treating gay, lesbian, and bisexual clients. *The Clinical Supervisor, 15,* 61–73. doi:10.1300/J001v15n01_05

Buhrke, R. A. (1989). Lesbian-related issues in counseling supervision. *Women & Therapy, 8,* 195–206. doi:10.1300/J015v08n01_16

Burkard, A. W., Knox, S., Hess, S. A., & Schultz, J. (2009). Lesbian, gay, and bisexual supervisees' experiences of LGB-affirmative and nonaffirmative supervision. *Journal of Counseling Psychology, 56,* 176–188. doi:10.1037/0022-0167.56.1.176

Council of Counseling Psychology Training Program, Association of Counseling Center Training Agencies, & Society of Counseling Psychology. (2009). Counseling psychology model training values statement addressing diversity. *The Counseling Psychologist, 37,* 641–643. doi:10.1177/0011000009331930

Croteau, J. M., Bieschke, K. J., Fassinger, R. F., & Manning, J. L. (2008). Counseling psychology and sexual orientation: History, selective trends, and future directions. *Handbook of Counseling Psychology* (4th ed.). New York, NY: Wiley.

Croteau, J. M., Lark, J. S., Lidderdale, M., & Chung, Y. B. (2005). *Deconstructing heterosexism in the counseling professions: Multicultural narrative voices.* Thousand Oaks, CA: Sage Publications.

Dillon, F. R., & Worthington, R. L. (2003). The Lesbian, Gay, and Bisexual Affirmative Counseling Self-Efficacy Inventory (LGB-CSI): Development, validation, and training implications. *Journal of Counseling Psychology, 50,* 235–251. doi:10.1037/0022-0167.50.2.235

Falender, C. A., & Shafranske, E. P. (2004). *Clinical supervision: A competency-based approach.* Washington, DC: American Psychological Association. doi:10.1037/10806-000

Falicov, C. J. (2003). Culture in family therapy: New variations on a fundamental theme. In T. L. Sexton, G. R. Weeks, & M. S. Robbins (Eds.). *Handbook of family therapy: The science and practice of working with families and couples* (pp. 37–55). New York, NY: Brunner-Routledge.

Fassinger, R. E., & Arseneau, J. R. (2007). "I'd rather get wet than be under that umbrella": Differentiating the experiences and identities of lesbian, gay, bisexual, and transgender people. In K. Bieschke, R. Perez, & K. DeBord (Eds.), *Handbook of counseling and psychotherapy with lesbian, gay, bisexual, and transgender clients* (2nd ed.; pp. 19–49). Washington, DC: American Psychological Association. doi:10.1037/11482-001

Gatmon, D., Jackson, D., Koshkarian, L., Martos-Perry, N., Molina, A., Patel, N., & Rodolfa, E. (2001). Exploring ethnic, gender, and sexual orientation variables in supervision: Do they really matter? *Journal of Multicultural Counseling and Development, 29,* 102–113. doi:10.1002/j.2161-1912.2001.tb00508.x

Halpert, S. C., Reinhardt, B., & Toohey, M. J. (2007). Affirmative clinical supervision. In K. Bieschke, R. Perez, & K. DeBord (Eds.), *Handbook of counseling and psychotherapy with lesbian, gay, bisexual, and transgender clients* (2nd ed.; pp. 341–358). Washington, DC: American Psychological Association. doi:10.1037/11482-014

Harbin, J. J., Leach, M. M., & Eells, G. T. (2008). Homonegativism and sexual orientation matching in counseling supervision. *Counselling Psychology Quarterly, 21*, 61–73. doi:10.1080/09515070801913569

House, R. M., & Holloway, E. L. (1992). Empowering the counseling professional to work with gay and lesbian issues. In S. H. Dworkin & F. J. Gutierrez (Eds.), *Counseling gay men & lesbians: Journey to the end of the rainbow* (pp. 307–323). Alexandria, VA: American Counseling Association.

Israel, T., Gorcheva, R., Walther, W. A., Sulzner, J. M., & Cohen, J. (2008). Therapists' helpful and unhelpful situations with LGBT clients: An exploratory study. *Professional Psychology: Research and Practice, 39*, 361–368. doi:10.1037/0735-7028.39.3.361

Lark, J. S., & Croteau, J. M. (1998). Lesbian, gay, and bisexual doctoral students' mentoring relationships with faculty in counseling psychology. *The Counseling Psychology, 26*, 754–776. doi:10.1177/0011000098265004

Lease, S. H., Horne, S. G., & Noffsinger-Frazier, N. (2005). Affirming faith experiences and psychological health for Caucasian lesbian, gay, and bisexual individuals. *Journal of Counseling Psychology, 52*, 378–388. doi:10.1037/0022-0167.52.3.378

Lebolt, J. (1999). Gay affirmative psychotherapy: A phenomenological study. *Clinical Social Work Journal, 27*, 355–370. doi:10.1023/A:1022870129582

Mair, D., & Izzard, S., (2001). Grasping the nettle: Gay men's experiences in therapy. *Psychodynamic Counselling, 7*, 475–490. doi:10.1080/13533330110087723

McCarn, S. R., & Fassinger, R. E. (1996). Re-visioning sexual minority identity formation: A new model of lesbian identity and its implications for counseling and research. *The Counseling Psychologist, 24*, 508–534. doi:10.1177/0011000096243011

Messinger, L. (2007). Supervision of lesbian, gay, and bisexual social work students by heterosexual field instructors: A qualitative dyad analysis. *The Clinical Supervisor, 26*, 195–222. doi:10.1300/J001v26n01_13

Mintz, L. B., & Bieschke, K. J. (2009). Counseling psychology model training values statement addressing diversity: Development and introduction to the major contribution. *The Counseling Psychologist, 37*, 634–640. doi:10.1177/0011000009331923

Mintz, L. B., Jackson, A. P., Neville, H. A., Illfelder-Kaye, J., Winterowd, C. L., & Loewy, M. I., (2009). The need for a counseling psychology model training values statement addressing diversity. *The Counseling Psychologist, 37*, 644–675. doi:10.1177/0011000009331931

Mohr, J. (2002). Heterosexual identity and the heterosexual therapist: An identity perspective on sexual orientation dynamics in psychotherapy. *The Counseling Psychologist, 30*, 532–566. doi:10.1177/00100002030004003

Mohr, J. J., Weiner, J. L., Chopp, R. M., & Wong, S. J. (2009). Effects of client bisexuality on clinical judgment: When is bias most likely to occur? *Journal of Counseling Psychology, 56*, 164–175. doi:10.1037/a0012816

Murphy, J. A., Rawlings, E. I., & Howe, S. R. (2002). A survey of clinical psychologists on treating lesbian, gay, and bisexual clients. *Professional Psychology: Research and Practice, 33*, 183–189. doi:10.1037/0735-7028.33.2.183

Pett, J. (2000). Gay, lesbian, and bisexual therapy and its supervision. In D. Davies & C. Neal (Eds.), *Therapeutic perspectives on working with lesbian, gay and bisexual clients* (pp. 54–72). Philadelphia, PA: Open University Press.

Phillips, J. C., & Fisher, A. R., (1998). Graduate students' training experiences with gay, lesbian, and bisexual issues. *The Counseling Psychologist, 26*, 712–734. doi:10.1177/0011000098265002

Rutter, P. A., Leech, N. N., Anderson, M., & Saunders, D. (2010). Couples counseling for a transgender-lesbian couple: Students counselors' comfort and discomfort with sexuality counseling topics. *Journal of GLBT Family Studies, 6*, 68–79. doi:10.1080/15504280903472816

Satterly, B. A., & Dyson, D. (2008). Sexual minority supervision. *The Clinical Supervisor, 27*, 17–38. doi:10.1080/07325220802221462

Schuck, K. D., & Liddle, B. J. (2001). Religious conflicts experienced by lesbian, gay, and bisexual individuals. *Journal of Gay & Lesbian Psychotherapy, 5*, 63–82. doi:10.1300/J236v05n02_07

Shidlo, A., & Schroeder, M. (2002). Changing sexual orientation: A consumers' report. *Professional Psychology: Research and Practice, 33*, 249–259. doi:10.1037/0735-7028.33.3.249

Singh, A., & Chun, K. (2010). "From the margins to the center": Moving towards a resilience-based model of supervision for queer people of color supervisors. *Training and Education in Professional Psychology, 4*, 36–46. doi:10.1037/a0017373

Tozer, E. E., & Hayes, J.A. (2004). Why do individuals seek conversion therapy? *The Counseling Psychologist, 32*, 716–740. doi:10.1177/0011000004267563

10

CONSIDERATIONS IN SUPERVISION WORKING WITH AMERICAN INDIAN AND ALASKA NATIVE CLIENTS: UNDERSTANDING THE CONTEXT OF DEEP CULTURE

JOSEPH E. TRIMBLE AND JEFF KING

Culture is embedded in every human interaction, at times almost imperceptibly shaping dialogue and understanding. Supervision provides a process to illuminate the handprint of culture. In this chapter, many of the elements described in the models in the present volume are demonstrated in the context of a specific cultural milieu: the worlds of American Indian and Alaska Native clients. Rather than presenting a set of supervision techniques, we intend to illustrate the interacting factors of culture, including the importance of age and generational knowledge as a cultural feature, that influence clinical and supervisory relationships.

The supervision of counselors working with American Indian and Alaska Native clients requires specific knowledge, skills, and values. The lens of culture in supervision is the subject of this chapter. Knowledge is related to (a) historical context, trauma that occurred historically and currently; (b) acculturation; and (c) healing practices, spirituality, and traditionalism. Skills and values

http://dx.doi.org/10.1037/14370-010
Multiculturalism and Diversity in Clinical Supervision: A Competency-Based Approach, C. A. Falender,
E. P. Shafranske, and C. J. Falicov (Editors)

associated with each are also addressed. In keeping with the model of Falender, Shafranske, and Falicov (see Chapter 1, this volume), therapist, supervisor, and client are all included in consideration. There is an unspoken acknowledgment among American Indians and Alaska Natives that elders, for example, are due respect and deference by younger tribal members (outsiders as well). However, what typically happens in session and supervision is that the elder will give permission for there to be equal relationships in those settings. Thus, the acknowledgment is there, and because it is already there, there is the freedom to make things equal in these counseling contexts. One endearing quality we have noticed about elders is that they make everyone feel equal and do not elevate themselves above others; rather, they make others feel comfortable in their presence. Historical understanding of American Indian and Alaska Native culture is a prerequisite for therapy and supervision of clients from these cultures.

CULTURAL HISTORY OF AMERICAN INDIANS AND ALASKA NATIVES

Destruction of American Indian and Alaska Native culture has been widespread throughout American history. Oppression, racism, genocide, and mistreatment have occurred repeatedly (King, 2009). Compulsory boarding school arrangements forced separation of young American Indian and Alaska Native children from their family and sent them to distant schools that attempted religious and cultural assimilation, disallowing native languages or culture. Upon their return, the children fit in neither world. Furthermore, Native religions were outlawed in the 1890s. In the 1950s, a large federal program relocated American Indians to urban centers from reservations. All of these factors contribute to historical knowledge, much of which is unknown to supervisees entering the field today. Such gaps in knowledge are a source of potential alienation and lack of trust—with a potential generational component. A supervisee could inadvertently re-traumatize a client or parent by recommending residential treatment for an adolescent with delinquent behaviors, unaware that the grandparent may have been separated traumatically from their family.

Supervisees need knowledge of American Indian and Alaska Native tribes and their history, as well knowledge of tribal and traditional ways. Heterogeneity exists among this population today because of differential patterns of acculturation and assimilation. Some of these may be generational, and multiple factors impact acculturation including education. A client's view of his or her Native identity can be a potent contributor to their receptivity to counseling (Trimble, 1987, 1996, 2000). Historically, healing practices have been well established to assist individuals who may find themselves living out of balance with life. Shamans or healers were delegated to conduct healing ceremonies, or they inherited this responsibility by birthright, so that healing traditions were handed down from one generation to the next with highly regulated rites of transmission and passage. There was variation among tribes and villages, and practices also evolved over time as a result of the exchanges of procedures, rituals, and ceremonies generated by contact with other groups and new insights gained by healers through personal and spiritual experiences. Central to an understanding of traditional American Indian and Alaska Native people is acknowledgment of the spiritual realm, ceremony, and the sacred quality of places, persons, and life. Individuals may be active participants in these activities but look to traditional healers—not counselors—for this knowledge. Choice of a mental health provider apart from traditional healers is a choice potentially associated with distrust, misunderstanding, apprehension, and the possibility that mental health practitioners may be ignorant of or insensitive to the cultural backgrounds, worldviews, and historical experiences of American Indian and Alaska Native clients. Client presenting problems may be distorted by Western protocols and diagnoses, which are guided by a different cultural worldview. For example, the mere placement of therapy in a therapy room may be difficult for the American Indian. To these clients, credentials or degrees, so valued by Western psychology, mean little compared with the genuineness and quality of the relationship. Such an understanding must be embodied in the supervisory relationship and client context with respect to the cultures of supervisor, supervisee, and client(s) and the relationships among them.

Cultural involvement and traditionalism may vary across generations. Great-grandparents may be Native speakers and traditional, and grandparents may live on a reservation and speak only English because of boarding school experiences. Grandchildren on the reservation may be bilingual because of Native language classes, and their peers in urban settings may speak only English (LaFromboise & Dixon, 1981). Most important, family is a source of connection and strength.

American Indians and Alaska Natives reside in all of Canada's provinces and in all of the United States. About 50% reside in urban areas; the remainder live in rural villages and small, rural communities and on reservations. There are 561 federally recognized American Indian tribes, with 210 distinct languages (LaFromboise & Dixon, 1981). Disproportionate numbers are below poverty level, have lower educational achievement, and have low levels of high school graduation. Health disparities in these populations include poor prenatal care, malnutrition, excessive deaths from cigarette smoking and alcohol abuse, and suicide (LaFromboise & Dixon, 1981). However, family structure, identity, and community affiliation are often strong, with families as a strong source of support and inspiration (LaFromboise & Dixon, 1981).

To work effectively with American Indian clients, supervisees need to thoroughly understand traditional ways of living that continue to be endorsed and practiced, such as the following:

- living in accord with the natural flow of life energy, having humility, viewing oneself as part of a greater cycle of life;
- speaking through neutral third persons to minimize face-to-face hostility (Garrett & Garrett, 1998);
- respecting extended families and informal caregiving through extended family members;
- using traditional healing practices;
- experiencing significant hardship or life difficulty before participation in a ceremony or sacred activity (this is important background for understanding the presenting "problem" for counseling); and
- gaining insight and deep knowledge from participation in pilgrimages, ceremonies, peyote meetings, or dances.

Supervisees also need to understand the specific skills characteristic of traditional healers. According to Inupiat members of an Alaska Native village, a healer has the following characteristics (Reimer, 1999):

- virtuous, kind, respectful, trustworthy, friendly, gentle, loving, clean, giving, helpful, not a gossip, and not one who wallows in self-pity;
- strong physically, mentally, spiritually, personally, socially, and emotionally;
- able to work well with others by becoming familiar with people in the community;
- good at communication, a skill achieved by taking time to talk, visit, and listen;
- respected because of his or her knowledge, disciplined in thought and action, wise and understanding, and willing to share knowledge by teaching and serving as an inspiration;
- substance free;
- knowledgeable of and adherent to the culture; and
- faithful and with a strong relationship with the Creator.

Herring (1999) provided the following guidance for counselors:

(1) address openly the issue of dissimilar ethnic relationships rather than pretending that no differences exist; (2) schedule appointments to allow for flexibility in ending the session; (3) be open to allowing the extended family to participate in the session; (4) allow time for trust to develop before focusing on problems; (5) respect the uses of silence; (6) demonstrate honor and respect for the [client's] culture(s); and (7) maintain the highest level of confidentiality. (pp. 55–56)

American Indian and Alaska Native Wisdom and Spirituality

Tribal spirituality is inseparable from tribal life. A general responsibility of life is to take care of Mother Earth and the beauty of the world (Garrett & Garrett, 1998). Plants and animals are part of the spirit world, as are people. Mind, body, and spirit are interconnected. All things are connected. *Mitakuye Oyasin* is a Lakota term that captures this concept. It means "all my relatives"—meaning people are in relationship to all things and also implying that all people have a responsibility to all things.

Multiple Identities

As is the case for countless people, those of American Indian and Alaska Native heritage have multiple identities. Falicov's (see Chapter 2, this volume) framework is particularly useful in considering the ecological niche and the multiple identities of the individual. Ecological structure, family organization, concept of healing, origins of mental health problems, and migration stories are all pivotal. In addition, the enactment and nature of an American Indian or Alaska Native individual's multiple identities can be influenced by that individual's tribal lifeways and thoughtways, which may be at variance with conventional expectations and proscriptions. A person's multiple identities in their sociocultural contexts must be considered in any counseling setting.

GENERAL SUPERVISION THEMES

The focus of supervision depends on the client's social–systemic context and which worlds he or she may currently be engaged in. Among tribal people, the supervisory relationship tends to be more effective if it reflects an egalitarian relationship with power and status categories either absent or minimized. This parallels the power dynamics within the tribal community.

As mentioned previously, connecting in authentic ways with American Indian and Alaska Native clients usually requires an emphasis on the subjective processes involved in building trust; identification of the nature of therapeutic relationship; acceptance and support of the client's worldview, values, relationship to the spiritual world, as well as their relationship to traditional healing, and external relationships and situations; and an understanding of what it is like to live with oppression and historical trauma. Thus, the supervisory relationship will involve the supervisee examining his or her own cultural heritage and how it has shaped his or her views of others and self as cultural beings; this examination includes the effects of academic training on his or her worldview and attitude toward both the scientific worldview and indigenous ways of knowing. Furthermore, supervision will explore the supervisor's willingness to accept mystery, healing processes different from their own experiences, and their ability to engage in the healing process themselves, both personally and as a therapist.

CASE EXAMPLE OF THE APPROACH

Two short counseling dialogues are presented to illustrate the essence of some of the culturally resonant relationships between the client and the counselor. The first dialogue occurs between a 30-year-old female Kiowa Indian supervisee and a middle-aged male, Muscogee (Creek) Indian supervisor; the second one is with the same supervisor and a male, 28-year-old non–American Indian supervisee. We describe the supervision session discussions and add in brackets what the thinking and reasoning is during the discussion.

Example 1: American Indian Supervisee and American Indian Supervisor

The following short supervision session description involves a 26-year-old female Navajo (Diné) client from Phoenix, Arizona, who was experiencing posttraumatic stress. She had been beaten and left for dead by two acquaintances after they had been at a bar for most of the night. She was referred through Victims Services and was currently involved in court proceedings regarding assault charges against the men.

Before the supervision, the supervisor was open to learning from the supervisee how she approached this case—recognizing the importance of respecting the process that occurred between her and her client. The supervisor purposely did not have a preconceived framework for supervision in order to allow the supervisor–supervisee relationship to develop according to the specific dynamics involved in the case being presented. This stance is reflected also in Duran's (2006, p. 125) comments on supervision in Indian Country.

Supervision Session 1

Supervisor:	How did things go in your first session?
Supervisee:	Well, as you know, she is still dealing with the trauma of her assault. She is very anxious about going to court to testify against the two men who abused her and left her for dead.
Supervisor:	How is she managing all this? [We are gathering information and determining how the process is unfolding—for both the client and the therapist.]

Supervisee: We talked about her spiritual beliefs, as this seemed central to how she copes. She wonders how she is getting support from the Creator.

Supervisor: What does she think? [In supervision, it is important to not formulate beforehand. Rather, simply hearing the story at this point is the most appropriate response. After the story is told, we get the whole picture; it is then that we can begin to discuss what the next moves will be.]

Supervisee: Well, she feels like she needs to be back in touch with her culture, especially her family. She has been out of touch for years. She feels like she has let her family down with her drinking and wild lifestyle. She'd like to get in touch with them, but thinks they won't have anything to do with her. She feels like maybe she brought this upon herself—that she shouldn't have been out at a bar at that time of the night and shouldn't have agreed to go with these guys— even though she knew them.

Supervisor: Regardless of whether they were friends or not, it was still wrong what they did. Even if she was in a bar drinking, it doesn't make it her fault what they did to her.

Supervisee: I know, but it's hard for her to let go of the guilt and that kind of thinking. I asked her to see if, as part of her healing, she could open herself up to the spiritual realm to allow for things to come her way that might be of help.

Supervisor: How did she respond? [Trying to get a whole picture of the client.]

Supervisee: She was very willing. She said she has been praying and trying to figure out what her lesson in this could be.

Supervisor: Has she had any dreams or anything happening in her life so far that are indications of healing? [Many clients have dreams and other events they would consider spiritual occurrences that they use to make sense of what is happening at this time in their healing process.]

Supervisee: I don't think she's used to thinking this way, but she seems to get a lot out of our sessions. She says they are helping her to think about things in a different way.

Supervisor: Different way? [Getting a sense for how the client is viewing her world—whether there is a spiritual perspective or whether it does not take culture into consideration. In this case, we were able to recognize that the client was beginning to revisit her spirituality and finding it helpful.]

Supervisee: She feels like there is hope. She is getting a sense that there is healing for her and that there are possibilities that she didn't know existed. She is excited about what might happen. She is recognizing that she is being helped by Spirit.

Supervision Session 2

Supervisee: I'm really excited to tell you about my session with Martha!

Supervisor: I'm interested! [Once again, trying to be totally open to the story of the therapeutic relationship as it unfolds and allows the supervisee to tell the story in the way that best suits her.]

Supervisee: Well, as you know, she has been praying and keeping herself open to Spirit for help. She was so excited to tell me what happened this week. As you know, she was so afraid of contacting her family and telling them what has happened but at the same time felt a deep need to reconnect with her culture. Well, she was taking the bus back home from shopping and wound up sitting next to an Indian guy that looked Navajo. They got to talking and found out that each other were Navajo. She felt this was an answer to her prayers.

Supervisor: Cool! [Supporting the notion that the client's healing process is active and affecting her life circumstances in unique and powerful ways.]

Supervisee: Yes. She explained that after he found out she was Navajo, he introduced himself in the traditional Navajo way, and she introduced herself in the same way. For her, this was profound to have this reconnection with her culture. She felt comforted by this.

Supervisor: This is amazing! She had wanted contact with her culture and it was brought to her. [Making sense of this situation from a spiritual perspective congruent with the client's Navajo views.]

Supervisee: Not only that, but since she felt this was an answer to her prayers, she told him her whole story, explaining how she felt she could not contact her brothers, fearing they would reject her.

Supervisor: Interesting. How did the man respond? [All aspects of life that present themselves to the client are part of the Navajo spirituality regarding all things being connected. Thus, the man's response would also inform us about how the healing is reaching and affecting the client.]

Supervisee: He was thoughtful and finally said that he thought her brothers would be open and welcoming if she were to call them.

Supervisor: Wow! There was her answer—do you think? [Not wanting to exert own thoughts but rather join with the supervisee and her perspective of what was happening.]

Supervisee: Well, she certainly thought so. She said as soon as she got home she called her brothers and they were willing to listen to her. Not only that, but they were very welcoming and supportive of her. In fact, they said they would come to Phoenix for her trial to support her.

Supervisor: Wow! The healing is connecting her to her family once again. Not only that, but they are coming here to support her. You know what is interesting? The trauma is about being abandoned and left for dead, and yet the healing is providing the opposite. It is showing her she is not alone and is bringing new life to her. [Feeling felt comfortable enough to offer this view, knowing by this time that the supervisee was viewing the situation in a very similar manner.]

Supervisee: That's how I feel. She has a new outlook on her life. I think it feels like she is getting her life back.

As is clear, the supervisor–supervisee relationship was more egalitarian than what is typical in this type of relationship, with the supervisor entering the supervisory session with an open mind and an attitude of supporting the therapist in her own journey with the client. Questions or comments were made in a manner to make it safe for the supervisee to tell the story in her words and from her perspective, without looking to the supervisor for his interpretation. This allowed the supervisee to fully express their process as a counselor.

Supervision Session 3

Supervisor: How did it go? [Again, belying any preconceived ideas before supervision.]

Supervisee: She is really frightened about testifying in court. However, she has been calling her brothers regularly and that is helping her—knowing they are coming to support her. She has also stayed in contact with the Navajo man she met on the bus.

Supervisor: That sounds good. [Being supportive.]

Supervisee: Yes, but she is feeling a bit uneasy about this guy now. He has been calling her a lot and has been a little weird, asking inappropriate questions of her and asking her to do things with him as though they are kind of like boyfriend–girlfriend.

Supervisor: What is she doing with those feelings? [Illustrating that all aspects of person, place, timing, feelings, and thoughts are considered related to each other and have meaning from a spiritual viewpoint. How one relates to the feelings that emerge are indications of how one is engaging the healing process.]

Supervisee: She doesn't know what to do with them. She feels confused. I suggested she listen to those feelings and see if she can make out what they are telling her, and she said she would try.

The supervisee was familiar with Native ways of viewing all things; thus, she was able to make a suggestion that was congruent with her client's worldview and encourage her to move forward with understanding how these feelings could be teaching her something valuable and essential to her process.

Supervision Session 4

Supervisee: Well, a lot more has happened. She called the Navajo guy and told him she did not want to continue the relationship.

Supervisor: How did this come about?

Supervisee: She said it was really hard, but she took time to make sense of her feelings and said she thought they were warning her about this relationship, so she called him and cut it off.

Supervisor: Wow! This is amazing! Previous to this time, she really wasn't paying attention to these feelings—in fact, she was ignoring them to continue to drink and hang out with people who were really unhealthy, and now she is setting healthy boundaries for herself.

Supervisee: Yes. And this is allowing her to feel more in touch with who she really is. She seems to be more confident each time I see her. She seems brighter each time as well. It is exciting to see her taking advantage of this time.

Supervisor: She seems very willing to trust the process you two have talked about.

Supervisee: Oh! She has taken to it incredibly! But so much has happened along the way to strengthen her relationship to her own spirituality and healing.

Supervisor: How is it for you? [Asking about this because part of supervision and cultural competence is that counselors be aware of how they are relating to the process that is occurring with their clients. Furthermore, it is imperative as part of the process that they are taking care of themselves.]

Supervisee: I feel like I am doing very little, which is fine! She is just going with it and amazing things are happening. I feel very privileged to see how powerful this healing is for her. I just encourage her to keep giving permission for these things to continue.

Supervisor: Another amazing thing is that this Navajo fella came into her life at the right time and said some very profound things to her that helped her along the way. But as she became healthier, he also became a helper by the fact that she was able to see his unhealthiness and set healthy boundaries for herself. [Here again, integrating person, place, timing, healing, and spirituality as part of the therapy process]

Supervisee: I think she recognizes this—that her guidance used him for a time but that he was not a person who could stay with her on this journey because he had his own issues.

Supervision Session 5

Supervisor: How'd your session go?

Supervisee: She had her court hearing, and her brothers came a couple of days early so they could help her with her nervousness and get reacquainted before the trial. She felt really good having her brothers there. They played cards, and she kind of showed them around town. But for the most part it was pretty laid back. They sat right in front at the trial where she could see them when she testified. She said it was amazing how supportive it felt. She was able to be strong while in the witness stand.

Supervisor: Powerful!

Supervisee: The men received some very stiff sentences. She was pleased to see that the judge did not blame her for being at the bar and did not entertain any input regarding her behavior causing this incident. The judge stated very clearly that this was a crime; a violent crime and that they needed to spend time in prison for this. She said he looked at her with kind of a compassionate look.

Supervisor: Wow! I bet this helped her with her own ability to distance herself from thinking of her behavior as part of the

	cause. [Commenting on the healing process and what it is teaching her]
Supervisee:	Yes. I think she had already done a lot of this, but having it happen in the courtroom I think reinforced it in a deeper way.
Supervisor:	Cool!
Supervisee:	She has a number of sessions left, and said she would like to continue in therapy because so much has opened up for her and she would like to explore it.
Supervisor:	Nice!
Supervisee:	She is going home with her brothers for a while and then coming back to Phoenix. She feels going home with her brothers will feel so much safer as she faces her relatives for the first time in years. She's a bit nervous but excited at the same time.
Supervisor:	I imagine this healing will continue to work as she moves forward. This is really courageous of her to go home! I'm betting she will be accepted, and this will be a very powerful coming home—at a lot of levels: her culture, her self, her family, her community, and her spirituality. Coming home. [Making a point to acknowledge the client's strengths as she moves forward and the confluence of all things working together in her personal healing journey]
Supervisee:	I think so. I said I would be praying for her and to call me if she could to let me know how things were going.

Example 2: Non–American Indian Supervisee and American Indian Supervisor

The client was a woman belonging to a Northwest tribe who was experiencing chronic paranoia and distrust, obsessive thinking about her health and diet, and social avoidance. The supervisee was a Euro-American/Anglo male intern in his last year of training. He was new to working with American Indians and had only minimal cross-cultural clinical and counseling training. Because this particular dynamic—a cross-cultural arrangement with a Euro-American/Anglo clinician in an American Indian setting—the time frame is much more extended in the learning process. There are many cultural facets that are fundamental to first contact with the client, to the early parts of therapy, and throughout therapy that are paramount for establishing trust, from type of introduction, the recognition of the unspoken space-in-between that is more often than not distrustful of Euro-American counselors, the counselor's own knowledge of his or her particular culture's history with American Indians and how he or she has come to terms with this in his or her own life, determining the pace of therapy, becoming sensitive to non-verbal cues that convey whether one has permission to ask certain questions or explore specific areas in the client's life, and openness to phenomenon that do not fit within the scientific grid (e.g., ghosts, spirits, visions, communication from animals or plants). Thus, supervision sessions are presented in order of significant supervisory interactions that are linear in time, but not necessarily session-by-session.

Supervision Session 1:

 Supervisor: How did things go in your first session?

 Supervisee: [Explaining the demographics for the client] Well, she seems very suspicious of her friends and relatives and wondered about why I was assigned to her.

 Supervisor: How did you respond to this? [Asking to explore the initial introduction between counselor and client—knowing the potential for distrust because he was non-Indian. Second, the supervisor wanted to get a sense for his supervisee in terms of how the supervisee approaches the messages that are conveyed to him through his clients.]

 Supervisee: I told her that she was assigned to me during our staff meeting. I thought her wondering about me being her therapist might be part of her paranoia. What do you think?

 Supervisor: Do you think she might have been asking about you as a Euro-American/Anglo person working with Native people? [Opening up the dialogue in terms of the supervisor–supervisee relationship as well as introducing the idea of how important trust is among Native people seeking counseling. Furthermore, it is common for therapists to assume that therapy techniques work on everyone—regardless of culture, so the supervisor is indirectly addressing this issue as well. The next bit of dialogue follows this same theme.]

 Supervisee: No! I hadn't even considered this. I guess I feel everyone is basically the same and we all experience the same kinds of problems, so I didn't think it would matter what race I was.

 Supervisor: Native people historically have had a lot of negative experiences in dealing with the Euro-American/Anglo world and White people in general. There is a lot of distrust toward Euro-American/Anglos in this community. I would think this would be enhanced all the more in a counseling session.

Supervisee: Well, I would assume that she would be able to know that I have had a lot of training as a psychotherapist and would have the skills to help address her problems. I did let her know my academic training history and therapeutic orientation.

Supervisor: What did you say?

Supervisee: Well, I told her I got my training at a prestigious university and will be getting my PhD within the year. I told her the types of training we received emphasized best practices and that my specialty was solution-focused therapy. I told her I thought this would work well with the issues she presented.

Supervisor: How do you see solution-focused therapy working with her? [Asking because, as mentioned previously, training programs commonly emphasize the effectiveness of therapy techniques with the assumption that they will work across ethnicities. The supervisor thus asks this to understand his supervisee's perspective on healing processes, techniques, and himself as a therapist.]

Supervisee: I try to conceptualize my client's problem within a framework of 8 to 10 weeks; so as she is telling me what is going on, I am figuring out what our schedule will be in addressing these problems so that we are able to deal with each one effectively within this time frame. I think she was pleased that therapy would only take a short amount of time in resolving these difficulties.

Supervisor: Typically, I try to work with a supervisee along the lines that their training has taken them and then add some of the cultural pieces to it as we encounter them. However, it seems to me in your case we will need to take a serious look at your therapeutic orientation as it relates to counseling in Indian Country. For example, with you being Euro-American/Anglo and being a counselor here on the reservation, it may take 8 to 10 weeks simply to build trust—if not longer. Secondly, Native peoples' problems have historically been minimized and their voices rarely heard by the broader community. So, it makes me wonder if she felt minimized by reducing her problems to a 10-week period of time. [Providing education regarding the importance of understanding the sociohistorical context through which to explain the deeper reason distrust may be present in the initial sessions]

Supervisee: I would've thought she would be relieved to know that we could deal with these issues in a shorter period of time.

Supervisor: That's why I think we are going to need to talk about your orientation and how it is likely to be perceived in this community. [Helping the supervisee, after hearing more about his perspectives, come to the extremely necessary understanding of himself as a cultural being and recognize the meaning this conveys across cultures. Second, the supervisor wanted to explore with him the dynamics that certain therapeutic techniques carry that can affect the therapeutic relationship and the therapy itself.]

Supervisee: Well, I'm open, but it might be a difficult adjustment for me since this has been the primary focus of my training.

Supervisor: Research has shown that the effective counselors in Indian Country are those who are flexible, meaning that they are willing to suspend their previous notions about how the world works and how therapy is supposed to work and be open to new information with an attitude of changing the way they do therapy based on new evidence.

Supervisee: I'm willing to give it a shot.

Supervisor: I am going to give you some readings and a couple of videos to watch about the Native American experience. Take your time with these, but while you are reading or watching them, try to do so with an open mind and try to take in what they are feeling given their circumstances. My own sense is that much of what you will read and see will be surprising and upsetting to you. But take it in and let the feelings that emerge from this inform you.

Supervisor: I am also going to share what I've learned in terms of Native ways of thinking that may be helpful in your own understanding of how to be effective in this community. [Expediting at this point the supervisory process by adding supplementary materials addressing the underlying issues that are likely to manifest themselves in the therapy room. The supervisor also wanted to build the supervisory relationship by sharing his own experiences as a means of conveying what areas need to be addressed to be an effective therapist in Indian Country. It is storytelling, and it fits what many clients will do in session—tell stories!]

Supervisee: I'm open!

Supervisor: The reason I gave you the readings and videos is because I think it's essential to know the worldview, values, lifeways, history, and current attitudes held by these tribal members. And that is not just head knowledge, but as I mentioned a minute ago, it has to be a connection of your own spirit with theirs, given all these things. You have to feel what these are about, experience the feelings of the pain that they have endured and continue to endure. Unless you can feel the pain, you will be ineffectual.

Supervisee: Wow! That's a lot to take in . . . that's a lot to think about. This is very different than my previous training.

Supervisor: I think at this point it might be best simply to listen to clients' stories and not to get into any problem solving. Since problem solving has been so much a part of your training, it may be necessary to give yourself permission to not think about solving the problem and to just listen. In this type of process, see what you learn about yourself as you attempt this. [Suggesting this was a necessary step in the supervisee's learning process, especially since his training had emphasized a certain therapeutic orientation that was not compatible with Native ways. The suggestion to simply listen and not problem solve was given to help him disengage with his previously held beliefs about how therapy works and allow him, through the stories, to experience the healing process through a very different venue.]

Supervisee: I think it will be hard, because my mind is geared toward this. Is this fair to the client? I mean, they *are* coming to me for help.

Supervisor: Storytelling is central to many tribes, including this one. I find that my clients will typically respond with a story after I ask them a question about a particular issue. However, it is in the story that the answer to my question is answered, plus a much more complete picture around what my question was about.

Supervisee: Geez! I guess there is a lot to learn.

Supervisor: Plenty! But part of the process is to be patient with yourself. [Providing instruction on becoming acquainted with the healing process and realizing one can learn from observing the process]

The following interchanges are excerpts from subsequent supervision sessions.

Supervision Session X

Supervisee: The videos were really powerful. I was not aware of the incredible tragedies tribes have gone through. The boarding school video really got to me. I can't believe we were so ignorant in trying to "civilize" Native people by stripping away their culture and teaching them to be Euro-American/ Anglo. How horrific and sad . . .

Supervisor: I would encourage you to let those feelings continue to teach you about yourself and about tribal peoples. [Using a strategy of having the supervisee begin to listen to his feelings as teachers is a parallel process to what many Native people benefit from in therapy. Thus, he will be on a similar journey to those of his clients.]

Supervisee: The readings were really informative as well. They seemed to echo what we've been talking about in our meetings. This is opening up a whole new world for me!

Supervisor: Part of becoming effective is letting go of your previously held assumptions and just listening to the stories, with an attitude that you'll change your ways if what you learn indicates that it is necessary to do so.

Supervisee: Well, already my attitude is changing. This stuff is kind of turning my training on its head! I feel like I'm starting new for the most part.

Supervisor: A good place to be! [For any counselor unfamiliar with the culture, it is a good indicator of progress when the counselor admit their confusion and lostness. It is important to support them and normalize this as a necessary process.]

Supervision Session XX

Supervisee: I really worked hard not to try to solve the problem but just to listen. It was hard! I saw how much my mind is programmed to problem solve. I had to fight it and tell myself to just listen—that it was not important to solve the problem but to just listen.

Supervisor: Good for you. What did you feel you learned from this experience?

Supervisee: I found that I could fully focus on the story and the person telling the story. I wasn't jumping ahead with problem solving or even figuring out all they were saying, but felt present—in the moment.

Supervisor: How did your client respond? [Commenting on the process, linking the supervisee's own learning with the impact it is having in session with his clients]

Supervisee: When she realized I wasn't going to problem solve like I did before, she told me some stuff that was happening with her family. She seemed to relax a bit. And you were right, she did tell about what was going on in her life by telling me a lot of stories. I realized that there is so much more information in the story than I ever expected. It's great! Oh! She also told me about her experience with Euro-American/Anglo people. She told me about the folks in town and how they have always looked down on her tribe. She told me about when she was younger; they would let the children from the tribe swim in their public pool on Saturday mornings until noon. Then they would drain the pool and refill it before the Euro-American/Anglo kids used the pool.

Supervisor: Do you think there was deeper meaning in her telling you this story? [Helping the supervisee realize there are deeper meanings in the stories told and acquainting him with a deeper kind of listening. This type of listening is what tribal people do all the time.]

Supervisee: Hmm. Well, it's a sad story and it resonated with all the stuff I've been reading and seeing on the videos, but I didn't really connect it to her telling me about her distrust of Euro-American/Anglo people—including me. Is that what you mean?

Supervisor: Yes. I'm wondering how you relate to this possibility—that she was telling you about her distrust of you.

Supervisee: Well, now that we're talking about it, it all makes good sense. I can see how it would take a lot of time to build any kind of trust.

Supervisor: True, but one of the powerful things about your session was that she did tell you. I would think this means she is willing to work on the trust issues with you. [Commenting on what was not said but was acted out in the session with his client. She did not say she didn't trust him, but she conveyed this by telling him about her distrust of Whites. If there was not the beginning of trust, he would not have heard this story.]

Supervisee: I think so . . . Boy! I'm afraid it will be so easy to mess up and lose her trust. She doesn't seem like a trusting person anyway.

Supervisor: Perhaps this is just right for her in terms of dealing with trust issues. And just right for you in terms of relating to the folks in this community, as well as understanding yourself in the larger context. [Again, commenting on process issues such as place, timing, and occurrences that fit within a Native worldview]

Supervisee: Yes, it does make sense in that way.

Supervision Session XXX

Supervisee: She stated that she was going to the meeting at the community center for a potluck this weekend. Her granddaughter will be performing as part of the traditional dance group from her school. This is going to be hard for her since she doesn't like to be around people.

Supervisor: Wow! This is taking a lot of courage on her part. Have you thought about attending? I know it's open to everyone. [Knowing that counselor involvement with clients outside of the therapy room has been typically discouraged in training programs, yet also knowing that not being seen in other community functions actually works against your credibility, the supervisor introduces this idea at this time. The supervisor also genuinely felt that this situation came up at the right time in the course of therapy to take trust to a new level. The client may not have even let him know about this event if the trust had not been built up by this point.]

Supervisee: Well, wouldn't that be sort of a dual relationship? I don't know what it will be like to be around her in a more public meeting. She may not want me there.

Supervisor: What I've found in Indian Country is that if you are not seen at other community activities, your credibility is questioned. Indians don't draw the therapist–client boundary lines in the same way we were trained to think. It is more seamless to them. Much like seeing a traditional healer at a gathering—no issues there. Further, it may help your relationship to her for her to see you there—in support.

Supervisee: I will have to think about that. It is making me reexamine my role as a therapist. I mean where do you set the boundaries?

Supervisor: Counselor flexibility is the core trait for effective work among Native people. That means stepping outside of your preconceived notions of what it means to be a therapist and see your role through their eyes.

Supervisee: That is a lot to think about. Can I get in trouble for this?

Supervisor: I'm your supervisor and I have the responsibility ethically to make sure you are conducting yourself in a professional manner. I have no problems with you attending the potluck.

Supervision Session XXXX

Supervisee: Well, I decided to go to the potluck. It was a bit awkward because I didn't know that many people. But some of the staff here came up to me and were really glad to see me. They took me around and introduced me to folks. That felt good!

Supervisor: Did your client interact with you?

Supervisee: She came later—probably because of her social anxiety, but when she saw me she smiled. She came over and introduced me to her daughter and granddaughter after the performance and things were winding down.

Supervisor: I'm glad you didn't go over to them and introduce yourself first. In most tribes, you wait to be invited. Sounds like a positive experience.

Supervisee: Well, there's more to this. In our next session, she seemed even more excited to see me than any previous session. She thanked me for coming to the center and said that it was nice to see me there.

Supervisor: I take it that she sensed your support for her.

Supervisee: I think so. I certainly felt that there was more trust in the room in our session than ever before. She seemed more open and talkative this time.

Supervisor: This is great! The two of you are moving forward.

Narrative Summary

It should be clear from these two different supervisor–supervisee interactions that there are significant cultural dynamics that affect the supervisory relationship. The fact that one of the counselors was American Indian allowed for much easier entrance into the client's life and trust. The Euro-American/Anglo counselor faced barriers from the beginning because of the historical distrust between cultures. The American Indian counselor was familiar with American Indian ways of thinking because they were part of her lifestyle. It was easy for her to be flexible, especially regarding the use of spirituality, even though they were from different tribes. There was a deep resonance between counselor and client because they were both American Indians.

This connection did not exist with the Euro-American/Anglo counselor. Furthermore, his training—although outstanding from a Western view—did not provide him with the information and skills necessary for working in a cross-cultural situation such as this. He felt confident in his skills as a solution-focused therapist and believed that exposure and training around best practices prepared him for any counseling setting.

What may not be as obvious in the narratives is the background for the supervisor—supervisee interaction. The Euro-American/Anglo counselor intern expressed difficulty in facing the necessary changes he would have to make to be an effective counselor in a tribal setting. This was primarily due to his training that gave him a structured approach to therapy and also an expectation that supervision would support and mimic this same approach. The reality is that most supervisors do have this same Western structural approach and tend to perpetuate this style without thinking about its implications cross-culturally.

Although the narratives focused on dialogue between supervisor and supervisee, the dynamic of supervision took on different styles dependent on where the counselor was in his or her own counseling style and understanding. Thus, supervisors must have the necessary cultural competence to have the same flexibility they are expecting of their supervisees. Effective supervisors need to be able to entertain and process events and situations related to the cultural context, as well as understand the unique dynamics that occur in the supervisory relationship. Supervision, as seen through the narratives presented, will take on different shapes and processes depending on multiple factors, including counselor ethnicity, knowledge, previous training, previous supervision, client factors, and attitudes toward change. The supervisory relationship must reflect the power dynamics present in the American Indian and Alaska Native culture, which are typically more egalitarian, are more process-oriented, and maintain a broader concept of what supervision is—similar to the counselor maintaining a broader concept of what psychotherapy is about. As this is reflected in the supervisory relationship, it reinforces this dynamic as the counselor seeks to employ it in therapy.

CONCLUSION AND RECOMMENDATIONS

In sum, it is imperative that supervisors possess the necessary knowledge and skills for working with American Indians and Alaska Natives. Otherwise, they are perpetuating a dynamic of supervision that is reflective of Western/Anglo psychotherapeutic approaches and not applicable to American Indian and Alaska Native culture. In fact, it carries with it bias and potential harm.

The egalitarian nature of the supervisory relationship tends to make it safer to focus on supervisee insensitivities, prejudices, and misinformation. In fact, it is assumed that the topics will be present with most, if not all, counselors working with American Indians and Alaska Natives, especially those who are not of American Indian or Alaska Native heritage. Moreover, an essential part of the supervisor–supervisee relationship is self-reflection, examination, and understanding oneself as a cultural being with a cultural heritage that has had an impact on different and similar American Indian and Alaska Native cultural groups. Typically, there is a naturally evolving process that brings the topics and issues to the surface for discussion. However, the supervisor may have to encourage the exploration of what are often referred to as taboo subjects, such as prejudice, racism, magical thinking, and so on. Sometimes, bibliotherapy and videotherapy are helpful for the supervisee—reading or watching personal stories that emphasize these culturally rich topics. In fact, they can be infused into part of the total supervisory process.

For supervisees, a transition occurs when they must let go of their preconceived notions of how to do therapy. It may feel as if they are abandoning all the training they have had through school. They also may feel various emotions related to the new knowledge they are acquiring, such as anger that they were never informed or taught these strategies or ways of being or anger at seeing the effects of historical oppression, poverty, and injustice on a tribal community. They will have to negotiate cognitively and emotionally the territory of integrating spiritual views into treatment. Many supervisees report a sort of paralysis of thought, emotion, and behavior when confronted with the overwhelming differences across cultures and healing traditions. Thus, it is imperative that a supervisor possess the ability to walk the supervisee through these transitions in a manner that is supportive, nonjudgmental, and strengths based. The egalitarian nature of the supervisory relationship nicely ties into this process.

The two case study narratives in this chapter that trace the dialogue between a non–American Indian supervisee and an American Indian supervisor and between an American Indian supervisee and an American Indian supervisor. These cases illustrate the value of cultural awareness—not just of American Indian and Alaska Native culture but also of the ability to embrace their perspective—in the therapeutic alliance and outcome. The ebb and flow of the dialogues reveal similarities and differences between the dyads that are derived from unique cultural perspectives, supervisee competencies, and the nature of the clients' presenting problems; other psychosocial idiosyncratic factors likely contribute to the dialogues' features, too. One contributing factor may be the symbolic or preconceived expectations of the supervisees and supervisors. Clearly, it is the supervisor's responsibility to provide ongoing commentary regarding how the supervisee is doing regarding providing counseling and grasping the cultural elements necessary for good therapy. In the case in which a supervisee is not receptive to supervision or for some reason is unable to grasp the concepts necessary for effective therapy in Indian Country, if it comes to the point where it is clear the supervisee is not grasping these necessary ideas, then other options need to be explored. Options include (a) not seeing clients but engaging in further cultural training and self-exploration, (b) recognizing that his or her style is better suited for ethnic populations similar to his or her own and seeking out a different place to complete the internship, (c) conducting conjoint therapy with the supervisor or another therapist with culturally competent skills, and/or (d) allowing the supervisee to provide services to individuals that are likely to benefit (and not be harmed) from his or her style of therapy.

Close cultural congruency and resonance are essential in promoting and advancing effective counseling relationships. Similarly, congruency and resonance are essential for supervisor–supervisee relationships as the concordant match between the two parties can promote and expedite supervision. Given tribal and village variability of American Indians and Alaska Natives, ideal supervisory congruence may be unlikely. Nevertheless, a good working relationship can be established, and much can be gained by recognizing the gaps in cultural differences and understanding that these will lessen in time. A focus on process rather than outcome allows for this relationship to flourish.

REFERENCES

Duran, E. (2006). *Healing the soul wound: Counseling American Indians and other native peoples*. Williston, VT: Teachers College Press.

Garrett, J., & Garrett, M. (1998). The path of good medicine: Understanding and counseling Native American Indians. In D. R. Atkinson, G. Morten, & D. W. Sue (Eds.), *Counseling American minorities* (5th ed.; pp. 183–192). New York, NY: McGraw-Hill.

Herring, R. D. (1999). *Counseling with Native American Indians and Alaska Natives: Strategies for helping professionals*. Thousand Oaks, CA: Sage.

King, J. (2009). Psychotherapy within an American Indian perspective. In M. Gallardo & B. McNeill (Eds.), *Intersections of multiple identities: A casebook of evidence-based practices with diverse populations* (pp. 113–136). Mahwah, NJ: Erlbaum.

LaFromboise, T., & Dixon, D. (1981). American Indian perceptions of trustworthiness in a counseling interview. *Journal of Counseling Psychology, 28*, 135–139.

Reimer, C. S. (1999). *Counseling the Inupiat Eskimo*. Westport, CT: Greenwood.

Trimble, J. E. (1987). Self-perception and perceived alienation among American Indians. *Journal of Community Psychology, 15*, 316–333. doi:10.1002/1520-6629(198707)15:3<316::AID-JCOP2290150305>3.0.CO;2-E

Trimble, J. E. (1996). Acculturation, ethnic identification, and the evaluation process. In A. Bayer, F. Brisbane, & A. Ramirez (Eds.), *Advanced methodological issues in culturally competent evaluation for substance abuse prevention* (Center for Substance Abuse Prevention Cultural Competence Series 6, pp. 13–61). Rockville, MD: Office for Substance Abuse Prevention, Division of Community Prevention and Training, U.S. Department of Health and Human Services.

Trimble, J. E. (2000). Social psychological perspectives on changing self-identification among American Indians and Alaska Natives. In R. H. Dana (Ed.), *Handbook of cross-cultural and multicultural personality assessment* (pp. 197–222). Mahwah, NJ: Erlbaum.

11

GROUP SUPERVISION AS A MULTICULTURAL EXPERIENCE: THE INTERSECTION OF RACE, GENDER, AND ETHNICITY

JEAN LAU CHIN, KIRSTEN PETERSEN, HUI MEI NAN,
AND LEAH NICHOLLS

Group supervision is a widely used but minimally addressed modality in the clinical training literature (Smith, Riva, & Cornish, 2012), and multicultural group supervision has received even less attention (Kaduvettoor et al., 2009). Generally, integrating multiculturalism and diversity into all aspects of the group supervision process has been found to facilitate peer vicarious learning (Kaduvettoor et al., 2009). In addition to considering the role of culture in client experience, collaborative exploration within group supervision brings into dialogue the multicultural identities of the participants. Rather than simply talking about culture, such group experiences (with significant supervisor involvement, as preferred by supervisees) provide a lived-world experience of the impacts of culture.

In the approach discussed in this chapter, emphasis is placed on describing a process for understanding the personal lens, worldviews, multiple identities,

http://dx.doi.org/10.1037/14370-011
Multiculturalism and Diversity in Clinical Supervision: A Competency-Based Approach, C. A. Falender, E. P. Shafranske, and C. J. Falicov (Editors)

and power issues brought to the clinical and supervisory relationships by the client, supervisee, and supervisor. Process analysis and self-reflection are central to the discussion of clinical case material, as well as to the supervision group process. The conduct of both the psychotherapy and the clinical supervision involve complex interpersonal relationships. Essential to these relationships is a fundamental understanding of the subjective experience of the other, for instance, the therapist's understanding of his or her client and the supervisor's understanding of the supervisee's conception of the client. Requisite competencies for supervision include skills, knowledge, and attitudes to infuse culture and diversity, such as the multidimensional ecological comparative approach (see Chapter 2, this volume), skills in self-reflection, and personal valuing of and respect for diverse others, consistent with Falender and Shafranske's (2004, 2012) model of competency-based clinical supervision. In addition, understanding current behavior and functioning as influenced by past events, life experience, and culture promotes therapeutic change and effective supervision. Such understanding fosters empathy and strengthens both therapeutic and supervisory relationships. A detailed illustration of the approach in practice, including commentary by participants in the group supervision, is offered to highlight the complexities and practice of multicultural group supervision.

MULTICULTURAL COMPETENCE

In group supervision, multicultural competence encompasses clients, supervisees/therapists, and supervisors. Simply acquiring knowledge about different cultural groups or specific skills to engage clients does not suffice. It is the acquisition of a framework of metaskills that enables therapists to observe, listen, and be empathic with those who are different from oneself and to recognize biases or beliefs that may be inherent in worldviews and in one's personal lens. The reflective capacity is necessary regarding the client and the supervisee–therapist's own process—and the trust established in supervision to allow the supervisor to address the emerging interaction and reflect on both the process and his or her own worldviews and their impact on that process.

Content areas important to establishing multicultural competence include

1. providing a group process that is safe, respectful, and collaborative;
2. addressing conflicts or misapplications of multicultural understanding;
3. providing informed consent regarding confidentiality among group members and limits of confidentiality for the supervisor

(e.g., for purposes of protection of the client and evaluation of the supervisee) and the importance attached to personal disclosures (a disclosure that is given in the program description before enrolling, in compliance with Ethical Standard 7.04 of the *Ethical Principles of Psychologists and Code of Conduct* (American Psychological Association, 2010);

4. being skilled to ask in a way that validates their importance about multiple identity statuses of clients, including age, sex, ethnicity, immigration, race, sexual orientation, and gender identity, and to reflect on these from the perspective of the supervisee–therapist in the interests of the therapy;

5. identifying the unique features, perspectives, and worldviews of the client or clients and how these overlap, or not, with those of the therapist and supervisor and the impact of all these on therapy and the supervision process (see, e.g., Chapter 2, this volume); and

6. addressing stereotypic or categorical approaches that may infer commonality in clients, supervisees–therapists, or supervisors from the same culture (Chin, 2009).

DIMENSIONS OF GENDER AND ETHNICITY

Stereotypic notions of race, ethnicity, and gender exist in the popular culture and may arise in psychotherapy and supervision. Individuals (supervisee–therapist or supervisor) may not know what they do not know, a factor called *metacompetence*, so the supervisor must be mindful of assumptions and biases. A challenge for the supervisor is to strike a balance between knowledge of a client's culture, avoidance of rigid perceptions and expectations of all individuals from that culture, and the need to model sensitivity to differences in beliefs, behavior patterns, and worldviews (Chin, 2009). Some of these notions about ethnicity may operate outside of consciousness because they are socially taboo, associated with power or privilege generally or in supervision. For example, stereotypes about aggressivity, passivity, laziness, intelligence, or emotional lability attributed to certain ethnic or racial groups may influence first impressions of clients, supervisees, or supervisors from those groups.

As clients present with psychological distress, gender and ethnicity and multiple diversity factors affect how they express that distress and the modes of coping they use. For example, a marital relationship gone awry may be influenced by cultural and religious notions about what women are expected to do (e.g., grin and bear the difficulties vs. get a divorce). Difficulties in parenting are influenced by culturally and societally driven views of what is good parenting (e.g., "My parents did it this way; this is the right way to do it. Children should obey their parents, you are a bad parent if they don't").

SUPERVISION EXAMPLE

Attention to race, gender, and ethnicity, indeed generally and to multicultural/diversity identities, is integral to all forms of clinical supervision. Furthermore, group supervision provides a unique opportunity to explore the multiple perspectives engendered by personal history, culture, and context that influence clinical and supervisory relationships, given the cultural differences of the group members. This section presents illustrations of group supervision of individual therapy cases, except for one case in which the client was receiving both group and individual therapy. Attention to culture was integrated throughout clinical training.

The Context of Supervision

The supervision took place in a university training clinic where doctoral clinical psychology student therapists are assigned to clients who may come from the university student population or the nearby community. The cases were part of the student's externship experience in the third year of training. Individual therapy was provided on a weekly basis. One of the clients was being seen in both individual and group psychotherapy.

The theoretical orientation of this program is psychodynamic, which in our view is consistent with multiculturalism. A psychodynamic approach addresses the meaning of current problems, conflicts, and issues within a historical understanding of past relationships and negotiation of developmental milestones. Multiculturalism adds to this the importance of family and social contexts and systems in how meaning is interpreted. It reinforces the importance of differences in social identities and the need to consider lived experiences among diverse clients, therapists, and supervisors in both the therapeutic and supervisory relationships.

Composition of the Supervision Group

The supervisor was a Chinese American female clinician and administrator with more than 30 years of clinical experience. The supervisees included (a) a White, Irish American, 31-year-old female student, born in the United States, who returned to graduate school after a 7-year hiatus as a freelance animator; (b) a 34-year-old female Taiwanese-Chinese student who returned to graduate school for her PhD after a 5-year career as a psychiatrist in Taiwan; and (c) a 31-year-old female Caribbean American student who was born in the United States. All of these individuals were women; however, the diverse mix of race and ethnicity enabled the group to explore the influence of different personal and worldview perspectives and life experiences.

Individual Supervision Sessions

The supervision provided by the first author (Jean Lau Chin) was weekly individual sessions for 1.5 hours over a 5-month period. Each supervisee presented three psychotherapy cases seen weekly. The focus of supervision included review of the psychotherapy sessions, review of process notes, and clinical write-ups to discuss the cases. Content and sequence analysis of clinical sessions, review of client history, and discussion of transference and countertransference reactions were conducted to arrive at a diagnosis, clinical formulations, and therapeutic interventions for working with the clients.

Group Supervision Preparation Protocol

The group supervision sessions provided the supervisees with the opportunity to present cases in a group format with the other supervisees and the supervisor. The group supervision meetings were both experiential and didactic. Preparation for the group supervision included a series of activities, all conducted in the first formal meeting.

First, supervisees were asked to read an article or articles on worldviews, and then engage in a discussion of multicultural issues in psychotherapy (Spinelli, 2006). Second was an identity circle exercise in which group members first identified the components making up their own identities and then assigned a percentage to the amount each component contributed to their overall identity. The second author (Kirsten Petersen) described 50% of her identity circle as that of a female graduate student; the rest: Irish, Norwegian, Taurus, artist, friend, woman, girlfriend, sister, and daughter. The third author (Hui Mei Nan) identified 35% as Taiwanese; 15%, gender; 15%, married; the remaining: education, professional, and age. The fourth author (Leah Nicholls) identified 30% as a student, 17% as Caribbean, 17% as American, 17% as black, and 29% as woman. Kirsten's emphasis on female gender compared with Hui Mei and Leah's emphasis on ethnicity and gender was important to understand in the context of the therapy and the group supervision. Part of the circle exercise was a discussion of competencies in which participants voiced their anxieties and insecurities about seeing clients so different from themselves or differing in various dimensions. They also discussed their own projections associated with religion and gender. This exercise helped them to identify themes about their diverse values and worldviews that included future plans for education, collectivistic beliefs about family, work ethic, gender roles, and different perceptions of feminine beauty.

Next, before the second group session, supervisees were asked to review a formal clinical case write-up by one of the supervisees and to reflect on how their own worldviews might influence their therapeutic approach with the client. Finally, before the third group session, supervisees were asked to reflect on what they had learned about themselves as they engaged in this process of self-reflection. The intent of these sessions was to engage supervisees in an exercise of self-awareness and self-reflection on the influence of ethnicity, gender, and other personal identities on their therapeutic work with diverse clients.

Clinical Cases

In the three clinical cases that were reviewed in group supervision, two of the clients were Latinas, all three clients were Catholic, and two were mothers. For the purposes of this chapter, we focus on Mrs. C, but we first describe the other two clients to illustrate how the supervisee and the other group participants responded differently depending on diversity factors and overlapping identities.

Mrs. A was a 45-year-old mother of four, from El Salvador. Her presenting problem was difficulty with her teenage son from her second marriage's school performance and oppositional and rebellious behavior. Her first marriage was at age 18, but she believed she had been too young and had married mainly to come to the United States. Her own parents were harsh and later divorced, and she split her time between them. In therapy, she came across as demanding and wanting answers yet rejecting of advice.

Ms. B was a White, Irish Catholic, 21-year-old female college student who presented with anxiety attacks; her demeanor was intellectualized and she appeared to struggle to present as competent. Her affect was constricted, and she was easily overwhelmed by minor mishaps, such as losing a lipstick, and she had crying bouts for no apparent reason. She had a significant fear of losing control and was uncertain about what she would do after graduation. Others saw her as successful, but she had self-doubts regarding her competency.

Mrs. C was a 37-year-old mother of a preadolescent, from Peru. She had separated from her husband of 15 years following disclosure that he was having an affair, although apparently he had had many over the course of their marriage. She was in the process of divorcing and selling the house where she resided with her daughter. Mrs. C and her husband came to the United States 1 month after they were married 15 years earlier.

Mrs. C presented with bulimia and complained of difficulties with her preadolescent daughter, whom she viewed as demanding. She talked readily in the sessions, communicating neediness and dependency. Mrs. C was of above average height with long dark hair, dark eyes, and a slim build. She was neatly and attractively dressed. She returned to individual therapy because of an increase in her bingeing behavior and because she wanted to "figure out" her life. She worried about her financial situation and said that her biggest fear was losing her job.

She had refused without explanation to see a therapist of Peruvian heritage. The supervisor hypothesized that Mrs. C wanted to distance herself from her cultural background and difficult past, including the domestic violence of her parents, their emotional remoteness, and the mental illness in the family. Mrs. C presented in her sessions as almost upbeat with a manic-like way of talking that sometimes made it difficult for the therapist to interject with questions. Her stories were generally long, with lots of detail so that it often took a while to get to the gist of what was bothering her. She used her hands, gesticulating frequently as she talked; her legs were always crossed. When questioned by the therapist, she frequently crossed her arms and seemed to tense up.

In the sessions, Mrs. C often appeared ambivalent about being in therapy and seemed to doubt the competency of the therapist. For example, she suggested that she hated to miss her eating disorders therapy but not her individual therapy. She continued to see another therapist initially because this other therapist was "in the field a long time" and said things "that were very true." She was consistently late to sessions (usually ranging from few to more than 20 minutes), denying that her lateness had to do with ambivalence toward the therapist or with anxiety aroused in the sessions, blaming her lateness on work and letting things pile up to the last minute. Mrs. C had been bingeing since the age of 7, when her mother had sent her to a Weight Watchers camp for teens to lose weight. At age 12, she began bingeing again when her mother's boyfriend moved into the house. Her bingeing has been on and off since then, never stopping for more than 6 months. Before reentering therapy, she had stopped bingeing for 6 months, but she had started up again just before she and her husband separated. She did not purge currently, was on a strict diet, and exercised most mornings. Although she tended to focus on the details about her bingeing, she showed increasing insight into its clinical significance. She described feeling "empty" before a bingeing session and had cravings for "sweet things," which she typically did not eat. Over the course of therapy, she had managed several times to stop the bingeing "before it got completely out of control." However, she took little if any pride in these successes because "the urge is still there."

Although relieved at some level that her husband was out of the house, she was lonely, uncertain about her ability to mother, and concerned that her daughter was becoming needy and dependent. However, even with all the turmoil and dislocation, she felt her daughter was better off than she herself had been as a child. Mrs. C was remorseful that her family was in Peru, but she was relieved she did not have to deal with their coldness and distance or with the fact they always ignored her bingeing. Mrs. C blamed the deterioration of her own marriage primarily on her pulling away, emotionally and physically, from her husband. Throughout her life she used food as a way to fill the void, which her mother "never noticed." Bingeing, although giving her a sense of control when feeling stressed and anxious, also served "as punishment" and to alleviate guilt. The symptom signaled her inability to view herself as the source of nurturing or parenting for her daughter and the inability of others to meet her needs.

The following excerpt reflects how Mrs. C's bingeing was tied to her feelings of incompetency as a mother. The vignette illustrates the anger and resentment she experienced when feeling abandoned or when demands were made on her, and how the bingeing was a way to fill herself up and to retaliate against those around her:

> Mrs C: I don't know what happened [after arriving 20 minutes late]. I left [work] at 5:30 and I still got here late!
>
> Supervisee: Traffic?
>
> Mrs. C: No. I don't know. I need to leave [work] at 5 pm. [Continues on to tell a story of her heating system not working the previous weekend and having to call the heating company to fix it. Her daughter, J, wound up spending a night at her father's while she stayed home. She became very stressed when it took more than one visit for the problem to be fixed.]
>
> Mrs. C: I just lay in bed crying. I almost binged but didn't.
>
> Supervisee: Why didn't you?
>
> Mrs. C: Because it wouldn't make me feel better—I would feel worse.
>
> Supervisee: So you recognized it wouldn't help.
>
> Mrs. C: Yes, but the urge was still there. J wanted me to help her with her book report, but I told her I couldn't, she would have to do it on her own. It's very hard being a mother to J. Sometimes I think she should stay with her dad.
>
> Supervisee: What's the hardest thing about mothering J?
>
> Mrs. C: The homework. J continues to struggle.
>
> Supervisee: When you were J's age, what kind of student were you?

Mrs. C:	I was OK. My mother occasionally helped me with homework when it was accounting, which was her job, but then she stopped.
Supervisee:	So you didn't get help from your mother?
Mrs. C:	No . . . I don't understand why she acts the way she does—clingy, demanding—J has it much easier than I did. I had *nothing*. No father who loved me, no computer. And she's so demanding! And my husband too. Both of them want so much.
Supervisee:	It sounds like there's some resentment there.
Mrs. C:	No, no, no. No . . . I once told J that I may not always be there for her but her father loves her and will be there for her.
Supervisee:	I know it's concerned you that J is not more independent. Your mother was not there for you, and you were very independent as a result. It sounds like you want J to be independent for her own sake and you also want her to be independent because you're not sure of your own ability to be a good mother. What do you think?
Mrs. C:	Yeah, I think that could be it. Maybe. It's just so hard being a mother. J wants a lot of affection, asks for it all the time from me but not so much from her father. Maybe because he gives it more? I was with J in the supermarket and I thought, "When was the last time I hugged and kissed her?" So I did and told her that she's beautiful and I love her. Expressing feelings does not come easy to me. It's easier for my husband and J.
Supervisee:	Is that something you think can work on within yourself?
Mrs. C:	I think so.
Supervisee:	Do you want to?
Mrs. C:	Yes and no. I would like to, but sometimes I don't because it's hard. Sometimes I just want to be left alone.

Supervisor Reflections for Group

Development of a Treatment Plan

Understanding Mrs. C in the context of her culture was an ongoing process in the group supervision. It was important to understand gender roles and expectations within Latin American cultures and how Mrs. C's views differed from or were consistent with those of her culture. Mrs. C's ambivalence about divorce reflected both inner dynamics related to abandonment and social and religious taboos about divorce. A reflective process was adopted in the group to address the supervisee's response to these factors and how the others viewed them.

The symbolic meanings associated with food both within the culture and through the client's personal lens afforded an opportunity to integrate cultural meaning with individual dynamics in shaping symptomatology and coping mechanisms. These were discussed in supervision to assist the supervisee and other group members in understanding them, reflecting on personal responses, and using them therapeutically and in formulating treatment goals that included

1. eliminating bingeing episodes through promoting greater awareness of triggers and the development of healthier coping mechanisms through increasing Mrs. C's understanding of the thoughts and emotions that come before, during, and after binge episodes;
2. helping Mrs. C to get her dependency needs and needs for affection met to enable her meet the needs and demands of others; and
3. promoting Mrs. C's awareness of her feelings of loneliness and anger, and her tendency to pull away from people to avoid getting hurt.

Supervision Group Process Interactions

Several issues are illustrative of the supervisory approach. The supervisee was urged to associate to her own strivings for independence and her needs to assert her femaleness as a means of enabling to examine how she responded to and was affected by Mrs. C's strivings and needs. Bridging the supervisee's lack of knowledge about Peruvian cultural norms, values, taboos, and worldviews and the intersection of Catholicism with the supervisee's identity as a White, Catholic, woman who was largely privileged and invisible was also central to the supervision. It was important in encouraging this process of self-reflection in the supervisee to ensure an empathic engagement and respect for the client's differences while helping her to negotiate therapeutic change. This process was also important in the group dynamics where each person came from a different perspective and could support and assist the supervisee.

Competence and Self-Efficacy—Gender

The supervisee and supervisor reflected on Mrs. C's fear of losing her job and its association with competence. The supervisee was urged by the supervisor and the others to consider how Mrs. C took pride in her independence but also to consider her strong dependency on men and to discuss her emotional response and her feelings about these factors. The supervisee suggested that without Mrs. C's experiencing a sense of her own competence, she was becoming overwhelmed by the demands of her daughter and the needs of others, so she tried to meet those needs at the cost of her own, all of which left her feeling resentful. Because of the differences in ecological maps among client, supervisee, other participants, and supervisor, the complexity of understanding, conceptualizing, and moving ahead with empathic engagement was challenging but rewarding. The participants provided vital insights into their own difficulties balancing their strivings with the needs of family members.

Mrs. C seemed unable to effectively parent. She resented her daughter's demands for attention and her insistence that Mrs. C be there for her. Sometimes issues of gender and ethnicity were not explicit, but they seemed to influence the nature of the therapeutic relationship. When her own needs were not met, it appeared that it was more difficult for Mrs. C to give to her daughter. It was difficult for the supervisee–therapist to understand Mrs. C's difficulty parenting, but she benefited from the knowledge, skills, and attitudes provided by the supervisor and the other participants on effective parenting and barriers to that.

Culture and the Marital Relationship

Culture, gender, and religious issues in the supervision interacted with the supervisee's independent strivings as a woman and her own distance from her cultural origins. For the supervisee, it was difficult to empathize with Mrs. C's declining to see a therapist from her own culture or the meaning or significance of her leaving her family and culture. The group processed and supported the supervisee's struggle and reflected on their own.

Meta-Issues in Supervision

As the supervision progressed, feelings of the supervisee vis-à-vis her clients emerged and were discussed. It became apparent that each of her cases evoked different feelings and responses. As she described it, Mrs. A was most difficult, communicating a foreboding sense of judgment about what the supervisee might say—increasing the pressure on the supervisee to perform as Mrs. A wanted her to. In looking for solutions and fixes for managing Mrs. A's son and the school, the supervisee began to doubt her own competency. How could she advise this mother when she has not been a parent? At the same time, she had many "you should" reactions (e.g., "You should set limits with your son. My mother would never have let us get away with that"). Prominent was the judgmental and critical tone of the sessions. Mrs. A was the parent of the trio vis-à-vis the supervisee. However, the supervisee identified most with Ms. B, who was intellectual like herself, a student still in the process of becoming who she is, and carried a demeanor of competency with her peers (even though she often did not feel competent). With Mrs. C, the supervisee felt most competent. Mrs. C was needy and talked readily without making demands on the supervisee. In many ways, she was the child of the trio.

As therapist, the supervisee was the adult of the trio. As supervisee, she was the child vis-à-vis the supervisor. The supervisee's different responses to each of her clients was illuminating in the dynamic of parent–peer–child relationship she held with them, and how it influenced the supervisee's affect, feelings of efficacy, and nature of therapeutic interventions. She felt judged by Mrs. A and even intimidated as she identified with the child in the parent–child relationship. She was most comfortable with Ms. B, and she wanted to comfort Mrs. C in a more maternal and nurturing manner.

The supervisor facilitated discussion of the supervisee's different responses to the three clients. The clients neatly represented the parent, peer, and child for the supervisee. The group examined how this role on the part of the supervisee facilitated or inhibited what occurred in therapy. The supervisee was clearly most comfortable with Mrs. C, that is, the child, with whom she could feel more empowered. We explored how issues of power emerged in all three cases as the supervisee felt judged or judgmental in her interactions. The supervisee's inclination to criticize Mrs. A for not being a good enough parent was initially disruptive to establishing a therapeutic alliance, whereas her overidentification with Ms. B resulted in a tendency to overclassify things as normal. In facilitating the supervisee to bring these reactions to the surface, for instance, identifying with Ms. B's reaction to her father's diagnosis of cancer or thinking about what "my mother would have done" in response to Mrs. A, the supervisee was able to question whether she was imposing her own culturally specific norms onto her clients. The supervisee could process Mrs. A's counters to her suggestions in therapy with "it won't work" and how this reduced them both to a sense of helplessness and powerlessness similar to Mrs. A's own experience with her son. We examined the supervisee's urge to reach out and hug Mrs. C in her moments of neediness; she began to realize that these affects followed by her resultant behaviors were preventing her from promoting Mrs. C's self-efficacy. They reflected the power she felt in the therapeutic relationship and were perpetuating the supervisee's tendency to infantilize Mrs. C in the relationship.

Although the two Latina cases dealt with parenting issues, they differed in that Mrs. C was dealing with her impulses and neediness and Mrs. A was dealing with superego issues of guilt and responsibility (i.e., rules). Ms. B, the White female client, was dealing with ego issues. In supervision, we examined the significance of these differences in how they evoked a underlying sense of "Why can't you be more like me?" from the supervisee toward her two Latina clients but did not elicit the same expectation for her White female client. The richness of the meanings associated with the supervisee's projections and expectations toward her clients illuminates the importance of attending to these cultural worldviews and social perceptions associated with race, ethnicity, and gender in supervision.

GROUP SUPERVISION: REFLECTIONS OF SUPERVISEES

All three supervisees were asked to describe in writing their reflections about the supervision experience. Each chose a different perspective, reflecting the impact of the exercise on their self-awareness.

Kirsten Petersen: Culture Versus Pathology

Her reflections focus on differentiating between culture and pathology. What is the impact of culture and gender? Would it make a difference if Mrs. C had a male therapist? How would a Peruvian therapist be different? Her thoughts follow.

> When working with a client, if I am not careful, I could easily find myself treating culture and pathology as one and the same. This certainly isn't a conscious decision on my part. The culture in which I grew up is a powerful influence on my beliefs, perceptions, and behavior. So innate is this influence that I will judge a person by the norms my culture has instilled in me. But what is "normal" in my culture can be viewed quite differently in another. My culture is not universal, which is why an important part of my work as a therapist is to tease apart culture from pathology. I have learned that it is all too easy for me to view my clients from my own worldview or culture and to pathologize their behavior.
>
> In my work with Mrs. C, a 37-year-old Peruvian woman seeking a divorce from her husband, I am sometimes frustrated by her seeming dependency on men. I come from an Irish Catholic background in which emotional independence and stoicism are highly prized traits. The women in my family did not depend on their husbands to be taken care of; they worked just as hard, if not sometimes harder, than their spouses to make ends meet. My own mother was the breadwinner of our household and obtained her master's in education when I was in elementary school. I realize now how these experiences have influenced my ideas on relationships between men and women.
>
> When I see Mrs. C avoid signing divorce papers, which her husband has asked her repeatedly to do, while continuing to seek a new romantic partner, I feel frustrated that she can't see that she really should be trying to take care of her emotional needs on her own! But then I realize that those are the values with which I grew up, whereas Mrs. C grew up in a

predominantly Catholic country with a mother who stayed married to her mentally ill and physically abusive husband. Divorce was simply not an option.

My work with Mrs. C is impacted not only by my cultural beliefs but also by my gender. I tend to take my gender for granted. I don't walk around consciously thinking, "I am a woman." Yet, how I feel about being a woman does influence how I conduct therapy. I generally operate against more stereotypical feminine behavior because I want to be perceived as a person, not as a gender. When I see a woman behaving girlishly, I tend to devalue her for it. Mrs. C often came across as girlish, and I sometimes found myself infantilizing her because of it, an urge against which I had to struggle. How Mrs. C feels about women, and about being a woman, will also affect her perception of me as a therapist. Her tendency to devalue women in general often made me feel devalued and incompetent—feelings that were compounded by the already existent anxieties of a fledgling therapist.

Although a Peruvian therapist might have been more culturally sensitive to Mrs. C's background, and her values about motherhood and marriage, it could also have acted as a blinder if Mrs. C's core values and beliefs were not questioned. Coming from a different ethnic background, I felt able to identify those differences provided I did not use my values to judge them.

But as hard as that has been at times, withholding my judgment, there is something even more difficult that I must confront, not only in my work with Mrs. C but also with any client from a non-White ethnic heritage, and that is my Whiteness. It is a very difficult thing to sit with a client knowing that, ethnically speaking, I am from a more privileged background. Being White has made my life easier in many ways, but I hate admitting it. "No, no!" I cry, "I grew up middle class, and my parents never owned a new car! No privilege here!" I can't stand the thought that my clients might be resenting me for my Whiteness and making assumptions about my level of wealth and where and how I live. If I don't address these potential assumptions, my Whiteness becomes the elephant in the room that no one talks about, and it can potentially interfere with the alliance and therefore stymie therapeutic work.

At this stage in my career, I cannot think of any weakness to this approach to supervision. I see nothing but benefits to supervisor, supervisee, and especially client, in exploring the dynamics of culture in therapeutic work. The conduct of psychotherapy has a history that is rooted in the society of upper class Caucasians. This is simply a fact we must be aware of to recognize the cultural lens through which psychotherapy has been practiced. It is too easy to talk about psychotherapy as if it were universal and not culture specific; doing so can blindside us to the experiences of others different from ourselves.

From my own experience, I have witnessed much resistance to this way of working with clients and supervisors, not just from other students but from experienced clinicians as well. Some want to believe that a psychodynamic understanding, for example, has no relevance to a client's cultural experiences, as if id, ego, transference, and counter-transference were pure constructs that operate independent of cultural factors. Although I myself have been tempted to think the same way, I no longer believe such a view is realistic or constructive. I now see this as resistance to working with differences and recognize the importance of therapists working through their initial biases and culturally neutral stances if they are to be effective with clients from diverse backgrounds.

Although maintaining an awareness of our own cultural lenses is essential, it is not sufficient. We must also assess our competency and ask whether the skills and issues of race and culture are being addressed in supervision. I now would ask the following questions: Is the client's culture (e.g., sex, gender, ethnicity, religion, sexual orientation) being discussed in supervision? Who is bringing it up, the supervisor or supervisee? Are either resistant to discussing these cultural constructs? Is the supervisee comfortable with bringing these issues things up with the client? Can the supervisee talk nondefensively about his or her own cultural heritage? Can the supervisee acknowledge that his or her cultural norms may contrast significantly from those of the client? These issues need regular examination in supervision, not just at the beginning of a therapeutic or supervisory relationship.

Hui Mei Nan: Learning From the Intercultural Supervision

Hui Mei's reflections draw on her immediate experience of transitioning between two very different cultures. Her thoughts follow.

When invited to participate in the discussion of intercultural supervision, I was in the midst of a cultural shock myself. I had moved to the United States less than half a year earlier. I was amazed by the diverse ethnic groups in my midst, in contrast to the homogenous Chinese society from which I came. I myself experienced a plethora of feelings, including novelty, confusion, surprise, and even fear aroused by being in New York City, the "Big Apple."

After we went through the identity circle exercise of pie charting, I discovered a new combination of my identity components. I realized that my current ethnic awareness was heightened and my sense of professional responsibility had decreased (given that I had been practicing as a psychiatrist and was now a student), and I felt my family role had increased in my current social context. My Chinese background and female identity, things I had taken for granted in the past, now played an increased importance in my transitioning to a graduate student in the United States. It reminded me how it is easy to take for granted that which we have become accustomed to and that which is habitual in our world.

Following this new heightened awareness, I found myself more able to pose questions about the client's life story and to consider the influence of culture and gender in the case formulation. I began to consider many questions about the client's experience of being raised in Argentina, her choice about distancing herself from her family of origin, and her determination to immigrate to the United States in early adulthood. I also began to entertain self-doubts about how I could possibly understand her world with my own limited understanding of her culture.

As we proceeded and the supervisor led a discussion about the similarities and differences between the client and therapist, I became more confident that I did indeed have something to contribute. If I focused not on the specifics of the client's culture but on how to look at difference, I had a framework for understanding clients coming from cultures different from my own. As the group members exchanged thoughts and elaborated on the possible differences in values and beliefs that emerged about gender roles, marriage, family, and the like, I could see how the client's conflicts could derive from several different cultural and personal perspectives. I began to see the value of this process of self-reflection. As we shared the different perspectives brought by the other group members, we were able to go beyond simply categorizing the client by his or her ethnicity or culture.

This sharing helped me to clarify the pros and cons of being in a not-knowing position, which freed me to organize treatment goals in a less biased and prescribed manner. My original belief that similarities between me and the client would reduce anxiety, as well as help to develop the therapeutic alliance, was challenged. In fact, I began to realize that the client may bring a totally different perspective to the therapeutic process. I realized that my initial concern about not knowing, which I took to be a disadvantage, could now be used with the client to explore areas to which she was unaccustomed. Instead of being trapped in my preoccupation about facts, I realized that these facts could sometimes serve to perpetuate stereotypic ideas. By focusing on the space between therapist and client in the session, I learned that I can expand the scope of my questions and engage the client in an open and curious manner that could facilitate the therapy. This new perspective enabled me to focus on the here and now, and how this process material could be useful in achieving psychotherapeutic goals.

Leah Nicholls: Viewing a Client From a Multicultural Perspective

Leah's reflection focused on her ability to integrate culture into psychotherapy and on how to avoid bias. Her thoughts follow.

Meetings with the group have changed my outlook on the client–therapist relationship. Sometimes cultural values, beliefs, and behaviors that are normal in a specific culture may appear pathological to those outside that culture. As therapists, it is important to be aware of specific cultural behaviors and beliefs that might influence our understanding of a client before formulating a diagnosis. A client's self-perceptions often are mirrored in his or her views of the therapist. If a client feels competent, a therapist is likely to be viewed as competent if the therapist is viewed as similar to oneself. Although client–therapist match based on ethnicity might facilitate shared views, it may also render some clients feeling pressured to behave according to cultural norms. If Mrs. C had been assigned a Peruvian therapist, it is possible that she might have felt more pressure to stay with her husband and resolve her marriage difficulties to conform with cultural norms about divorce and separation.

Being a woman, Black, and a student has shaped my development and experiences and has influenced how I view the world and interpersonal problems. In looking through the lens of my identities, I have become aware that clients who are different from me by gender, culture, or race may not experience the world in the ways I do. I am aware that being a Black woman affects my interactions with others and influences their perceptions and comfortability with me. If I am outspoken, it may be viewed as aggression. If I am passive, then I may be viewed as incompetent or weak. It is a work in progress of finding the proper balance to be perceived as assertive and competent. As individuals become more aware of how their stereotypes affect therapy, it will be easier for people of different cultures to understand one another and to view differences in a positive, as opposed to a negative, light. At the same time, I have learned that my identity can result in bias or limit the ways in which I view my clients. To be multiculturally competent, I must be aware that difference matters.

EVALUATION AND OUTCOME

The written exercise presented above enabled the supervisees to evaluate the impact of supervision, and the learning process within supervision. To evaluate the therapeutic relationship and treatment outcomes, the supervisees were asked to provide write-ups of treatment summaries that were discussed in a clinical case presentation format.

For the supervisor, the challenge was how to engage the supervisees in a process that was self-reflective while remaining focused on the clients' issues. While pushing the limits of how the supervisees felt and exploring what they bring to the therapeutic relationship and to the supervision process, the supervisor was always careful to respect the boundaries that distinguished supervision from therapy. Issues of culture and gender are not necessarily intuitive in the practice of psychotherapy; how to evoke the supervisee's attention to such issues requires, at times, stepping back to a metaperspective rather than going with the flow of a session. It also means making links between events in the past to those in the present, thinking about relationships with parental figures and significant others by gender, and eliciting meaning from cultural norms without stereotyping those behaviors.

CONCLUSION AND RECOMMENDATIONS

The value of using this group supervision approach is its enhancement of attention to process and self-reflection. It draws on belief systems and biases of individuals to view the world from their own cultural lens, not as a negative but as a way to foster a questioning and critical inquiry. There are concrete skills to be learned and specific tools that can be used to (a) promote the understanding of personal identity and how it contributes to one's practice of psychotherapy; (b) cultivate self-reflection; and (c) direct attention to issues of race, gender, and ethnicity in the practice of psychotherapy. Attention to the issues of transference and countertransference is essential to identify and correlate those biases experienced by both client and therapist. The recognition of how these are mirrored in the supervision is then important to address. Supervisors and therapists using this approach need to themselves have participated in experiential learning and training exercises or groups that elicit these issues.

REFERENCES

American Psychological Association. (2010). *Ethical principles of psychologists and code of conduct (2002; amended June 1, 2010)*. Retrieved from http://www.apa.org/ethics/code/index.aspx

Chin, J. (2009). *Diversity in mind and in action: Vol. 1. Multiple faces of identity*. Santa Barbara, CA: Praeger/ABC-CLIO.

Falender, C. A., & Shafranske, E. P. (2004). *Clinical supervision. A competency-based approach*. Washington, DC: American Psychological Association. doi:10.1037/10806-000

Falender, C. A., & Shafranske, E. P. (2012). *Getting the most out of clinical training and supervision: A guide for practicum students and interns*. Washington, DC: American Psychological Association. doi:10.1037/13487-000

Kaduvettoor, A., O'Shaughnessy, T., Mori, Y., Beverly, C., Weatherford, R. D., & Ladany, N. (2009). Helpful and hindering multicultural events in group supervision: Climate and multicultural competence. *The Counseling Psychologist, 37*, 786–820. doi:10.1177/0011000009333984

Smith, R. D., Riva, M. T., & Cornish, J. A. E. (2012). The ethical practice of group supervision: A national survey. *Training and Education in Professional Psychology, 6*, 238–248. doi:10.1037/a0030806

Spinelli, E. (2006). Existential psychotherapy: An introductory overview. *Análise Psicológica, 24*, 311–321.

12

REFLECTIVE PRACTICE:
CULTURE IN SELF AND OTHER

CAROL A. FALENDER, EDWARD P. SHAFRANSKE,
AND CELIA J. FALICOV

What does a fish know of the water in which it swims every day?
—Albert Einstein

Each of us (supervisors, supervisees, and clients) lives "embedded in a continuous flow of experience" in which "taken-for-granted schemes" organize perceptions and bring order to life (Eraut, 1994, p. 104). The history and cultures we inhabit continuously shape these schemes, often outside of our conscious awareness. Our multicultural identities contribute as well to our sense of self and influence our understanding of the world in which we live. And yet, it is as if we are like Einstein's fish: We live our lives swimming in a great multicultural ocean, at times hardly noticing its features or the effects of its currents. Culture is so immanent that we are usually not aware of it (Qureshi, 2005).

An overarching principle in this volume concerns raising awareness of the multicultural identities of clients and, with this awareness, tailoring treatment to incorporate clients' preferences and values. In our view, these aims are best accomplished by taking a proactive, intentional stance to diversity

http://dx.doi.org/10.1037/14370-012
Multiculturalism and Diversity in Clinical Supervision: A Competency-Based Approach, C. A. Falender,
E. P. Shafranske, and C. J. Falicov (Editors)

awareness and to developing multicultural competence. Such a stance requires effort and mindful attention to the assumptions, values, and loyalties stemming from our own multicultural identities, which shape our understanding of our clients. As Eraut (1994), drawing on the work of Schutz (1967), observed, "The 'act of attention' brings experiences, which would otherwise be lived through, into the area of conscious thought" (p. 104). Further, such acts may reveal the "inescapable framework" of beliefs and assumptions (Taylor, 1989, as cited in Falender & Shafranske, 2004, p. 32) we bring to our understanding of the client's experience. Such acts of attention are difficult to perform. In fact, unless confusion or misunderstanding surfaces, it is likely that the impacts of individual differences and culture will largely remain unnoticed. We will simply go on understanding the client with little or no appreciation for the influence of culture or subtle misunderstandings of the client's subjective experience. The development of reflective practice provides the means to better attune to the subjective experience of the client and to bring awareness to the cultural, contextual, and historical factors that shape his or her experience. Further, such efforts are not limited to clinical relationships because multicultural factors also influence supervisory relationships.

CLINICAL SUPERVISION, METACOMPETENCE, AND REFLECTIVE PRACTICE

In supervision, efforts to develop multicultural competence involve acts of attention in which supervisor and supervisee collaboratively explore the multiple factors influencing the clinical and supervisory relationships and processes. Collaboration is essential because relying on self-awareness alone is fraught with problems and limitations. Self-assessments of multicultural competence have not been found to be highly correlated with more objective measures and are influenced by social desirability (Johnson, Barnett, Elman, Forrest, & Kaslow, 2012). Further, the accuracy of self-appraisals is limited by self-enhancing behaviors commonly found in self-knowledge (Sedikides, 2007). Supervision provides the means to draw out the cultural features by encouraging self-reflection, observing supervisee and client behaviors in recorded sessions, sharing observations, providing feedback and modeling and encouraging reflective practice in supervision. Self-observations by means of video have been found to improve people's awareness of their behavior and its impact on others (Bollich, Johannet, & Vazire, 2011) and, in this way, improve self-knowledge. Video observation, in addition to other important functions it serves in supervision, may be an important tool in enhancing awareness of the impacts of multicultural similarities and differences. The aforementioned processes aim at enhancing *metacompetence*, by which we mean simply knowing what one knows and what one does not know (Falender & Shafranske, 2007).

The notion of metacompetence has particular relevance for multicultural competence because it focuses on the tension between what a supervisee (or supervisor) knows and does not know about the client, as well as considers the means by which the culture of the client is being brought into awareness. For example, a supervisee may hold beliefs about a client's worldview, such as, "He's very machismo," yet upon reflection and questioning, it becomes clear that this opinion is highly inferential and actually little is known about the client's disposition, attitudes, and behaviors. Supervision provides a remedy to what could develop into a misalliance or rupture by drawing attention to what is not known, by initiating self-assessment and observation, and by providing ongoing feedback. Not only is the understanding of the client enhanced, so too is metacompetence. Positive experiences in supervision can lead to a deepening appreciation of metacompetence as a clinical and supervisory ally—knowing what one does not know is not an acknowledgment of a deficiency or a failure; rather, it is an acknowledgment that more needs to be learned or understood. Internationally, and across disciplines, the challenges of metacompetence as it relates to self-assessment, specific to multicultural competence and other clinical competencies, lie behind licensure debates and challenges to lifetime licensure. Indeed, the development of metacompetence is the key to career-long development and ethical professional practice.

Cultural Humility

Metacompetence as related to efforts to understand the culture of the other builds on the application of the concept of cultural humility. As Falender and Shafranske (2012) described:

> The concept of cultural humility facilitates reflective process and translation. Cultural humility incorporates lifelong commitment to self-evaluation and self-critiquing, addressing and redressing power imbalances in the client–therapist–supervisor dynamic. . . . By formalizing the essential aspect of self-appraisal in combination with self-critiquing, adding humility to the equation, a transformation occurs. Instead of conceptualizing particular behaviors, humility is a mind-set of openness and awareness. Implementation of cultural humility involves not simply understanding concepts but also integrating them into one's clinical work, worldview, and supervision. (p. 56)

Metacompetence and cultural humility, taken together, set the stage for collaboration. The incorporation of humility with metacompetence encourages a stance of openness to the client's experience and fosters the client's self-inquiry concerning cultural, societal, and political influences and loyalties. Through these efforts, a critical consciousness can be nurtured that takes into consideration that some clinical problems are situated in social and political contexts in which psychological oppression plays a central role and requires structural, as well as personal, solutions (Hernández, 2008).

Reflective Practice

Reflective practice has been identified as a competency benchmark and is a marker of readiness at each stage of professional development. For example, readiness for internship requires "broadened self-awareness; self-monitoring; reflectivity regarding professional practice (reflection-on-action); use of resources to enhance reflectivity; [and] elements of reflection-in-action" (Fouad et al., 2009, p. S10). As applied to multicultural competence, reflectivity involves developing an awareness of the appearance and influence of culture in the here and now of clinical engagement and in supervision. Further, by means of reflectivity, supervisors and supervisees are encouraged to refer back to themselves and to reflect on their involvement in the clinical or supervisory interaction, which provides the means to evaluate ways of thinking (Hoshmand, 1994). Attention is directed not only to the client but also to awareness of cultural influences affecting the interactions between client–supervisee–supervisor within the unique context and setting of psychological treatment. Supervision provides an opportunity to observe how the personal subjectivities and multicultural identities of supervisor and supervisee influence understanding the client, as well as impact the supervisory relationship itself. Willingness on the part of the supervisor to disclose their reactions with respect and sensitivity models multicultural awareness and invites the supervisee to examine the personal factors influencing their grasp of the client's worldview. A particular challenge is when supervisee and client (or supervisor) share cultural borderlines (Falicov, 1995) and there is the misperception of absolute similarity, which forecloses consideration of the unique perspectives of each party in the interaction.

Reflective practice also involves drawing attention to emotional responses and to hunches or personal intuitions that shape clinical understanding. Reflection using "loose descriptions" and drawing on personal experiences and self-knowledge provides "a basis for the recognition of and guesswork about contexts hidden in the intersubjective processes" (Krause, 2006, p. 198). In fact, at times our conclusions are more guesswork than scientific, verifiable facts. Such an acknowledgment is consistent with perspectives drawn from metacompetence and cultural humility and reaffirms the importance of taking a stance of receptivity and learning from the client about his or her multicultural identifies and subjective, culture-informed meanings.

Initially in supervision, reflectivity takes the form of *reflection-on-action* (Schön, 1983, 1987, as cited in Falender & Shafranske, 2012):

> When events transpire quickly in a clinical session [the supervisee] has to make quick sense of what is going on; capture the essential components of what has transpired to bring to supervision; and, then independently and in supervision, engage in reflection and self-assessment. (p. 213)

Later, with increased awareness, *reflection-in-action* (Schön, 1983, 1987) occurs, in which reflection occurs in real time during the session. For the supervisee and supervisor, reflection in the immediacy of the clinical or supervisory interaction marks a critical development in multicultural competence. The in-the-moment awareness of the influence of cultural worldviews demonstrates the internalization of sophisticated understanding and attunement to the cultural backdrop that influences all interaction. Reflective practice is advanced through self-observation of personal reactions and the linkage of these reactions to cultural loyalties.

Mindfulness and Reflective Practice

Reflective practice involves a number of capacities, including openness, self-observation, self-awareness, self-reflection, metacognition, and emotional awareness. Reflectivity, including reflection-on-action and reflection-in-action, involves a fundamental ability to be present to one's experience. As such, the framework of mindfulness provides an approach to enhance skills in the ability to more fully experience one's experience in supervision and in the clinical interaction. Although a comprehensive discussion of mindfulness is beyond the scope of the chapter, it is important to discuss the potential benefits of incorporating mindfulness when reflecting on the clinical interaction considering the role of culture and one's personal reactions.

Principles derived from mindfulness, such as attentive openness, when practiced in supervision, may encourage supervisor and supervisee to practice "a careful and attentive waiting for knowledge" (Childs, 2011, p. 296). Such an approach is based on experiential knowledge that is formed in the clinical and supervisory interactions. Safran, Muran, Stevens, and Rothman (2008) described their use of a mindfulness induction exercise in group supervision, which can

> set the tone for each session by focusing trainees' awareness on the present and helping them adopt a sense of nonjudgmental awareness of their own sensory and emotional states . . . this kind of mindfulness work helps trainees increase their awareness of subtle feelings, thoughts, and fantasies that emerge when working with the client, which provide important information about what is occurring in the relationship. (p. 145)

The inclusion of such practices is consistent with the processes involved in reflective functioning.

INCORPORATING FRAMEWORKS IN REFLECTIVE PRACTICE

Organizing frameworks, such as competency-based clinical supervision (Falender & Shafranske, 2004) and the multidimensional ecological comparative approach (MECA; see Chapter 2, this volume), provide theoretical anchoring that can situate the process and outcomes of reflection. For example, in competency-based clinical supervision, efforts are made to identify with precision the specific knowledge, skills, and values/attitudes that are assembled to compose a competency. Applied to multicultural competence, such an approach assists supervisees and supervisors in identifying areas for targeted growth and development. MECA provides a comprehensive orientation to approach culture throughout the supervisory and clinical process. For example, understanding the cultural lens through which the supervisor or supervisee views the client, supervisee, or clinical interaction provides an entry into the impacts of culture. Incorporating diversity through MECA into the supervision process, as described in Chapters 2 and 4 of this volume, provides distinctive training and practice protocols for instilling competent multicultural supervision and building metacompetence.

As illustrated throughout this volume, the development of self-awareness and multicultural competence is a complex undertaking that requires commitment and intentionality. Each chapter in this volume highlights areas that require particular consideration and provides perspectives and information drawn from the literature. Rather than presenting a cookbook approach to these specific multicultural features, the contents provide points for reflection and the means to contextualize the supervisor's and supervisee's personal observations within the field. Cultural relativism (see Chapter 2); power, privilege, and social hierarchies (see Chapter 3); cultural histories and group identities (see Chapters 6 and 11); and sources of anxiety in diversity (see Chapter 4) are all issues that stimulate reflection and self-assessment.

COMMITMENT AND INTENTIONALITY
IN REFLECTIVE PRACTICE

Reflective practice cannot be developed in clinical training or sustained throughout one's career without commitment and intention. This is particularly the case when self-reflectivity is directed to the embedded multicultural features that influence clinical and supervisory interaction. Indeed, the fish must make an effortful commitment (with a lot of reminders) to know the water in which it swims every day. Put another way, the commitment to multicultural competence requires deliberate practice.

Self-reflective practice and efforts to develop multicultural competence can be enhanced by a number of supervisor-initiated means (see, e.g., Dressel, Consoli, Kim, & Atkinson, 2007; Falender & Shafranske, 2012, Chapter 4; Orchowski, Evangelista, & Probst, 2010). These include

1. making explicit that reflectivity and attention to diversity and multicultural factors are a supervisory and professional responsibility;
2. creating a safe environment by attention to the supervisory relationship and alliance by providing openness, genuineness, warmth, empathy, respect, and a collaborative, nonjudgmental stance;
3. modeling reflectivity and cultural humility, including disclosing multicultural identities and challenges to multicultural competence;
4. valuing and respecting the supervisee's multicultural identities and perspectives;
5. considering with the supervisee the impacts of diversity and multicultural identities within the supervisory relationship;
6. presenting, discussing, and providing didactic material about the ways in which gender, class, and ability (as well as other multicultural factors) contribute to relationships of privilege and oppression (Hernández, 2008);
7. directing and supporting reflective activities, such as mindfulness, both in session and outside of session;
8. using self-assessment and inquiry tools to enhance reflection;
9. addressing barriers to multicultural competence by empathy-based attention to sources of discomfort related to difference (see Chapter 4, this volume); and
10. engaging in collaborative reflection and assessment of the effectiveness of supervisory activities aiming to support the development of multicultural competence and eliciting recommendations for improvement.

Much work is before us to fully implement multiculturally sensitive practices in clinical and counseling psychology. Values and commitment are fundamental to efforts to fully understand the culture in self and in other. Reflection on one's values and commitments is the starting point in such a process.

REFERENCES

Bollich, K. L., Johannet, P. M., & Vazire, S. (2011). In search of our true selves: Feedback as a path to self-knowledge. *Frontiers in Psychology, 2*. doi: 10.3389/fpsyg.2011.00312

Childs, D. (2011). Mindfulness and clinical psychology. *Psychology and Psychotherapy: Theory, Research, and Practice, 84,* 288–298. doi:10.1348/147608310X530048

Dressel, J. L., Consoli, A. J., Kim, B. S. K., & Atkinson, D. R. (2007). Successful and unsuccessful multicultural supervisory behaviors: A Delphi poll. *Journal of Multicultural Counseling and Development, 35,* 51–64. Retrieved from http://www.counseling.org/Publications/Journals.aspx doi:10.1002/j.2161-1912.2007.tb00049.x

Eraut, M. (1994). *Developing professional knowledge and competence. Developing professional knowledge and competence.* New York, NY: Routledge.

Falender, C. A., & Shafranske, E. P. (2004). *Clinical supervision: A competency-based approach.* Washington, DC: American Psychological Association. doi:10.1037/10806-000

Falender, C. A., & Shafranske, E. P. (2007). Competence in competency-based supervision practice: Construct and application. *Professional Psychology: Research and Practice, 38,* 232–240. doi:10.1037/0735-7028.38.3.232

Falender, C. A., & Shafranske, E. P. (2012). *Getting the most out of clinical training and supervision: A guide for practicum students and interns.* Washington, DC: American Psychological Association. doi:10.1037/13487-000

Falicov, C. J. (1995). Training to think culturally: A multidimensional comparative framework. *Family Process, 34,* 373–388. Retrieved from http://www.familyprocess.org/ doi:10.1111/j.1545-5300.1995.00373.x

Fouad, N. A., Grus, C. L., Hatcher, R. L., Kaslow, N. J., Hutchings, P. S., Madson, M. B., . . . Crossman, R. E. (2009). Competency benchmarks: A model for understanding and measuring competence in professional psychology across training levels. *Training and Education in Professional Psychology, 3*(4, Suppl.), S5–S26. doi:10.1037/a0015832

Hernández, P. (2008). The cultural context model in clinical supervision. *Training and Education in Professional Psychology, 2,* 10–17. doi:10.1037/1931-3918.2.1.10

Hoshmand, L. T. (1994). *Orientation to inquiry in a reflective professional psychology.* Albany: State University of New York Press.

Johnson, W. B., Barnett, J. E., Elman, N. S., Forrest, L., & Kaslow, N. J. (2012). The competent community: Toward a vital reformulation of professional ethics. *American Psychologist, 67,* 557–569. doi:10.1037/a0027206

Krause, I.-B. (2006). Hidden points of view in cross-cultural psychotherapy and ethnology. *Transpersonal Psychiatry, 43,* 181–203. doi:10.1177/1363461506064848

Orchowski, L., Evangelista, N. M., & Probst, D. R. (2010). Enhancing supervisee reflection in clinical supervision: A case study illustration. *Psychotherapy: Theory, Research, and Practice, 47,* 51–67. doi:10.1037/a0018844

Qureshi, A. (2005). Dialogical relationship and cultural imagination: A hermeneutic approach to intercultural psychology. *American Journal of Psychotherapy, 59,* 119–135.

Safran, J. D., Muran, J. C., Stevens, C., & Rothman, M. (2008). A relational approach to supervision: Addressing ruptures in alliance. In C. A. Falender & E. P. Shafranske (Eds.), *Casebook for clinical supervision: A competency-based approach* (pp. 137–157). Washington, DC: American Psychological Association. doi:10.1037/11792-007

Schön, D. A. (1983). *The reflective practitioner: How professionals think in action.* New York, NY: Basic Books.

Schön, D. A. (1987). *Educating the reflective practitioner: Toward a new design for teaching and learning in the professions.* San Francisco, CA: Jossey-Bass.

Schutz, A. (1967). *The phenomenology of the social world.* Evanston, IL: Northwestern University Press.

Sedikides, C. (2007). Self-enhancement and self-protection: Powerful, pancultural, and functional. *Hellenic Journal of Psychology, 4,* 1–13.

INDEX

Diversity lens, 8
Diversity mindfulness, 63, 65. *See also*
    Feminist, gendered, multicultural,
    ecological, and antiracist frame-
    work
Domenech Rodriguez, M. M., 131
Double discourse, 43–44
DSI (differential status identity), 148–149
Duran, E., 236
Dysfunctional family patterns, 125–126

Early treatment withdrawal rates,
    xii–xiii
Eating disorders, 46
Ecological context. *See also* Feminist,
    gendered, multicultural, ecologi-
    cal, and antiracist framework
    in case illustration, 135
    as ecological domain, 47, 48–49
    of race-related issues, 87
Ecological niches
    in MECA, 39–40
    and race-related issues, 86–87
    in supervisory sessions, 51, 53
Ecological rescuing, 132, 133
Ecological systems theory, 86
Ecomaps, 117
Economic factors, 149
Ecosystemic domains, 46–50
Education For All Handicapped Chil-
    dren (Public Law 94-142), 8
Egalitarian relationship, 235, 252
Einstein, Albert, 273
Elicitation and disclosure (in three-step
    supervision strategy), 97–101
Empathic exploration, 85, 105
Empirical grounding, 86–88
Empirical support, 15
Empowerment
    family, 141
    psychosocial, 124
    and sociopolitical lens, 46
    by supervisors, 172
Eraut, M., 273, 274
Erickson Cornish, J. A., 165
Ethical-decision-making model, 9, 72
Ethical dilemmas, 131
*Ethical Guidelines for Supervision in Psy-
    chology* (CPA), 10–11
Ethical imperative, 182–183

*Ethical Principles of Psychologists and Code
    of Conduct* (APA), 10, 257
Ethnic-focused position, 35
Ethnicity, in group supervision, 257–258
Ethnicity and Family Therapy (McGold-
    rick, Giordano, and Pearce), 8
Ethnic stereotyping
    and cultural assessment, 132–133
    in ethnic-focused position, 37
Ethnocentrism, 132
Euro-American clinicians, 242–243,
    250–251
Euro-American culture
    in cultural diversity lens, 45
    and family life cycle, 49–50
    and psychological theory, 30
Evaluation
    of competency-based approach,
        159–160
    of group supervision, 271
    in IAS model, 224, 225
    in three-step supervision strategy,
        104–105

Falender, C. A., 5–7, 16, 52, 70, 165,
    210, 213, 223, 225–226, 256,
    274, 275, 277
Falicov, C. J., 4–5, 8, 32, 38, 47, 53,
    83–84, 86, 119, 153, 214, 217, 235
Family empowerment, 141
Family intermediary, 122, 125, 128
Family life cycle
    in case illustration, 136–137
    as ecological domain, 47, 49–50
Family nuclearization, 141
Family organization
    in case illustration, 136
    as ecological domain, 47, 49
Family sessions, 140
Fassinger, R. E., 210, 211, 213, 214, 217,
    218, 226
Females, depression in, 61, 62
Feminist, gendered, multicultural, eco-
    logical, and antiracist framework,
    59–78
    advocacy for women, 77–78
    case illustration of, 72–77
    and collaborative self-reflection, 72
    and gender inequality, 61–63
    multicultural issues in, 69–72

social class worldview model, 149
strengths and limitations of competencies, 152
Social class groups, 146
Social class worldview model, 149
Social constructivist narrative theory, 92
Social identity, 188–189
Social injustice, 37
Social intermediary, 122–124, 128, 139
Social justice, xiii, 5, 45–46
Social movements, xii
Social stigma, 211
Sociocultural background, of supervisee, 45
Sociocultural identities, 214–215
Socioeconomic status (SES). *See* Social class and socioeconomic status
Sociological imagination, 138
Sociopolitical lens, 44–46
Sociopolitical movements, xii
Soldiers, disabled in war, 166
Spiritual exclusivism, 186
Spiritual illiteracy, 187
Spiritual intolerance, 186
Spiritual Issues in Supervision Scale, 194
Spirituality. *See* Religion and spirituality
Spiritually conscious care, 191
Standardised Index of Gender Equality (SIGE), 62
Standards, for multicultural supervision, 10–11
Stereotypic notions
in group supervision, 271
in psychotherapy, 257–258, 271
Stevens, C., 277
Storytelling, as cultural heritage, 246
Stresses, of migration, 113
Sue, D. W., 5, 7
Suicide attempts, 125
Sulzner, J. M., 215
Supervisees
acculturation of, 269
affirmation of sexual minorities by, 216–217
biases of, 219
bibliotherapy for, 252
in competency-based supervision, 17

cultural humility of, 14
difficulty grasping cultural concepts by, 252–253
in group supervision, 267–271
in IAS model, 218–219
and knowledge of American Indian and Alaska Native tribes, 232–233
reactivity of, to clients, 17, 75–77
refusing to provide therapy, 13–14
and sexual minority issues, 218–219
sociocultural background of, 45
Supervision. *See* Clinical supervision
Supervision approach, 152
Supervision contract, 17
Supervision as cultural encounter, 32–34
Supervision diversity competence, 6–7
Supervision of supervision
defined, 4
in multicultural supervision, 18–19
Supervision processes, 154
Supervisor-initiated means, 279
Supervisors
affirmative environment created by, 215, 218, 226
competence of, and race-related issues, 106
competence of, and sexual minority issues, 214
in competency-based supervision, 17
and diversity perspectives, 19
intentional orientation of, 182–183
lack of competence of, 12, 77, 178
multicultural competence for, xi
role of, in MECA, 54
Supervisory alliance
developing, in competency-based supervision, 16–17
and race-related issues, 83, 93, 96
and self-reflection, 68
with women, 66–67
Supervisory relationships
collaboration in, 274
countertransference in, 173
power analysis in, 70–71
race-related dialogues in, 85
Supervisory sessions, 51, 53
Symbols, use of, 118

ABOUT THE EDITORS

Carol A. Falender, PhD, is coauthor of *Clinical Supervision: A Competency-Based Approach* (2004) and *Getting the Most Out of Clinical Training and Supervision: A Guide for Practicum Students and Interns* (2012), with Edward P. Shafranske, and coeditor of *Casebook for Supervision: A Competency-Based Approach* (2008), also with Edward P. Shafranske. She directed American Psychological Association (APA)–approved internship programs for more than 20 years and has served as a member of the Supervision Guidelines Group of the Association of State and Provincial Psychology Boards and as chair of the APA Supervision Guidelines Task Force, Board of Educational Affairs.

Edward P. Shafranske, PhD, ABPP, is coauthor and coeditor, with Carol A. Falender, of numerous publications in clinical supervision, including *Clinical Supervision: A Competency-Based Approach* (2004), *Getting the Most Out of Clinical Training and Supervision: A Guide for Practicum Students and Interns* (2012), and *Casebook for Supervision: A Competency-Based Approach* (2008). He is professor, Muriel Lipsey Chair of Clinical and Counseling Psychology, and director, PsyD program, Pepperdine University, and he lectures in the psychiatric residency programs at the University of California,

Los Angeles, and the University of California, Irvine. He is actively involved in clinical supervision and maintains a practice in clinical psychology.

Celia J. Falicov, PhD, is an internationally known family therapy author, teacher, and clinician. A licensed clinical psychologist, she is a clinical professor in the Department of Family and Preventive Medicine, and directs mental health services at the Student-Run Free Clinic Project, University of California, San Diego. She is past president (1999–2001) of the American Family Therapy Academy. She pioneered writings on family transitions, migration, and cultural perspectives in psychotherapy practice and training, and she has received many professional awards for this work. Dr. Falicov is the author of *Latino Families in Therapy* (2nd ed., 2014).